JAPANESE WOW FACTOR

REDEFINING DOTS, LINES, AND PLANES IN DESIGN

sendp●ints

PREFACE: PERMANENCE IN IMPERMANENCE

● In the vast realm of graphic design in Japan, a specific aesthetic idea gleams quietly, illuminating the creative sky like an ancient star. This idea is encapsulated as "Permanence in Impermanence," which embodies a profound philosophical quest concerning life, time, and existence. *JAPANESE WOW FACTOR: Redefining Dots, Lines, and Planes* is a book that embarks on this pilgrimage, offering a poetic narrative on the aesthetic concept of "permanence in impermanence" about Japanese graphic design.

● In this philosophical interpretation of dots, lines, and planes, we will explore the unique artistic essence of Japanese graphic design, which, rather than a simple arrangement and combination, interweaves "impermanence" and "permanence," aiming to capture the ephemeral and circumfluent beauty of life through abstract graphics.

● With the revelation of the true essence of life as its core idea, Japanese graphic design resonates with the swift transformations in life, probes into the true nature of beings, and articulates the profound philosophy of "permanence in impermanence." A Japanese design master, Tadao Andō[1], once said, "Design is the unceasing pursuit of permanence in impermanence." In accordance with this concept, his works demonstrate the resilience and beauty of life amid transience through subtle changes in light and shadow.

1. Tadao Andō (1941–) is one of Japan's leading contemporary architects. He is best known for his minimalist concrete buildings.

● Under such an aesthetic philosophy, dots, lines, and planes—once viewed as static elements—become dynamic forces constantly seeking eternity. Dots evolve into the continuation of lines, and intermingling with each other, these lines transform into multi-dimensional planes, outlining an aesthetic philosophy that transcends the boundaries of time.

● All these factors, with the ingenuity of designers, give birth to a series of works imbued with philosophical depth, inviting people to explore the boundless possibilities and embrace the unceasing beauty of life in appreciation. *Victory 1945*, crafted by a renowned Japanese graphic designer named Shigeo Fukuda[2], is based on the composition of dots, lines, and planes. Through adept graphic design, it strikingly juxtaposes the brutality of war with the yearning for peace. The dots and lines in this work serve as both poignant reminders of the scars and agonies left by war and as symbols of the relentless pursuit of peace. Such a profound probing into the true meaning of life captures the very essence of "permanence in impermanence," a concept deeply cherished in Japanese graphic design.

2. Shigeo Fukuda (1932–2009) was a Japanese design prodigy and creative multipotentate as a sculptor, graphic artist, and poster designer. Most importantly, Shigeo Fukuda was greatly influential as a designer of optical illusions.

● "Permanence in impermanence," transcends the realm of design, representing a profound meditation on aesthetics. Just as Kenya Hara[3], a Japanese design master, believed, design is not merely a skill, but rather an ability to deeply sense and discern the essence of things. While emphasizing that the wellspring of designers' creativity stems from their sensitivity to beauty, he attaches more importance to their capacity to grasp and reflect the core of existence. Another renowned Japanese graphic design master, Ikko Tanaka[4], is celebrated for his exceptional ability to convey complex ideas to readers through simple, easy-to-understand visual symbols composed of elemental lines and graphics. His works unfold the permanent beauty in impermanence and therefore please both eyes and minds. Kohei Sugiura[5], another designer master, is adept at creating distinctive visual effects with the composition of dots and planes while integrating words and images, as he believes that design is more than visual expression—it is a comprehensive comprehension and articulation of the essence of things.

3. Kenya Hara (1958-) is a renowned Japanese designer and the artistic director of Muji, who has curated a number of exhibitions on the theme of Japanese culture and aesthetics. He is one of Japan's most iconic designers, and his books *Designing Design* and *White* are recognized as essential readings for the study of design theory and aesthetics.

4. Ikko Tanaka (1930–2002) was a prolific and influential graphic designer in Japan. He has created visual identities for a wide range of brands, corporations, and cultural events. He has also worked on posters, books, and exhibitions, and was known for his use of color, typography, and Japanese aesthetics.

5. Kohei Sugiura (1932-) is a leading Japanese graphic designer and design theorist, known for his profound influence on book design and visual language systems.

● This book will take you on an evolutionary journey through early 20th-century Japanese graphic design. It traces the rise and influence of dots, lines, and planes, delving into the aesthetic principles that underpin it, and reveals how designers—aided only by these simple elements—demonstrate their quest for eternal beauty. This journey will guide you into a realm beyond forms, where you can fathom the philosophical depth in Japanese design.

● At the heart of Japanese graphic design lies the key to infinite creativity, rooted in the intricate interplay of dots, lines, and planes. The book will explore how these elements evolve independently and then gradually converge into novel artistic forms. Delving deeper, we will discover that these components are not isolated but rather intersect and interact with each other, weaving a richer design tapestry. It is within this dynamic interaction that the aesthetics of "permanence in impermanence" are most vividly expressed.

● *JAPANESE WOW FACTOR* will venture into the distinctiveness of Japanese graphic design, guided by the aesthetic motto of "permanence in impermanence." In this sense, this book serves as a beneficial philosophical dialogue between time, life, and art—an intellectual odyssey into the beauty of "permanence in impermanence."

CONTENTS

USAGE GUIDE

DA. DESIGN AGENCY
AD. ART DIRECTION
D. DESIGN
TD. TYPE DESIGN
MD. MOTION DESIGN
SD. SPATIAL DESIGN
I. ILLUSTRATION
PT. PHOTOGRAPH
PRT. PRINTING
CL. CLIENT
C. COPYRIGHT

- PHILOSOPHICAL PURSUITS
  IN JAPANESE PLANAR COMPOSITION — **6**

- DOT, LINE, AND PLANE WITH THE
  DEVELOPMENT OF
  JAPANESE GRAPHIC DESIGN — **18**

- THE ESSENCE OF JAPANESE GRAPHIC
  DESIGN: DOTS, LINES, AND PLANES — **30**

  - ● DOT —————— 34 ———— ○ DOT TO LINE ———— 76
  - ◇ LINE —————— 102 ———— ◆ LINE TO PLANE ———— 158
  - ■ PLANE —————— 186 ———— ▦ PLANE TO DOT ———— 242
  - ●◇■ DOT, LINE, AND PLANE ———————————— 264

- PHILOSOPHY IN DESIGN AND
  THE SOURCE OF CREATIVITY:
  SYMBOLIC AESTHETICS — **338**

- INDEX — **358**

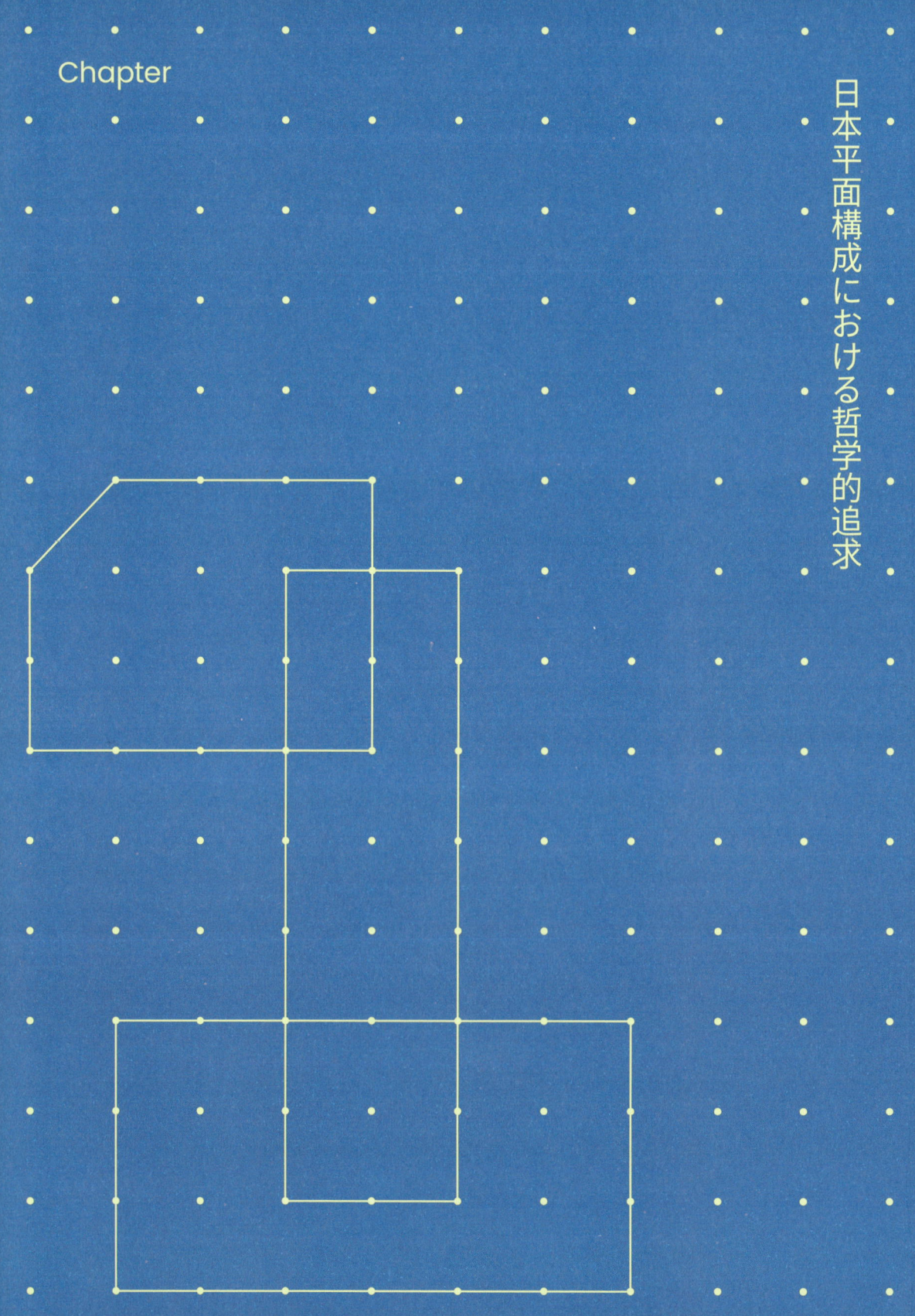

Chapter

日本平面構成における哲学的追求

PHILOSOPHICAL PURSUITS IN JAPANESE PLANAR COMPOSITION

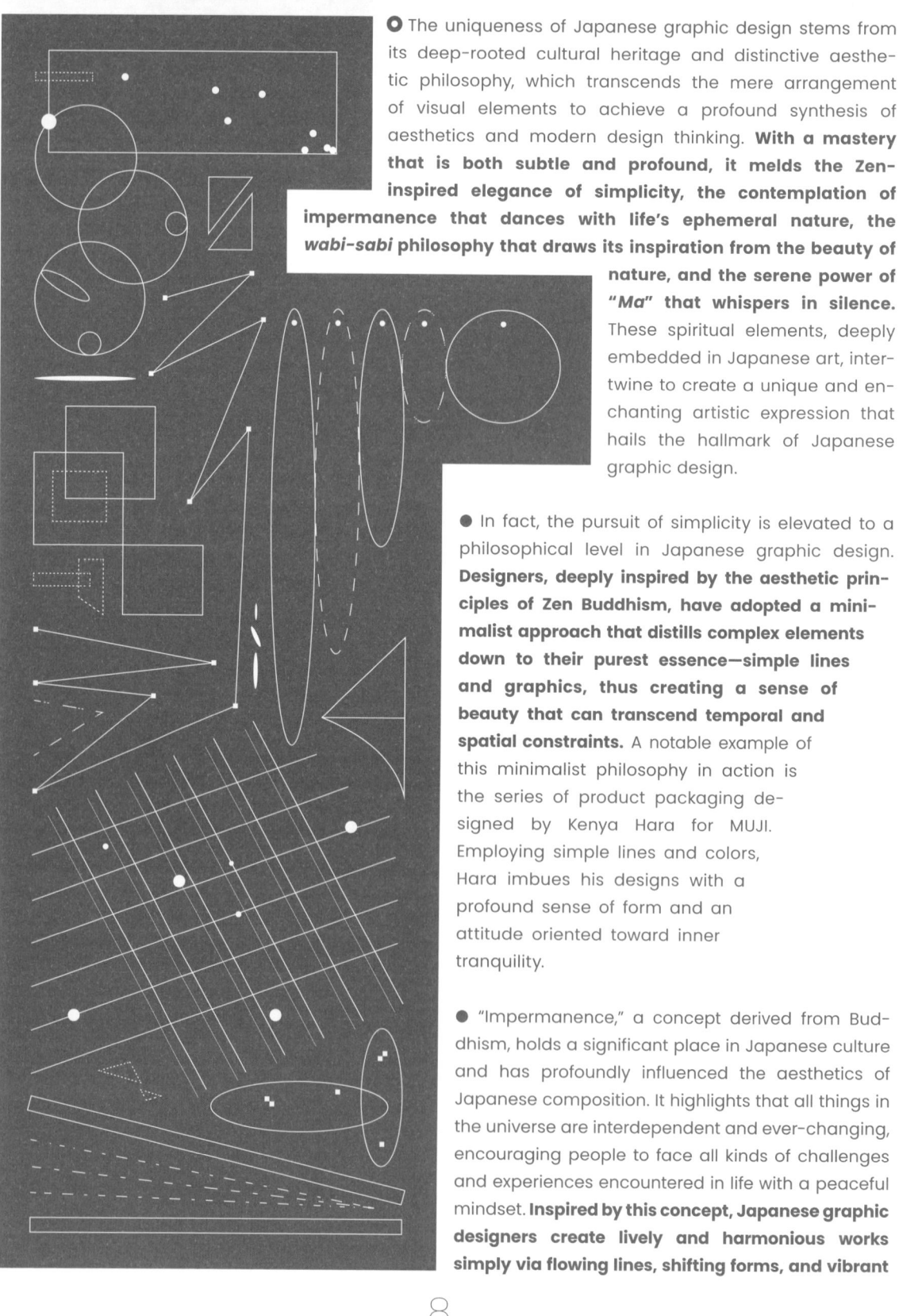

○ The uniqueness of Japanese graphic design stems from its deep-rooted cultural heritage and distinctive aesthetic philosophy, which transcends the mere arrangement of visual elements to achieve a profound synthesis of aesthetics and modern design thinking. **With a mastery that is both subtle and profound, it melds the Zen-inspired elegance of simplicity, the contemplation of impermanence that dances with life's ephemeral nature, the** *wabi-sabi* **philosophy that draws its inspiration from the beauty of nature, and the serene power of "Ma" that whispers in silence.** These spiritual elements, deeply embedded in Japanese art, intertwine to create a unique and enchanting artistic expression that hails the hallmark of Japanese graphic design.

● In fact, the pursuit of simplicity is elevated to a philosophical level in Japanese graphic design. **Designers, deeply inspired by the aesthetic principles of Zen Buddhism, have adopted a minimalist approach that distills complex elements down to their purest essence—simple lines and graphics, thus creating a sense of beauty that can transcend temporal and spatial constraints.** A notable example of this minimalist philosophy in action is the series of product packaging designed by Kenya Hara for MUJI. Employing simple lines and colors, Hara imbues his designs with a profound sense of form and an attitude oriented toward inner tranquility.

● "Impermanence," a concept derived from Buddhism, holds a significant place in Japanese culture and has profoundly influenced the aesthetics of Japanese composition. It highlights that all things in the universe are interdependent and ever-changing, encouraging people to face all kinds of challenges and experiences encountered in life with a peaceful mindset. **Inspired by this concept, Japanese graphic designers create lively and harmonious works simply via flowing lines, shifting forms, and vibrant** color combinations, and these designs not only reflect the dynamic beauty of life but also guide viewers to appreciate the true meaning of life behind the constant changes.

● **Wabi-sabi aesthetics, complemented by Zen aesthetics and the concept of "impermanence," places great emphasis on the discovery of beauty in simplicity and fragmentation.** It also advocates for the acceptance of life's impermanence and incompleteness, which has made it an indispensable aesthetic concept in Japanese culture. Japanese graphic designers, upholding a simple and unpretentious style, utilize solely raw materials and asymmetrical layouts to honor natural forms and material textures. Occasionally, such a design conveys a desolate and solitary aesthetic, but makes it possible for viewers to perceive the resilience and transcendence of life in quietness.

● "Ma," a specific Japanese cultural concept, holds a distinctive and crucial position in graphic composition. **It denotes not merely the physical intervals and blanks but also conveys a sense of voidness and serenity that resonates within the mind. By skillfully incorporating the concept of "Ma," Japanese graphic composition achieves a delicate visual balance between simplicity and complexity, fostering an atmosphere of tranquility and calmness that transcends the visual realm.** The great benefit of this design approach is that it not only evokes a sense of openness and freedom in the spatial arrangement but also inspires viewers to reflect deeply on the essence of life.

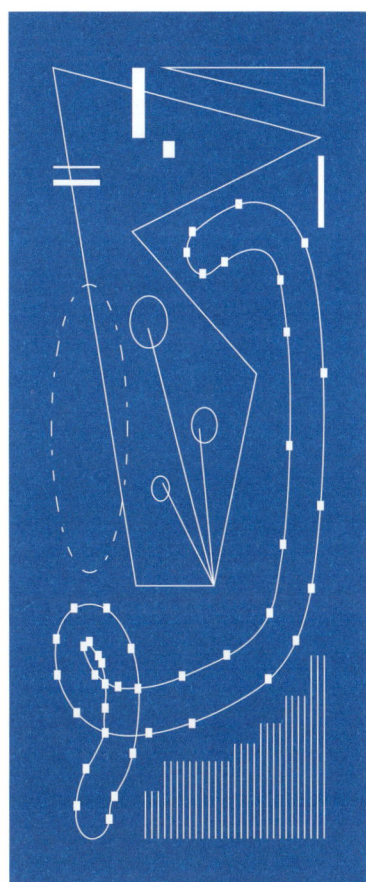

O With the core value of Japanese spirit guiding their graphic design endeavors, designers often find inspiration in traditional Japanese culture and channel into works their reverence for nature, tradition, and beauty. As a result, the creations embedded with the cherished values of Japanese society are both uniquely individual and universally resonant. Owing to the deep exploration and inte-gration of cultural elements, Japanese graphic designers oc-cupy a distinctive position in the global design landscape.

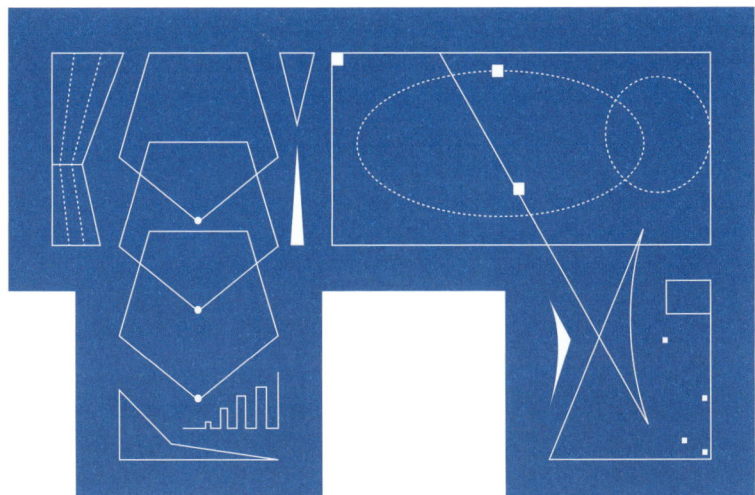

THE CONCEPT OF ZEN
FLOWING IN THE JAPANESE CULTURE

○ **Zen, as an integral component of Eastern philosophy, carries immense significance in both Chinese and Japanese culture.** Zen Buddhism, ever since its initial introduction to Japan from China in the late 12th century, has marked another milestone of cultural exchange between the two countries. Despite the failure to gain widespread popularity during the Heian period (794–1185), Zen Buddhism gradually captured the hearts of Japanese intellectuals and elites amidst the social turmoil of the Sengoku period (1467–1615). In this period, its quest for inner peace and the exploration of the true nature of things struck a chord with many Japanese scholars and monks, who later passionately embraced Zen and incorporated its principles into their literary works, artistic pursuits, and everyday lives. This fusion of Zen with Japanese culture gradually shaped the nation's distinctive aesthetic ideals, philosophy of life, and societal norms.

● **Significantly influenced by the philosophy of Zen, Japanese literature also imparts a deep understanding of nature, life, and the cosmos. Such an impact can be manifested in the works of numerous Japanese writers in whose depictions of natural landscapes and explorations of existence, we can find a unique aesthetic emotion and perception of life.** Among them, Yasunari Kawabata[1] stands out, as his works often carry a subtle fusion of melancholic emotion and Zen wisdom. In one of his masterpieces *The Dancing Girl of Izu*, Kawabata, with his delicate portrayal of the dancing girl and her surroundings, unveils such a transcendent beauty that rises above the mundane and strives towards inner purity. This beauty is not confined to the superficial form of the work but is also embedded in its profound insights into life and human emotions.

● **Zen Buddhism has also deeply influenced the realm of art, with its essence permeating various forms such as painting, sculpture, and architecture.** The three major aesthetic principles of Japanese traditional art—mono no aware, Yugen, and wabi-sabi—are vivid manifestations of Zen philosophy. These principles emphasize a genuine appreciation and meticulous attention to detail, seeking a beauty that goes beyond physical form and resonates deeply within the heart.

● Zen design, a perfect integration of Zen aesthetics and modern design principles, embraces simplicity, austerity, elegance, and tradition. By prioritizing negative space and steering clear of excessive decoration, Zen design stresses that its creations are not only the realization of Zen philosophical ideals but also uphold the responsibility of preserving and evolving traditional Japanese aesthetics. Three core principles, namely mushin, kanso, and yugen, can be cited to define the simple yet profound aesthetic vision of Zen design. Mushin strives for mental freedom and purity, allowing the design to demonstrate its purest form. In graphic design, mushin is often translated into a commitment to simplicity, where superfluous decorations are stripped away to achieve a pristine existence that helps foster a sense of freedom and spirituality in the observer. Kanso, on the other hand, involves the removal of redundant elements, retaining only those that are essential and meaningful. The precise and minimalist use of typography, color, and graphics creates such a subtle yet striking impact that viewers cannot help but immerse themselves in the sheer beauty of the work. Finally, yugen stresses subtle elegance and concealed beauty, inviting people to delve into the depths of design. Thanks to the skillful utilization of negative space, gradient colors, and layering, designs are more layered and thought-provoking, inviting viewers to contemplate an infinite beauty beyond the surface.

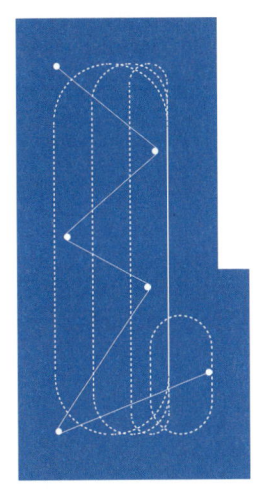

1. Yasunari Kawabata (1899–1972) was a renowned Japanese novelist and short story writer whose prose is characterized by simplicity, lyricism, and subtle tones, and who became the first Japanese author to be awarded the Nobel Prize for Literature in 1968 for his outstanding literary achievements. His works have had a wide international impact and are still widely read today.

2. Daisetsu Suzuki (1870–1966), was a renowned Japanese essayist, philosopher, religious scholar, and translator, especially known for his studies of Buddhism, especially Zen and Shingon Buddhism. He played an important role in spreading Eastern religions and philosophies to the West, and made outstanding contributions to the translation of Chinese, Korean, Japanese, Vietnamese and Sanskrit classics.

● Ever since Daisuke Suzuki[2]'s introduction of "Japanese Zen" to the world in the mid-20th century, Zen design has captured global attention and praise with its unique charm and rich cultural heritage. As more and more designers incorporate Zen concepts into their works, they are creating numerous masterpieces that blend oriental charm with modern aesthetic sensibilities. At the same time, Zen design breaks the boundaries between tradition and modernity, which profoundly influences the global design across East and West and offers designers fresh perspectives and new sources of inspiration.

● In addition to its far-reaching influence on art and design, Zen has evolved into an indispensable element and permeates the daily lives of Japanese society, with more and more people seeking inner peace and tranquility through activities such as meditation, tea ceremonies, and flower viewing. These practices not only foster personal self-cultivation but also serve as a unique symbol of Japanese culture.

◉ Furthermore, the concept of Zen has extensively influenced various facets of Japanese society, including architecture, gardens, and cuisine. It is especially evident in Japanese architecture and garden design, where beauty and functionality come together to inspire deep contemplation and reflection. Similarly, the concept of Zen is fully embodied in Japanese cuisine with a strong emphasis on health, simplicity, and the pursuit of pure, authentic flavors.

THE VIEW OF "MUJO" AGAINST VOIDNESS

○ **Zen culture really took root and began to develop in the Kamakura period (1185-1333), but traditional Japanese culture can be traced back to somewhere around the 6th century, which is marked by a major cultural "shock": the introduction of Buddhism.** For the first time, the Japanese were faced with an advanced and structured continental belief/value system with tangible objects such as temples, statues, and scriptures that seemed stunningly advanced. Awed, they tried to absorb it as much as possible, but at the same time, they tried to reconcile it with their own values to reconfirm their identity. For example, the Japanese followed animistic beliefs in multiple gods/deities, a religion of "eight million gods in nature"—meaning that gods resided in every element in nature, constantly changing their places. For the Japanese, gods followed an elusive, mysterious, and undefinable existence. In contrast, Buddhism was a philosophical religion that could guide you in the right direction and help you deal with death and other sufferings. The stark contrast divided Japanese leaders, who had to fight to decide if the country had to accept this new religion or reject it.

● Through this paradigm shift, one of the main teachings of Buddhism resonated with Japanese aesthetics despite the spiritual collision: Mujo, or "impermanence." Buddha maintained that everything on Earth constantly changed; hence, nothing was everlasting nor absolute. What we think is "A" today could become "B" tomorrow, even in those things whose consistency is taken for granted. Buddha further taught that we shouldn't rely on external supports such as money, status, products, or relationships to feel happy, because they could also disappoint us by changing or being gone tomorrow.

● The notion of mujo (impermanence) is closely connected to the Buddhist concept of "kuu (空)," a central idea in Mahayana philosophy. The character "kuu," meaning "emptiness," "void," or "sky," expresses the understanding that all things, including the self, lack inherent existence and can only be defined through their relationships to other things. In Japanese, "kuu" can also be read as "utsu," a word used to describe feelings or

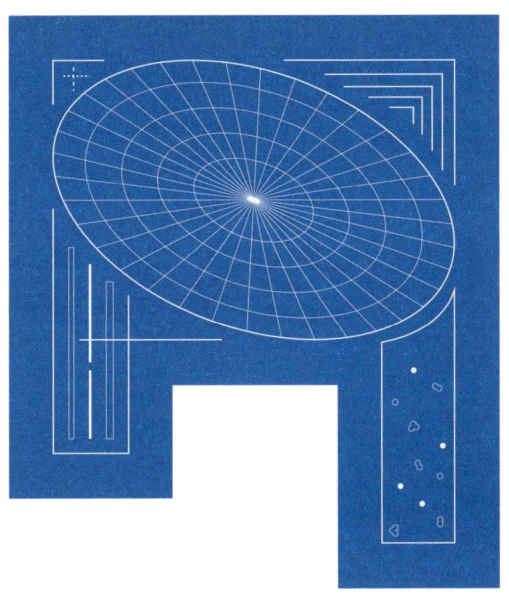

states that are empty, hollow, or vain, further emphasizing the transient and insubstantial nature of reality.

● In the book A Method Called Japan: The Culture of Facades and Realities (日本とある方法: おもかげ・うつろいの文化), NHK Books, 2006, Seigo Matsuoka, an influential editorial director, observed that the Japanese traditionally considered that "utsu" (emptiness) and "utsutsu" (reality) were on the same spectrum, and used the verb "utsurou" (虚无) to describe the transition from one state to another. For example, "four seasons utsurou," "people's feelings utsurou," and "love utsurou." The power could also "utsurou" and escape our grasp. We are in a world of "mujo." Japanese people found beauty in "utsurou." Rather than trying to keep real things real or disguise empty things as full, they embraced the utsurou nature of things as they are. They spent an enormous amount of time and energy "observing utusou" things, appreciating moments that were real or beautiful. When those moments were gone, they used their memory or experiences to fill the voids. Ultimately, such an attitude helped cement Japanese aesthetics.

● **Concerning the graphic design, the influence of impermanence aesthetics can be manifested through distinctive and unconventional elements.** To achieve dynamic and unexpected effects, designers strive to innovate by introducing temporary and ephemeral elements, which include the use of fleeting graphics or unconventional typography. The impermanence aesthetics also profoundly influence their choice of colors. By skillfully employing a spectrum of shadows, gradients, and lighting effects, designers break the traditional color norms and unveil multifaceted layers of reality. This versatile application of color not only enriches the expressiveness of the design but also conveys a sense of reverence for diversity and transformation. In terms of layout and composition, designers draw inspiration from impermanence aesthetics to creatively break the balance by introducing asymmetrical, dislocated, or irregular elements, resulting in more tense and vibrant designs. With such an approach, designers aim to evoke viewers' awareness of impermanence, inviting them to immersive contemplation of the fluidity of time and space.

◐ **Guided by such an aesthetic philosophy, graphic design is able to break the constraints of static artwork and evolve into a visual narrative full of vitality and changes.** For viewers, the works are not only designers' manifestos of their pursuit of beauty but also their specific interpretations of life, the fleeting moments, and endless changes. This design offers a novel and profound aesthetic experience, leading people to think about the transient flow of life and the diversity of things.

WABI-SABI AESTHETICS
IN PURSUIT OF THE TRUTHFULNESS OF NATURE

○ The roots of wabi-sabi (侘寂) aesthetics can be traced to ancient Chinese Taoism and Zen Buddhism. It emphasizes the beauty of nature and the poignant experience of impermanence. In traditional Japanese art, it stands as an aesthetic sphere that transcends stylistic confines, embodying a state of mind. Initially, wabi-sabi symbolized the solitude, impoverishment, and loneliness of hermits. Over time, the self-imposed isolation and voluntary poverty of hermits and ascetics, however, begin to be perceived as a path to attaining spiritual richness. While "wabi" literally means poverty, its underlying meaning goes beyond the absence of material possessions. Rather, it signifies a refined state that disdains material wealth, reveres the transcendence of the material world, and advocates for a life of simplicity.

● "Sabi," as an external manifestation of aesthetic values, is based on the metaphysical and spiritual tenets of Zen Buddhism, translating these principles into artistic and tangible attributes. It laments the passing of time and the impermanence of all existence while alluding to the beauty inherent in irregularity, simplicity, and the ambiguity shaped by natural forces. These objects mirror a universal flux: impermanence that is transient but pleasing and thought-provoking, guiding the viewer or listener to a state of reflection and contemplation—a return to wabi-sabi and solitude, which is intended to elicit an aesthetic experience of tranquility and transcendence.

● Wabi-Sabi, as an intuitive appreciation of the "instantaneous beauty" of the material world, maps the irreversible flow of life in the spiritual world. This subtle and profound beauty, which dwells in simplicity, rusticity, imperfection, and even decay, skillfully integrates the impermanence of time into the current aesthetics of space. It embodies a deep awareness of the ephemeral nature of all things, permitting one to sense the fragility and pain of traditional aesthetics within the contemporary moment. Unlike Western aesthetics, wabi-sabi takes root in an Eastern perception of nature and human relationships, rejecting the Western philosophical premises of power, authority, dominance, participation, and control. The art that emerges from this philosophy is not only a visual and tactile expression but also a profound interpretation of the values behind it. In wabi-sabi, these two dimensions are intricately woven and inseparable.

● **Up to now, wabi-sabi has been widely understood as a profound experience of nature, time, and existence in the world of aesthetics, standing in contrast to the modern world's relentless pursuit of perfection. It signifies a preference in Japanese graphic composition for natural things and the pursuit of simplicity and imperfect beauty.** Designers' skillful incorporation of wabi-sabi aesthetics has translated this concept into guiding principles and techniques for captivating works. Concerning the use of colors, muted and natural palettes are favored to highlight the raw texture of materials. This design approach instills the works with such an intrinsic sense of calm and inner strength that viewers can easily connect themselves with the authenticity and beauty of nature. When it comes to formal expression, designers forsake excessive embellishments and focus on the simplicity and purity of design elements, thus creating works with a sense of breath, freedom, and spirituality. Furthermore, the perception of nature, time, and existence advocated by wabi-sabi aesthetics is transformed in graphic design into a keen attention to detail and a profound awareness of life's irreversibility.

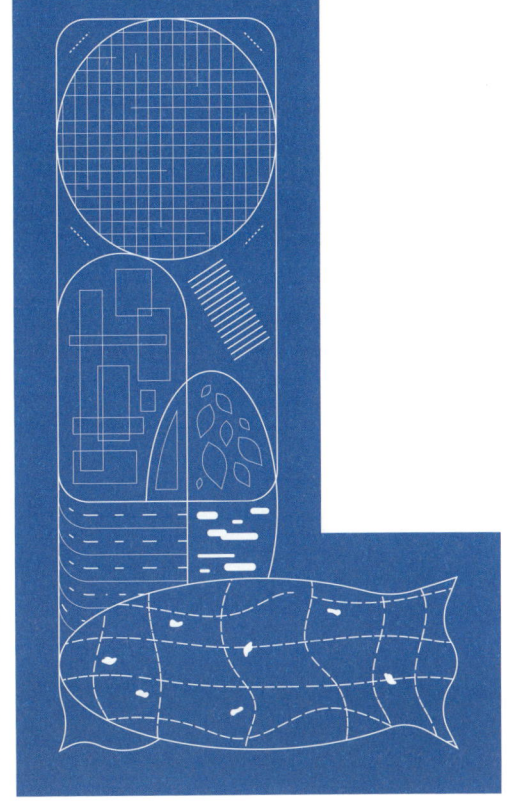

In his book *Designing Design*, Japanese designer Kenya Hara shares his experience with designing the playbill for the opening and closing ceremonies of the 1998 Nagano Winter Olympics. To create a breathtaking spectacle against the wintery backdrop, Hara drew inspiration from his childhood memories. He recalled the translucent imprints of his footsteps on the soft surface of the snow, revealing the dark soil beneath and forming distinctive patterns. To transform this nostalgic vision into a visual design, Hara developed a kind of special paper with a white, fluffy texture. When debossed, some parts of the paper looked translucent, like the footprints on ice or in the newly fallen snow. The texture of the material elicits the images of this festival of snow and ice. Mainly relying on the use of natural elements and simple forms, Hara displayed the refined elegance of wabi-sabi aesthetics through subtle hues and organic textures. While observing this design style, viewers can not only sense the flow of nature and time but also feel inspired by the fragility and preciousness of life.

"MA" FOR THE CREATION OF BALANCE AND SERENITY

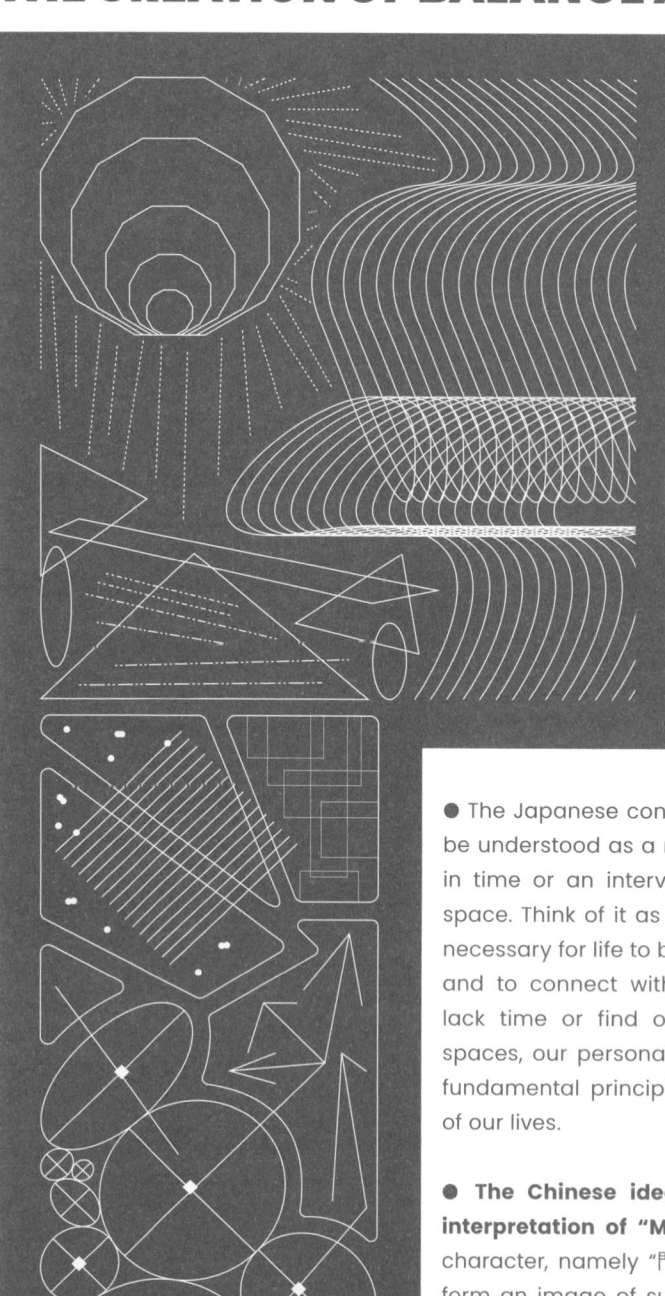

◐ In the fields of art, design, and philosophy, there is an aesthetic concept deeply entrenched in Japanese culture—"Ma"—a term in Japanese that is multifaceted and somewhat challenging to define precisely in English because it encompasses various aspects related to space, time, and the interval between objects or events. However, it is commonly translated as "negative space," "pause," "interval," or "emptiness." Reducing it to these simplistic translations, though, does not capture the full depth and complexity of the concept. "Ma" is about the space in-between, the intervals, and the silence, alluding to the beauty of harmony and balance.

● The Japanese concept of "Ma" can be understood as a moment of pause in time or an interval of emptiness in space. Think of it as the time and space necessary for life to breathe, to experience, and to connect with the world. When we lack time or find ourselves in constrained spaces, our personal growth is hindered. This fundamental principle applies to every aspect of our lives.

● **The Chinese ideograph "間" offers a perfect interpretation of "Ma."** The two ideograms of the character, namely "門" (door) and "日" (sun), together form an image of sunlight gently streaming through a doorway. This image captures the idea of "Ma" beautifully, illustrating metaphorically the importance of openings and pauses in our lives, just like a door slightly ajar to let light and fresh air in.

● **The concept of "Ma" has exerted a profound influence over the composition, style, and aesthetics of traditional

Japanese paintings. These artworks frequently embrace negative space, where the empty or unpainted areas hold as much significance as the painted elements themselves. The deliberate employment of negative space encourages viewers to contemplate the subject matter and discover the beauty within simplicity. Moreover, traditional Japanese paintings often emphasize suggestion rather than explicit representation. This allows viewers to engage with the artwork and fill in the details with their imagination, creating a sense of "Ma" in the gap between what is painted and what is implied. For example, the use of fog in landscapes deliberately employs negative space to evoke a sense of transcendence and atmosphere.

● "Ma" in art refers to the empty space around and between elements, and is also referred to as "blank space." While the form or image itself constitutes the positive element, the empty surrounding or "blank space" around it is deemed negative. "Negative space" is also known as the ground in graphic design, referring to the blank space between images. Kenya Hara, in his book *White*, emphasizes that "white" is not an empty void but a space brimming with vitality and potential, inviting imagination and evoking a sense of reminiscence. Similarly, Ikko Tanaka utilizes the concept of "Ma" in his designs, always thinking about how to make the images more concise and powerful. Designers can skillfully use "negative space" to create a sense of visual balance and tranquility, illustrating the importance and value of "Ma" in Japanese culture.

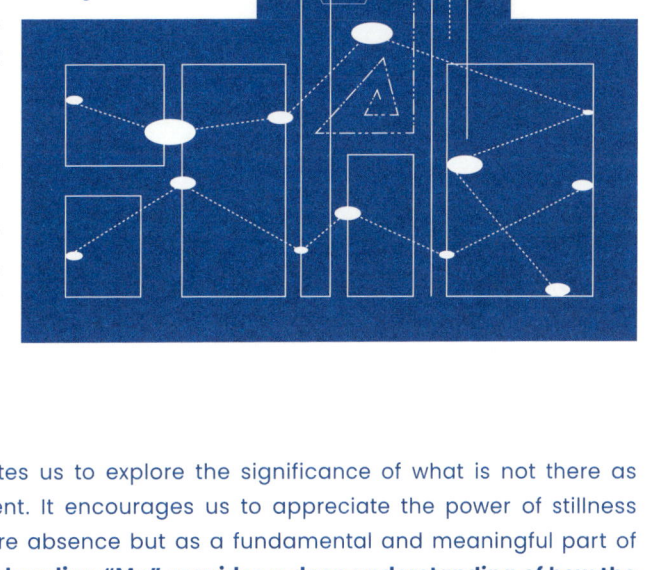

○ In essence, "Ma" invites us to explore the significance of what is not there as much as what is present. It encourages us to appreciate the power of stillness and silence, not as mere absence but as a fundamental and meaningful part of our experience. **Comprehending "Ma" provides a deep understanding of how the Japanese people view and engage with their surroundings, offering a valuable perspective on the elegance of simplicity and the significance of what exists in the spaces between.**

DOT, LINE, AND PLANE WITH THE DEVELOPMENT OF JAPANESE GRAPHIC DESIGN

○ Japanese graphic design is a precious gem in the world of design, marked by a winding journey of exploration and a glorious renaissance in its development. When the shadow of World War II finally receded, Japanese graphic design managed to rise from the ruins and secure a position on the international design stage. During this process of transformation, it developed a distinctive style that blends the profound essence of traditional culture with the innovative concepts of modern Western design. Among them, simple yet expressive elements of design—dots, lines, and planes—have played a crucial role, and as the cornerstones of the visual world, they reflect the Japanese design philosophy and aesthetic pursuit. This chapter will embark on a journey through the golden era of Japanese graphic design, exploring the evolving expressiveness of dots, lines, and planes in different periods. It also tells the story of how Japanese graphic design has embraced new ideas, internalizes influences, and transcends boundaries in search of spectacular charm and everlasting vitality.

SEARCHING FOR THE "JAPANESENESS" IN MODERN DESIGN

● **The early 20th century marked a profound transformation in Japanese graphic design. Heavily influenced by Western ideas, this period saw the emergence of new artistic styles and creative inspiration.** Encouraged by modern art trends such as Constructivism, Cubism, Futurism, and Bauhaus, designers were eager to experiment with geometric shapes and expressive design languages. These innovations not only influenced Japanese graphic design but also laid a solid foundation for the development of its styles centered on dots, lines, and planes. In such a context of modern design, designers, rather than settling for mere imitation, attempted to seek a balance between universal design principles and their unique cultural identity, which consequently led to designs blending an international perspective and a deep sense of "Japaneseness."

● **This concept, known as "glocalization" (a blend of globalization and localism), has played an important role in the development of modern Japanese graphic design.** The term comes from a Japanese word, "dochakuka," which calls for designers to adopt an international way of thinking while at the same time tailoring their work to suit the unique characteristics of local culture. Such an approach ensures that designs remain deeply rooted in their cultural origins while resonating with global audiences. It is this deep reflection on and practice of "glocalization" that has made Japanese graphic design unparalleled in the scope of global design, providing valuable inspiration and insight to designers worldwide.

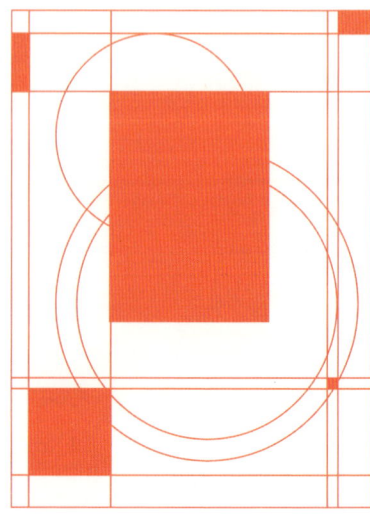

● In the mid-20th century, the Nippon Kobo, a group with prominent figures such as Yusaku Kamekura[1], Takashi Kono[2],

1. Yusaku Kamekura (1915–1997) was a pioneering figure in modern Japanese graphic design. In the postwar period, he actively promoted the internationalization of Japanese design. His iconic works include the poster for the 1964 Tokyo Olympics. He was also one of the founding members of the Japan Graphic Designers Association (JAGDA).

2. Takashi Kono (1906–1999) was a distinguished Japanese poster designer, renowned for his visually powerful style characterized by simple compositions and restrained use of color. He was one of the key figures in shaping the visual language of postwar Japanese advertising.

3. Yōnosuke Natori (1910–1962) was a prominent Japanese photographer, editor, and publisher. He was dedicated to advancing photojournalism and played a key role in founding Nippon Kobo and the magazine NIPPON. His works have a profound impact on visual communication and graphic design in Japan.

4. Ken Domon (1909–1990) was one of Japan's most influential documentary photographers. Known for his realism, he specialized in capturing social issues and the cultural heritage of Buddhism.

Yonosuke Natori[3], Domon Ken[4], and so on, actively explored the "Japaneseness" in design. Via their globally distributed magazine *NIPPON*, they presented a unique Japanese design style featuring high-quality photography and bold, minimalist layouts that were simple yet vibrant, rich, and substantial. This approach is closely linked to the philosophy of Japanese tradition, and like an enduring underground current, it is continuously nourishing the evolution of Japanese graphic design to this day.

POSTWAR AWAKENING OF DESIGN CONSCIOUSNESS

● **To explore the achievements and unique styles of modern Japanese graphic design, we must first trace its origins to an era deeply intertwined with industrial manufacturing. Japanese graphic design didn't come out of thin air; instead, it was gradually conceived and developed in the wave of industrialization.** The prosperous development of the industrial manufacturing industry brought unprecedented opportunities and challenges for Japanese graphic design. On the one hand, the acceleration of industrial production fueled a rising market demand for design, which provided a vast stage for designers to display their talent and creativity. On the other hand, designers faced the critical task of creating a modernized and internationalized image of Japan while simultaneously addressing market needs.

● **The war reduced the Japanese economy to ruins; amidst this adversity, though, the nation demonstrated spectacular post-war resilience and creativity.** As the economy gradually recovered, a wave of Japanese manufacturing companies such as Honda (1946) and Sony (1946) emerged one after another. These companies not only secured their place in the domestic market but also set their sights on vast international markets. At that time, design took on a new and vital mission—to drive exports and enhance Japan's global competitiveness. With active encouragement and guidance from the government, industrial design gained increasing prominence in the national economy. In 1947, the *American Life and Culture Exhibition* held in Japan provided a chance to introduce American culture and lifestyle. Through real objects and photographs, it demonstrated the application of American industrial design in people's lives, which further sparked Japan's yearning for "external perspective" to redefine itself.

● **A turning point came when Konosuke Matsushita[5] embarked on his first visit to the United States.** Through this visit, Matsushita was deeply inspired by the widespread application of advanced electronics in the U.S.. Returning to Japan, he actively advocated for the establishment of Japan's in-house design department and boldly predicted, "The future will be an era of design." This vision was quickly accepted by Toyota, Hitachi, Mitsubishi, and other companies, which followed suit in setting up in-house design departments, marking the beginning of a new manufacturing paradigm in Japan—a trinity of technological innovation, quality management, and industrial design. In the subsequent year, the Japan Industrial Design Association was founded and it organized the nation's first postwar industrial design exhibition. These two events, equally important in the history of Japan's industrial design development, signaled the commencement of its standardized development.

5. Kōnosuke Matsushita (1894–1989) was a renowned Japanese industrialist and the founder of Matsushita Electric, known today as Panasonic. Revered as the "God of Management" in Japan, he had a profound impact on corporate management and production innovation. His unique management philosophy and emphasis on talent development played a significant role in Japan's rapid postwar economic growth.

● **The establishment of industrial design awards and design magazines further propelled the globalization of Japanese design.** To encourage outstanding design works, the Mainichi Newspapers Co. launched the Mainichi Industrial Design Award (later renamed the Mainichi Design Award). Even today, it stands as one of the most esteemed design awards in Japan, serving as an important driving force in the growth of Japanese design. At the same time, the establishment of numerous design magazines, such as *Idea*, *Publicity Meeting (Sendenkaigi)*, and *Design for Life*, played a crucial role in promoting global perspectives and nurturing international exchanges within the design community.

ESTABLISHMENT OF GRAPHIC DESIGN

● **Designs originating in the manufacturing industry significantly influenced the development of modern Japanese graphic design, contributing to its stylistic definition and the establishment of its cultural status. A series of designs were created with designers continually drawing inspiration from traditional culture and combining it with modern design concepts to exhibit unique Japanese attributes.** These works have not only won widespread domestic recognition and acclaim but also gained prominence on the international stage, symbolizing Japanese cultural and design leverage.

6. Yoshio Hayakawa (1917–2009) was a Japanese graphic designer and art director who was active in the postwar advertising and publishing industries. He was known for his elegant and minimalist design style, as well as his exploration of modern visual language.

● **The year 1952 marked a crucial moment in the history of Japanese graphic design.** Headed by Yusaku Kamekura, Yoshio Hayakawa[6], and other top Japanese designers, the graphic design group "Japan Advertising Artists Club" (referred to as JAAC) was established. As the first nationwide organization for graphic designers in postwar Japan, JAAC signaled the dawn of an organized and strategic phase

7. Kazumasa Nagai (1929–) is a prominent Japanese graphic designer and printmaker, and one of the founding members of the Nippon Design Center (NDC). He is renowned for his distinctive style that blends traditional natural motifs with modern graphic expression. His works span posters, corporate identity, and public campaigns.

8. Tadanori Yokoo (1936–) is one of Japan's most influential graphic designers, illustrators, and painters. He is celebrated for his vivid visual language that combines psychedelic colors, collage techniques, and traditional Japanese cultural symbols. His works span advertising, publishing, theater posters, and contemporary art, making him a key figure in postwar Japanese visual culture.

of graphic design development in the country, functioning as an annual platform for soliciting and exhibiting design works. The organization later evolved into the predecessor of the Japan Graphic Designers Association (JAGDA). In fact, ever since the founding of JAAC, both professional designers and amateurs have eagerly participated and exhibited their works with the aspiration of becoming the designers of a new era. From the JAAC platform walked many designers who have subsequently shaped contemporary Japanese graphic design, including Ikko Tanaka, Kazumasa Nagai[7], and Tadanori Yokoo[8].

Fig. 1 Poster for the 16th Nissenbi Exhibition, designed by Tadanori Yokoo, 1966.

● **In 1955, *Graphic'55* was hosted at the Takashimaya Department Store, bringing Japanese graphic design to new heights.** The exhibition presented an internationalized design scenario with the presence of many core members of JAAC, such as Yusaku Kamekura, Takeshi Kono, and Ryozo Hayakawa, as well as American design master Paul Rand. Rather than enforcing a singular standard, the exhibition encouraged designers to delve into their creative potential. Despite the integration of a wide variety of modern design techniques, such as photography, illustration, photoengraving, printing, it demonstrated the unique flavor of Japanese national aesthetics. These works, printed in practice, clearly demonstrated the close relationship between graphic design and society. A standout piece was Yusaku Kamekura's poster for the exhibition (Fig. 2), which employed geometric shapes and the interweaving of fundamental circles to convey the designer's ideas succinctly yet powerfully. **This exhibition stands as a milestone, marking the true "dawn of graphic design" in Japan and signaling the year the field established its unique identity.**

● In 1960, Japan ushered in the World Design Conference (WoDeCo), the first of its kind in Asia. At this conference, the *Tokyo Declaration* was issued under the theme of "Our Century: What Designers Can Contribute to the Human Environment of the Coming Age?" The declaration explored in depth the social responsibility and ethical boundaries of design, and further advanced the construction of design theories and principles in Japan. Since then, a new generation of Japanese designers has continued to combine modern design concepts with Japanese aesthetics, producing many outstanding works that have further solidified Japan's position in the global design arena.

Fig. 2 Poster for the exhibition *Graphic'55*, designed by Yusaku Kamekura, 1952.

GRAPHIC DEVELOPMENT IN JAPAN

● Dots, lines, and planes are essential visual languages indispensable in visual art and design, as these basic compositional elements can combine to form countless geometric shapes, which then produce a wide range of visual effects through various permutations and combinations, profoundly influencing the fields of art and design.

● **Dots, lines, and planes, ubiquitous in Japanese art, constitute the basic elements of a picture and an important carrier for artists to express their emotions and aesthetic concepts.** Early Yamato-e[9] is characterized by its depiction of landscapes, where spatial dynamics are created solely through fine lines. However, during the Edo period, those basic lines and dots were deliberately utilized in ukiyo-e[10] to highlight details and layers. Occasionally, they serve as decorative components to enhance the artistic appeal of a painting. The famous "Korin[11] ripples" from the Korin school paintings are the exemplary practice of this technique, in which lines of different thicknesses are skillfully used to achieve visually decorative expressions.

Fig. 3 Korin ripples.

9. *Yamato-e* is a native Japanese painting style that emerged during the Heian period, around the 10th century. Characterized by distinctly Japanese themes, compositions, and techniques, it marked a departure from the then-prevalent Tang-style Chinese paintings in Japan.

10. Ukiyo-e, literally meaning "pictures of the floating world," was one of the most significant art movements of the Edo period (1603–1867). Its aesthetic combines the narrative realism of emaki (painted handscrolls) from the Kamakura period with the decorative sophistication developed during the Momoyama and early Edo periods.

11. Ogata Korin (1658–1716) was a Japanese artist of the Tokugawa period (1603–1868), regarded, along with Sotatsu, as one of the masters of the Sotatsu-Koetsu school of decorative painting.

● **In the modern era, as Japan gradually engaged with Western artistic concepts and techniques, its graphic designs have been profoundly influenced by the vertical and horizontal structure of European Constructivism as well as the simple and rational design style of the Bauhaus.** Striving not only for simplicity and clarity but also for dynamic interplay and variation between elements, Japanese designers deftly incorporate dots, lines, and planes into their works to achieve a simple and layered visual effect. The creative combination and arrangement of dots, lines, and planes result in varied dynamic geometric shapes that are both strikingly dynamic and rich in emotional and conceptual depth. Geometric shapes are often used extensively in Japanese graphic design works, not only for their aesthetic appeal but also for their inherent cultural significance. Squares and rectangles represent artificial forms, curves symbolize intuition and inspiration, and especially, circles, called "円" in Japanese, embody enlightenment, perfection, strength, and elegance.

● **The more design practice Japanese designers engage in, the more diverse and flexible approaches they adopt in their use of dots, lines, and planes.** Over time, designers tend to refine and simplify complex shapes into geometric forms to make their works simple in form but profound in meaning. The natural environment has significantly shaped their perception of nature, as we can easily find the evident appreciation of flora and fauna in Japanese design. In their depiction of these natural elements, designers frequently apply geometric processing to imbue their creations with a distinctive Japanese aesthetic. Moreover, Japanese graphic design is deeply rooted in traditional culture and traditional elements such as clothing and logos become a rich source of inspiration for creation. These featured design concepts and techniques have won Japanese graphic design an international reputation and made it a model for many designers to follow.

THE GEOMETRIC SHAPES TO BRIDGE MODERNITY AND TRADITION

● **Yusaku Kamekura is the founder of the first generation of Japanese graphic design. His early training at Bauhaus instilled a strong preference for basic elements such as dots, lines, and planes, and as a result, his works exemplify the principles of modern design.** Kamekura is also keen on the elements of traditional Japanese culture, and his works display the perfect fusion of modernization with national identity. One of his most iconic works is the poster for the Tokyo 1964 Summer Olympics (Fig. 4). At that time, postwar Japan urgently needed to convey a positive image to the world. With the Olympic Games, such a grand worldwide event, graphic posters could act as a universal language to share this message. Looking for a way to transcend linguistic barriers, Japanese graphic designers, led by Kamekura, came up with an ingenious graphical system that was unique, clear, and modern: Pictograms. The poster made by photoengraving featured a large red circle on a white background, hovering above five golden interlinked rings. The depiction of the "rising sun" symbolized Japan's resurgence and evoked national pride in the Japanese people. In another famous poster entitled *Peaceful Use of Atomic Energy* (Fig. 5) he

Fig. 4 Poster for the 1964 Tokyo Olympic Games, designed by Yusaku Kamekura, 1964.

Fig. 5 *Peaceful Uses of Atomic Energy,* designed by Yusaku Kamekura, 1956.

created an image of radial lines around a central axis to represent the state of an atomic energy explosion. The simple yet striking depiction delivered a powerful visual impact, addressing the issue with precision and depth. In Yusaku Kamekura's view, Japanese graphic design should meet global standards and simultaneously display the unique Japanese visual aesthetics. His creation with simple geometric shapes helped define the unique and enduring aesthetics of Japanese graphic design, setting a good example of how to connect Japanese design to the modern world and resonate with the traditional Japanese pursuit of simplicity and beauty.

Fig. 6 Cover of *Design News*, Issue No. 218, designed by Ryohei Kojima, 1992.

● The same feature can be observed in the work of Japanese graphic designer Ryohei Kojima[12]. For over 20 years, he has been designing covers for the journal *Design News*, which targets a predominantly international design audience. To meet the diverse visual needs of readers, Kojima extensively employs simplified geometric shapes in his compositions. For example, *Design News* Issue No. 218 (Fig. 6), designed by Kojima, focused on the theme "Diseño España" (The Explosion of Spanish Design). The centerpiece features a fusiform shape created with various styles of lines and filled with shades of red, purple, and magenta, generating a sense of elasticity and outward expansion. The relatively symmetrical cones radiating out from the center symbolize the reversibility and interoperability of international information.

12. Ryohei Kojima (1939-) is a renowned contemporary Japanese graphic designer, best known for his poster works. He has also created a wide range of commercially influential designs. Kojima's visual language is clean and powerful, balancing artistic expression with functional clarity. His works span various fields, including advertising and publishing.

● **In addition to the use of simple geometric shapes, Japanese designers also excel at abstracting geometric elements.** They distill and generalize the geometric features of natural forms, transform them into simple geometric shapes, and then combine and arrange these shapes to create a design work. This process of abstraction not only enhances the simplicity and recognizability of their works but also conveys a philosophical connotation beyond the concrete form.

● **Another world-renowned Japanese design master, Shigeo Fukuda, also favors the geometric use of dots, lines, and planes. His proficient mastery of such elements as lines and planes results in vivid symbols of the objects he sees. Through simple geometrical shapes and lines, he creates complex and meaningful graphic works with a visual effect of absurdity while maintaining the sense of order.** Benefiting from this stylistic language, even viewers of different languages and cultures can obtain a deeper resonance in his posters. For example, his most famous poster, *Victory 1945*,

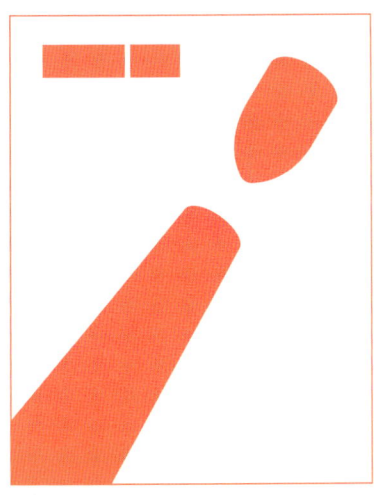

Fig. 7 *Victory 1945*, designed by Shigeo Fukuda, 1975.

utilizes simple lines and planes to feature the image of the cannonball flying back into the cannon. The cannonball's return path creates a concise and witty graphic language, conveying a profound and thought-provoking meaning.

● Apart from designing, Shigeo Fukuda is constantly interested in the complementary relationship between "figure" and "ground" to explore the principle of trompe l'oeil. Fukuda skillfully uses the relationship between black and white, the positive and negative spaces formed by interspersing and juxtaposing planes, and the virtual and the real to create a simple and captivating effect. This design approach demonstrates Fukuda's mastery of geometric aesthetics and the infinite potential for visual creativity.

● **The design of Kazumasa Nagai centers on the portrayal of plants and animals. Stripping away realistic details, he prefers to abstract their forms through geometric simplification, using the basic elements of dots, lines, and planes.** Therefore, his works are always metaphorical, aiming to "denounce human actions on behalf of silent animals and plants." Nagai avoids intricate colors and elaborate shapes; instead, he mainly relies on the simplicity and power of geometric elements—dots, lines, planes, and basic forms—to convey his profound inner emotions, inviting viewers to delve deep into the themes.

● In the skilled hands of Japanese designers, the basic elements of dots, lines, and planes are endowed with new life and meaning. Using geometric shapes, designers distill complex forms to their most essential components and create visually striking and culturally profound works that interpret Japanese design concepts.

Fig. 8 *Kazumasa Nagai Design Life*, designed by Kazumasa Nagai, 1993.

INTERMINGLING WITH TRADITIONAL CULTURE

● In addition to the influence of the Western modernist design movement, the traditional cultural consciousness deeply rooted in the hearts of the Japanese people has also shaped their preference for geometric graphics, adding aesthetic interest and cultural significance to the simplicity of the shapes.

● **In graphic composition, the typical symbol of a family crest is widely incorporated in Yusaku Kamekura's posters, though in an abstract way.**

Fig. 9 *Progress and Harmony for Mankind*, Poster for *Expo '70 Osaka*, designed by Yusaku Kamekura, 1967.

Simple yet symbolic, it reflects the unique cultural psychology and protocols of the Japanese nation. Kamekura uses the family crest as a visual language throughout the poster to express the cultural identity of Japan. The poster designed by Kamekura for *Expo'70*, for example, simplifies Sakura, a flower representative of Japan, into the geometric symbol of the family crest—the cherry crest—and places it at the center of the poster. The colorful beams of light radiating from the cherry blossom emblem not only enhance the visual impact but also create a dynamic beauty through the balanced arrangement of radial lines. Moreover, the beams, designed to resemble cherry blossom petals, further emphasize the essence of Japanese culture while conveying a positive and optimistic spirit. This geometric treatment of dots, lines, and planes makes the poster a design that is simple and powerful.

● **Japanese graphic designer Ikko Tanaka also incorporates a great deal of traditional Japanese cultural elements into his works, aided by abstract geometric "planes" to form more recognizable forms. Through this approach, he blends modernity with distinct "Japaneseness," allowing his graphic compositions to convey deeper cultural meanings.** One of his most famous pieces, *Japanese Dance*, depicts fully a woman with Japanese characteristics. In this piece, large geometric shapes are employed to represent traditional clothing and hair accessories, while highlighting the distinctive Japanese aesthetic. Tanaka also introduces "ingenious tricks" within the purely geometric composition, such as stacking two circles of different sizes to form the lips and combining circles and semicircles to design the eyes. Due to this thoughtful treatment, the eyes of the woman are imbued with emotional depth, creating a sense of rhythm and movement that breaks the otherwise equal and symmetrical design.

● **In its evolutionary process, Japanese graphic design has consistently upheld a respect for and inheritance of traditional culture.** When designers incorporate dots, lines, and planes in their creations, they often combine traditional elements with modern design techniques, resulting in works rich in national characteristics while still reflecting contemporary sensibilities. This fusion of tradition and modernity is evident not only in the selection of graphic elements but also in the continuity and innovation of design concepts.

Fig. 10 *Japanese Dance*, designed by Ikko Tanaka, 1981.

TECHNOLOGICAL DEVELOPMENT AND JAPANESE GRAPHIC COMPOSITION

● With the rapid advancement of technology, digital technology has penetrated every corner of graphic design. Japanese designers have increasingly embraced a variety of digital design software and tools in their creative processes. This not only enhances the precision and efficiency of their works but also enables designers to effortlessly achieve complex graphic manipulations and visual effects, revitalizing the composition of dots, lines, and planes in the digital era.

● **Mitsuo Katsui, a pioneer of modern digital design in Japan, has dedicated his career to exploring new realms of graphic design, particularly possible ways to integrate emerging technologies like computers into the design process.** His most famous works mainly use the color of light as a design language, employing gradient compositions between different colors to create mesmerizing effects with the aid of computer technology. Additionally, Katsui utilizes technology to form more complex geometric shapes and skillful arrangements of lines to construct more diverse patterns. It is worth mentioning that he often incorporates psychological principles into his designs to easily capture the attention of viewers and arouse deeper level of interaction and emotional resonance.

● **The development of computer graphics has greatly accelerated the progress of graphic design in Japan.** From simple visual displays to advanced image processing techniques, these technologies have allowed designers to express their creativity with more freedom. During the 1990s, the widespread adoption of DTP technology, the rise of programming, and the growing interactivity of the Internet further enriched the scope of graphic design. Today, computers have become an essential tool in the design process, enhancing both the efficiency and quality of work while continually expanding the boundaries and possibilities of design. In a nutshell, technology has made graphic design more diverse, dynamic, and interactive.

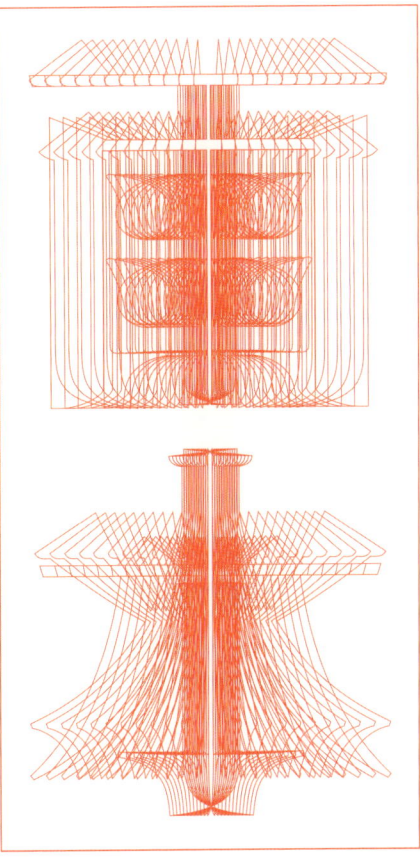

Fig. 11 *Letters and Life–Rain Water*, Morisawa typeface, designed by Mitsuo Katsui, 2008.

Chapter

日本グラフィックデザインの精髄　点・線・面

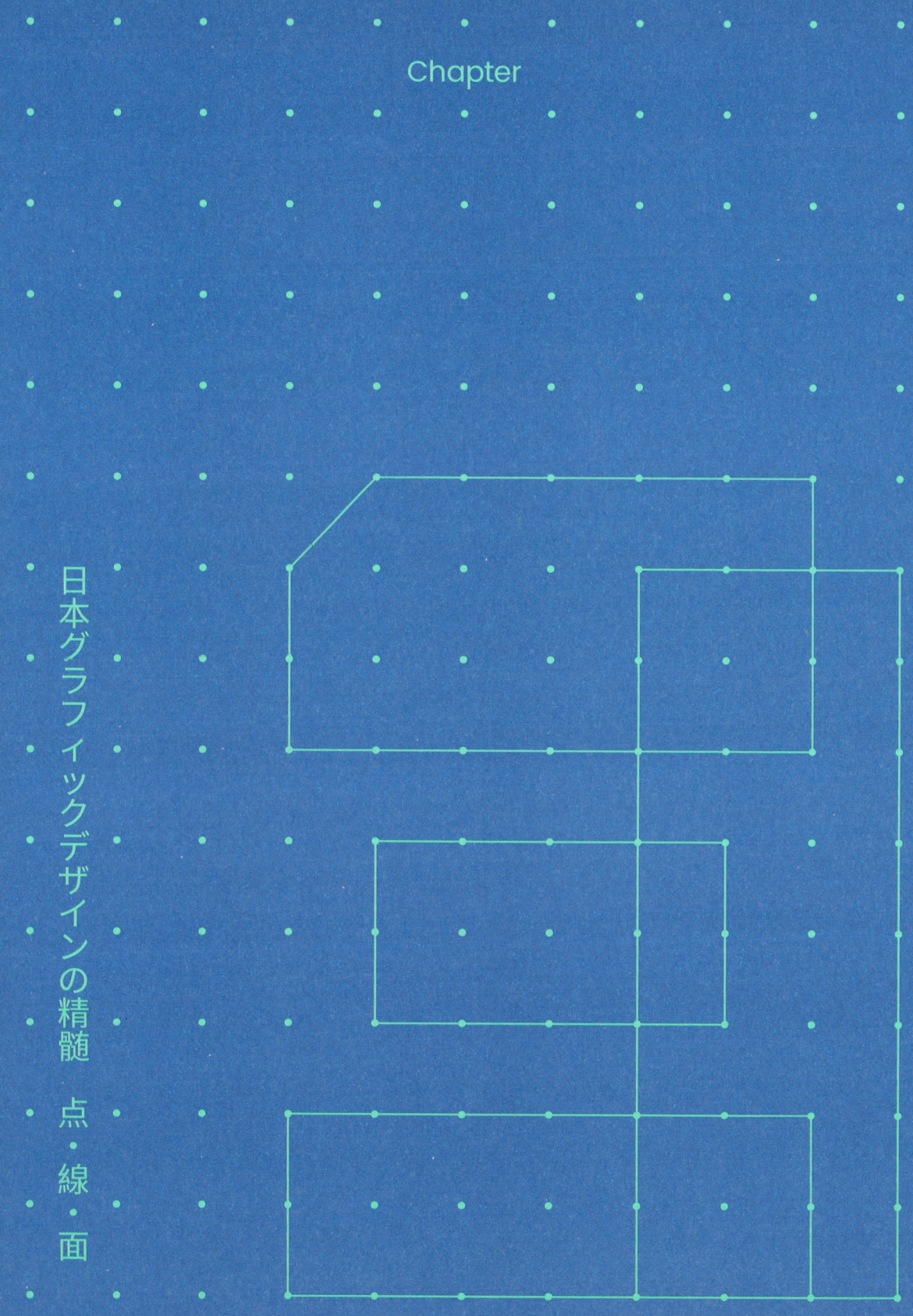

THE ESSENCE OF JAPANESE GRAPHIC DESIGN: DOTS, LINES, AND PLANES

Dots, lines, and planes—the basic elements of artistic expression in Japanese graphic design—are more than mere shapes and structures; they represent a profound philosophical pursuit. With unparalleled aesthetic principles embedded in it, this style serves as the unique artistic language of Japanese graphic design.

● The "dot" serves as the smallest visible unit and the starting point of abstract expression, imbued with rich symbolism and emotional resonance. Far from being a mere geometric element, the dot is a powerful and expressive visual language. Through subtle variations, designers can craft delicate and layered visual effects within a two-dimensional space. This sensitivity to the dot and its refined treatment can be traced back to traditional Japanese art. For instance, in ukiyo-e prints, artists skillfully used variations in dots to portray facial expressions and the flowing texture of clothing, breaking the constraints of flat visual space and endowing the image with vivid expressiveness. In modern art, artists like Yayoi Kusama[1] have elevated the dot into an autonomous artistic language. Through repeated experimentation with the size, shape, and arrangement of dots, Kusama creates works with strong visual impact and psychological depth. As dots accumulate and overlap, they begin to form lines, guiding the viewer's gaze and serving as a foundation for constructing the overall design context.

1. Yayoi Kusama (1929-) is a Japanese contemporary artist who works primarily in sculpture and installation, and she is also active in painting, performance, video art, fashion, poetry, fiction, and other arts. Her works are grounded in conceptual art and incorporates stylistic elements of feminism, minimalism, surrealism, primitivism, pop art, and abstract expressionism. They often carry autobiographical, psychological, and gender-related themes.

● The "line" plays a key role in guiding, separating, and defining shapes in Japanese graphic design. The precise use of lines grants the design dynamics and structure. Through the interweaving of lines, designers can create rhythmic images that guide the viewer's eyes and emotions. This technique is especially common in Japanese logo and packaging design. For example, a simple and smooth line can present product information in a way that is both distinct and eye-catching, without sacrificing aesthetic appeal. Lines can be further categorized into two basic forms: straight lines and curved lines. If we say straight lines are the result of the visual persistence effect between two neighboring dots, then curved lines are formed by changes in position or direction. The variations in thickness, curvature, and density of these lines can trigger different emotional resonances and create different feelings and expressions. Intertwined and overlapped lines together form a "plane," and thus rich and multi-layered planes can be obtained through the arrangement and combination of different lines.

● The "plane" is a two-dimensional space formed by dots and lines together. This spatial extent is not only the definition of shape but also the basis of the entire design composition. The natural extension of dots and lines forms a plane, which provides a wider space of expression for design. In Japanese graphic design, a plane is not just a graphic but also an expression of space. By skillfully utilizing planes, designers can create visual depth and hierarchy, a technique prominently displayed in poster design, magazine layouts, and other creative fields. Japanese designers often create visual tension and dynamism by adjusting the size, shape, and arrangement of planes, resulting in compositions that feel both rich and well-ordered. At the same time, a plane can also be seen as an enlarged dot or a thickened line. In this sense, a plane can be further deconstructed into countless dots and lines, reflecting the interplay and transformation between different formal elements in design.

● Dots, lines, and planes are intertwined and interdependent, collectively shaping the multifaceted variations of the flat visual world. The arrangement and change of dots define the shape of lines, while large enough dots can be directly viewed as a plane. Similarly, planes emerge from the spreading and interweaving of lines with new possibilities of dots nurtured within them. This dynamic interplay creates a closer relationship among dots, lines, and planes, presenting a more complex and deeper design context. Japanese graphic designers are skillful at interacting with them. By combining dots and lines, they create a sense of rhythm and make the overall design more dynamic and vibrant. Furthermore, a skillful plane user can weave dots and lines into a cohesive, organic composition, forming more complete and harmonious images. This interaction is evident not only in static designs, such as posters and layouts, but also in dynamic works, including animations and interactive designs.

○ Through the skillful use of basic elements such as dots, lines, and planes, Japanese designers create depth and movement within limited two-dimensional spaces, achieving a balance of simplicity and tension. This precise control over form and perception reflects a uniquely Japanese aesthetic of "permanence in impermanence"—a pursuit of inner balance and enduring visual experience amidst constant change. The design language of dots, lines, and planes runs through various fields such as posters, logos, and packaging, forming a fundamental pillar of Japanese graphic design. It is this meticulous attention to everyday details that sets Japanese design apart on the global stage, consistently revealing its distinctive and profound artistic allure.

DOT

What's a dot?

● In graphic design, the dot is the most fundamental geometric element and the smallest unit of visual composition. It has no inherent direction, size, or specific shape, yet its simplicity grants it remarkable expressive power. A dot can function independently as a focal point in a design, or it can serve as the starting point of lines and shapes. Through arrangement, repetition, and transformation, it helps construct a rich and versatile visual language.

The Compositional Aesthetics of Dots

● **First, a dot's visual properties—such as position, size, color, and density—make it highly adaptable.** In symmetrical compositions, a centered dot conveys stability and balance; placed lower, it creates a grounded, calming effect; positioned higher, it draws the viewer's gaze upward. A dot placed at a golden ratio point within the layout captures attention more effectively and strengthens the overall composition.

● **Second, the dot is the structural foundation of lines.** It marks the beginning, end, or nodes along a path. By arranging dots in either an orderly or a free-form manner, designers can create straight lines, curves, or intricate patterns, thus introducing rhythm and structure into their designs.

● **In ordered compositions, the repetition and alignment of dots generate a rhythmic visual flow.** In more spontaneous arrangements, variations in size and spacing produce a dynamic, playful rhythm, adding vitality and fluidity to the visual experience. The interaction between dots and surrounding space introduces tension and enhances the sense of depth and rhythm in the layout.

● **More importantly, dots are imbued with a sense of symbolism.** As the most elemental unit of visual language, a dot can represent a beginning, a seed, life, energy, or limitless potential. In Japanese design, the subtle use of dots often conveys a sense of order and poetic nuance found within the microcosm, embodying a quiet but profound expression of beauty.

Various Dots in Design

- **SIZE OF DOTS:**

Large Dots:

Small Dots:

- **SHAPE OF DOTS:**

Regular:
Basic Geometric Shapes:

Composite Polygons:

Irregular:
Pictorial Dots:

Textual Dots:

d	点	o	點	t
ぎ	3	ㅎ	포	୧

- **ORIENTATION OF DOTS:**

Horizontal:

Vertical:

- **POSITION OF DOTS:**

Upper Dot: A dot located toward the upper part of the composition.

Central Dot: A dot placed in the center of the layout.

Lower Dot: A dot situated in the lower section of the layout.

Golden Ratio Dot: A dot positioned according to the golden ratio, dividing a line into two parts such that the ratio of the smaller to the larger is approximately 0.618.

- **DENSITY OF DOTS:**

Isolated Dot: A single, stand-alone dot in the composition.

Dispersed Dots: Dots spaced relatively far apart from each other.

Dense Dots: Dots placed close together, forming a concentrated arrangement.

Radial: Dots radiating outward or converging inward.

WHERE THE DOT BEGINS

DAIGO DAIKOKU

Art Director
Graphic Designer

Daigo Daikoku is a graduate of the Kanazawa College of Art, one of the few public art schools in Japan. He began working at Nippon Design Center (NDC) in 2003 and founded Daikoku Design Institute in 2011. To successfully expand into global markets, Daigo moved to Los Angeles in 2018. At NDC's LA office (NDCLA), he envisions a global multidisciplinary design studio—one that aggregates diverse experiences and channels them into a holistic, intimate practice. Daigo acknowledges that technology has brought our world closer together; however, barriers still exist. He believes visual communication can help bridge the divide and create a higher social consciousness. At NDCLA, Daigo and his team focus on bringing ideas to life through simple, clear, and bold design, and the serendipity that occurs at the crossroads of culture. Daigo serves on the board of directors at NDC in Tokyo today and is involved with the company's strategic planning.

Daigo communicates essential information while also forging emotional and philosophical connections between his works, his clients, and their audiences. Projects include: creative direction for Takao 599 Museum, the nature-themed museum for Mount Takao (2015–present); exhibition design for The Art of Bloom, a multi-sensory experience that focuses on the symbiotic relationship between humans and nature (2019); exhibition design for HIDA: A Woodworking Tradition in the Making for Japan House Los Angeles (2020); book design for *New Language*, a textbook used for language classes in Japanese elementary schools (2020); book design for *Waka* poetry by Empress Michiko (2015); art direction and production for MUJI's annual, cross-media, global holiday campaign (2009–2014); brand identity for Pristine, Japan's renowned organic cotton brand (2010–present); and package design for Koshi no Kanbai, one of Japan's premium sake brands (2015–present).

◯ As a starting point for form, emotion, and meaning, a single dot can hold immense potential. For Daigo Daikoku, the dot is not only a fundamental element of graphic composition but also a vessel for the diverse expressions of graphic design. In this interview, he reflects on how abstraction can be distilled into the concrete, how a "dot" interacts and harmonizes with its surrounding space, and the potential of graphic composition in the digital age. Guided by a practice rooted in Japanese aesthetics and shaped by global experiences, he shares his creative process—distilling core information from complexity, seeking meaning in the smallest elements, and emphasizing the tactile quality of real experience. His approach reveals a design philosophy grounded in curiosity, sensitivity, and an embrace of imperfection.

ZERO IN: THE 1% THAT MATTERS

● **One of the most widely praised aspects of Daigo Daikoku's work is his ability to distill complexity into its purest visual essence.** When discussing his approach to abstraction, he emphasizes that distillation is not merely about reduction, but about starting from a place of richness and intricacy. His creative process begins with broad and in-depth research—casting a wide net to gather as much information and inspiration as possible. From this abundance of material, he meticulously filters out what truly matters, discarding 99% of irrelevant data to uncover the 1% core idea. Though this process can seem daunting, he believes that only by identifying that 1% of true value can a design communicate its purpose with clarity and precision.

● **He illustrates this method with inspiration drawn from nature, likening it to the formation of smooth river stones.** Over time, the stones shed their rough edges and excess mass, gradually revealing a refined form. What may appear insignificant at first becomes something beautifully polished through patience and persistence. In his own works, Daikoku applies a similar philosophy—continually refining and focusing his concepts until the remaining core feels honest, powerful, and complete.

● **The same principle applies to commercial brand design.** For example, a logo design demands that designers capture a wealth of ideas and emotions, but trying to include everything often dilutes the essential message. For Daikoku, the designer's role is to guide clients in identifying their core narrative,

Fig. 1 Dear Mayuko (Yokohama) Brand identity, designed by Daigo Daikoku, 2016.

stripping away noise, and constructing a clear and impactful visual framework that effectively communicates the brand's message. His design thinking is consistently sharp and deliberate, favoring simplicity, boldness, and clarity. While he values the precision of language, he believes images are better at conveying subtle feelings through ambiguity—offering what words cannot. His goal is to make these elusive sensations visible through imagery.

● **Throughout his design practice, Daikoku also maintains a strong belief in avoiding overly didactic design.** He insists on leaving room for the viewer's interpretation and curiosity. For him, trusting the audience is as important as trusting the design itself—an approach that continues to shape his distinct and evolving visual language.

THE DOT AS A UNIVERSE: PRESENCE, SPACE, AND RHYTHM

● **Daigo Daikoku's exploration of abstraction finds rich expression in his treatment of the "dot"—a fundamental element in his visual language.** For him, the dot is a starting point, a zero state full of potential from which any form can emerge. A dot can stand alone or evolve into a line, a plane, a letter, or an image. It possesses infinite flexibility, adapting to its surroundings to take on different personalities—at times subtle and restrained, supporting the overall composition; at other times bold and expressive, commanding attention within the frame. He aims for each dot in his design to embody its own character and purpose.

● **More compelling to Daikoku than the dot itself is the space surrounding it—the environment that gives the dot its meaning.** He compares this to a rock climber plotting a route or a flower arranger composing a bouquet: in both cases, the goal is not to dominate the space but to shape it with intention and meaning. This is a deeply Eastern way of thinking. He cites the rock garden at Ryoan-ji in Kyoto as an example, where meaning does not reside in the rocks alone, but in the spatial relationships they create. In his own works, the movement of a single dot can transform the mood and dynamics of an entire composition, creating a unique rhythm specific to each piece. Through this rhythm, new spatial relationships emerge.

Fig. 2 Poster for Musashino Art University "Personality", designed by Daigo Daikoku, 2016.

● **Even the smallest dot in his works possesses a distinctive presence.** For Daikoku, each dot reflects a deliberate intention. As a designer, he sees his role as understanding, guiding, and fully expressing that intention. Whether a dot takes the form of a square, rectangle, or circle, its placement within a defined space imbues it with context and meaning. In one of his posters, for instance, he positioned a character's eye outside the face—a bold decision that defies visual convention and generates striking tension. By exploring the interaction between form and space, he breathes individuality and emotional resonance into even the simplest of dots.

BETWEEN CULTURES: JAPANESE SIMPLICITY AND AMERICA DYNAMISM

● **Now based in Los Angeles, Daigo Daikoku acknowledges that his visual instincts remain deeply rooted in Japanese aesthetics.** He believes that simplicity, refinement, and an attentiveness to lived experience are at the core of his design philosophy. In Japanese culture, even the everyday presentation of food is considered an art form—one that heightens awareness of the present moment through color, arrangement, and taste. Experiences are often layered, much like the ritual of entering a traditional home: with every turn, a new scene unfolds, framed by shōji screens and tatami in a harmonious and poetic progression. For Daikoku, such multi-sensory, multi-layered experiences shape how he constructs visual narratives. Even the simplest forms, in his view, can hold profound beauty and meaning.

● **At the same time, the spontaneity and visual optimism of American culture have been equally inspiring.** Living in the U.S. has deepened his understanding of this contrast and sparked his exploration of how Japan's restrained minimalism might intersect with the bold, fast-paced energy of American graphic expression. This interplay—between clarity and complexity, order and spontaneity—continues to shape and evolve his design philosophy, guiding him to create works that are both personally distinctive and widely resonant.

Fig. 3 Tsubaki Hills Screen, designed by Daigo Daikoku, 2010.

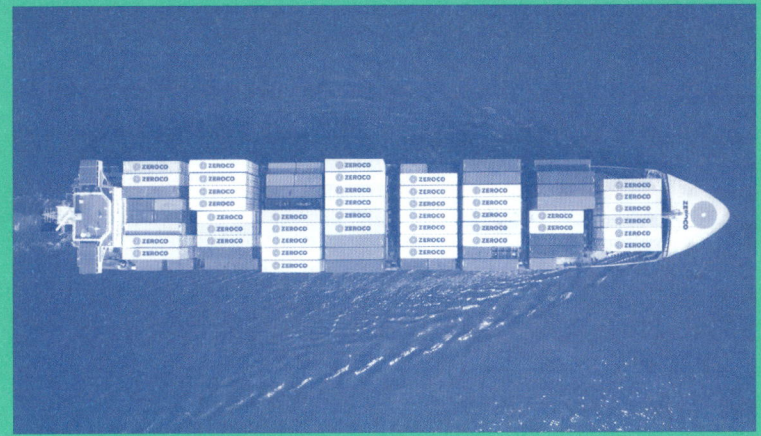

Fig. 4 ZEROCO Brand Identity, designed by Daigo Daikoku, 2023.

DIGITAL FUTURE: EMBRACING IMPERFECTION AND THE UNKNOWN

● **When Daigo Daikoku first began his creative journey, he primarily worked on posters and other print-based projects. His approach was closer to that of a painter, focused on the physicality of visuals and textures. As digital tools have evolved, so too have his working methods and design strategies.** While he is excited by the new forms of expression and experiences enabled by digital media, he approaches these tools with caution. For example, he acknowledges that social media has transformed how designers share their works and ideas, fostering stronger connection within the design community. Yet, he also notes that our attention tends to gravitate toward the most popular or easily consumable content, while truly original ideas often remain hidden, unable to be "notificated" to the forefront. In an era shaped by "algorithm-friendly" content, the future will be, as he puts it, "Like an Amazon or Google experience, we end up searching for something different in a sea of sameness."

● **Artificial intelligence adds another layer of reflection to the design conversation.** Daikoku recognizes the astonishing capabilities of AI tools, particularly their ability to generate highly complex and refined images in an instant. However, he finds this kind of "perfection" unsettling, as it often lacks soul. What truly captivates him are imperfections—visual irregularities or traces of human error that bring emotion and depth to the work. For him, the vitality of design doesn't lie in flawless repetition but in the unexpected, in the gaps that spark curiosity. It is precisely in these imperfections that creativity takes root and flourishes.

TOUCH LIFE: CULTIVATING SENSITIVITY THROUGH AUTHENTIC EXPERIENCE

● **At the end of the interview, Daigo Daikoku emphasized the importance of grounding design in real-life experience.** For the younger generation of designers, he offered a simple yet profound piece of advice: "Look at real things with your own eyes, and pay close attention to how those experiences make you feel." He recalled his visit to the Louvre to see the *Mona Lisa*. What struck him most wasn't just the unexpectedly small size of the painting, but the worn floorboards surrounding it. The creaking sound of the wood, smoothed by generations of visitors, quietly testified to the passage of time and the enduring presence of art. For Daikoku, the key lies in cultivating a heightened sensitivity—only by immersing oneself in genuine life experiences can one sharpen one's perception of the world.

Fig. 5 Zhuanzhuan Visual Identity, designed by Daigo Daikoku, 2023.

● **After all, design never exists in a vacuum.** It is always in dialogue with its context—its environment, history, and audience. As a designer, your fundamental task is to communicate meaning through visuals. Expanding one's reservoir of real-life experiences, he believes, directly enhances a designer's capacity to engage in meaningful communication. In his view, this ongoing investment in visual and emotional literacy is one of the most valuable tools a designer can possess.

• DEAR MAYUKO BRAND IDENTITY

Dear Mayuko is an aspirational lifestyle cosmetics and beauty brand known for its use of ceresin, a natural moisturizing ingredient derived from silkworm cocoons. The brand's sensory qualities—fluffy, bubbly, silky, glossy—are reflected in various rounded shapes inspired by the cocoon's form. At the brand's launch, NDCLA oversaw the entire art direction, designing and directing all elements from the logo, packaging, and storefront to promotional materials and advertisements.

DA. Nippon Design Center
AD. Daigo Daikoku
D. Mayumi Sano
PT. Mikiya Takimoto, Kei Iwasaki
CL. Dear Mayuko Co., Ltd.

 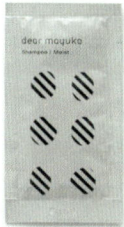 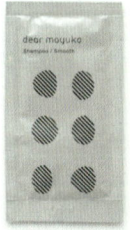    

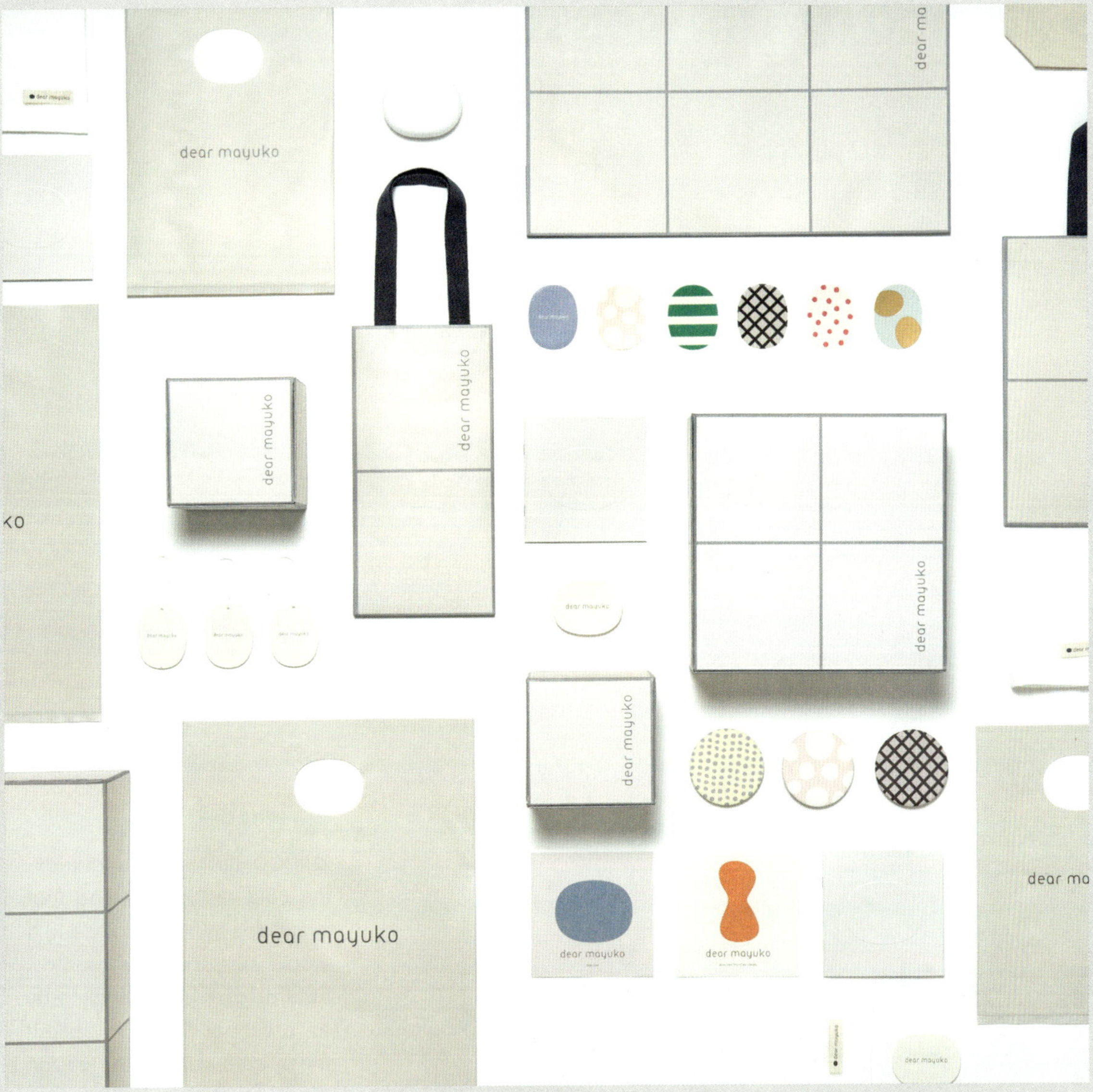

● Why Dot?

Inspired by the cocoon's rounded form, the design team created a range of circular graphics to evoke feelings of comfort, softness, and gentleness. In contrast, elements such as store interiors, paper bags, and gift boxes were designed using a square grid system. This interplay between round and square forms enhances the circular motif, bringing harmony and clarity to the overall brand experience.

Basic Dot

- ● C20 M15 Y15 K0 / R211 G212 B211
- ● C45 M20 Y20 K0 / R152 G182 B194
- ● C20 M20 Y20 K0 / R211 G203 B197
- ● C60 M40 Y20 K0 / R116 G140 B173
- ○ C0 M0 Y0 K0 / R255 G255 B255
- ● C0 M0 Y0 K100 / R0 G0 B0

● ZEROCO BRAND IDENTITY

● Why Dot?

ZEROCO uses a groundbreaking cold storage method that maintains 100% humidity and a stable ±0°C, offering the most natural and eco-friendly way to preserve food. To reflect these core values, the design team created a bold, generous "0" as the symbol mark—a confident, open form that expresses the brand's strong presence and commitment to solving global food challenges.

The design team collaborated with logistics company ZEROCO to build a lasting visual identity and strategy, positioning it as a global sustainability leader. Anticipating a future of 10 billion people facing food shortages and environmental decline, ZEROCO developed a 0°C, 100% humidity storage unit that preserves produce far longer than conventional methods. The design work helped establish ZEROCO as a pioneering solution in food distribution and agriculture, delivering Japan's finest produce worldwide.

DA. Nippon Design Center
AD. Daigo Daikoku
D. Kai Watanabe, Kosuke Tsurube
CL. ZEROCO

Basic Dot **ZERCO**

- ● C65 M25 Y5 K0 / R88 G158 B209
- ● C60 M10 Y0 K0 / R94 G183 B232
- ○ C0 M0 Y0 K0 / R255 G255 B255
- ● C0 M0 Y0 K100 / R0 G0 B0

NORIKKO PACKAGING DESIGN

This package design is for Norikko, a traditional dish prepared by local women on Ieshima, an island in the Seto Inland Sea. The black-and-white design intuitively reflects the visual contrast of dark Norikko served over white rice.

DA. Nippon Design Center
D. Daigo Daikoku
CL. NPO Ieshima

● Why Dot?

The idea is to capture a sense of deliciousness through minimal design. Inspired by the simple, familiar image of freshly cooked white rice topped with *nori tsukudani*[1], the packaging evokes a comforting scene that stirs warmth and nostalgia for many Japanese people.

1. Nori Tsukudani is a Japanese dish made by simmering nori (seaweed) with soy sauce, mirin, and other seasonings. It is typically served as a side dish, often enjoyed with rice.

Basic Dot

○ C0 M0 Y0 K0 / R255 G255 B255
● C0 M0 Y0 K100 / R0 G0 B0

⛩ CHINZAN-SŌ TOKYO GARDEN THREE-STORY PAGODA

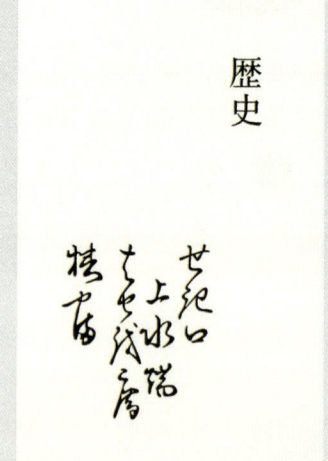

Entsukaku, a three-story wooden pagoda dating back to the 12th century, is now located in the garden of the Hotel Chinzan-sō Tokyo. For the ceremonies surrounding the renovation of this pagoda, erected by Japan's most renowned Shogun, Daigo Daikoku took charge of the art direction and graphic design for two folding booklets. These booklets featured camellia motifs, paying homage to the garden's reputation as a prime camellia-viewing location, alongside architectural drawings that delve into the deeper significance behind the pagoda's construction. The pagoda has been designated by Japan as a Tangible Cultural Property.

DA. Nippon Design Center
AD. Daigo Daikoku
CL. Fujita Kanko Inc.
C. Norimitsu Korekata

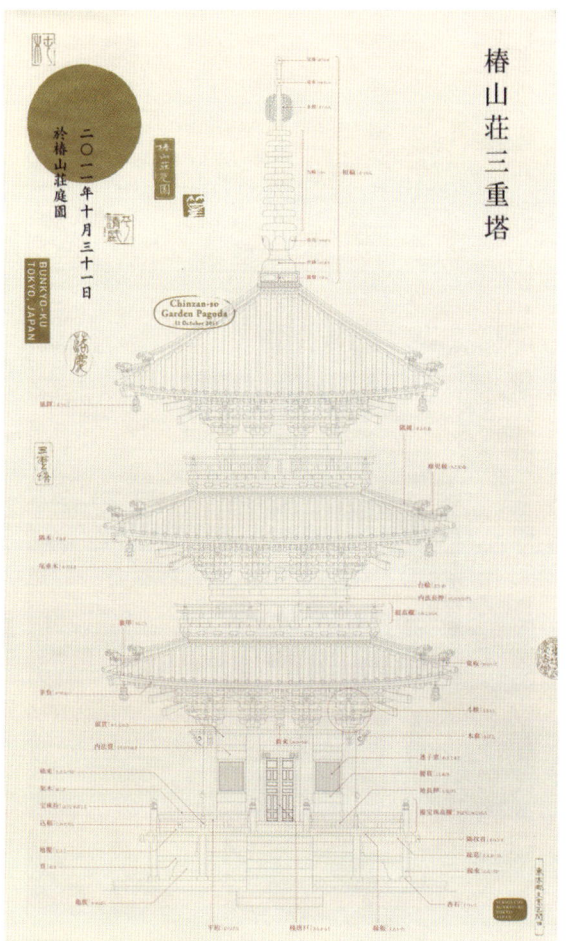

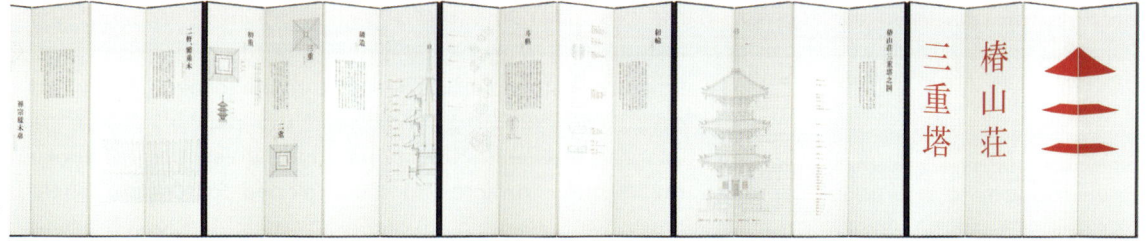

🟢 Why Dot?

The design team drew inspiration from the essence of the three-story pagoda, with its gracefully overlapping roofs, to create a mark that is both clear and dignified. The gentle curves of the roofs and the serene continuity of the three layers were thoughtfully expressed to convey a sense of elegance and quiet strength—enhancing gracefully, yet maintaining a calm, poised presence.

Basic Dot

- 🟤 C25 M25 Y50 K0 / R202 G187 B137
- 🔴 C45 M20 Y20 K0 / R152 G182 B194
- ⚪ C0 M0 Y0 K0 / R255 G255 B255
- ⚫ C0 M0 Y0 K100 / R0 G0 B0

49

○ BANLAN BRAND IDENTITY

Daigo Daikoku developed the logomark and supporting applications, including packaging and retail displays, for the Banlan brand store opening in 2024. Banlan channels Chinese aesthetics into modern, high-quality furniture built to withstand the test of time. Defined by its unique "Chinese Modern" style, Banlan draws inspiration from the minimalist ceramics of the Song Dynasty (960-1279), a period renowned for its flourishing arts and culture. NDCLA collaborated with Banlan's president and creative team to rebrand the visual identity, emphasizing the brand's core values and its unwavering confidence in the quality of its products, which come with a 10-year guarantee.

DA. Nippon Design Center
AD. Daigo Daikoku
D. Kosuke Tsurube
CL. Guangzhou Banlan Furniture Co., Ltd.

● Why Dot?

For the client, the philosophy of "Chinese Modern" was instrumental in shaping the design of the symbol and logo. Banlan's aesthetic draws deeply from the refined pottery and sculptures of the Song Dynasty, with a particular focus on the interplay between straight lines and curves. Daigo Daikoku meticulously explored and developed a design where these two elements create a dynamic tension, resulting in a beautiful contrast. The circular shape of the symbol represents this aesthetic in its purest form, embodying both the quality and philosophy behind Banlan's craftsmanship. The letter "B" is rendered with graceful curves and sharp straight lines, reflecting the meticulous refinement of form, akin to the careful honing of a piece of art to perfection.

Basic Dot

● C20 M40 Y70 K0 / R211 G163 B88
● C15 M20 Y25 K0 / R222 G207 B207
● C75 M70 Y65 K30 / R70 G67 B69
● C60 M55 Y65 K5 / R120 G112 B92

ZHUANZHUAN

NDCLA has refreshed the visual identity of ZHUAN ZHUAN, the world's largest used goods e-commerce platform, with over 200 million users. In an age of mass production, how can we build a sustainable world without placing further strain on the environment? Responding to this urgent global challenge, ZHUAN ZHUAN is leading the way—strengthening ties with both the market and its users, and doing so with a long-term vision for sustainability over the next 30, even 50 years.

DA. Nippon Design Center
AD. Daigo Daikoku
D. Mika Tohmon, Kosuke Tsurube, Kai Watanabe
CL. ZHUAN ZHUAN

Why Dot?

In redefining the core value of a service used by over 300 million people, Daigo Daikoku introduced the design concept of "Valuable Circulation." The new logo features two circles rotating along a single ring—a visual metaphor aligned with ZhuanZhuan's commitment to sustainability. This simple yet intuitive design clearly communicates the brand's values. The original bear icon was retained as a distinctive brand element, reimagined in a flattened form that subtly echoes the silhouette of a bear. The word ZHUANZHUAN (转转), which conveys a sense of repetition and movement, is integrated into the logotype to form a continuous graphic pattern. This pattern extends into the packaging design, embedding the idea of "Valuable Circulation" throughout the entire brand experience.

Basic Dot

● C0 M85 Y70 K0 / R233 G71 B63
○ C0 M0 Y0 K0 / R255 G255 B255
● C0 M0 Y0 K100 / R0 G0 B0

● KIYOSATO SHOCHU PACKAGING DESIGN

At 44° North latitude, at the foot of the Shiretoko Mountains in Kiyosato, Hokkaido, stands Japan's only shochu brewery operated by a local government. In 1975, the town's residents brewed Japan's first white potato shochu. In 2014, the brand's concept and design were renewed to promote Kiyosato as a culturally rich agricultural town to a global audience. Rooted in human connection, the project was developed through close dialogue with the townspeople, ensuring that local pride grows alongside the product.

DA. Nippon Design Center
AD. Daigo Daikoku, Masashi Tentaku, Yui Takada
PT. Takaya Sakano
CL. Kiyosato Shochu Distillery
C. Norimitsu Korekata

● Why Dot?

Kiyosato, located in the northernmost part of Japan in Hokkaido, is a region blessed with rich natural surroundings. To reflect its unique character—pure water, expansive snowy fields, and agricultural heritage—the design team developed a custom bottle design. The logo features three circles symbolizing "people," "landscape," and "nature." These organic forms, inspired by the shape of potatoes—the key ingredient in Japanese shochu—capture both the spirit of the region and the warmth of its community.

Basic Dot

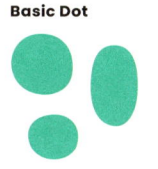

● C25 M25 Y50 K0 / R202 G187 B137
● C85 M85 Y30 K0 / R67 G62 B120
○ C0 M0 Y0 K0 / R255 G255 B255

● SNOW DROP

The designer created a book of *Grimms' Fairy Tales* using his custom font. For the story of *Snow Drop*, which features many exciting scenes, the designer aimed to offer a fresh perspective—one that diverges from the traditional image people have of the tale. To achieve this, he expressed it through graphic and typographic elements that evoke a sharp, almost piercing sensation, like needles pricking the eyes.

AD. TD. D. Zin Nagao

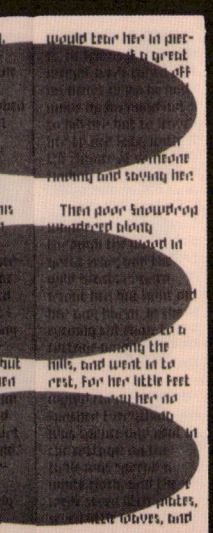
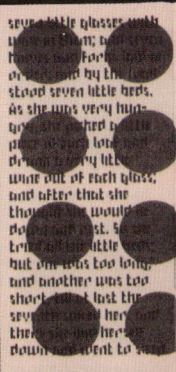

Why Dot?

The designer used dots of different shapes and sizes to cover the text of the book, creating a highly intuitive visual experience for the reader—one that lets them guess where the story is going based on the graphics.

Basic Dot

○ C0 M25 Y15 K0 / R249 G209 B203

● C0 M0 Y0 K80 / R89 G87 B87

I'M INSANELY CURIOUS

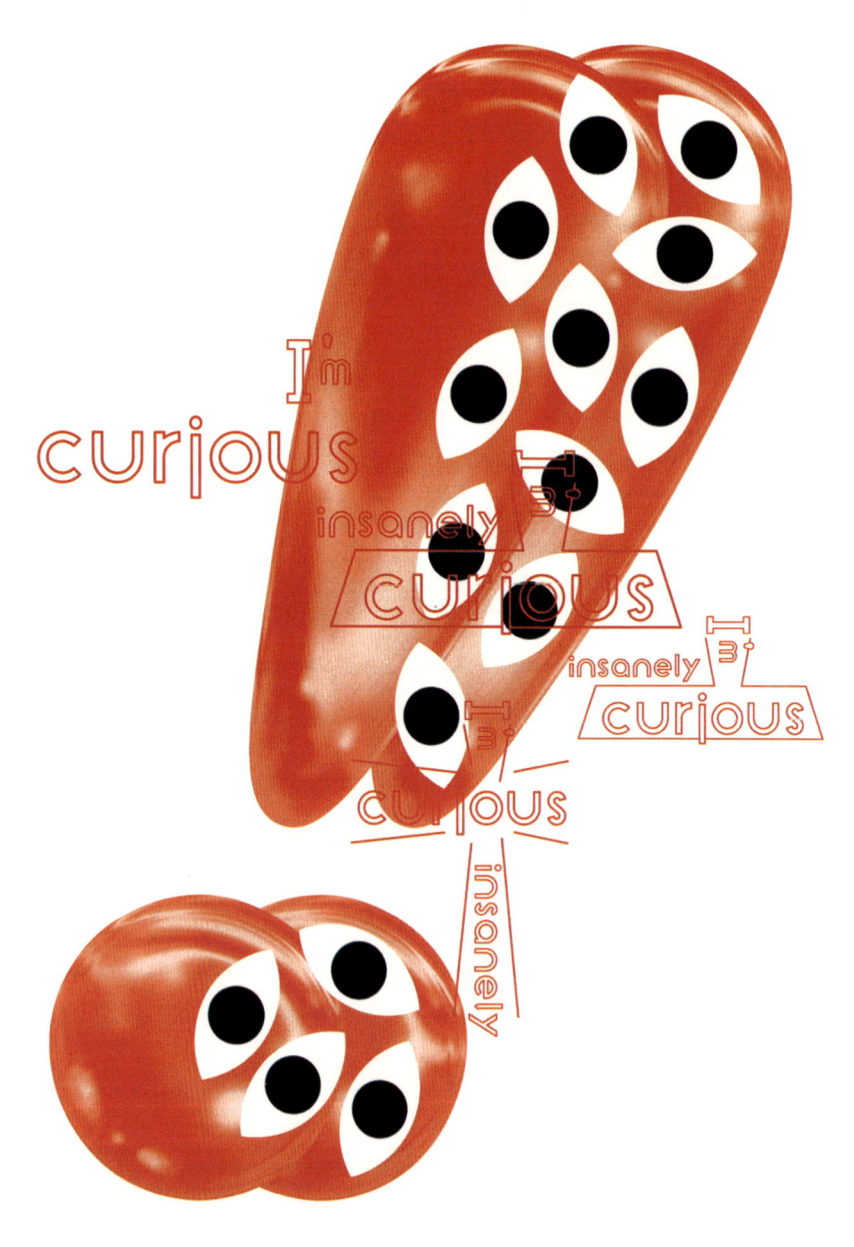

This work was specially created for the "Buy-in" themed exhibition of the X Sign Space in Hangzhou (China). It humorously reflects the phenomenon of the once lightweight paper bag now often serving as a symbol of wealth. The designer draws inspiration from the various glances directed at paper bags (and the people proudly carrying them)—ranging from casual envy to unabashed admiration—to highlight the social significance behind the paper bag.

DA. Ito Kashiwagi Design Office Inc.
D. Mitsuki Kashiwagi

🔴 Why Dot?

Although this paper bag design was not directly put into production, the entire design process remained firmly focused on the essence of the paper bag as a medium for information and visual communication. In order to maximize the visual perception of the viewer within the limited display space, the designer used the graphic of the eye and maximized the repetition of this specific graphic within the limited space to form a strong visual impact. The intention is to tell the viewer that when you are judging something according to the handbag, the handbag is also judging you.

Basic Dot

- 🔴 C10 M85 Y95 K0 / R219 G71 B28
- ⚫ C0 M0 Y0 K100 / R0 G0 B0
- ⚪ C0 M0 Y0 K0 / R255 G255 B255

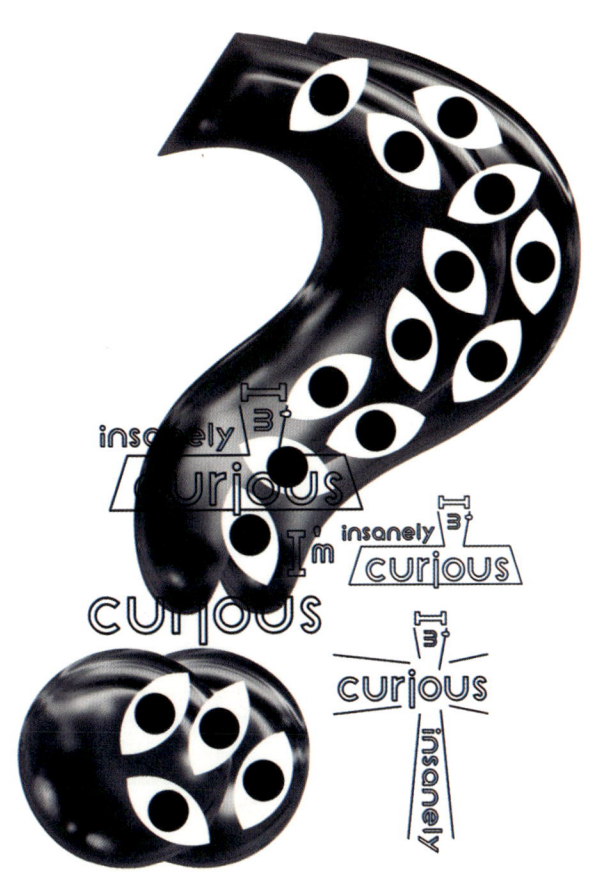

JAGDA INTERNATIONAL STUDENT POSTER AWARD 2020

The JAGDA International Student Poster Award is an esteemed international poster competition. This poster explores the theme of "Money" by creatively overlapping coins from around the world with textual information. The design creates a strong visual impact by scattering the coins across the poster, effectively drawing the viewer's attention.

DA. iyamadesign inc.
D. Koji Iyama
CL. Japan Graphic Designers Association Inc. (JAGDA)

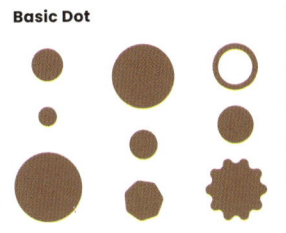

Why Dot?

The design was intended to appear as a simple dot at first glance, but upon closer inspection, it reveals itself to be a coin, highlighting the theme of the International Poster Competition.

Basic Dot

- C45 M65 Y85 K0 / R159 G109 B60
- C0 M0 Y0 K100 / R0 G0 B0
- C0 M0 Y0 K0 / R255 G255 B255
- C0 M0 Y0 K20 / R220 G221 B221
- C0 M0 Y0 K50 / R159 G160 B160
- C50 M100 Y100 K15 / R135 G31 B36

BIRD

The designer observes the world from the perspective of geometric shapes, and in his eyes, all kinds of birds can also be presented in this kind of geometric patchwork. The designer first sketched the design by hand with a compass and ruler, and then used computer software to transform it into a graphic. Finally, the designer then colored the birds and animals according to their own colors to complete the design.

DA. SOBOKU DESIGN
D. Yusei Oi

Why Dot?

The designer uses basic geometric shapes to represent various bird forms. Each shape represents a part of a bird's body, e.g., the head is represented by a dot and the beak by a triangle. All these basic dots are put together to form a bird with a special style.

Basic Dot

- C0 M0 Y0 K90 / R63 G59 B58
- C15 M15 Y30 K0 / R223 G214 B184
- C25 M0 Y5 K50 / R124 G145 B152
- C45 M20 Y90 K0 / R158 G176 B58
- C0 M50 Y10 K0 / R241 G157 B181
- C55 M60 Y65 K40 / R96 G76 B63
- C0 M35 Y85 K0 / R248 G182 B45

▲ OGIHARA FARM

Why Dot?

The logo design focuses on the presentation of a specific scenario, namely the shape of grapes and hills. The designer followed the concept of minimalism and avoided adding unnecessary information as much as possible. The designer believed that the minimalism of the design would allow the high quality and craftsmanship of the product to be visualized.

This creation focuses on crafting a unique brand identity for a vineyard. The small farm treasures its bond with customers and has never engaged in online sales. To accurately align with this sincere and pure business philosophy, the design emphasizes a simple and natural aesthetic expression. In the early morning, under the lush grapevines, ripe fruits hang amidst the greenery, with the distant Mount Komagatake quietly coming into view. This breathtaking scene is a special gift from nature to the hardworking cultivators. The design faithfully presents this touching image, aiming to allow viewers to directly experience the unrefined yet distinctive charm of "Ogihara Farm."

DA. Ito Kashiwagi Design Office Inc.
D. Mitsuki Kashiwagi
CL. Ogihara Farm

Basic Dot

● C50 M10 Y70 K0 / R142 G186 B105
○ C0 M0 Y0 K0 / R255 G255 B255

● MARU-EXERCISE

These small cards, made from circular stickers, serve as tools for the designer's daily practice of fostering divergent thinking. During the creative process, the designer breaks free from the constraints of specific themes and objectives, following only a few simple rules while freely exploring and striving to uncover diverse and unique creative expressions. Through this daily practice, the designer has clearly felt her own transformation and growth.

D. Sakura Kashiwazaki

● Why Dot?

To achieve the goals presented in the introduction, the designer intentionally set moderate rules, using only a limited color palette and specific-sized circles for the creation. Circular stickers are simple to handle and easily accessible, making them more suitable for long-term creative engagement compared to traditional art materials.

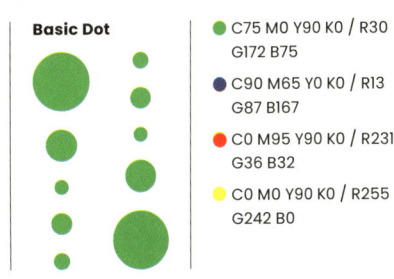

Basic Dot

● C75 M0 Y90 K0 / R30 G172 B75
● C90 M65 Y0 K0 / R13 G87 B167
● C0 M95 Y90 K0 / R231 G36 B32
● C0 M0 Y90 K0 / R255 G242 B0

● FRUITS REPORT

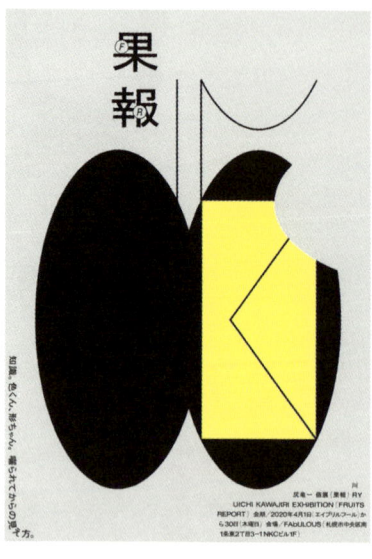
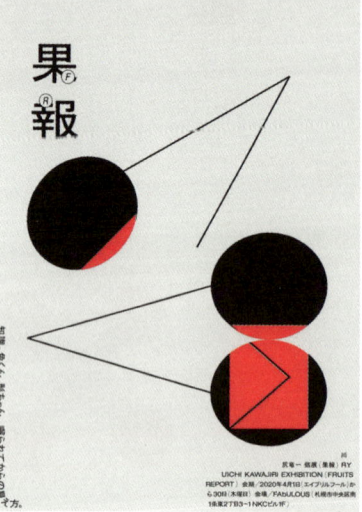

FRUITS REPORT is a series of works themed around "fruit and reports," with its title derived from the words "果" (FRUITS) and "報" (REPORT). The design approach is unique, using black outlines to depict the contours of fruits, with the interiors filled with colored mail icon symbols. The combination of these elements naturally evokes images of fruits such as apples, grapes, and cherries. The inspiration for the promotional poster comes from the story of Adam and Eve gaining knowledge after eating the forbidden fruit. Visually, the designer intentionally removed part of the fruit graphic to leave space for reflection and interpretation.

DA. Kawa
D. Ryuichi Kawajiri

● SANZUI'S SELF-INITIATED PROJECT

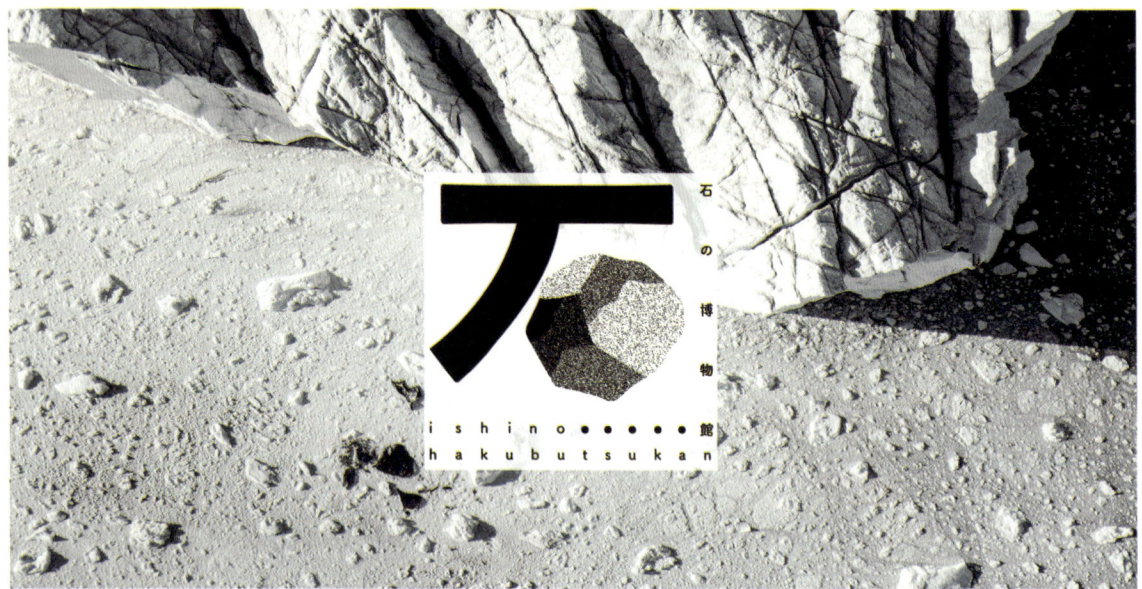

Designer sanzui is dedicated to creating work that highlights the intrinsic character of each motif. Through careful analysis, sanzui translates these elements into visuals that deeply resonate with viewers.

Sanzui aims to create designs that effectively convey the essence of each motif. With a focus on visual appeal and clarity, he ensures the motif is both eye-catching and easily recognizable. By combining these elements, the result is a strong, memorable design that reflects the true value of the design.

D. sanzui

● Why Dot?

The designer used the Chinese character "石" as a recognizable visual basis for his design. By replacing the original character "口" with a stone with many visible surfaces, the design is close to the meaning of the character itself and visually conveys the meaning to viewers who do not recognize the character. The surrounding dotted rows of Chinese characters, letters, and dots create the feeling of gravel strewn across the ground and dotted with stars.

Basic Dot

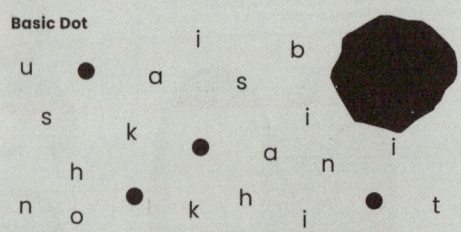

○ C0 M0 Y0 K0 / R255 G255 B255
◐ C0 M0 Y0 K50 / R159 G159 B160
● C0 M0 Y0 K100 / R0 G0 B0

■ CHIBA ART FESTIVAL 2019

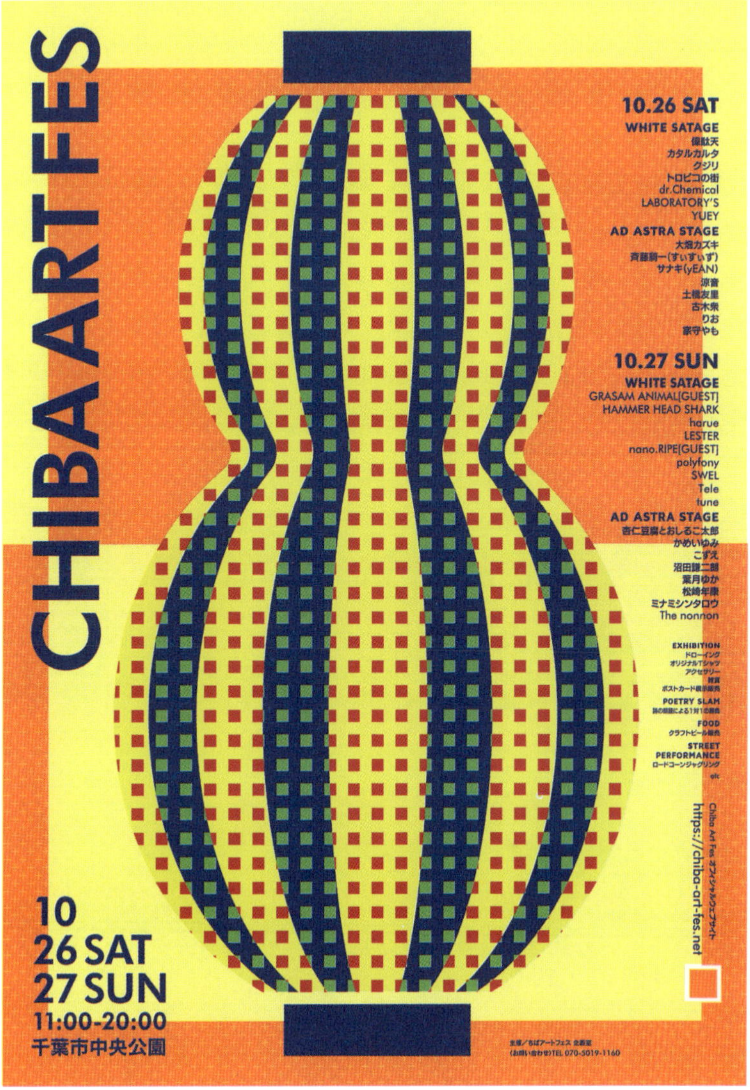

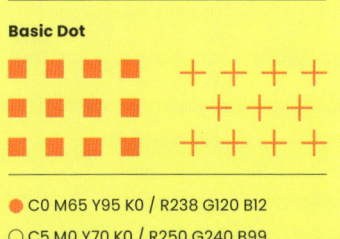

Why Dot?

The designer used the square dots to convey the texture of the peanut skin.

Basic Dot

- C0 M65 Y95 K0 / R238 G120 B12
- C5 M0 Y70 K0 / R250 G240 B99
- C100 M85 Y25 K0 / R0 G60 B126
- C15 M100 Y80 K0 / R208 G15 B49
- C60 M5 Y100 K0 / R112 G181 B44

This poster for the Chiba Art Festival 2019 combines peanuts, a local specialty, with chochin lanterns under the theme of a festival. The peanut pattern symbolizes the lanterns that brightly illuminate the event.

DA. TARO inc.
D. Hiroyuki Masuda
CL. Chiba Art Festival

▲ TOKYO MIDTOWN DESIGN HUB KIDS WEEK

● Why Dot?

The designer used basic geometric shapes for the typeface design, which is childlike and at the same time expresses the theme of the exhibition.

Basic Dot

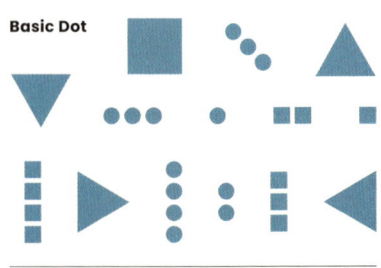

- ● C65 M20 Y15 K0 / R86 G165 B199
- ● C10 M65 Y5 K0 / R221 G118 B166
- ● C50 M5 Y75 K0 / R142 G192 B96
- ● C10 M100 Y75 K0 / R216 G8 B53
- ● C16 M12 Y11 K0 / R221 G221 B222
- ○ C0 M0 Y0 K0 / R255 G255 B255
- ● C0 M0 Y0 K100 / R0 G0 B0

Since this event takes place during children's summer vacation, the design team aimed to create a fun and engaging atmosphere while maintaining the sophistication of the event venue. The posters were thoughtfully designed to balance playfulness with visual refinement. One poster features a composition of dots forming graphics of the sun, mountains, and ocean, evoking the essence of summer. The other takes a more interactive approach, presenting a puzzle-like design with the event title and silhouettes of two children, inviting curiosity and engagement.

DA. iyamadesign inc.
D. Koji Iyama
CL. Tokyo Midtown Design Hub

YOTSU

Why Dot?

The logo features the shape of a slice of French bread to enhance its interest. The logo uses vertical typography to visualize the bread when it is freshly sliced.

Basic Dot

- C0 M0 Y0 K100 / R0 G0 B0
- C0 M0 Y0 K0 / R255 G255 B255
- C20 M25 Y30 K0 / R211 G193 B175

This is a brand logo design done by the designer for a bakery. This bakery logo was designed to reflect the shop's concept of simplicity, clarity, and playfulness. The design captures a warm and inviting feel, ensuring it is both easily recognizable and visually engaging.

DA. Econosys Design Inc.
AD. Mitsutaka Nakao
D. Takayuki Isomi
CL. Yotsu

◆ COUPLE CRANES

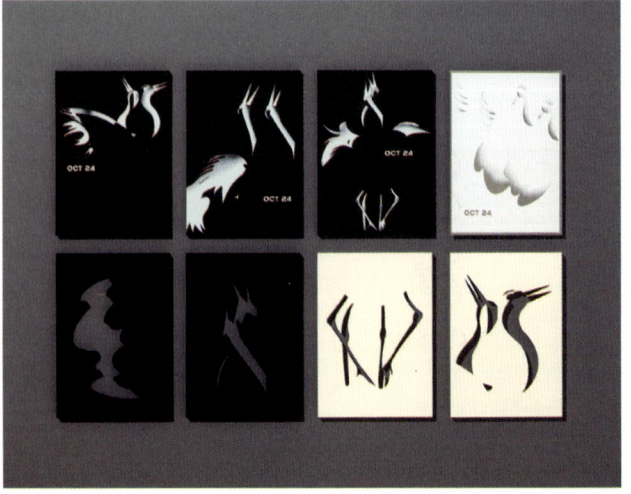

This wedding tool was created for a ceremony held at Sankeien, an important cultural landmark in Yokohama, Japan. The designer crafted posters, invitations, and various items for the event. In Japan, wedding invitations are often overly ornate and cluttered. In contrast, the designer sought to use the natural qualities of paper to create a simple yet beautiful invitation, one unlike any seen before. By boldly incorporating black—traditionally considered taboo in Japanese weddings—the designer aimed to express an avant-garde perspective on marriage, challenging conservative norms.

D. Miharu Matsunaga (Hami)
CL. Couple Cranes

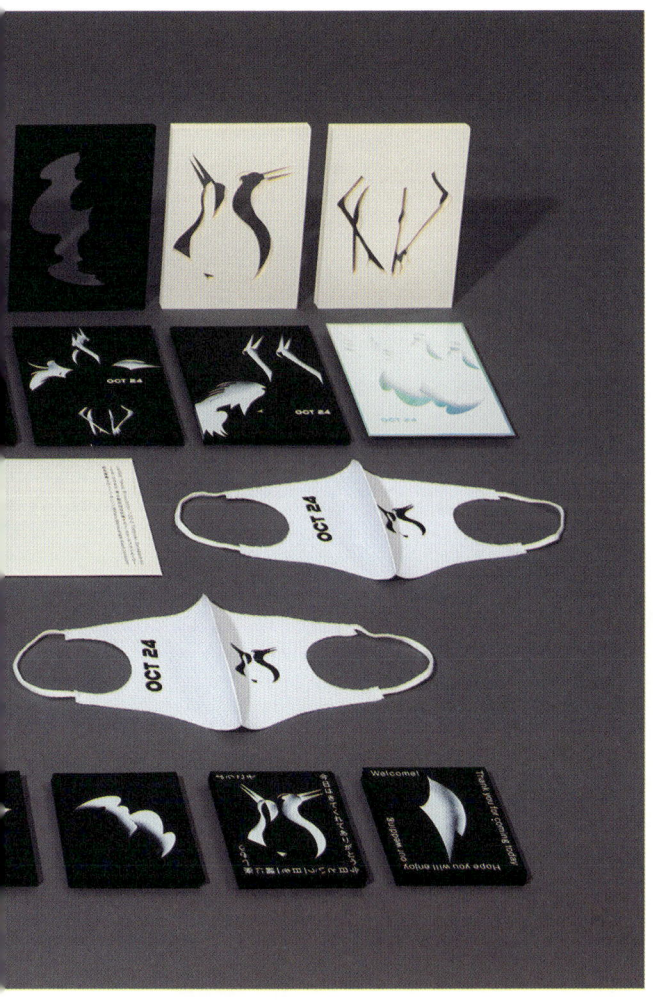

● Why Dot?

In order to convey a simple and refined visual effect, the designer used the silhouette of cranes for the design, then split a complete crane graphic so that its parts are distributed on different carriers. Each small part is a delicate visual point.

Basic Dot

- ● C0 M0 Y0 K100 / R0 G0 B0
- ○ C0 M0 Y0 K0 / R255 G255 B255
- ○ C20 M20 Y30 K0 / R212 G202 B180

● SWIM WORLD

This is the branding for SWIM WORLD, a swimming school in Japan. The core element of this branding is the logo, which is designed based on the Chinese character "泳" (meaning swim). This design approach connects the visual identity to the essence of swimming while incorporating a cultural reference. One of the key features of the logo is its adaptability—it can freely change depending on the media in which it is used. For example, on a poster, the logo can appear as a dynamic splash of water, conveying movement and energy. On a badge, it can transform into various facial expressions, creating a fun and engaging visual element. This versatility allows the brand to communicate a playful and approachable image.

By integrating these dynamic design elements, the branding makes swimming feel more enjoyable and accessible for people of all ages, from children to adults. The fluidity of the logo reflects the nature of water and movement, reinforcing the core theme of swimming. Overall, this branding enhances the connection between the audience and the swimming experience, making it more visually appealing and emotionally engaging.

DA. DENTSU INC.
D. Taichi Tamaki
CL. SWIM WORLD

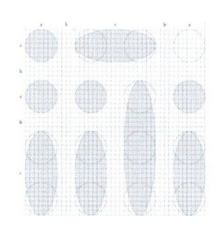

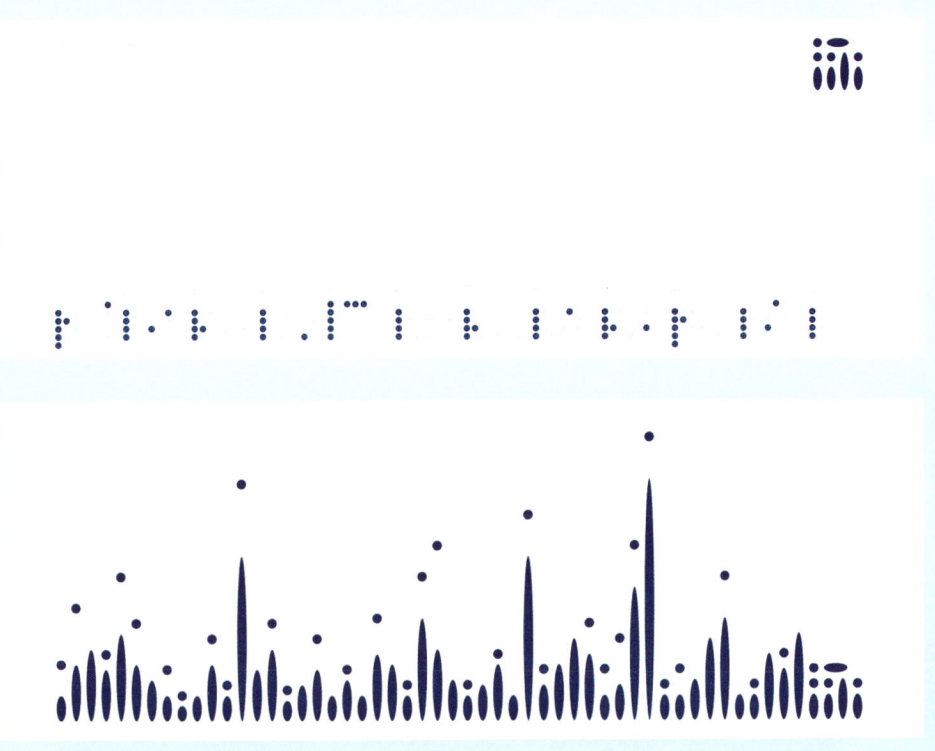

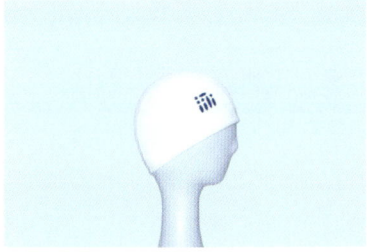

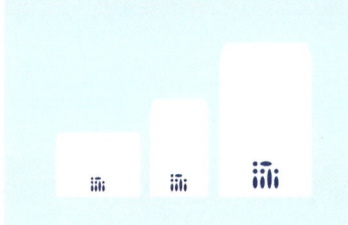

● Why Dot?

This logo is created using a very simple design system. Blue dots are systematically arranged within a square, where they expand and contract to form the shape of the Chinese character "泳." The logo is highly adaptable depending on the media in which it is used. It can transform freely, sometimes appearing like a splash of water, effectively and playfully representing the image of swimming. In fact, achieving diverse and flexible expressions while maintaining a strong brand identity is often challenging. However, the structured composition of dots and planes within this simple design system enables the creation of a cohesive brand identity.

Basic Dot

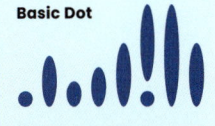

● C100 M65 Y0 K0 / R0 G84 B167

○ C0 M0 Y0 K0 / R255 G255 B255

● GOOD DESIGN EXHIBITION 2024

The design team was responsible for the graphics for the 2024 Good Design Exhibition.

DA. 6D
AD. D. Shogo Kishino
D. Norika Kato
SD. Keiji Ashizawa
PT. Shingo Fujimoto
CL. Japan Institute of Design Promotion

🔴 Why Dot?

The red circle logo, symbolizing the Good Design Exhibition, was used as the visual motif of dots.

The design team expressed the diversity of "good design" (works) by gathering the G Mark (red circle) in various forms and using dots of different sizes.

Basic Dot

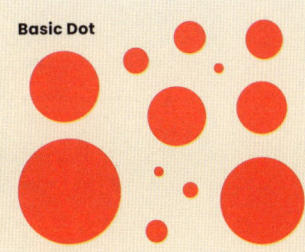

- 🔴 C0 M100 Y100 K0 / R230 G0 B18
- ⬤ C20 M40 Y55 K0 / R210 G164 B117
- ⚪ C0 M0 Y0 K0 / R255 G255 B255
- ⚫ C0 M0 Y0 K100 / R0 G0 B0

DOT TO LINE

The Concept of Dot to Line

● The essence of "Dot to Line" lies in the idea that when multiple "dots" are continuously arranged or set in motion, they generate a "line" endowed with direction, rhythm, and logic.

● In different contexts, "dots" may take the form of visual elements, action nodes, pivotal events, or sparks of thought, while "lines" emerge as the overarching paths, processes, or visual guides woven from these dots.

● In visual art, scattered dots are arranged in an orderly manner to form lines, which guide the viewer's gaze and infuse the composition with rhythm.

● In spatial and behavioral design (such as the visiting route in a museum), each stop functions as a focal "dot" for attention, and together these dots link up to form a coherent visiting "line."

● On a conceptual level, "Dot to Line" can also be seen as beginning from a single idea, gradually unfolding and linking related content, and ultimately shaping a systematic framework of knowledge or creativity.

● In short, "Dot to Line" is both a mindset and a design strategy—transforming the fragmentary into the continuous, and the partial into the whole.

Various Kinds of Dot to Line

● **Lines Formed by Dots of Varying Sizes:**
Uniform in size:

Gradually shifting in size:

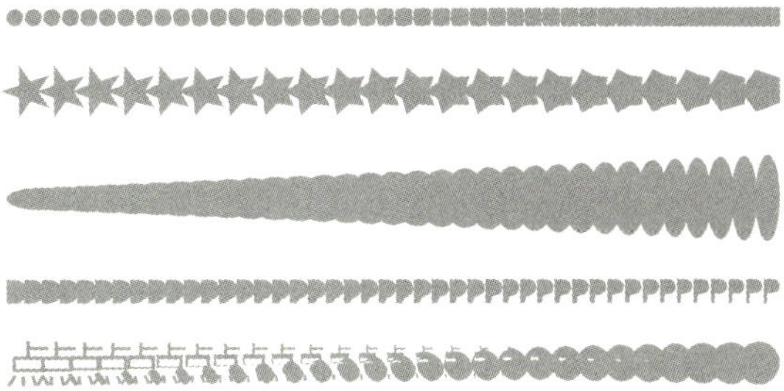

● **Lines Formed by Dots with Varying Density:**
Regular:

Irregular:

● **Lines Formed by Dots of Diverse Shapes:**
Same dots:

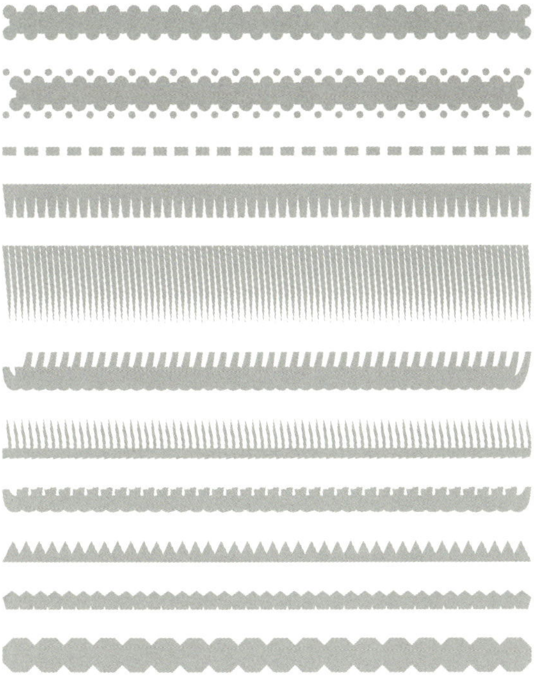

Different dots:

● **Lines Formed by Dots in Different Trajectories:**

● **Lines Formed by Stretching a "Dot":**

FLYERS FOR "PHILOSOPHICAL DIALOGUE PARA SHIF" AT LIFESTYLE DESIGN CENTER

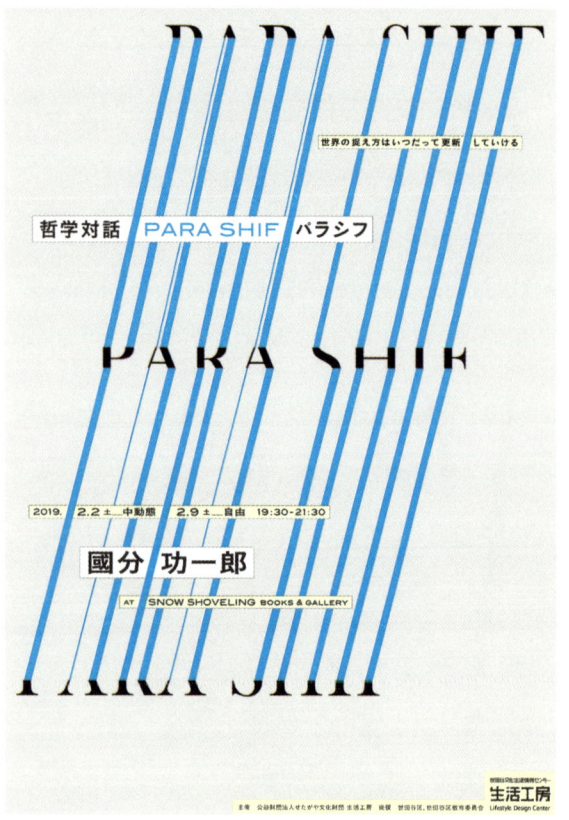

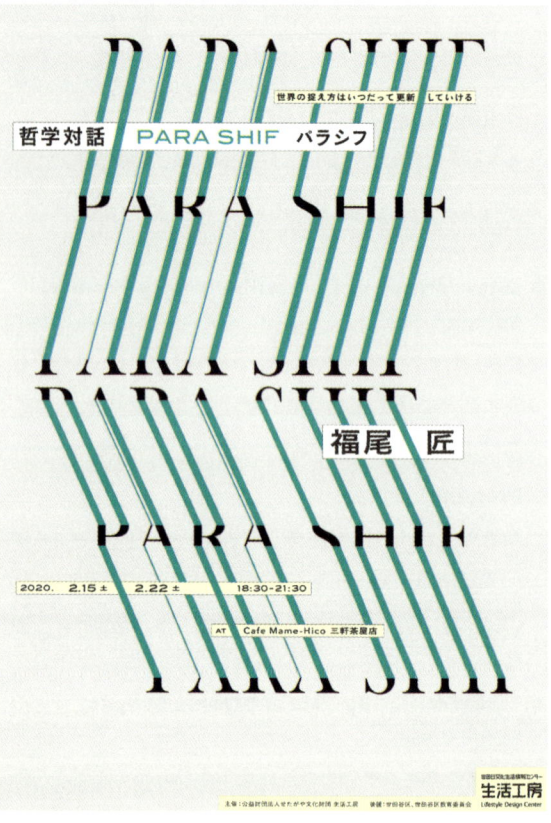

As the event promoted by this flyer revolves around the expression of concepts through words and dialogue, it does not feature a specific visual motif. The designer was tasked with translating this abstract concept into a compelling visual representation while ensuring clarity and coherence. To achieve this, letters and geometric forms were carefully integrated to evoke the essence of a "paradigm shift," allowing viewers to intuitively grasp its significance.

AD. woolen Co., Ltd.
D. Naoko Fukuoka
CL. Setagaya Cultural Foundation

◯ Why Dot to Line?

The designer was tasked with visualizing both the concept of a "paradigm shift" and the event's title. When approaching abstract concepts, various methods were considered. In this case, the designer chose to use the ends of extended letters to form lines that are either angled or vertical, in keeping with the theme of the project, to create a special and compelling visual effect.

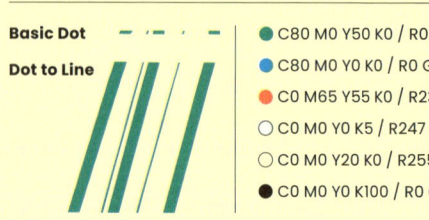

- ● C80 M0 Y50 K0 / R0 G172 B151
- ● C80 M0 Y0 K0 / R0 G175 B236
- ● C0 M65 Y55 K0 / R238 G121 B197
- ○ C0 M0 Y0 K5 / R247 G248 B248
- ○ C0 M0 Y20 K0 / R255 G252 B219
- ● C0 M0 Y0 K100 / R0 G0 B0

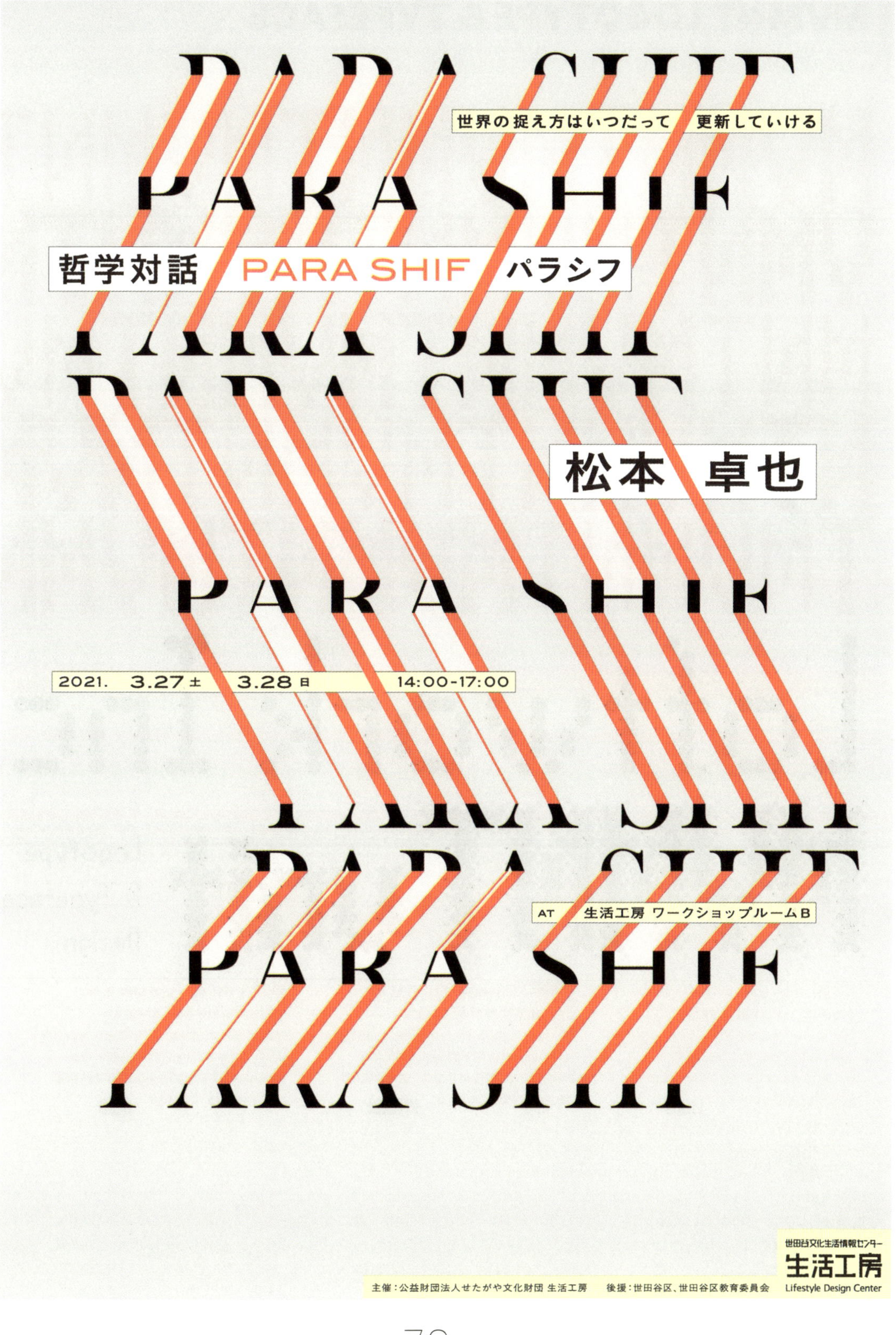

世界の捉え方はいつだって　更新していける

哲学対話　PARA SHIF　パラシフ

松本　卓也

2021.　3.27 土　3.28 日　14:00-17:00

AT　生活工房 ワークショップルーム B

主催：公益財団法人せたがや文化財団 生活工房　　後援：世田谷区、世田谷区教育委員会

MVMNT LOGOTYPE & TYPEFACE

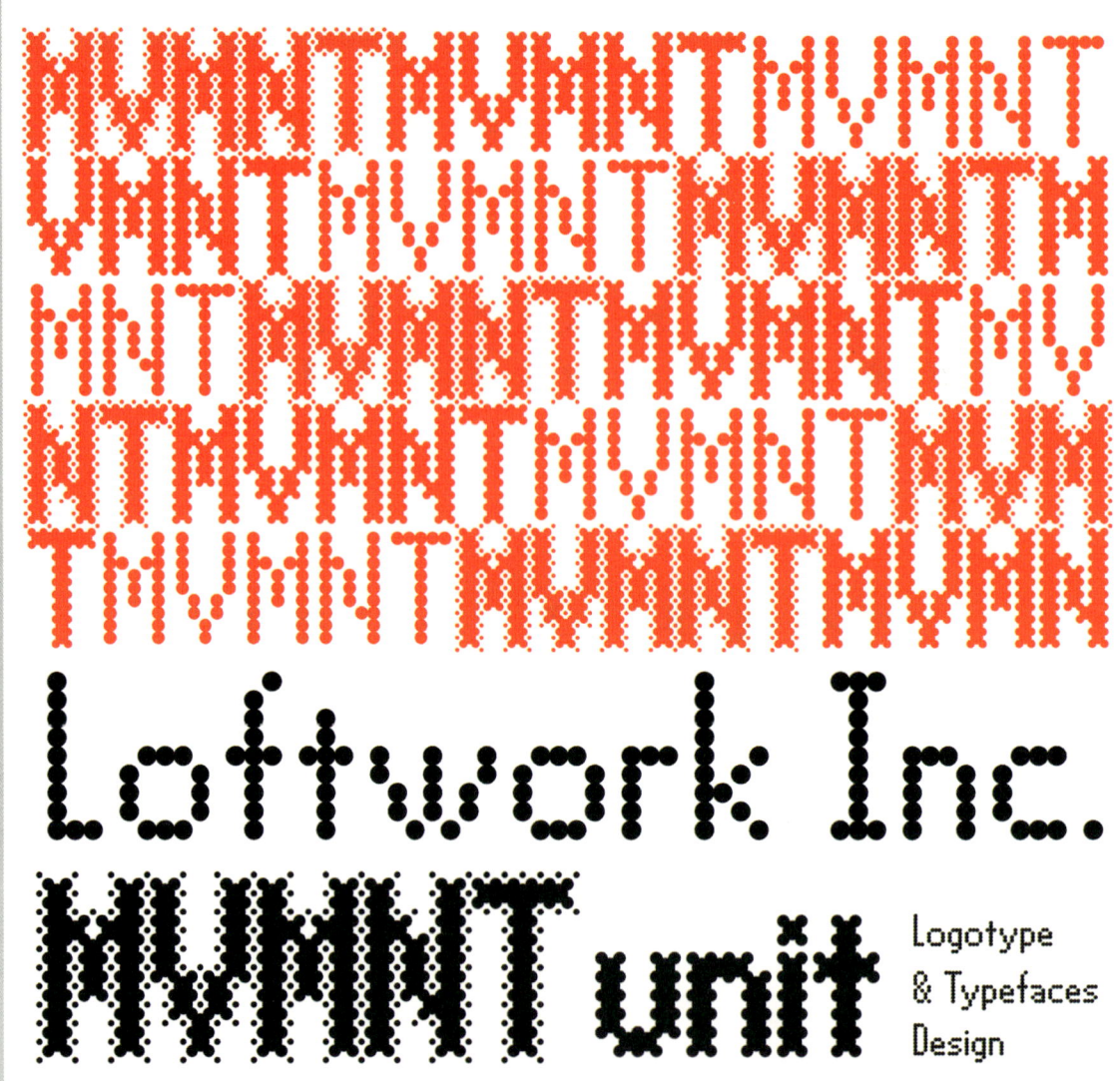

MVMNT (Movement) unit is an organization that creates unknown movements (new legends) with artists/creators with the mission of creating an emotional society and culture. **LIGHT**

MVMNT (Movement) unit is an organization that creates unknown movements (new legends) with artists/creators with the mission of creating an emotional society and culture. **MEDIUM**

MVMNT (Movement) unit is an organization that creates unknown movements (new legends) with artists/creators with the mission of creating an emotional society and culture. **BOLD**

For this project, the designer crafted the logotype with a focus on "change" and "movement," establishing a visual identity that will become a new option for the future. The design was meticulously calculated so that, as the weight transitions from Light to Bold, the shadows increase in a halftone-like progression. The logotype and typefaces were designed to be both pop and fashionable, while maintaining readability without resorting to trends that may only appeal to a select audience.

AD. TD. D. Zin Nagao
CL. MVMNT

MVMNT

The concept is to create a "legend" for the year 20XX.

What is the "legend"

An event that is not an everyday occurrence, that seems unusual at first glance, but that motivates one to act.

It influences later thought, values, culture, and lifestyle in more than a few ways.

We aim to prototype art-driven, thought-provoking and socially relevant content (new meanings, worldviews, and triggers), create communication systems that hack legacy methods, and create creative movements from XS to XXXL through the power of community.

For the future we want, we are committed to the R&D spirit of both business and culture.

In a time when society and people's values have changed drastically and the formula for success of the past has collapsed, we believe that the attitude of artists who observe society and challenge to deconstruct it without being bound by preconceived ideas is important in business as well, in order to achieve the future we want to have.

We are committed to the challenge of collaborating with Artists/Creators **to support the social penetration phase of** Marketing/Communication **as well as** brand development, such as business, service, product development, and worldview.

In addition to client work, the unit plans to develop its own media and businesses. We regularly hold thought experiment gatherings with **Artists/Creators.**

○ Why Dot to Line?

The designer has maximized the use of halftone dot elements in the design of this typeface, which are clustered together and regularly arranged to form the strokes of the English alphabet. The designer considers the process of composing the typeface and adjusting its weight to be very dynamic.

Basic Dot

Dot to Line

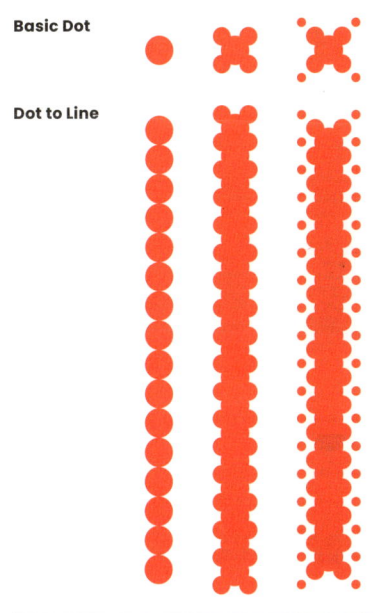

- ● C0 M0 Y0 K100 / R0 G0 B0
- ○ C0 M0 Y0 K0 / R255 G255 B255
- ● C0 M95 Y95 K0 / R231 G36 B24

DENTSU LIVE 19

This graphic design was created for 2019 greeting tools by Dentsu Live, a company specializing in event and space production. By employing typography that evolves while maintaining a consistent structural framework, the designer sought to reflect the company's intelligent and sophisticated image.

AD. TM INC.
D. Yuto Tamura
CL. Dentsu Live Inc.

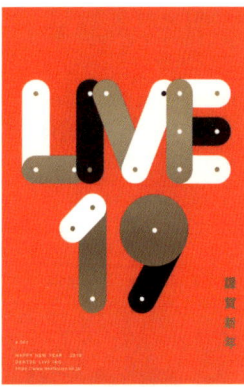

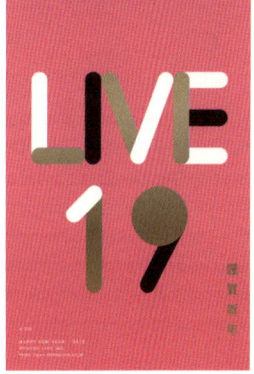

◯ Why Dot to Line?

In order to give a dynamic feel to the images in the main visualization, a visual connection is created between them. The designer established a set of design rules based on the size of the endpoints and, the width and combination of the lines. The simplicity of these elements not only enhances the clarity of the underlying logic but also makes the design more eye-catching and visually appealing.

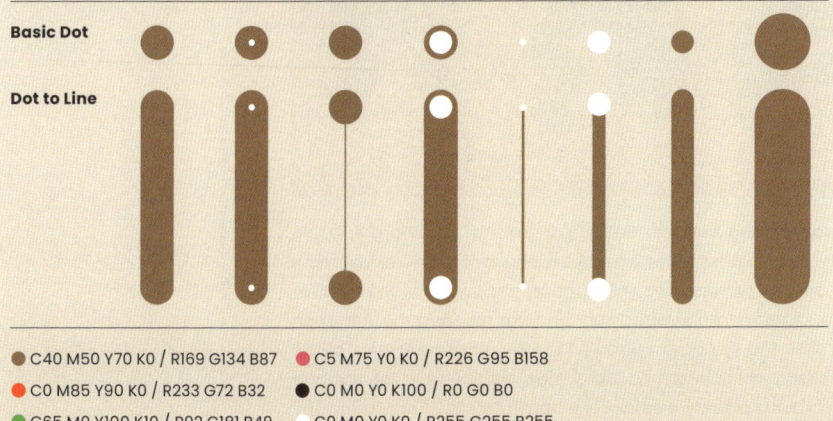

- C40 M50 Y70 K0 / R169 G134 B87
- C5 M75 Y0 K0 / R226 G95 B158
- C0 M85 Y90 K0 / R233 G72 B32
- C0 M0 Y0 K100 / R0 G0 B0
- C65 M0 Y100 K10 / R92 G181 B49
- C0 M0 Y0 K0 / R255 G255 B255
- C85 M50 Y0 K0 / R3 G110 B184

 **SMAKE**

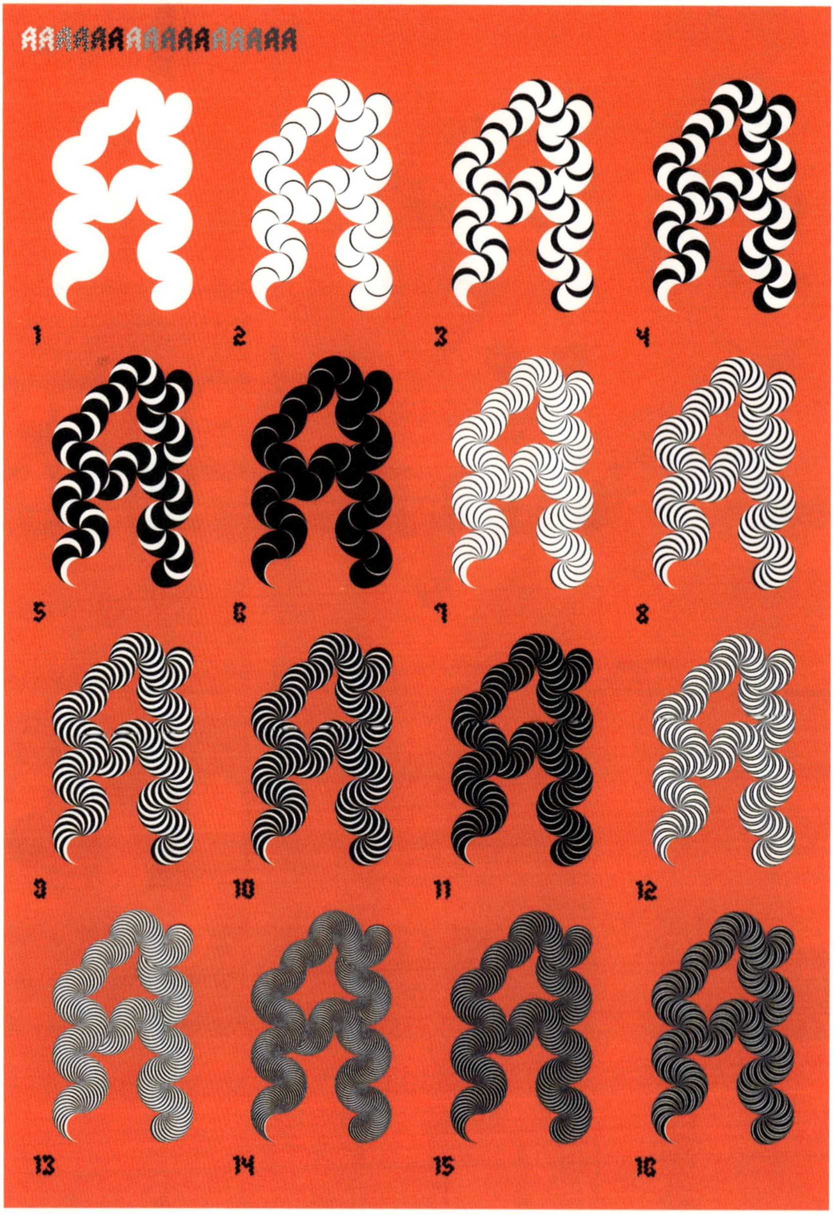

This is a flat yet three-dimensional display typeface, featuring 16 pattern variations suitable for diverse applications. The design is mathematical, incorporating twists and turns in key areas. The designer embarked on this project with the goal of creating a typeface that boldly embraces geometric principles while embodying an organic beauty. Although the process was challenging at first, the designer identified the key characteristics of the ellipse and its rotation around its axis, which informed the design. Additionally, the shape's resemblance to a snake coiling around a body inspired the name "SMAKE," capturing the essence of its serpentine form.

AD. TD. D. Zin Nagao

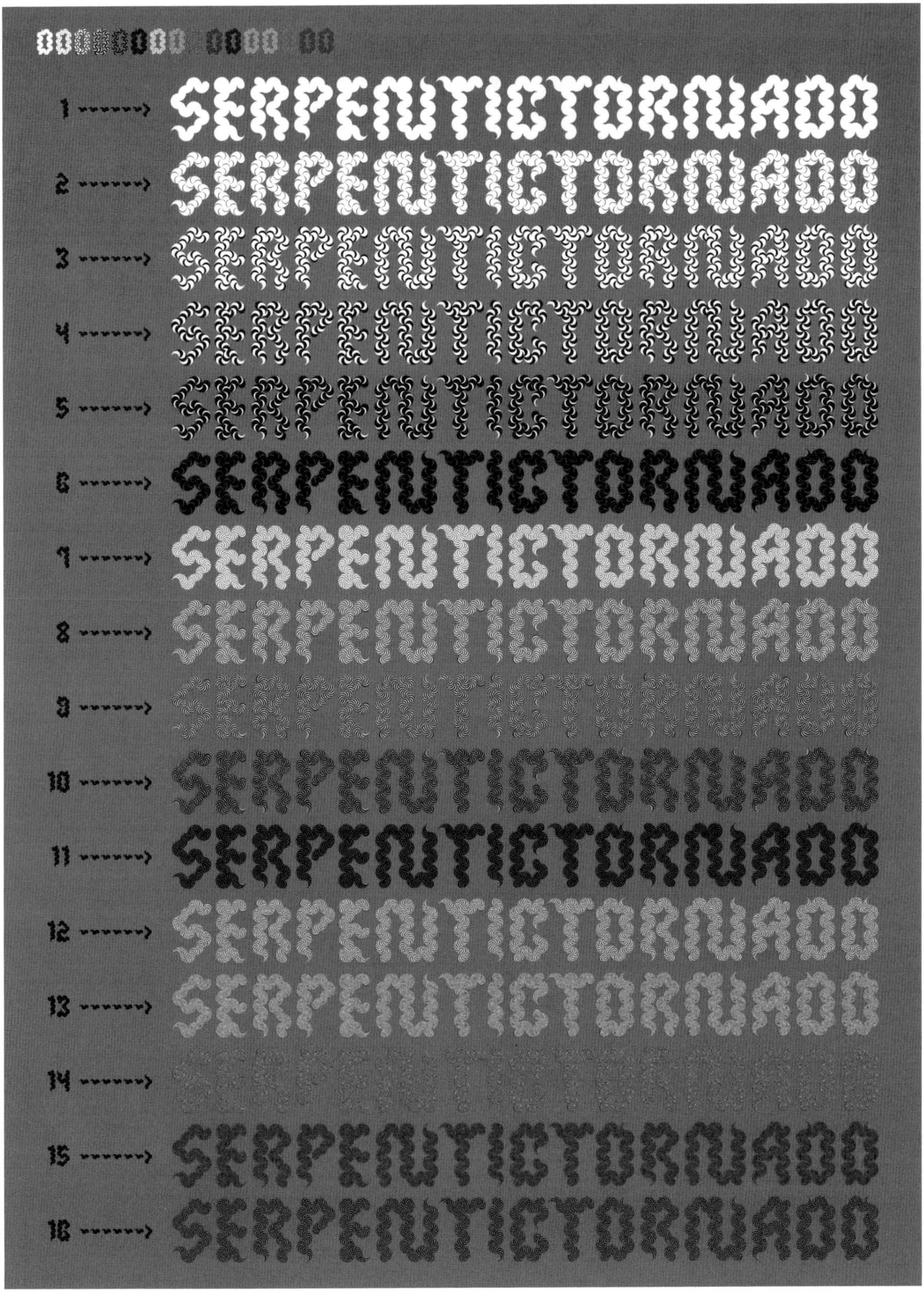

1 ──────> SERPENTICTORNADO
2 ──────> SERPENTICTORNADO
3 ──────> SERPENTICTORNADO
4 ──────> SERPENTICTORNADO
5 ──────> SERPENTICTORNADO
6 ──────> SERPENTICTORNADO
7 ──────> SERPENTICTORNADO
8 ──────> SERPENTICTORNADO
9 ──────> SERPENTICTORNADO
10 ──────> SERPENTICTORNADO
11 ──────> SERPENTICTORNADO
12 ──────> SERPENTICTORNADO
13 ──────> SERPENTICTORNADO
14 ──────>
15 ──────> SERPENTICTORNADO
16 ──────> SERPENTICTORNADO

◯ Why Dot to Line?

In this typeface, dots of different lengths are arranged in a crisscross pattern. After forming the basic lines, they are twisted into a spiral pattern to form individual letters.

● C0 M85 Y100 K0 / R233 G71 B9
● C0 M0 Y0 K100 / R0 G0 B0
○ C0 M0 Y0 K0 / R255 G255 B255

SHIROKUMA MIKAZUKI COFFEE

◯ Why Dot to Line?

The designer used letters of the alphabet to form smoke-like shapes, representing the scent of food, coffee beans and croissants, which is an innovative approach. The curves representing the scents are readable and convey product information to the viewer, which is aesthetically pleasing and functional at the same time.

Basic Dot
Dot to Line

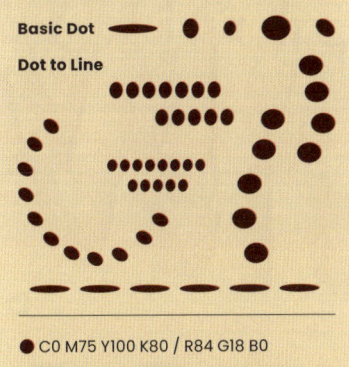

- C0 M75 Y100 K80 / R84 G18 B0
- C5 M10 Y30 K5 / R241 G223 B184
- C0 M65 Y100 K10 / R223 G122 B0

The project is designed for a café that recommends freshly made croissants and freshly ground coffee. A Japanese logotype is incorporated to evoke the enticing aroma of freshly baked goods and coffee, thereby enhancing the overall sensory experience.

DA. STUDIO WONDER
D. Sou Nomura
CL. Shirokuma Mikazuki Coffee

SMALL VOICE, BIG IMPACT

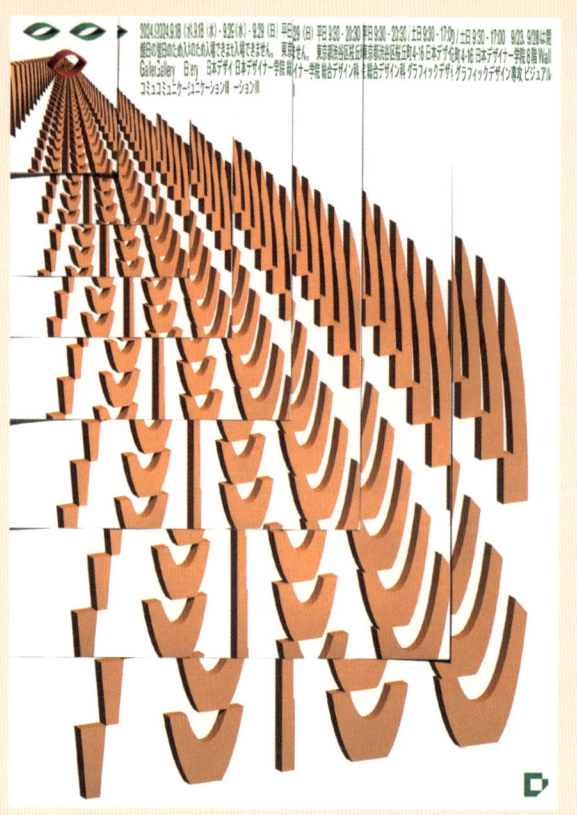
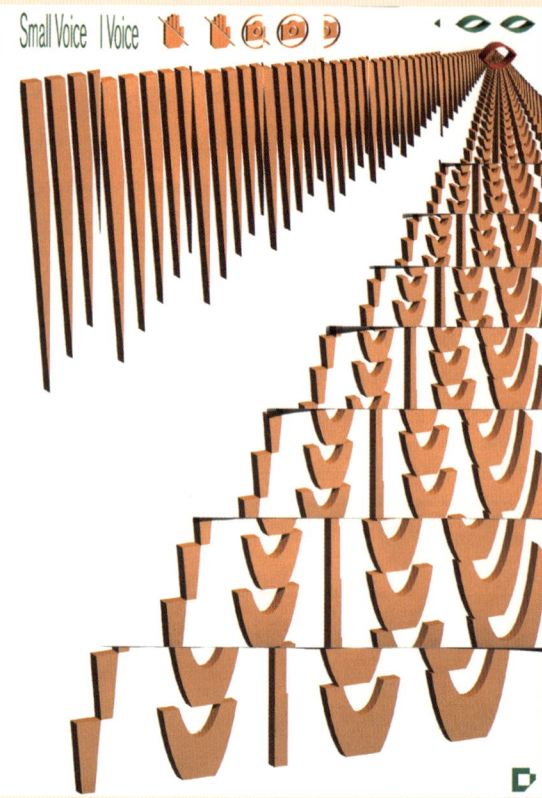

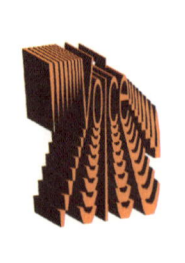

Nippon Designers School presented *Small Voice*, an exhibition amplifying hidden, unspoken voices. The designer led its graphic design, crafting a visual identity that embodies the power of subtle yet significant messages. The student-created works tackled real social issues—including blood type stereotypes, family structure bias, sexual harassment, and workplace harassment—offering raw perspectives of young creatives.

The key visual transforms the word "Voice" from small to expansive, symbolizing how even the quietest voices can drive profound change. This dynamic concept was applied across posters, motion graphics, cards, and the exhibition catalog, where a single "voice" evolved into various forms, achieving a sculptural, commanding presence. Through thoughtful typography, the project amplifies the strength of emerging voices, proving that even the smallest voice can create a powerful impact.

AD. Nippon Designers School
D. Taichi Tamaki
CL. Nippon Designers School

◯ **Why Dot to Line?**

The designer translated the word "Voice" into a graphic, extracting part of the shape of the letters and repeating and extending them to create a sense of sound expansion. He believed that graphics can tell a story that was constantly changing through time, scale, or form. The transformation from dot to line creates a narrative within the graphic itself, reinforcing the exhibition's theme of amplifying small but important sounds.

Basic Dot

Dot to Line

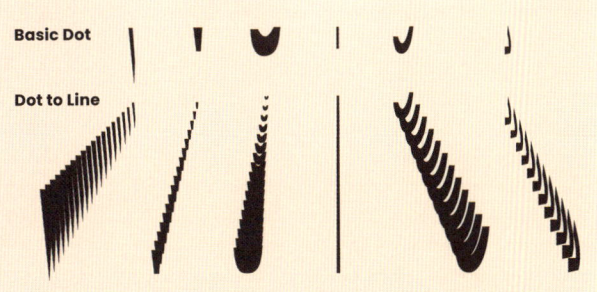

- C5 M50 Y60 K0 / R235 G152 B100
- C60 M80 Y100 K45 / R85 G46 B21
- C95 M20 Y90 K0 / R0 G139 B78
- C25 M100 Y100 K0 / R193 G25 B32
- C0 M0 Y0 K100 / R0 G0 B0
- C0 M0 Y0 K0 / R255 G255 B255

SHINKENCHIKU RESIDENTIAL DESIGN COMPETITION

This is a poster announcing the historic architectural design competition held annually since 1964. Each year, a new jury is selected, and a distinct theme is introduced. In 2020, "Big Data and the City: Spatial Design for Well-Being" was presented by Yuji Yoshimura, a researcher at the University of Tokyo specializing in the relationship between cities and science. The competition challenges entrants to explore how vast amounts of data—comprising countless small pieces of information—can reveal unseen aspects of urban life. Beyond the visual beauty of architecture, participants are tasked with interpreting this data to envision a better, more connected future. The designer's approach visually conveys how individual data dots converge to form lines, planes, and layers, ultimately shaping the spatial design of the city.

DA. PINHOLE
D. Minako Izumi
CL. Shinkenchiku-sha

Why Dot to Line?

The designer created posters for Mr. Yoshimura's previous lecture at the university, titled "About the Future of Shibuya." The design for that lecture featured fine dots to symbolize the long, linear, towering skyscrapers of Shibuya, gradually dissipating into the sky. The concept represented a mature city becoming increasingly informatized and, in contrast to its size, seemingly empty. Mr. Yoshimura appreciated this visual approach and invited the designer to apply a similar concept for this competition, using dots as a representation of data.

The designer's use of slightly elongated vertical dots, which exist between lines and dots, draws from an early digital experience—specifically, the appearance of TV monitors in the 1990s. At the time, all TV and computer monitors had a slightly spherical, protruding surface, and if you observed them closely, you could see vertical dots. This nostalgic memory informed the designer's choice to use elongated dots as the smallest unit of visual information, representing something that is typically invisible to the naked eye. While modern high-resolution screens make these dots virtually undetectable, the designer sought to evoke the sense of invisible data by reinterpreting these memories and transforming them into a visual form.

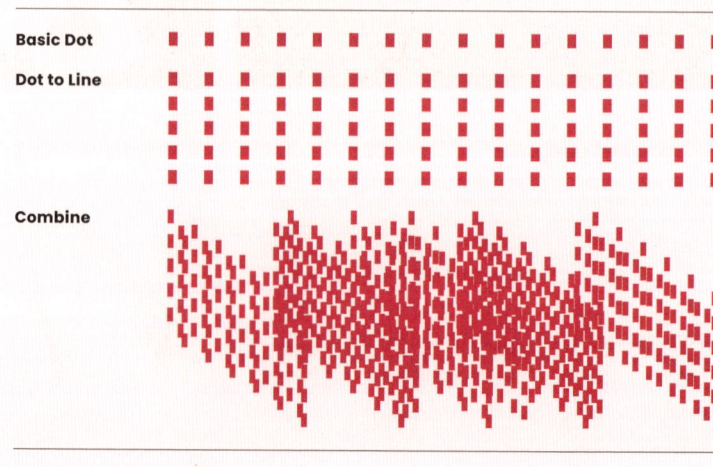

Basic Dot
Dot to Line
Combine

● C10 M100 Y15 K0 / R214 G0 B116
○ C0 M0 Y0 K0 / R255 G255 B255

新建築住宅設計競技
SHINKENCHIKU RESIDENTIAL DESIGN COMPETITION

Big Data and City
Spatial design for well-being

Deadline: NOVEMBER 1st, 2022 6:00 p.m. JST
Web entry & application

課題｜ビッグデータと都市
―ウェルビーイングな空間デザイン―
審査員｜Yuji Yoshimura 吉村有司
登録・提出締切｜2022年11月1日（火）日本時間 18:00

入選発表 Announcement of the Winner
月刊『新建築』2023年3月号（2023年3月1日発売）、および月刊『a+u』2023年4月号（2023年3月27日発売）、当WEBページを予定しています。
Winner(s) will be announced in the 2023 March issue of SHINKENCHIKU (published on Mar 1, 2023) and April issue of a+u (published on Mar 27, 2023) magazines and on the competition website.

入選賞金 Prize
総額 **1,000,000 Japanese yen**
入選点数および賞金の配分は審査員の決定に従います。
total: **1,000,000 Japanese yen**
The number of winners and the amount of prize will be determined by the judges.

主催｜一般財団法人吉岡文庫育英会 株式会社新建築社
後援｜吉岡文庫育英会　新建築

審査員｜吉村有司 Yuji Yoshimura
愛知県生まれ／2001年～渡西／ポンペウ・ファブラ大学情報通信工学部博士課程修了／バルセロナ都市生態学庁、カタルーニャ先進交通センター、マサチューセッツ工科大学研究員などを経て2019年～東京大学先端科学技術研究センター特任准教授
Born in Aichi Prefecture and moved to Spain in 2001. Ph.D in Information, Communication and Audiovisual Media Technology, Pompeu Fabra University. After working at the Barcelona Urban Ecology Agency, Center for Innovation in Transport (CENIT), and as a researcher at the Massachusetts Institute of Technology, he became project associate professor at the Research Center for Advanced Science and Technology (RCAST) at the University of Tokyo in 2019.

sk-jutaku.shinkenchiku.net

登録・詳細は専用WEBページより

WURFACE

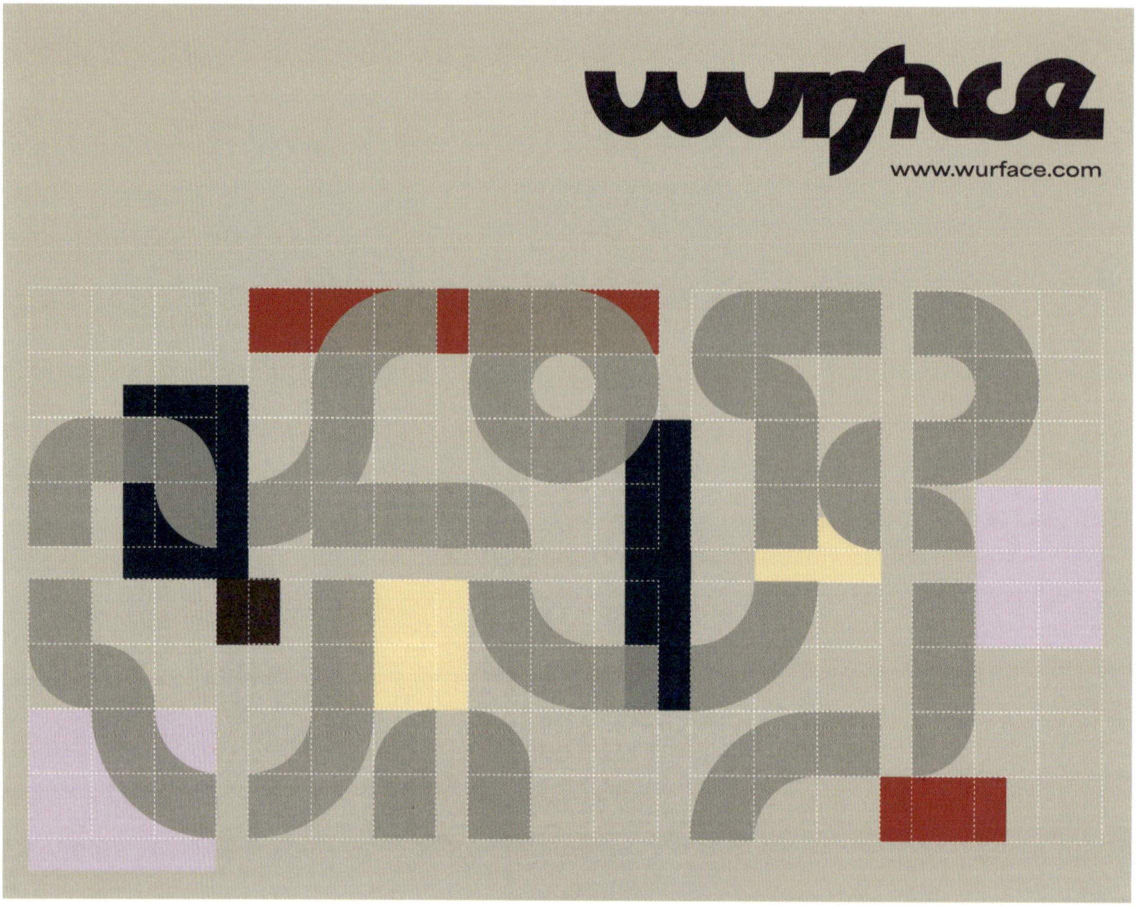

Wurface is the visual identity of a tile supplier located in Hong Kong, designed to appeal to interior design professionals with a vibrant, architectural aesthetics. Inspired by the fluid, sharp motion of mortar binding tiles, the branding integrates this motif to reflect the tiling process and emphasize design versatility. This cohesive approach highlights Wurface's creativity, expertise, and innovation in a competitive market.

D. Josephine Grenier
CL. Wurface

◯ **Why Dot to Line?**

The designer first mapped out a standard grid as the basis for the design. Then the base graphics were set to represent the tiles, and these base graphics were stitched together and typed to form the brand's main visual system. The base graphics were incorporated into the grid lines to convey the brand's focus on structure, uniformity, and precision. The grid was organized into different planes to ensure versatility across formats to enhance the adaptability and consistency of the brand image.

Basic Dot

Dot to Line

- C20 M20 Y30 K25 / R175 G167 B150
- C20 M20 Y30 K0 / R212 G202 B180
- C65 M55 Y55 K60 / R55 G57 B56
- C90 M50 Y55 K50 / R0 G67 B71
- C15 M25 Y0 K0 / R220 G199 B155
- C5 M10 Y40 K0 / R245 G229 B169
- C20 M100 Y100 K15 / R181 G16 B24
- C15 M10 Y15 K0 / R223 G224 B217

IMITATIVE BEHAVIOUR: IN THE FOOTSTEPS OF MY DAUGHTER IN HONG KONG

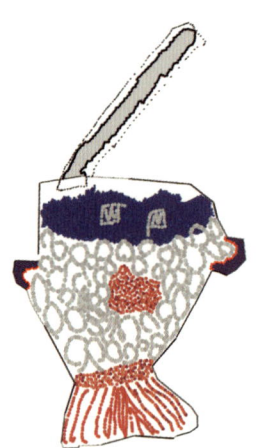

Dad: This is cute.
Mashiro: It's a dessert.
Dad: What flavor is it?
Mashiro: Um, It's blueberry jelly flavor.
Dad: That sounds delicious.
Who did you eat it with?
Mashiro: Kokona.

Mashiro: It's a mixed juice.
Dad: A mixed juice, huh!
Mashiro: It's from the song that goes,
"Once, the Crybaby God cried at the sunrise and cried at the sunset, and red tears fell down."
Dad: So that's the song!

Mashiro: It's a fairy.
Dad: What kind of fairy is it?
Mashiro: An ice fairy.
Dad: Is it riding in a carriage?
Mashiro: No, It's just an ice fairy.

This project is a collaboration with the designer's daughter, inspired by the drawings and paintings they create together. Sometimes she imitates his works; other times, he imitates hers. Their creations influence each other in a continuous exchange.

The process is simple: The designer selects his daughter's drawings, scans them, and digitally traces her lines with dots. Typically, children mimic their parents, but here, he follows in his daughter's footsteps—an experience that has deeply enriched his artistic practice.

Artists often look to the past for inspiration, but this project looks to the future—his daughter's creativity. He once heard a line in a zombie movie: "Choosing adults is choosing wisdom. Choosing children is choosing hope." Through design, he seeks to build a relationship with the future—one rooted in "hope."

D. Naonori Yago / Mashiro Yago

Dad: Is this a bad fairy?
Mashiro: Yes.
Dad: Why is it bad?
Mashiro: Because it prevents snow
from falling on Christmas.
Dad: That's really bad!
What a naughty one!

Imitative Behaviour: In the Footsteps of My Daughter
Typically, "imitative behavior" refers to children mimicking their parents.
But in this case, I am imitating my daughter's creation.
A few years ago I watched a movie where someone said:
"Suppose you can only help one: either adults or children.
Choosing adults is choosing wisdom. Choosing children is choosing hope".
I want my designs to bring "hope" and build a relationship with the future.

Mashiro: It's a bear.
Dad: What kind of bear?
Mashiro: Um, I think It's a small, cute and gentle bear.
Dad: I see. It looks gentle with its head tilted.

Imitative Behaviour: In the Footsteps of My Daughter

Typically, "imitative behavior" refers to children mimicking their parents.
But in this case, I am imitating my daughter's creation.
A few years ago I watched a movie where someone said:
"Suppose you can only help your eldest adults or children.
Choosing adults is choosing wisdom. Choosing children is choosing hope."
I want my designs to bring "hope" and build a relationship with the future.

Dad: Were you practicing a signature?
Mashiro: Aoha-chan asked me to write it.
Dad: She asked you to write a signature?
Mashiro: No, she asked me to write wiggly letters that aren't any real letters. Unreadable letters.

Imitative Behaviour: In the Footsteps of My Daughter

Typically, "imitative behavior" refers to children mimicking their parents.
But in this case, I am imitating my daughter's creation.
A few years ago I watched a movie where someone said:
"Suppose you can only help your eldest adults or children.
Choosing adults is choosing wisdom. Choosing children is choosing hope."
I want my designs to bring "hope" and build a relationship with the future.

Imitative Behaviour: In the Footsteps of My Daughter

Typically, "imitative behavior" refers to children mimicking their parents.
But in this case, I am imitating my daughter's creation.
A few years ago I watched a movie where someone said:
"Suppose you can only help your eldest adults or children.
Choosing adults is choosing wisdom. Choosing children is choosing hope."
I want my designs to bring "hope" and build a relationship with the future.

Dad: Is this a snow fairy?
It looks really cold, doesn't it?
You did a great job.
Mashiro: Yeah.

Imitative Behaviour: In the Footsteps of My Daughter

Typically, "imitative behavior" refers to children mimicking their parents.
But in this case, I am imitating my daughter's creation.
A few years ago I watched a movie where someone said:
"Suppose you can only help your eldest adults or children.
Choosing adults is choosing wisdom. Choosing children is choosing hope."
I want my designs to bring "hope" and build a relationship with the future.

Imitative Behaviour: In the Footsteps of My Daughter

Typically, "imitative behaviour" refers to children mimicking their parents. But in this case, I am imitating my daughter's creation. A few years ago I watched a movie where someone said: "Suppose you can only help non-older adults or children. Choosing adults is choosing wisdom. Choosing children is choosing hope." I want my designs to bring "hope" and build a relationship with the future.

Dad: This is displayed at home.
Dad and mum's wedding!
Mashiro: Yes.
Dad: There's a unicorn!
Is this unicorn celebrating dad and mum?
Mashiro: Yes. I got angry while drawing it, so I stopped halfway and coloured it later.

Imitative Behaviour: In the Footsteps of My Daughter

Typically, "imitative behaviour" refers to children mimicking their parents. But in this case, I am imitating my daughter's creation. A few years ago I watched a movie where someone said: "Suppose you can only help non-older adults or children. Choosing adults is choosing wisdom. Choosing children is choosing hope." I want my designs to bring "hope" and build a relationship with the future.

Dad: This is a giraffe drawn on a wood, isn't it?
Mashiro: I stopped midway.

Imitative Behaviour: In the Footsteps of My Daughter

Typically, "imitative behaviour" refers to children mimicking their parents. But in this case, I am imitating my daughter's creation. A few years ago I watched a movie where someone said: "Suppose you can only help non-older adults or children. Choosing adults is choosing wisdom. Choosing children is choosing hope." I want my designs to bring "hope" and build a relationship with the future.

Mashiro: This is Mount Fuji.
There are palm trees.
Dad: Who's in the car?
Mashiro: It's Mashiro and Neiro.

Imitative Behaviour: In the Footsteps of My Daughter

Typically, "imitative behaviour" refers to children mimicking their parents. But in this case, I am imitating my daughter's creation. A few years ago I watched a movie where someone said: "Suppose you can only help non-older adults or children. Choosing adults is choosing wisdom. Choosing children is choosing hope." I want my designs to bring "hope" and build a relationship with the future.

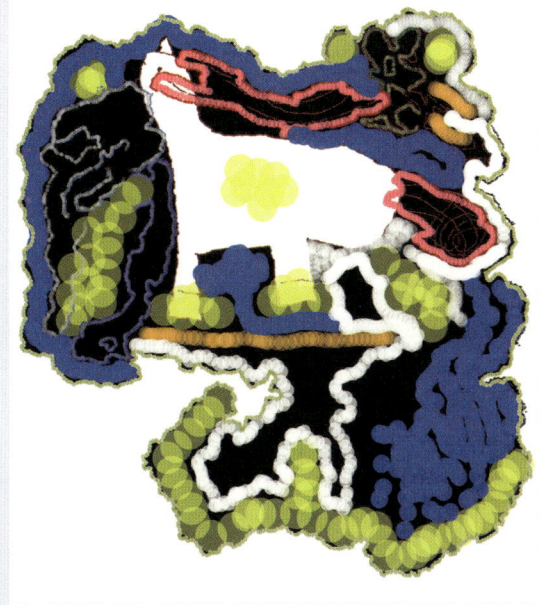

◉ Why Dot to Line?

They began creating this project when the designer's daughter was three years old. She struggled to control her arm strength to draw these lines, some too faint, some too bold. The designer transformed this lack of control into an art form by depicting the lines again through the software—the greater the force the more dots that make up the line, the less the force the fewer dots that make up the line.

The designer saw this as a way to express the handmade elements of the sense of craftsmanship through geometric forms. Dots converge to form lines, and lines merge to form planes. This concept of dot, line, and plane became the basis of the project.

Basic Dot

Dot to Line

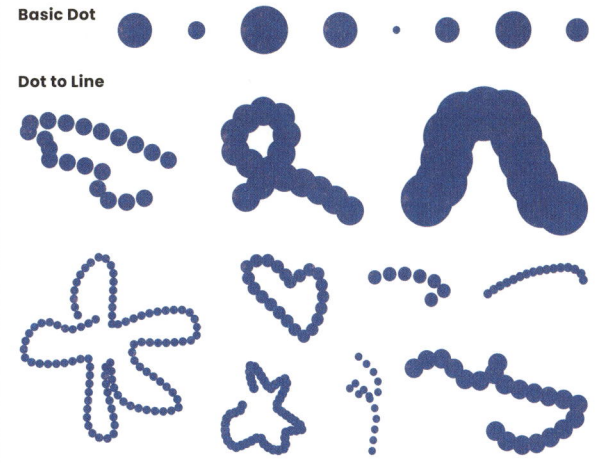

- C0 M0 Y0 K100 / R0 G0 B0
- C0 M0 Y0 K0 / R255 G255 B255
- C10 M0 Y80 K0 / R240 G235 B69
- C0 M95 Y95 K0 / R231 G36 B24
- C80 M25 Y65 K0 / R20 G144 B112
- C0 M85 Y65 K0 / R46 G89 B167
- C0 M80 Y25 K0 / R233 G83 B125
- C70 M15 Y0 K0 / R46 G167 B224
- C50 M90 Y60 K10 / R139 G52 B76
- C25 M20 Y20 K0 / R201 G199 B197
- C25 M90 Y80 K0 / R193 G58 B54
- C70 M60 Y50 K0 / R99 G104 B114
- C75 M100 Y20 K0 / R97 G33 B118
- C55 M0 Y100 K0 / R127 G190 B38
- C35 M35 Y85 K0 / R182 G161 B62
- C90 M55 Y100 K35 / R3 G76 B40

LINE

What's a line?

● In graphic design, a line is defined by its geometric length and direction, but not its thickness. When a dot remains stationary, a line is the trajectory of the dot's movement. Lines have multiple attributes such as position, length, width, direction, shape, and character, and are extremely crucial to design.

● Lines are rich in forms. Their various forms—whether perceivable or invisible, straight or curved, bold or delicate, solid or dotted, thick or thin—greatly influence the viewer's perception. The subtle variation of lines provides endless opportunities for designers to manipulate their attributes to achieve specific visual effects.

The Compositional Aesthetics of Lines

● **Lines can be distinct and indistinct.** Distinct lines, such as straight and curved lines, exhibit clear shapes, while indistinct lines, such as dotted or blurred lines, are often used to imply movement, connection, or depth, adding a sense of hierarchy to a design.

● **Tangible lines can take the form of straight lines or curves.** Curved lines evoke fluidity and softness, while straight lines represent rigor and stability. The interplay between these two elements creates a diverse range of styles.

● **The bold and soft edges of lines can create either visual tension or harmony.** Some lines look hard and sharp, while others look soft and rounded.

● **Solid and dotted lines convey richness and hierarchy in design.** Solid lines delineate clear outlines and boundaries, while dotted lines evoke a sense of lightness or remoteness.

● **The thickness of lines affects the overall atmosphere of a design.** Thick lines can highlight and emphasize the elements, while fine lines are better suited to convey nuances.

● **Shades of line create a visual hierarchy.** Deep lines bring elements to the foreground, while light lines allow elements to float lightly in the background.

Various Lines in Design

- **THICKNESS OF LINES:**
  Thin Line:
  Thick Line:

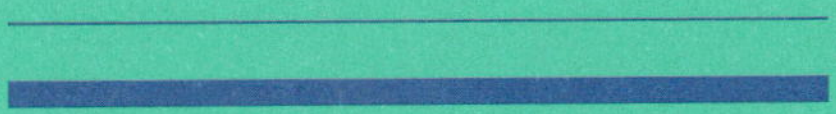

- **FORM OF LINES:**
  Straight Line:
  Curved Line:
  Closed Curve:

  Regular Wavy Line:

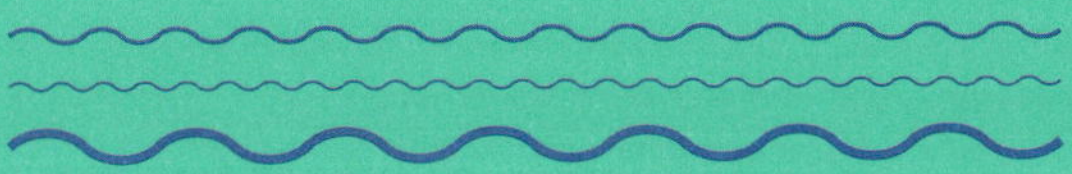

  Irregular Wavy Line:

- **ORIENTATION OF LINES:**
  Horizontal Line:

  Vertical Line: Inclined Line:

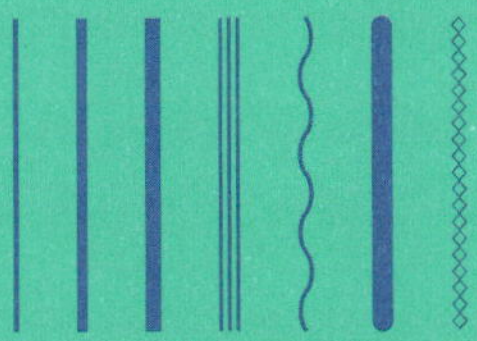

  Zigzag Line:

- **ARRANGEMENT OF LINES:**
  Ordered:
  Parallel Line: Perpendicular Line:

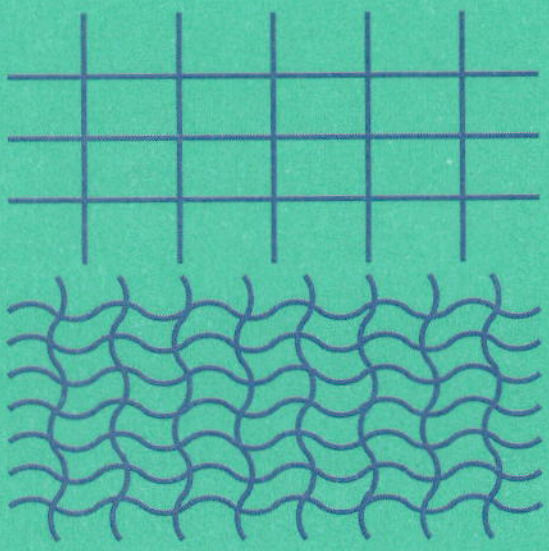

- **Disordered:**
  Intersecting Line: Entangled Line:

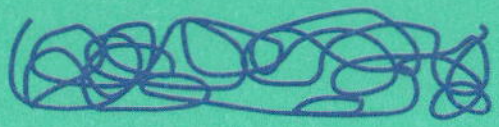

- **COMBINATION OF LINES:**
  Encircling Line:

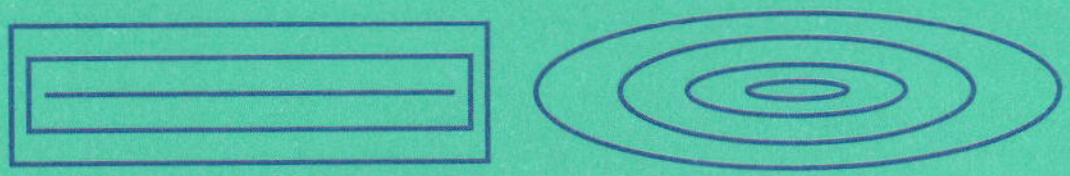

  Double Line:

  Multiple Line:

- **DENSITY OF LINES:**
  Sparse Line:

  Dense Line: Even a single line can convey a sense of density when marked by sufficient irregularity.

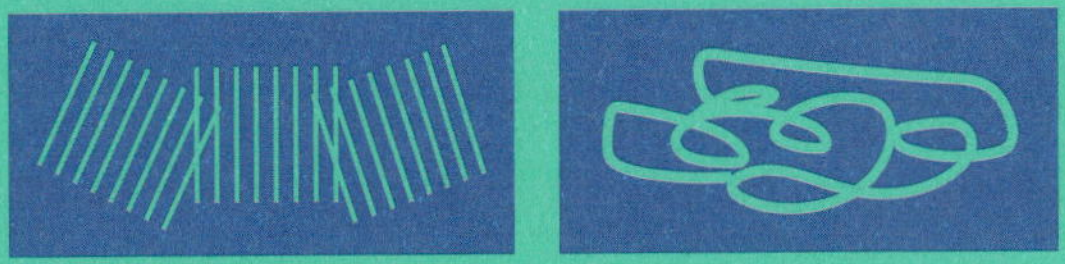

- **FUNCTION OF LINES:**
  Division: Used to divide elements within a composition to create clear boundaries.

  Connection: Used to connect elements within a composition to create smooth transitions.

- **TEXTURE OF LINES:**
  Pencil
  Chalk
  Crayon
  Brushe
  Marker

MULTI-DIMENSIONAL EXPERIMENTS GUIDED BY THE LINE

Art Director
Graphic Designer

Born in Shizuoka in 1986. Graduated from Musashino Art University, Department of Visual Communication Design in 2008, after which Naonori Yago joined Hakuhodo in 2009. Affiliated with SIX since 2014. Major awards include Tokyo ADC, JAGDA New Designer Award, D&AD, NY ADC and ONE SHOW.

○ In the landscape of contemporary Japanese design, Naonori Yago is a name that consistently pushes the boundaries of graphic expression. His works revolve around the motif of the "line," stretching from the surface of the page into physical space and from visual language into bodily perception. Whether it's the creation of "paper jewelry" crafted from metal and paper, or his reimaginings of children's drawings through dots and planes, Yago's ongoing exploration of the line prompts viewers to reconsider the relationships between image and reality, senses and consciousness.

○ In this interview, we will follow the thread of the "line" once more—discussing its connection to the body, its role in shaping materials and space, and Yago's recent focus on installation art and the creative power of children. Through it all, Yago reveals not only a graphic designer's sharp sensitivity and multidimensional design thinking, but also a deep-rooted humanistic vision and an educational ideal behind his artistic practice.

BETWEEN ORDER AND EMOTION

● **In the works of Naonori Yago, geometric precision and hand-drawn lines spontaneity often coexist—like a visual dialogue between structure and sentiment unfolding across the canvas.** This distinctive language of contrast not only defines his creative style but also reflects a profound understanding of both the world and the self.

● "The precision of geometry brings us social order, the freedom of hand-drawn brings us personal emotion." This is Yago's general view on these two modes of expression. For him, geometry is more than a stylistic choice—it is a way of observing and responding to both the cosmos and society. Take the circle, for example: To Yago, it represents nature itself—after all, the Earth is a sphere, the most primordial form granted by the universe. The square, by contrast, is a human invention. We trim the world into squares: To build architecture, frame windows, crop photographs and images—organizing the chaos of life into clean divisions. And then there's the triangle, which Yago sees as the foundation of physical stability. No object can stand without at least three points of contact; it is the minimal unit of support in our physical world.

● Beneath these symbolic forms lies a deeper message: geometric shapes embody rules, logic, and societal systems—they shape the very framework through which we rationally perceive the world. In contrast, the hand-drawn line conveys bodily sensation and subjective feeling. "Emotion originates from the body's sensations," Yago explains. "That's why the hand-drawn expresses emotions."

● In his graphic design practice, geometry and hand drawing aren't adversaries locked in a zero-sum game. Instead, they depend on and enrich each other. **Yago seeks a tensioned balance—allowing both to "appear" while also letting them "disappear."** It's a design philosophy that hovers between order and emotion, reason and feeling—giving his works a rational beauty without losing its human warmth.

Fig. 1 *Imitative Behaviour: In the Footsteps of My Daughter* in Tokyo, 2024.

THE BODY AND THE LINE: A PRACTICE OF PERCEPTION

● **For Naonori Yago, the line is far more than a visual design element—it is an extension of the body's own perception.** Winding across the skin as jewelry or piercing the canvas as visual glyphs, his lines take jagged, irregular, undulating, or supple forms. More than a traditional "graphic language," these lines act as a second language of the body—flowing, breathing, and stretching naturally through his creations.

● "Our bodies are constantly changing, we should face it when we create graphic design and artwork," Yago says. He doesn't see the body as merely a tool of creation—it is the origin of perception and expression. He describes his process like this: if he has a restful night of sleep, his arms move with greater ease; if he has too much to drink, his movements slow the next day. Yet for him, no bodily state is better or worse—each holds the potential for good work. "The important point is to arrange the drawing direction according to my body's condition," he explains. When feeling well, he tends to compose with strict lines and control; when off balance, he might use more spontaneous and idiosyncratic lines to build a different kind of rational order. Regardless of the state, a dynamic tension between precision and freedom runs through his works. He calls this approach: "making strict dots and unique dots." Through this rhythm, his works maintain a living connection with the body—as though the works themselves are also breathing, also alive.

Fig. 2 *Imitative Behaviour: In the Footsteps of My Daughter* in Tokyo, 2024.

● This awareness didn't come to him all at once. In his early years, Yago admits he was overly focused on "concept" and "purpose," often sidelining the body's own agency. He recalls a time when he felt like a lone figure wandering the universe—without direction, unable to touch or feel anything around him. Then came the turning point: the COVID-19 pandemic. During isolation, he began drawing again, bringing it back into his graphic design practice. It started with a single bouquet of wilted flowers he had brought home from an exhibition. With no concept, no theme, just instinct, he began to draw. "My arm moved smoothly, step by step," he recalls. And the drawing was done. That moment marked a shift in his creative journey. He realized, "To create something, body action must come first." Creation doesn't begin in the head—it begins in the body, in sensation. And through this process, the power and vitality of the work will emerge on its own.

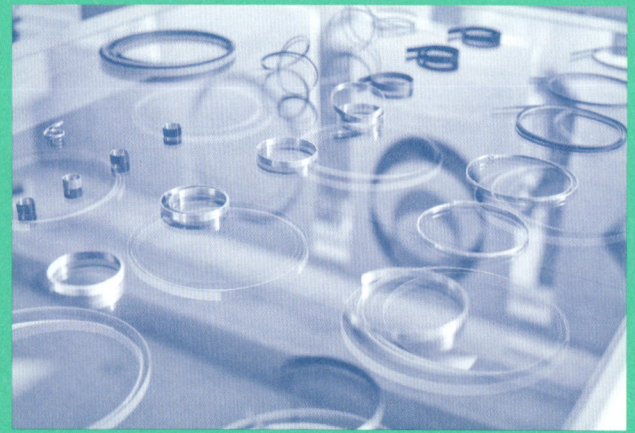

Fig. 3 *Imitative Behaviour: In the Footsteps of My Daughter* in Tokyo, 2024.

MATERIAL PLAY: HOW LINES TRAVERSE THE TWO- AND THREE-DIMENSIONAL SPACE

Fig. 4 *Imitative Behaviour: In the Footsteps of My Daughter* in Tokyo, 2024.

● Naonori Yago's visual language is not confined to the flat plane. His lines do not merely dance across the page—they extend outward into physical space. Through his hands, materials like paper and brass are reimagined into sculptural forms he calls "paper jewelry," transforming what is typically seen as lightweight or rigid into expressions of dynamic visual tension and sculptural potential.

● **"Rigid materials are both interesting and playful to work with,"** Yago admits. To him, such materials not only provide structural support but also enhance the spatial impact of his lines. He offers an example: when drawing with a hard pencil, the resulting lines display sharp, angular edges. Though they exist on a flat sheet of paper, these lines evoke a chiseled, almost sculptural depth. This strategy—creating apparent two-dimensionality imbued with three-dimensional depth tension—allows his flat compositions to generate a striking sense of space.

● As a graphic designer, Yago constantly explores the shifting boundary between two and three dimensions. He notes that successful graphic works often evoke a sense of volume, while effective three-dimensional designs often reclaim the clarity of flat composition. In practice, this means that when creating an object, he seeks a visual angle from which it appears as a planar graphic form. It's within these shifting viewpoints that his lines find new directions to grow—guiding not just the composition, but also the viewer's experience of spatial perception.

● However, material and design are by no means a game of unrestricted freedom. **Yago is fully aware of the unavoidable constraints in the creative process. "We have to design within a world bound by economic and production limitations," he says.** Whether it's the choice of color, the cost of materials, or the limitations of printing technology, designers must always complete their works within an imperfect reality. Yet in his view, it is precisely these constraints that spark much of our creativity.

● "If we had no limitations, it would be a very boring world to creation." For Yago, limitations are not obstacles, but the very engine of invention. Through the ongoing negotiation between the properties of a material and the goals of design, he has cultivated a visual language that moves fluidly between softness and rigidity—celebrating both the flow and structure of the line. In this way, his "paper jewelry" is more than an accessory; it becomes an architectural expression of material, line, and space.

FROM SURFACE TO SPACE: THE EXPANSION OF LINES IN INSTALLATION ART

● In recent years, Naonori Yago's practice has gradually extended into the realms of physical and installation art. As his work transitions from the page to three-dimensional space, his understanding and use of the "line" have undergone subtle transformations.

● "Physical and installation works are very meaningful challenges for me," Yago says. Compared to the structural and symbolic qualities of lines in his two-dimensional works, installations demand greater attention to the interplay between light, materials, and the viewer's movement. He must constantly consider how these elements interact and shape the experience of the piece.

● A representative example is his spatial installation for the Azabudai Hills Summer Festival. The central concept of the project was "semi-transparent forms," aimed at offering a refreshing outdoor experience during the sweltering city summer while also echoing Mori Building's vision of "community." Yago created a signature goldfish figure composed of dots, and cleverly chose the traditional Japanese sudare screens (bamboo blinds) as the main material. The inherent transparency of sudare screens allowed the dots and lines to create subtle veiling effects—at close range, the fine details seemed to vanish, only to re-emerge when the viewer stepped back. It is in this fluctuating distance of perception that Yago constructs a sense of breath between line and space.

Fig. 5 Azabudai Hills Summer Festival, designed by Yago Naonori, 2024.

● As he has said before, "I try to discover a two-dimensional view in the three-dimensional works." In his installations, lines are no longer just compositional elements—they become channels of perception, gaining new forms and rhythms through shifts in angle and lighting. This tension between the flat and the spatial has become a recurring theme in his sculptural explorations.

● In Yago's visual world, the "line" is no longer confined to the stroke of a pen—it becomes a medium that structures space and awakens the viewer's bodily awareness. He liberates the line from the surface, allowing it to breathe and meander through the real world, ultimately merging with light, material, and the shared experience between people.

THE FUTURE OF CREATIVE POTENTIAL

● For years, Naonori Yago has explored the multifaceted expressions of fundamental elements across both graphic design and installation art. Yet

Fig. 6 *Imitative Behaviour: In the Footsteps of My Daughter* in Hong Kong, 2024.

beyond this steady trajectory, his interests have quietly shifted toward a new frontier—kids' creativity.

● "I have an interest in implementing kids' creativity in social situations," Yago shares. This curiosity stems from a personal project he began four years ago, one that continues to this day: a creative collaboration with his daughter. In this ongoing exchange, his daughter draws freely, and Yago later scans, traces, and transforms her lines into graphic artworks. In doing so, he uses dots to articulate her raw, energetic marks. When this project began, his daughter was only three years old, and her motor control was still developing. The lines she drew varied in strength, so Yago responded by placing denser dots in stronger areas and sparser ones where the lines weakened.

● What might seem like a technical treatment is, in fact, Yago's most honest response to creativity in its purest form. He explains that by using dots to re-configure his daughter's irregular lines, he aimed to translate their raw energy into a visual language—an iconic form of flat representation. **The resulting tension between his daughter's unstable, expressive lineworks and his geometric order yields a unique dynamic, turning childlike creativity into explosive visual experiments with line and composition.**

● "I've gained a lot of impressions and inspirations from this project," Yago reflects. For him, this collaborative method—initiated by a child and interpreted by an adult—is not only an exploration of visual expression but also a form of social practice. He hopes to expand the project beyond his daughter, inviting more children to take part. He envisions a series of workshops designed to systematically nurture and harness children's innate talents and imagination. All kids have creativity in themselves already, but that creativity is disappearing year by year," he says. In today's educational and social systems, children's imaginations are often suppressed by rigid structures. Through art, design, and visual experimentation, Yago hopes to reignite their original and unfiltered desire for expression.

● **"I've already found my own creativity, now I want to support kids to find theirs."** For Yago, this is not just a shift in methodology; it could represent a new horizon for graphic design itself. A fresh visual language might be hiding in those unpolished, crooked lines—waiting to be sparked, to be seen.

Fig. 7 Naonori Yago with his daughter at the exhibition, 2024.

IMITATIVE BEHAVIOUR: IN THE FOOTSTEPS OF MY DAUGHTERS IN TOKYO

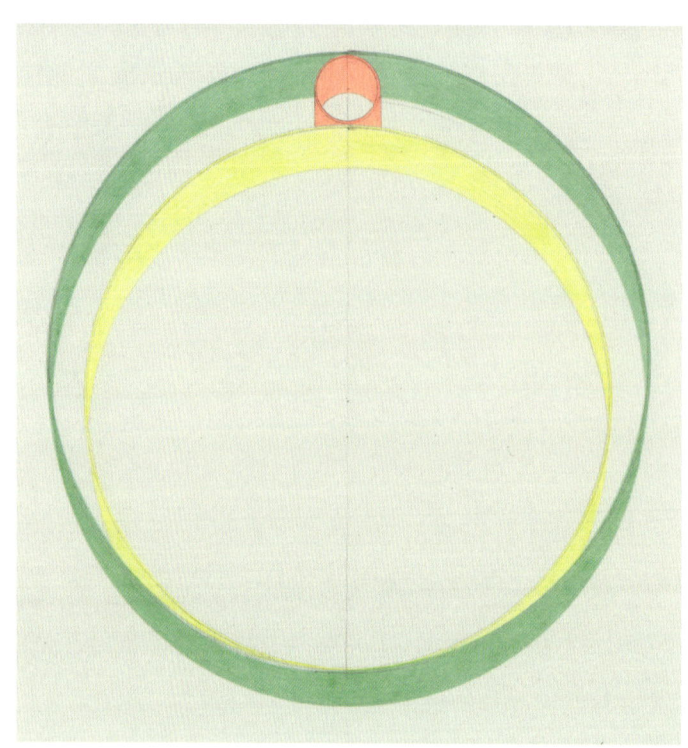

Imitative Behaviour: In the Footsteps of My Daughters

Imitative Behaviour: In the Footsteps of My Daughters

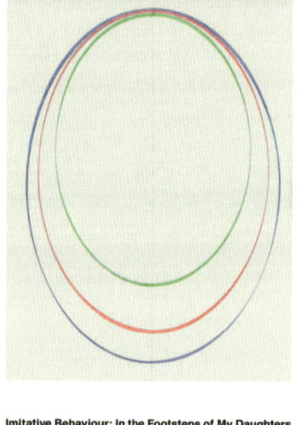

Imitative Behaviour: In the Footsteps of My Daughters

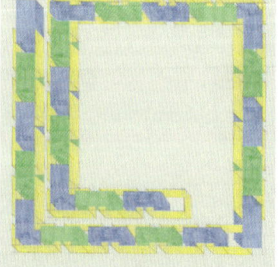

Imitative Behaviour: In the Footsteps of My Daughters

Watching his daughter create and play with her own paper jewelry, the designer wondered—why don't adults do the same? Surely, there must be a way to craft beautiful paper jewelry that adults can wear. This idea led him to design his own paper jewelry, eventually evolving it into contemporary jewelry. The exhibition showcased both entry-level paper jewelry and high-end metal jewelry, offering a glimpse into the transformation of a simple material into sophisticated adornments.

D. Naonori Yago

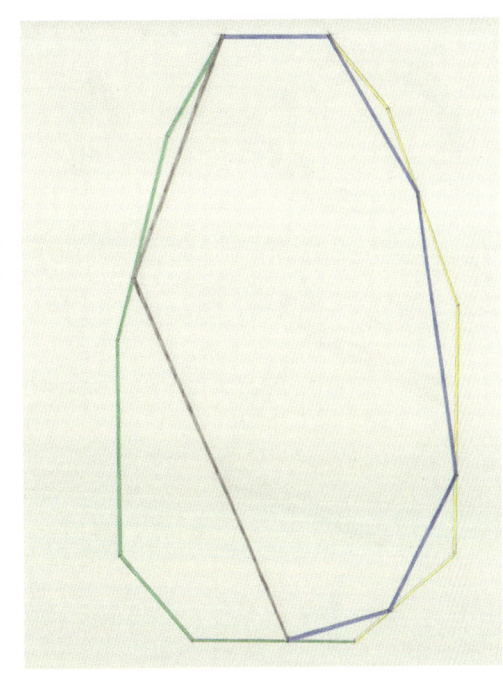

Imitative Behaviour: In the Footsteps of My Daughters

Imitative Behaviour: In the Footsteps of My Daughters

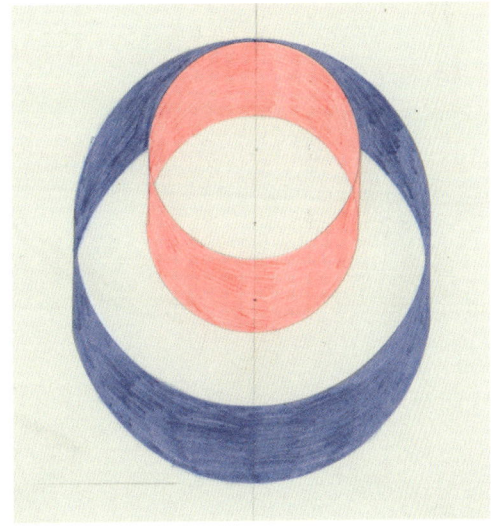

Imitative Behaviour: In the Footsteps of My Daughters

Imitative Behaviour: In the Footsteps of My Daughters

◇ Why Line?

The designer took the paper decorations made by his daughters as a basis, extracted their outlines, and turned them into graphics to create the posters for this exhibition. He also changed the original paper material to brass to make durable decorations. Unlike ordinary decorations, which are soft and changeable in shape, some of these decorations have sharp corners, and their bendable lines contrast with the softness of the body.

Basic Line

- C45 M0 Y50 K0 / R152 G206 B151
- C10 M0 Y55 K0 / R238 G238 B140
- C0 M65 Y45 K0 / R237 G121 B113
- C75 M50 Y0 K0 / R71 G116 B185
- C0 M45 Y15 K0 / R243 G168 B180
- C0 M0 Y0 K0 / R255 G255 B255
- C0 M0 Y0 K100 / R0 G0 B0

○ TATAMI REFAB PROJECT

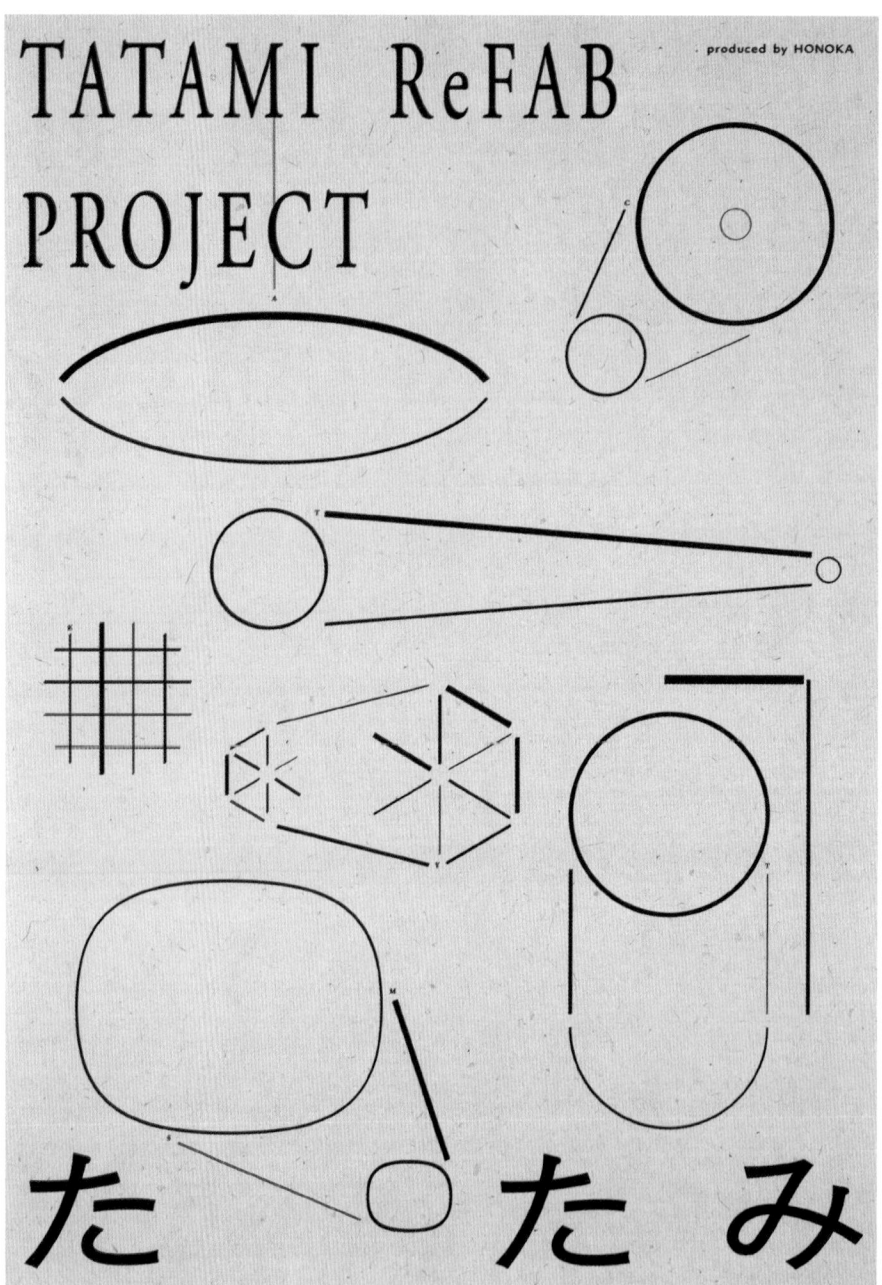

This design is part of the "TATAMI ReFAB PROJECT," an initiative that upcycles discarded materials from Japan's traditional tatami flooring, transforming them into new furniture. The project was showcased at Milan Salone, the world's largest furniture fair.

DA. TM INC.
D. Yuto Tamura
CL. HONOKA lab.

◇ Why Line?

Tatami is made by weaving dried, slender leaves known as *igusa*. The designer symbolized igusa through irregular lines, layering them over the newly reborn furniture. This approach serves as a visual element that complements the story of the material's transformation into its final form.

Basic Line

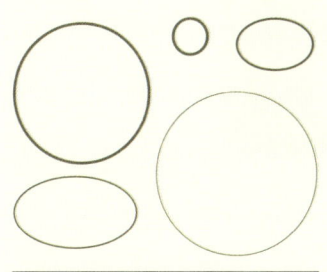

- C20 M10 Y35 K0 / R214 G218 B178
- C0 M0 Y0 K100 / R0 G0 B0
- C65 M55 Y85 K10 / R105 G105 B64

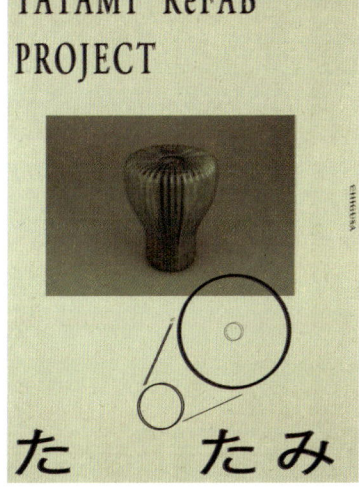

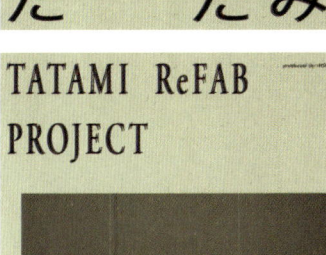

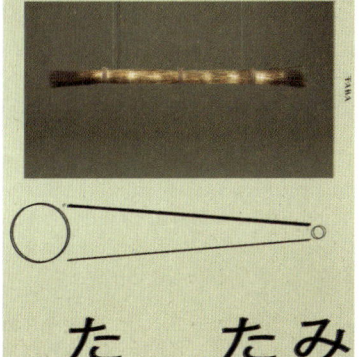

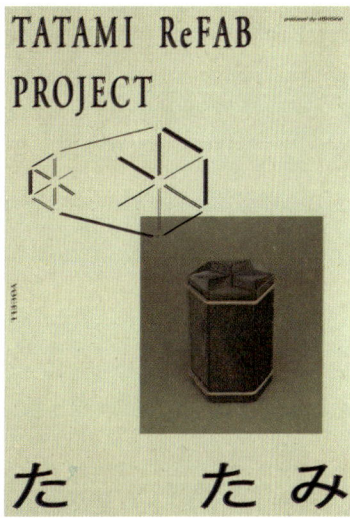

↑ B4A

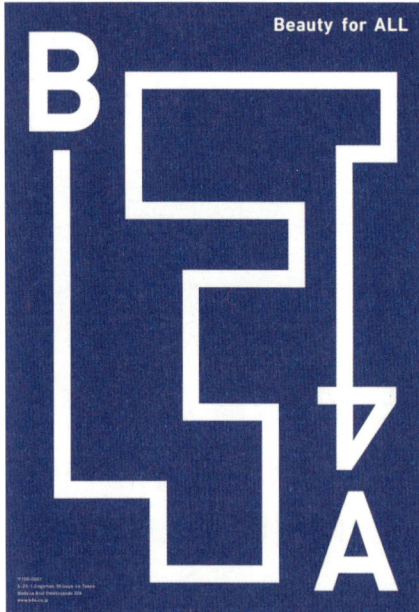

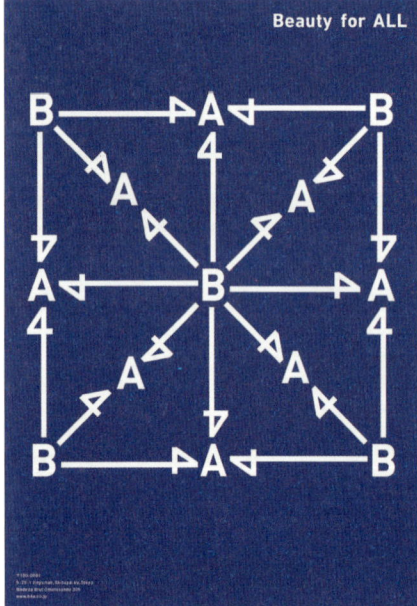
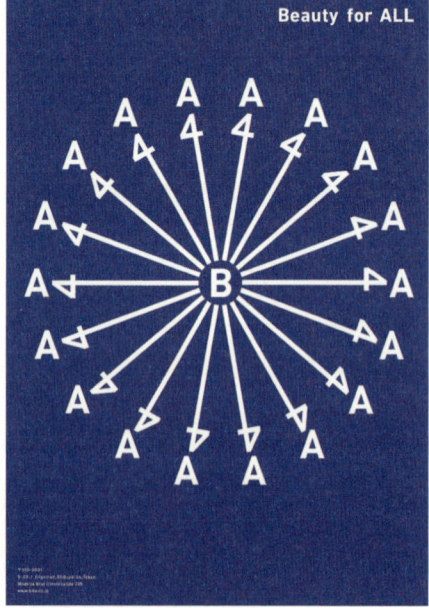

This is the logo and visual identity for B4A, an IT company specializing in backend systems for the aesthetic medicine industry. The company name, B4A—short for Beauty for All—embodies its mission to make high-quality aesthetic treatments more accessible to everyone. The logo design reinforces this vision by incorporating a stylized "4" as an arrow, visually representing the seamless delivery of "B" (Beauty) to "A" (All) with clarity and simplicity.

DA. TM INC.
D. Yuto Tamura
CL. B4A

 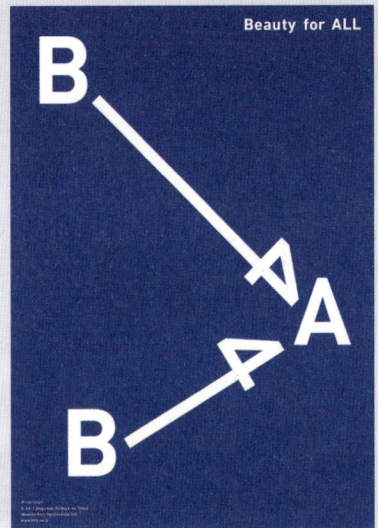 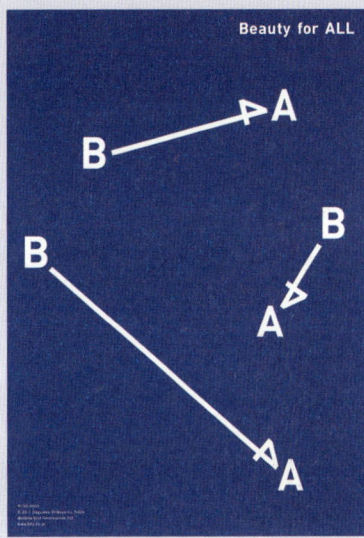

◇ Why Line?

To convey the seamless accessibility from "B" to "A" across various contexts, the designer developed a dynamic visual system in which the arrow stretches, bends, and transforms freely. This fluid movement reflects adaptability and openness, while the continuous line serves as a symbol of infinite possibilities.

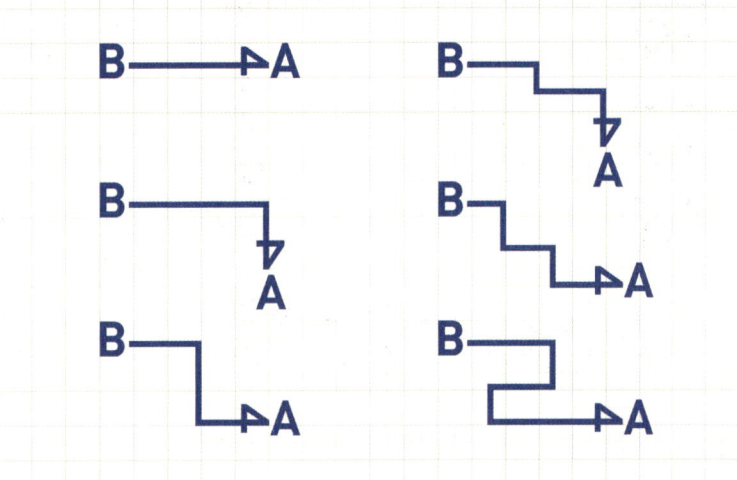

Basic Line

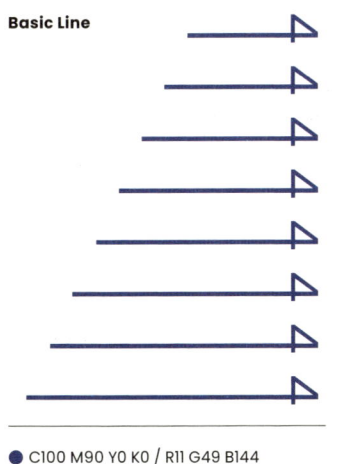

● C100 M90 Y0 K0 / R11 G49 B144
○ C0 M0 Y0 K0 / R255 G255 B255

DESIGN FOR *MUSEUM OF THE PEOPLE, BY THE PEOPLE, FOR THE PEOPLE*

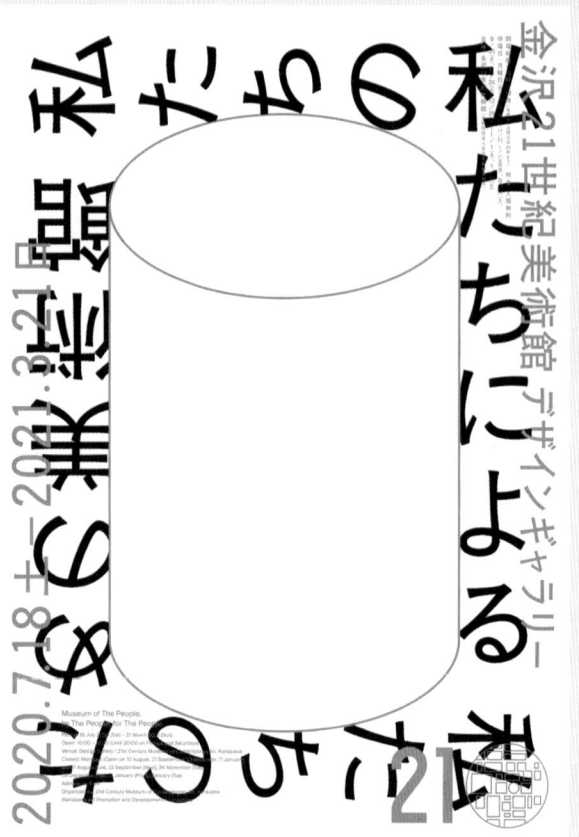
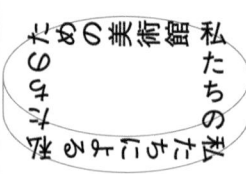
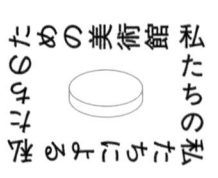
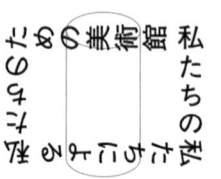

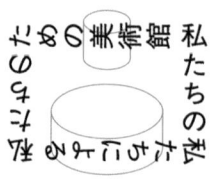
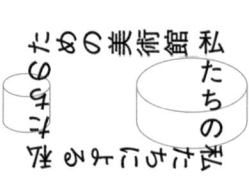
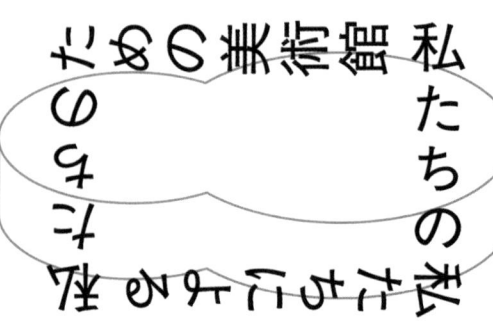

The book design was created for the exhibition *Museum of the People, by the People, for the People* held at the 21st Century Museum of Contemporary Art, Kanazawa. This exhibition, marking the 16th anniversary of the museum's opening, reflects on its history and contemplates its future. The main visual features a cylindrical object, crafted with lines to evoke the iconic architecture of the museum's building. The overall design, including the logo, posters, wall graphics, venue layout, animated videos, and booklet design, was undertaken.

DA. emuni
D. Masashi Murakami
CL. 21st Century Museum of Contemporary Art, Kanazawa

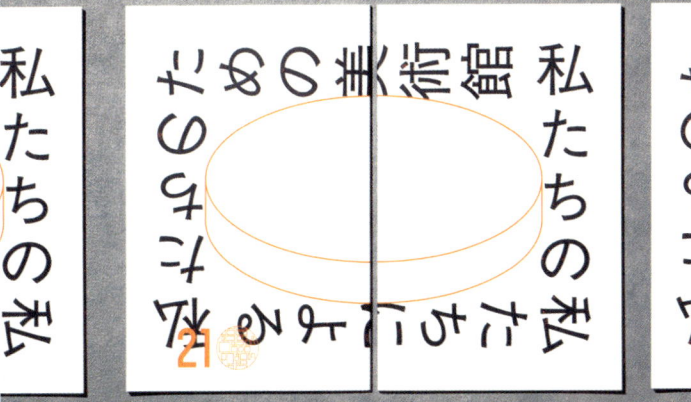
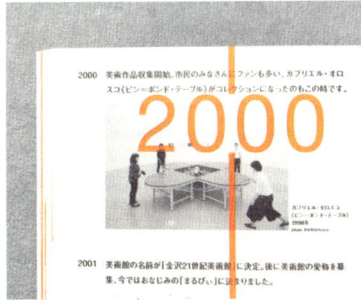
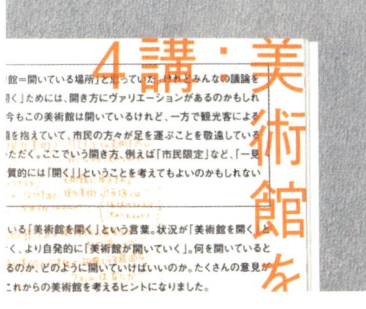

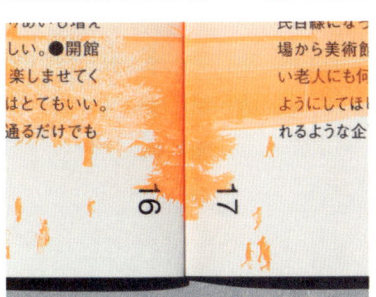

◇ Why Line?

The designer used lines to express the continuity of time. The exhibition board was simplified into a cylinder made of lines, making it the main identifying graphic, which was simple and representative, deepening the viewer's impression of the exhibition. At the same time, the designer enlarged the text of the title, which made the strokes of the text more obvious and had the feeling of a line.

Basic Line

● C0 M60 Y85 K0 / R240 G131 B44

● C0 M0 Y0 K100 / R0 G0 B0

○ C0 M0 Y0 K0 / R255 G255 B255

THEATRE VISUAL IDENTITY

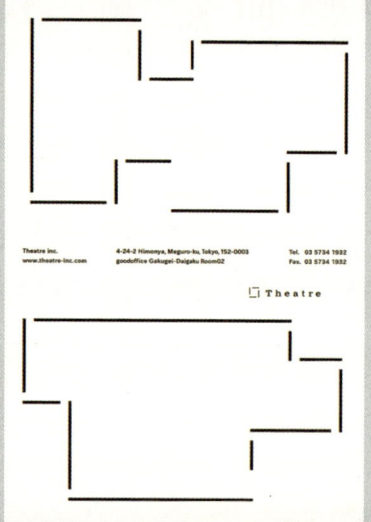

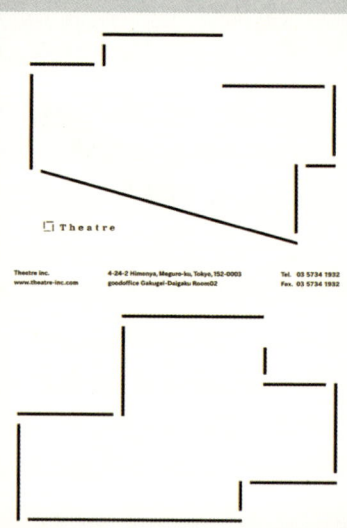
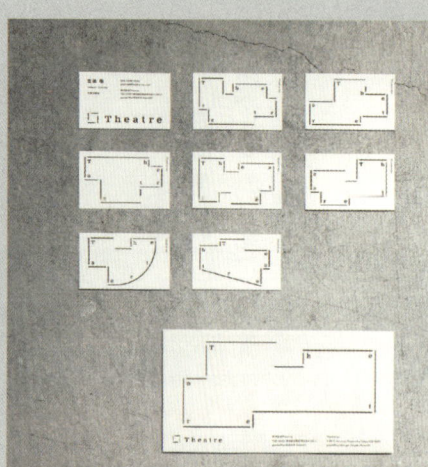
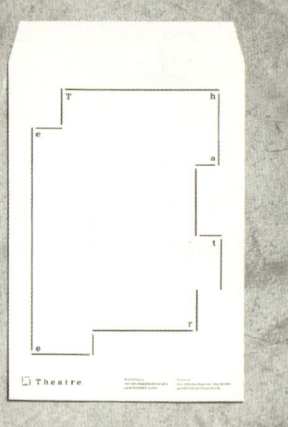

This is the logo and visual identity for Theatre, a real estate company providing office solutions. The design loosely encloses four sides while leaving the center open, embodying the traditional Japanese spatial concept of "emptiness." Developed based on the structured rules that define the logo, the visual system allows for infinite expansion, evoking the excitement of unfolding blueprints and envisioning new possibilities.

DA. TM INC.
D. Yuto Tamura
CL. Theatre

◇ Why Line?

"Emptiness" serves as a vessel—an invitation for the viewer's imagination. By simply enclosing space with lines, the contours naturally emerge, encouraging the mind to visualize the form. The designer's intention was to fully harness the power of negative space, creating a dynamic interplay between presence and absence.

Basic Line

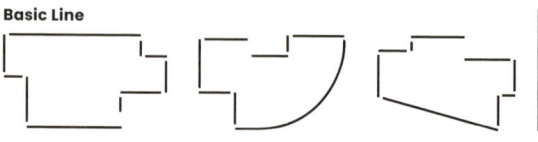

● C0 M0 Y0 K100 / R0 G0 B0
○ C0 M0 Y0 K0 / R255 G255 B255

YUKISAWAYA

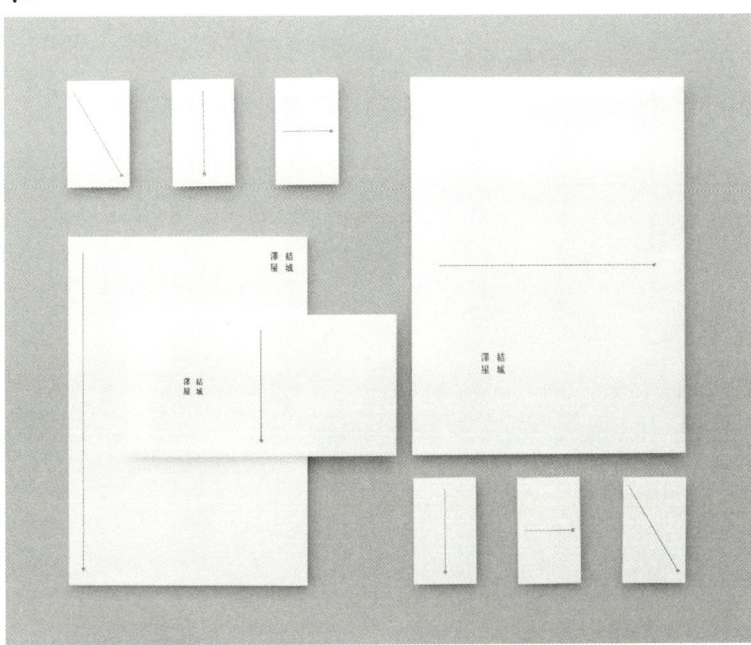

A long-established wholesaler of the 2,000-year-old intangible cultural asset "Yuki-Sugi" in Yuki City, Ibaraki Prefecture, has launched a new kimono brand VI.

DA. 6D
AD. D. Shogo Kishino
D. Miho Sakaki
PT. Shingo Fujimoto

◇ **Why Line?**

The brand's logo uses a thread, a finger spinning cotton thread, a long line of spun threads, and its history to express Yuki-Sugi's long heritage and the enormous amount of work required to make a single piece of fabric! The logo is expressed with a thread and a finger, while the letters are understated like a seal. While satisfying the basic principle of simple expression of the logo, the subtleties of the logo deviate from the norm, reflecting Sawaya's philosophy of preserving tradition while enjoying kimono for the "present day."

Basic Line

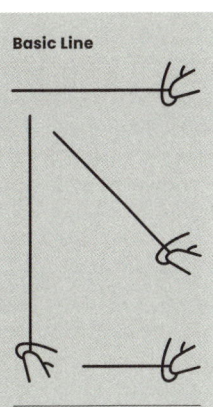

● C0 M0 Y0 K100 / R0 G0 B0
○ C0 M0 Y0 K0 / R255 G255 B255

⟲ THE GOAL

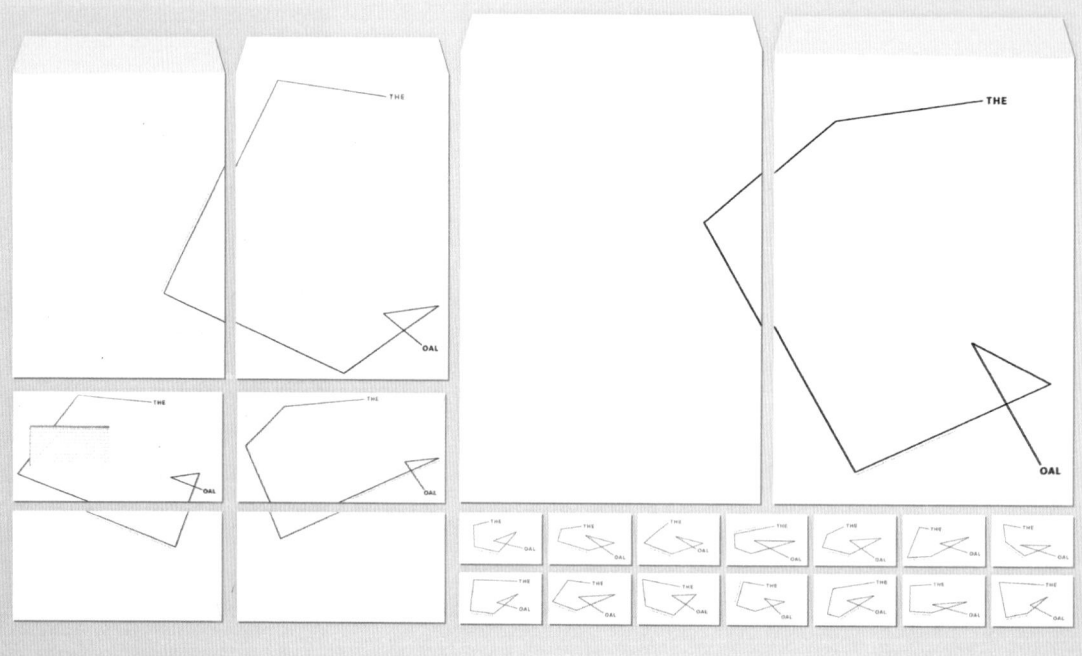

THE GOAL Co., Ltd., a fashion advertising company based in Ginza, Tokyo, aims to address social issues through the power of fashion. Its core business philosophy needs to be directly communicated through the CI logo, and presenting it in a minimalist way has become the key to this design.

The design team introduced the corporate philosophy CI logo—"GO WITH FASHION," where "GOAL" symbolizes "goal." With diverse clients, the goals are equally varied, much like the countless paths to a destination. Different people come together, advancing toward a shared goal. To visually represent this concept, the team created a new, groundbreaking, and intuitive brand logo, which was applied to the back of employees' business cards. The team also developed a unique algorithm for THE GOAL, dynamically linking the personalized logos of 70 employees with the company's CI logo, displaying 70 variations on the homepage. As the CI visual window, the website presents the journey of individuals moving toward their goals, with line elements running throughout, symbolizing the "posture of striving toward a goal."

D. Miharu Matsunaga (Hami)
CL. The GOAL

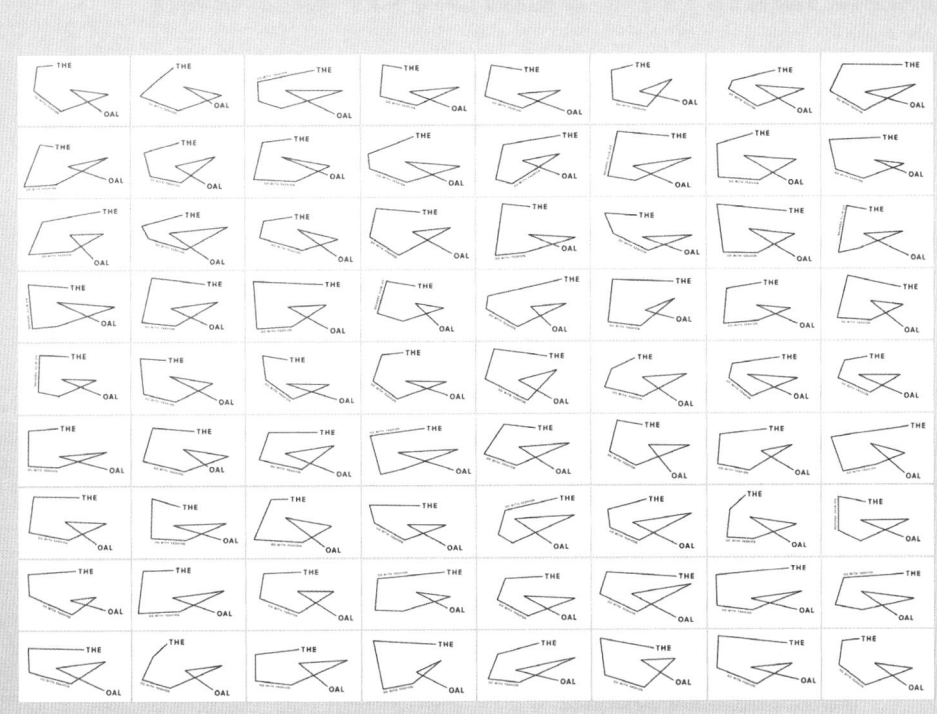

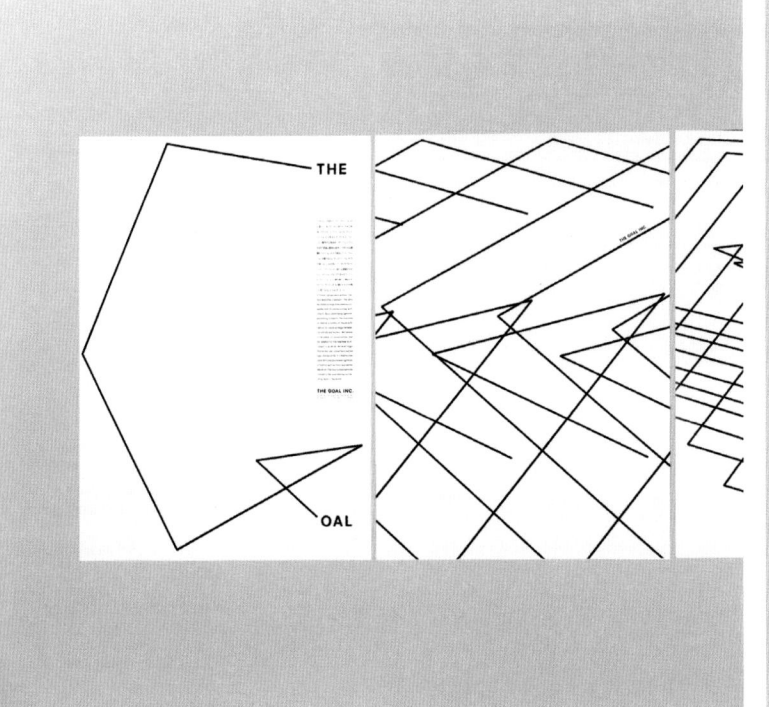

◇ Why Line?

The designer used minimalist lines to interpret the complex corporate philosophy. An ordinary line, once imbued with meaning, transcends its existence as a simple form. The key to the design lies in the value that can be conveyed at the end of this line.

Basic Line

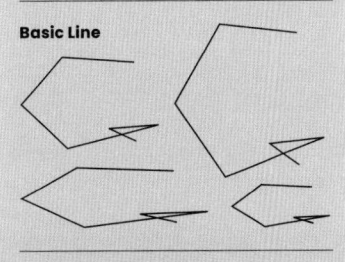

● C0 M0 Y0 K100 / R0 G0 B0
○ C0 M0 Y0 K0 / R255 G255 B255

(VISUAL IDENTITY DESIGN OF OIZUMI

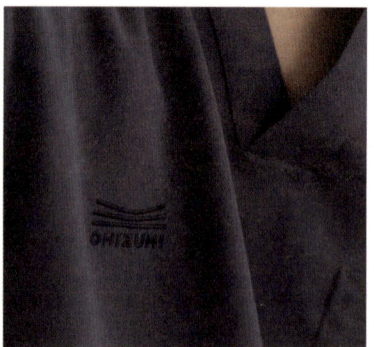
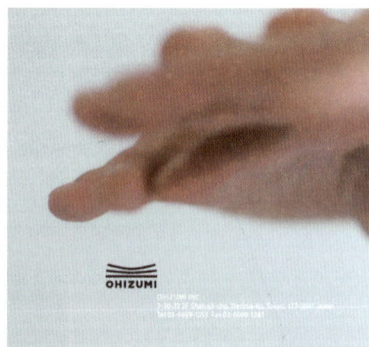

Oizumi is an osteopathic clinic based in Tokyo. For its logo mark, the designer emphasized proper alignment and balance, visually representing a well-aligned and straightened body.

D. Arata Kubota
CL. Oizumi

◇ **Why Line?**

People of all ages and nationalities visit this osteopathic clinic, making simple, non-verbal communication essential. To address this, the designer created a logo using only lines, visually representing the body's improvement and alignment in a clear and universally understandable way.

Basic Line

● C0 M0 Y0 K100 / R0 G0 B0
○ C0 M0 Y0 K0 / R255 G255 B255

FUREN

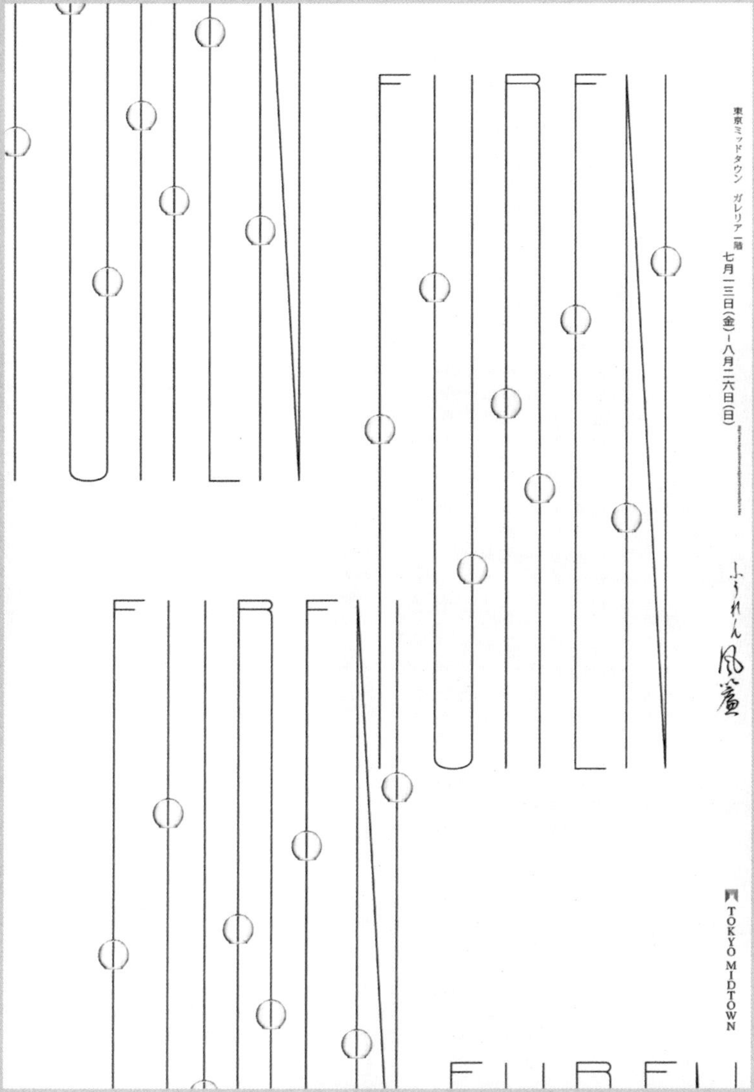

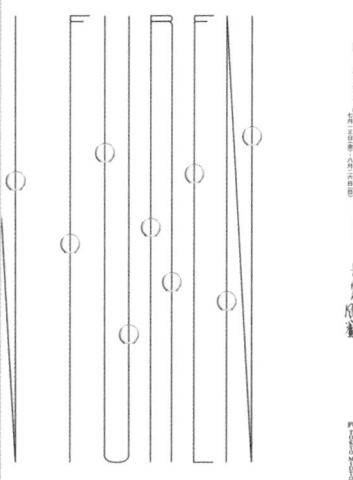

◇ Why Line?

By stretching typography, lines naturally emerge—mirroring the visual effect of the actual installation. In the design, the lines function both as textual elements and graphic components, seamlessly integrating language and imagery to create a cohesive visual experience.

Basic Line

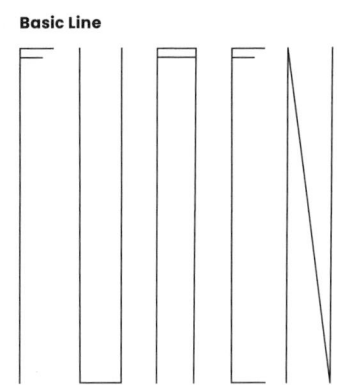

● C0 M0 Y0 K100 / R0 G0 B0
○ C3 M2 Y3 K0 / R249 G250 B249

This is a seasonal event design for Tokyo Midtown, a multifunctional urban complex that embodies a modern and refined lifestyle in the heart of the city. The designer created an installation piece titled "FUREN" (Blind Wind), inspired by the essence of a traditional Japanese summer, and visualized its underlying concept through design.

DA. TM INC.
D. Yuto Tamura
CL. Tokyo Midtown

QUARTERLY MAGAZINE YAMABIKO

The quarterly magazine *Yamabiko* is part of Yamabiko Corporation's efforts to promote its corporate philosophy. The internal newsletter is used as a communication tool with a sense of warmth.

DA. fff Inc.
D. Maehara Shoichi
CL. Quarterly Magazine *Yamabiko*

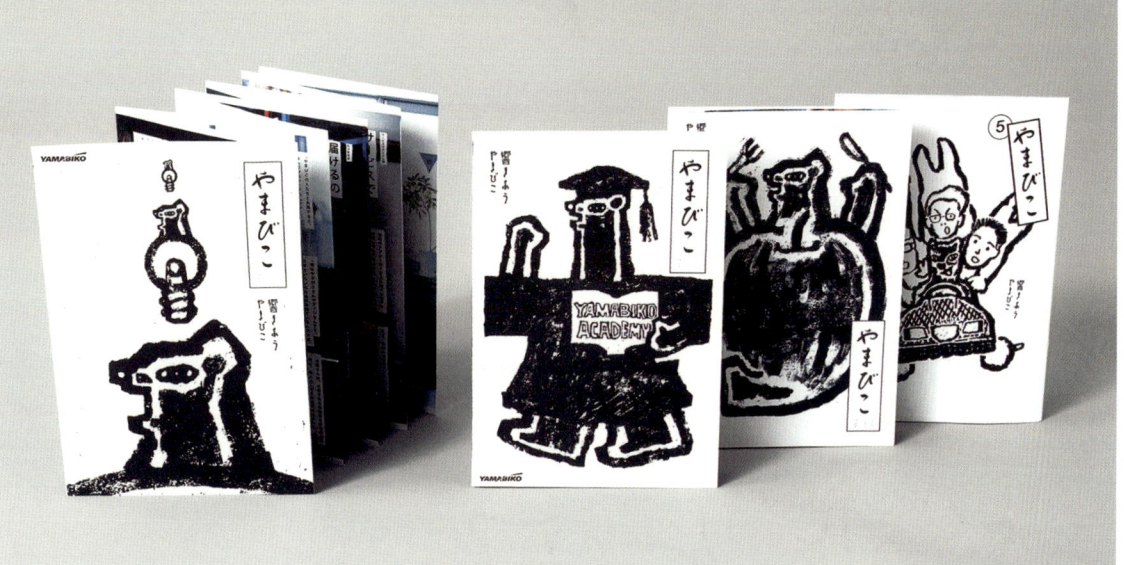

◇ Why Line?

The purpose of the quarterly *Yamabiko* is to keep employees informed about what is happening within the company. When planning its design, the core principle was to keep it simple yet impactful, aiming to convey a raw and powerful visual language that avoids lengthy explanations and speaks directly to the heart. To realize this design concept, the designer adopted a rough line style, resembling the strokes of a child's hand, outlined in pure black ink. This approach is both unpretentious and full of strength.

Basic Line

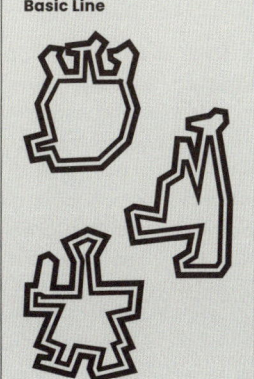

○ C0 M0 Y0 K10 / R239 G239 B239

● C0 M0 Y0 K100 / R0 G0 B0

○ C0 M0 Y0 K0 / R255 G255 B255

꒱ PENINSULA TIME

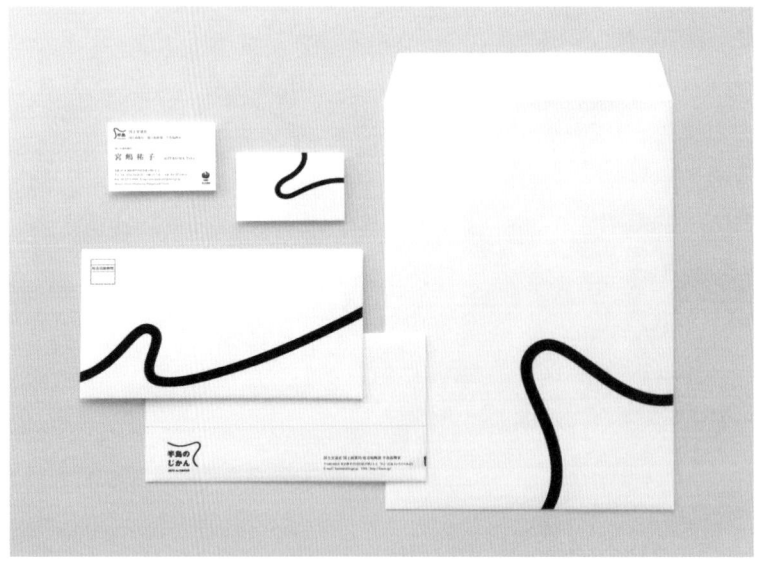

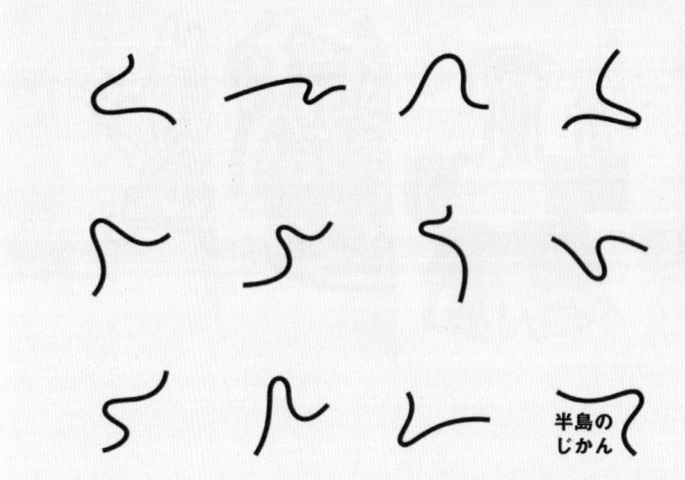

◇ **Why Line?**

By definition, a peninsula is a landform surrounded by the sea on three sides. The designer sought to express this concept using the simplest possible element—a single line. Recognizing that peninsulas around the world come in many forms, he aimed not to depict a specific place, but rather to capture the diversity of peninsula-like shapes through a collection of curved lines. This approach allowed for a bold, simple, and clear representation of landforms shaped by the Earth itself.

Hanto no Jikan (Peninsula Time) is an exhibition promoting the 23 peninsular regions of Japan. Peninsulas, by definition, are nearly surrounded by water and therefore possess an enviable environment with beaches, villages, and mountains all in one area. At the same time, peninsulas are characterized by a rich multiculturalism, having served as the gateway to Japan throughout history. Hanto no Jikan takes a candid look at peninsular areas, with the main focus on photographs depicting the scenery, people, and produce of the peninsulas. The exhibition offered an opportunity to reexamine the definition, value, and future of peninsulas.

DA. Nippon Design Center
AD. Daigo Daikoku
CL. The Ministry of Land, Infrastructure, Transport and Tourism (MLIT)
C. Norimitsu Korekata

Basic Line

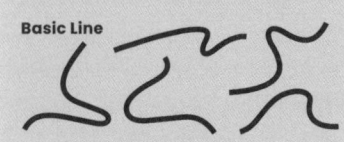

● C0 M0 Y0 K100 / R0 G0 B0
○ C0 M0 Y0 K0 / R255 G255 B255

HARAPPA

Designers were in charge of the VI and signage for the 4th floor Harappa, located on Harakado in Harajuku, Tokyo. The entire floor serves as a public space where visitors can engage with art and content centered on the theme of sustainability.

PLANNING & PRODUCE. RGB · KADOWSAN
AD. D. Shogo Kishino
D. Norika Kato
PT. Shingo Fujimoto
CL. TOKYU LAND CORPORATION

Why Line?

Since this is a public space, the designer did not emphasize individuality in the design. The logo design was inspired by insects or animals hidden in the grass, with a hand-drawn grass texture covering the surface to create a natural and friendly visual effect.

Basic Line

- C75 M15 Y100 K0 / R56 G167 B56
- C75 M30 Y60 K100 / R63 G141 B118
- C100 M80 Y85 K40 / R0 G47 B45
- C0 M0 Y0 K100 / R0 G0 B0
- C0 M0 Y0 K0 / R255 G255 B255

MT SHOPPER

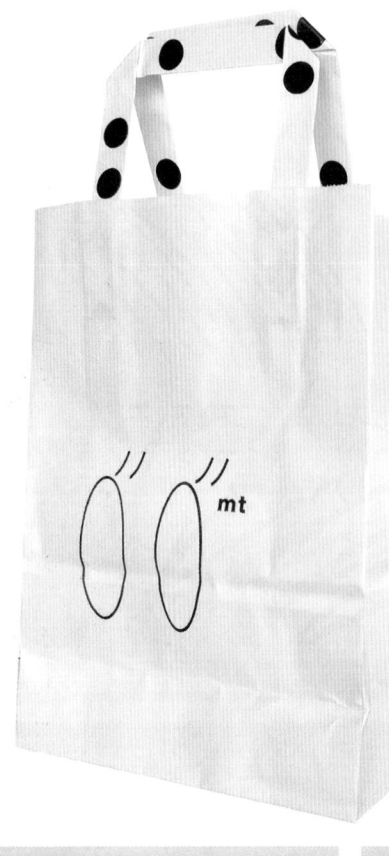
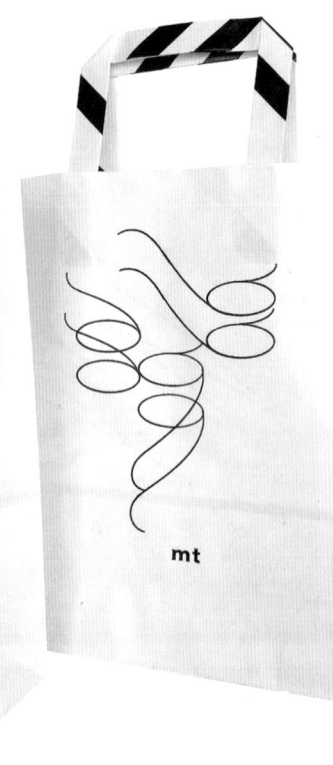
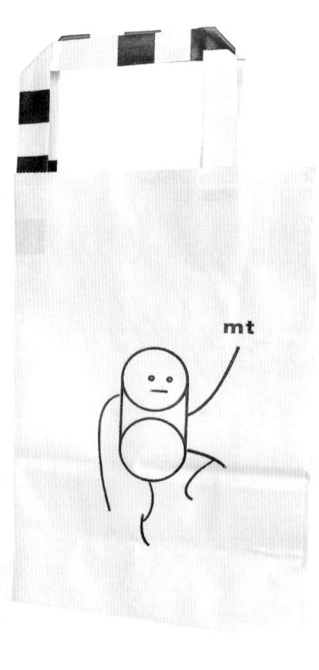

◇ Why Line?

By combining simple shapes and colors, the shoppers were designed to stand out with their monochrome hues and dynamic patterns, creating a bold and eye-catching visual appeal.

Basic Line

● C0 M0 Y0 K100 / R0 G0 B0
○ C0 M0 Y0 K0 / R255 G255 B255

The shopper design at the MT store showcases the bold silhouette of masking tape, with playful dots and lines randomly scattered across the handles. This design aims to create a unique and vibrant atmosphere, adding a touch of spontaneity and character.

DA. iyamadesign inc.
D. Koji Iyama

HAKOBE

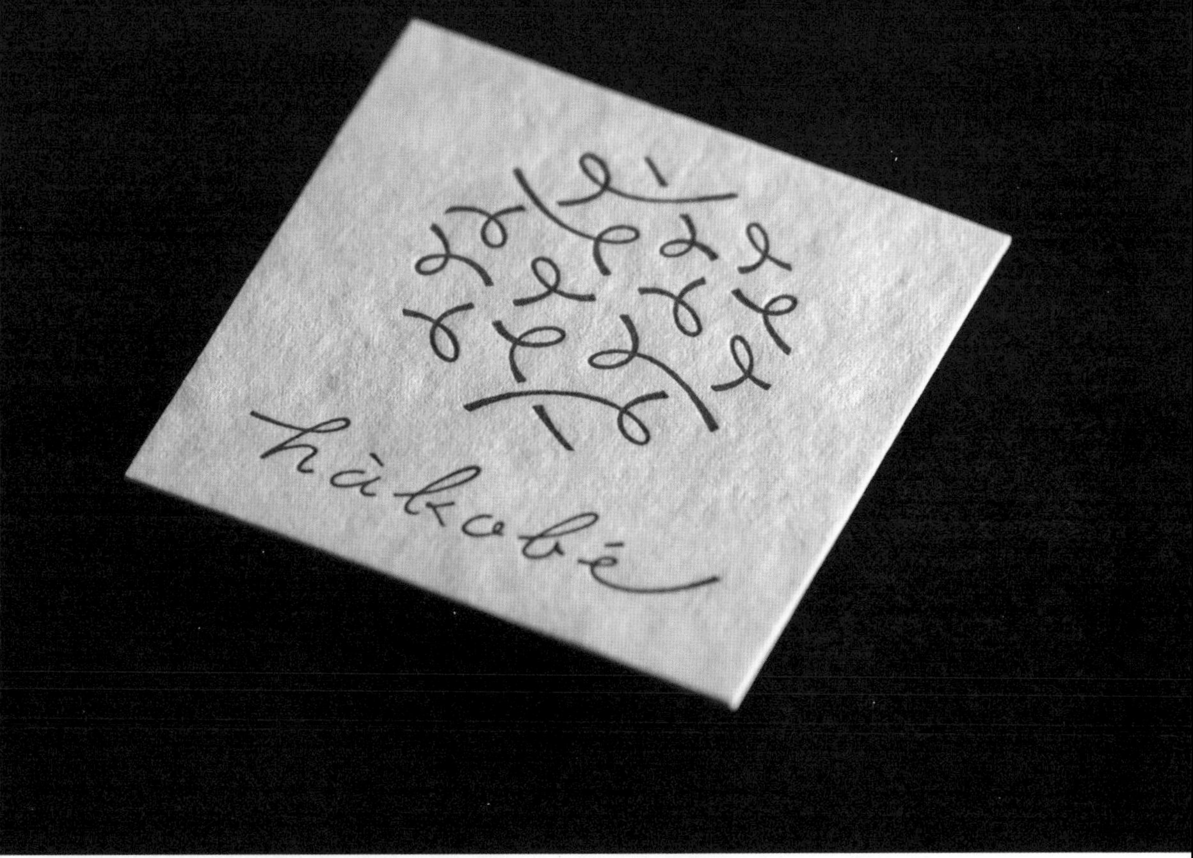

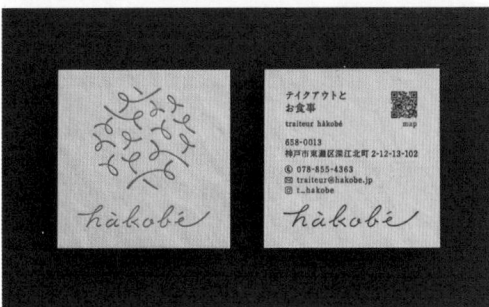

Why Line?

The logo reflects the owner's vision for the restaurant's gradual expansion, much like the steady growth of Stellaria. Inspired by the image of Stellaria plants spreading across the landscape, the logo uses lines to evoke a sense of interconnected growth and continuous development.

Basic Line

● C85 M50 Y100 K30 / R32 G87 B43
○ C0 M0 Y0 K0 / R255 G255 B255
● C0 M0 Y0 K100 / R0 G0 B0

The project focuses on designing the logo and signage for the French restaurant "Traiteur Hàkobé." Hàkobé, or Stellaria, refers to a group of small yet steadily growing plants found across France.

DA. Econosys Design Inc.
AD. Mitsutaka Nakao
D. Wakana Touge
CL. Traiteur Hàkobé

TSUKURU LAB.

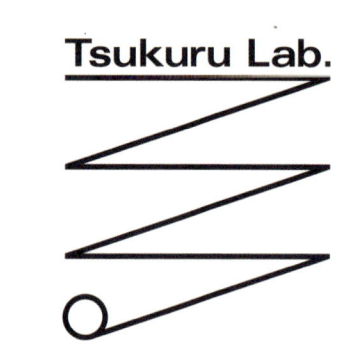

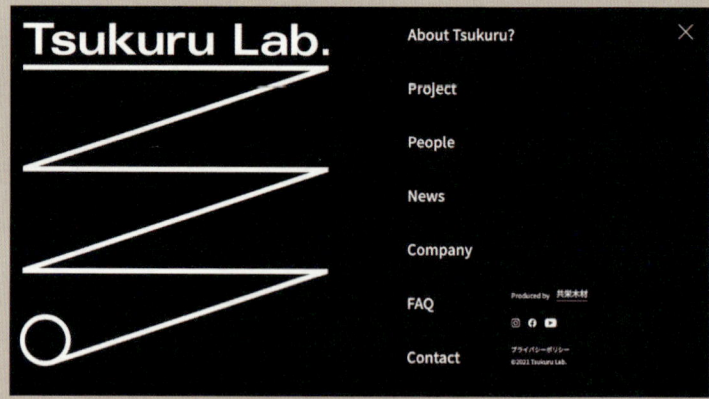

This is the new logo for Tsukuru Lab.—a woodworking company based in Ehime Prefecture. Using the Hiragana characters for "Tsu," "Ku," and "Ru" as a starting dot, the design team crafted a dynamic graphic that conveys motion and innovation in pushing ideas forward.

DA. Econosys Design Inc.
AD. Mitsutaka Nakao
D. Onyoo Jeon / Shoji Miyai
PT. Mitsuyuki Nakajima (external)
CL. Kyoei Lumber Inc.

 Why Line?

The logo can be interpreted as a piece of wood rolling on a wooden board, vividly representing the continuous development of Tsukuru Lab.

Basic Line

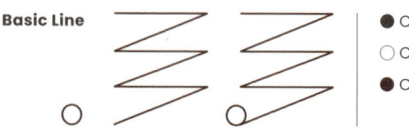

● C0 M0 Y0 K100 / R0 G0 B0
○ C0 M0 Y0 K0 / R255 G255 B255
● C60 M80 Y100 K45 / R85 G46 B21

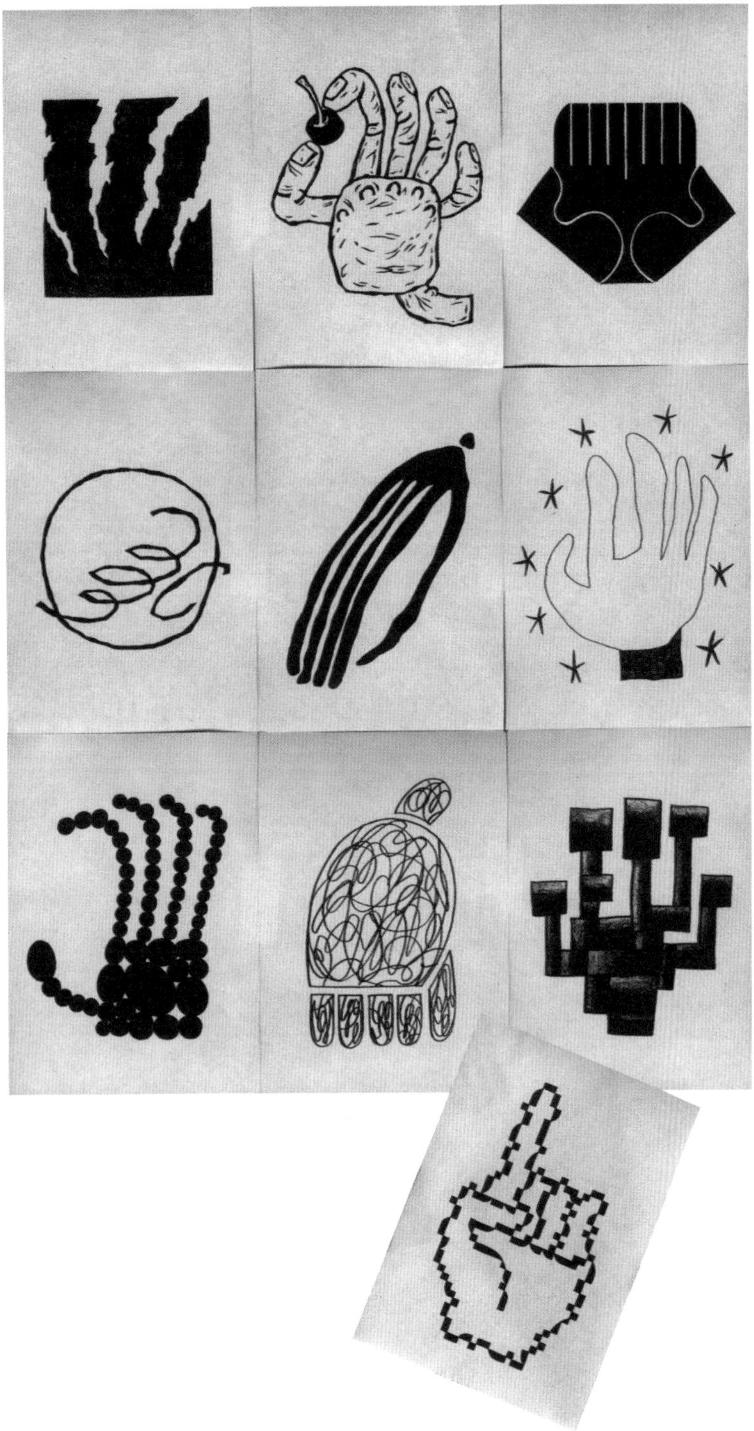

FREE HAND

◇ **Why Line?**

The designer used many different random, hand-drawn lines to depict hands of various shapes and textures, presenting a rich and vibrant form of expression in a simple composition.

Basic Line

○ C10 M12 Y25 K0 / R234 G224 B197
● C0 M0 Y0 K100 / R0 G0 B0

This standalone work uses the hand as a motif to create many distinctive hand-painted images. It explores the limits of figurative expression within the constraints of the hand, offering a creative challenge that also serves as valuable training for other crafting activities.

D. Tasuku Matsuo

IKIMONOGAKARI 10TH ALBUM " 〇 " (MARU)

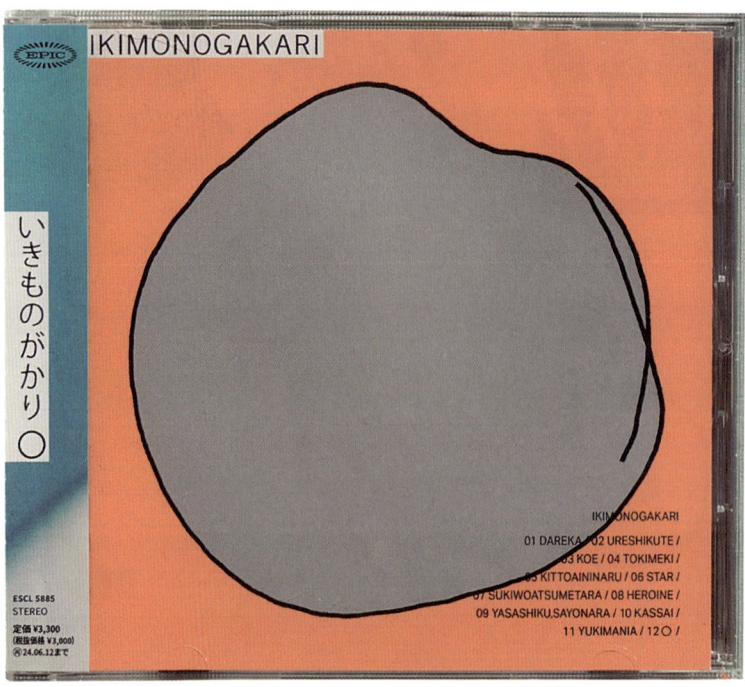

◇ Why Line?

The minimalist symbol "〇" evokes countless associations. After a deep discussion with the music group Ikimonogakari about the meaning of the circle, the design team unanimously agreed that they were not aiming for a perfect circle, but rather one that bears the traces of life, slightly flawed. This choice was intended to convey a philosophy: humanity, being inherently imperfect, should embrace and cherish its flaws, for that is where true beauty lies. In the design, the interior of the circle was made with a mirrored effect, so when listeners pick up the CD to play the music, they see their own reflection, thus creating an interactive experience and resonance with the music.

Basic Line

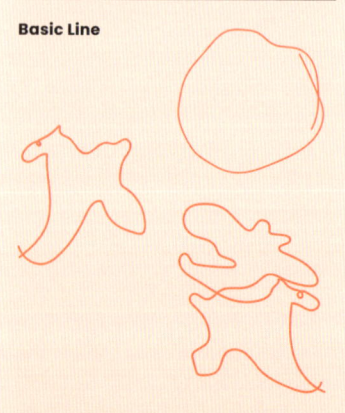

- ● C0 M60 Y50 K0 / R239 G133 B109
- ● C0 M0 Y0 K100 / R0 G0 B0
- ○ C0 M0 Y0 K0 / R255 G255 B255
- ● C0 M0 Y0 K40 / R181 G181 B182

This album is the tenth release by the Japanese music group Ikimonogakari, titled "〇" (Maru).

DA. fff Inc.
D. Maehara Shoichi
CL. Ikimonogakari

"KIGUU" MAHO OKAMOTO, RUI MARUYAMA

The project is a collection of works by two poets, each with a distinct style represented by the colors gold and silver. Though the line may appear dual, it is in fact a single form, inspired by Euler's Polyhedron Formula. This mathematical theorem, discovered either accidentally or conjecturally, first surfaced in a correspondence between Euler and his friend Goldbach.

D. I. Hirokazu Matsuda

◇ Why Line?

In abstracting the two artists, the designer arrived at a mathematical figure. Viewing mathematics as a way to describe the world, the designer felt it would be a fitting counterpart to the work of two individuals who convey the world through words. Inspired by the Möbius strip and Klein bottle, the designer referenced these forms to express the complexity and depth of the poets' perspectives.

Basic Line

- ● C25 M40 Y75 K0 / R201 G159 B79
- ● C0 M0 Y0 K40 / R181 G181 B182
- ● C0 M0 Y0 K100 / R0 G0 B0
- ○ C0 M0 Y0 K0 / R255 G255 B255

YOKUBARI PARCO

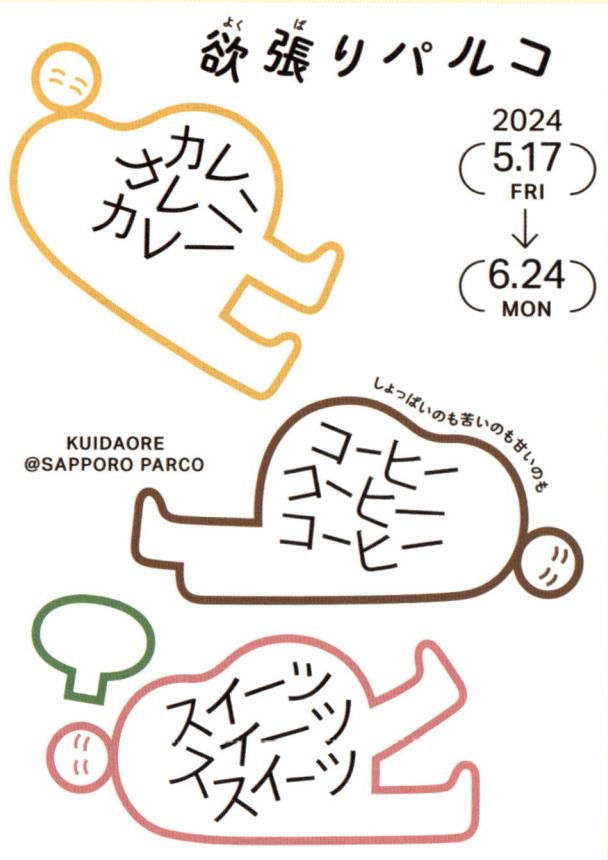

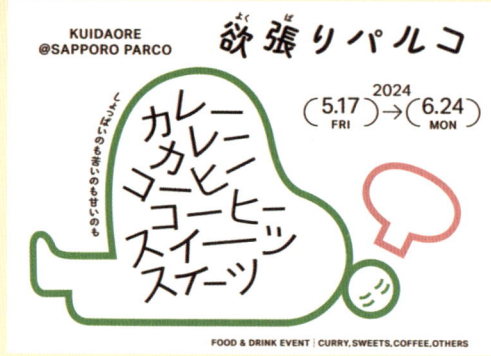

◇ Why Line?

Given the mischievous tone of the Japanese project name "Greedy," the design team aimed to craft a playful and slightly whimsical atmosphere. By abstracting the human silhouette with lines rather than solid shapes, the design achieves a simple yet striking main visual. The team also carefully considered the size and placement of the text to ensure a harmonious balance across the composition.

Basic Line

- C45 M75 Y100 K5 / R154 G84 B37
- C5 M30 Y90 K0 / R241 G188 B26
- C5 M60 Y20 K0 / R231 G132 B154
- C70 M20 Y000 K0 / R84 G155 B53
- C0 M0 Y0 K100 / R0 G0 B0
- C0 M0 Y0 K0 / R255 G255 B255

This is the main visual for the event period during which three food-related projects were held in succession. The concept was inspired by the idea of indulging in a variety of flavors—spicy, sweet, and bitter—through dishes like curry, donuts, bagels, and coffee. To reflect this, the design team used the words "curry," "coffee," and "sweets" to evoke a sense of satisfaction, depicting people lying down with joyful expressions, with their stomachs full. The design emphasizes the "greediness" of the project's theme by showing people eagerly opening their mouths, devouring the information and the experience.

DA. STUDIO WONDER
D. Sou Nomura / Mayu Sugihara

"ARABESQUE" FUROSHIKI CLOTHS

The "Arabesque" Furoshiki[1] cloths, designed by Masashi Murakami, were on display at the Charity Exhibition *Furoshiki Kaleidoscope* at the Creation Gallery G8 in Ginza in 2019.

1. Furoshiki: In Japanese culture, "furoshiki" refers to a traditional wrapping cloth with a rich cultural heritage. It is widely used for carrying and storing various items, embodying Japan's refined sense of aesthetics, practicality, and the enduring tradition of craftsmanship.

DA. emuni
D. Masashi Murakami

◇ **Why Line?**

Three-dimensional lines are randomly combined on the white plane, bringing a new visual experience to traditional Furoshiki products.

Basic Line

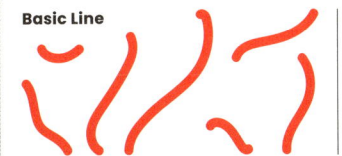

● C0 M100 Y90 K0 / R231 G36 B16
○ C0 M0 Y0 K0 / R255 G255 B255

COMMA

Comma is an experimental project that brings visual innovation to ambient perfume, offering a unique sensory experience. It encourages individuals to pause and take a breath, promoting relaxation in daily life. The use of cans as incense containers reflects the project's goal of making relaxation accessible and convenient. With a simple twist of the cap, users can easily enjoy moments of tranquility, turning ordinary moments into opportunities for rejuvenation. Comma combines practicality and mindfulness, helping users prioritize self-care amidst the hustle and bustle of modern living.

D. Josephine Grenier

Drawing Inspiration from Traditional East Asian Aesthetics

As a French designer living in Japan, the unique blend of cultural perspectives allows for a fresh and nuanced approach to traditional East Asian aesthetics. Unlike locals who may take their cultural surroundings for granted, this designer's outsider perspective cultivates a deeper appreciation of Japan's heritage. Everyday elements, such as the intricate patterns of Kamon crests, the refined architecture of shrines, and the subtle elegance of Japanese typography, captivate her imagination and shape her design sensibilities. The works of graphic design masters like Tadanori Yokoo and Kazumasa Nagai, who merge traditional motifs with modern simplicity, influence her approach, guiding her to balance respect for tradition with a contemporary design sensibility.

Incorporating Japanese Culture to Transcend Language Barriers

Design, as a universal form of communication, becomes even more powerful when it transcends language barriers. For the designer, this realization came shortly after arriving in Japan as a recent graduate, where her portfolio became the primary means of communication. Initially, her works reflected a European essence, which captivated their audience. However, over time, immersion in Japanese daily life led to a more intuitive understanding of the cultural nuances that inform design. Elements like the circle, rich in symbolic meaning in Japanese culture, and the flat compositions found in traditional Ukiyo-e art began to influence her works. By blending European and Japanese design elements, she creates a fusion that resonates with local sensibilities, bridging the gap between traditional and modern aesthetics.

Cultural Differences in Basic Design Elements

The designer believes that cultural background profoundly shapes one's interpretation of basic design elements like dot, line, and plane. These elements take on different meanings depending on cultural context. For example, the circle holds significant symbolism in Japan, not only as a national symbol on the flag but also in the design of traditional emblems, reflecting the Japanese preference for symmetry and balance. In contrast, the circle in France is primarily appreciated for its geometric properties, devoid of the same cultural weight. Lines, too, carry different meanings in different cultures. In Asian cultures, particularly within the context of Chinese characters and calligraphy, lines are fundamental to the writing system, with their number and direction carrying intrinsic meaning. This contrasts with the flowing, curvilinear nature of Latin script, where lines are more fluid and expressive.

Balancing Traditional and Modern Elements in Design

While the designer is unsure if integrating diverse cultural elements constitutes innovation, it is clear that such integration reflects the interconnected nature of today's globalized society. In design, as in the broader world, cultural influences continuously intermingle, facilitated by global transportation and information exchange. In her own creative practice, the designer strives to maintain a connection to traditional aesthetics, believing that ancient craftsmanship provides a meaningful foundation that resonates with viewers. However, she also recognizes the importance of modernity, incorporating minimalist, graphical, and geometric elements that reflect the digital age. By balancing traditional motifs with contemporary design principles, the designer creates works that are both rooted in heritage and oriented toward the future, offering a unique and innovative perspective on design.

◇ Why Line?

Comma employs deliberate, repetitive lines inspired by the rhythmic cadence of breathing exercises. The abundance of curved lines throughout the composition creates a fluid, undulating motion, reminiscent of gentle breaths. These lines intertwine and flow gracefully, producing an immersive visual experience that evokes a sense of tranquility.

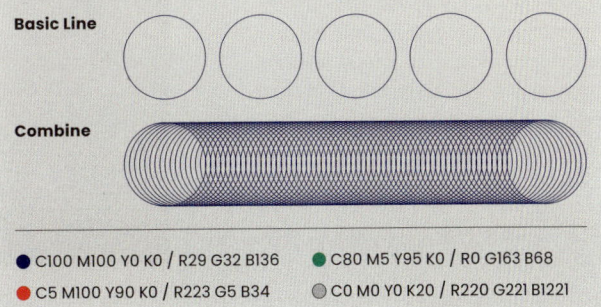

Basic Line

Combine

● C100 M100 Y0 K0 / R29 G32 B136   ● C80 M5 Y95 K0 / R0 G163 B68
● C5 M100 Y90 K0 / R223 G5 B34   ○ C0 M0 Y0 K20 / R220 G221 B1221

MASAYA MAKINO 2ND ALBUM *CITY*

This is the visual design for Masaya Makino's second album, *City*, which includes the CD cover, promotional leaflet, and a handkerchief design. In the designer's view, Makino's music is incredibly captivating, with its charm rooted in a subtle psychological distance—neither overly intimate nor distant, creating a pleasant listening experience. The melodies are intricate, the rhythms balanced, and there is an intentional use of space, allowing the listeners to interpret the music in their own unique way based on their personal experiences and current state of mind. Therefore, the designer focused on the album's "city" theme, incorporating these musical qualities into the design.

D. Sakura Kashiwazaki
CL. Masaya Makino

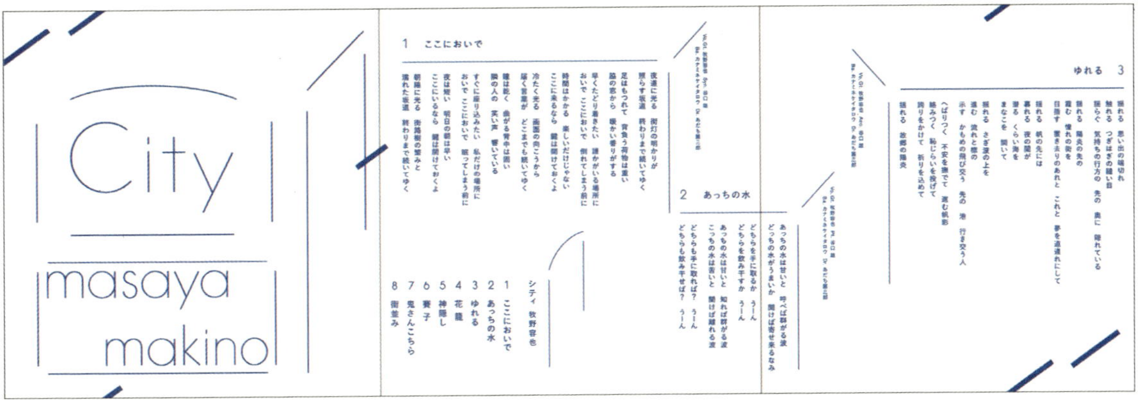

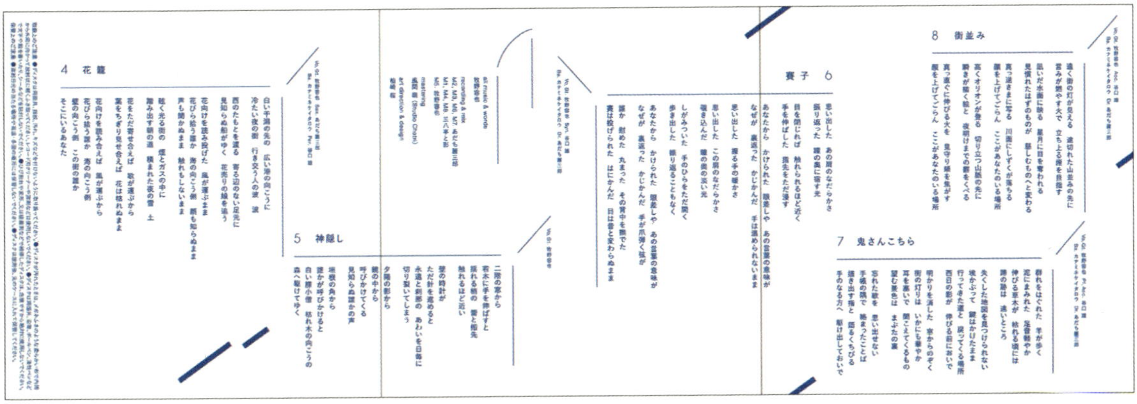

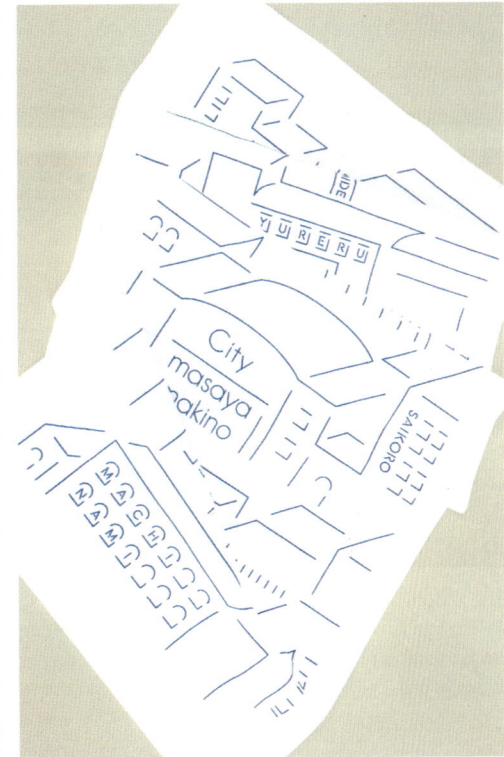

◇ Why Line?

The designer was also responsible for the design of Makino's debut album. As it marked his first introduction to the public, the designer approached the project with a passion to convey his musical philosophy and personal style, carefully refining every detail of the design. For the second album, she aimed to create a relaxed and effortless atmosphere, contrasting with the first album. To achieve this, she boldly simplified the design, using only clean, short straight lines and curves to express the carefree energy within the music.

Basic Line

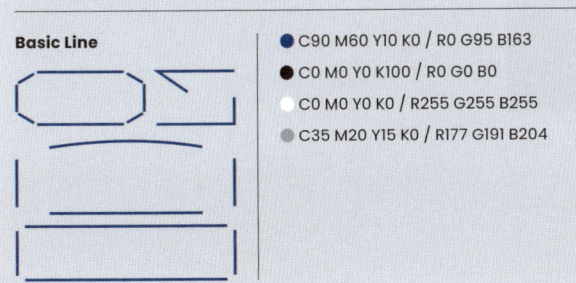

- C90 M60 Y10 K0 / R0 G95 B163
- C0 M0 Y0 K100 / R0 G0 B0
- C0 M0 Y0 K0 / R255 G255 B255
- C35 M20 Y15 K0 / R177 G191 B204

ALBUM DESIGN FOR MACARONI EMPITSU

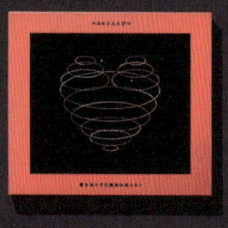   

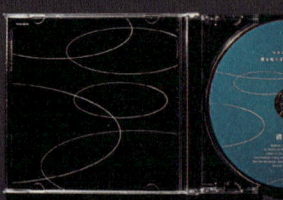  

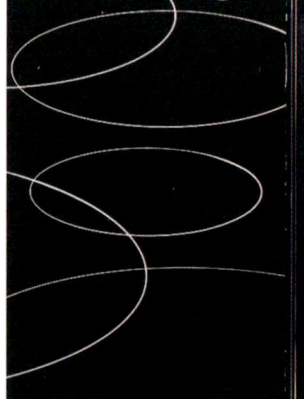

The album is titled "Love Without Knowing Magic Can't Be Used." The CD jacket design abstracts the concepts of "love" and "magic" from the album title. The hearts are composed of overlapping rings, a visual motif often used to represent magic in animation.

D. Shimizu Kango
CL. TOY'S FACTORY Inc.

◇ Why Line?

The designer used circles of different sizes and lines to create a combination that prevents the image from appearing monotonous. The illustrations on the album's inner pages also use the same method to ensure visual consistency.

Basic Line
Combine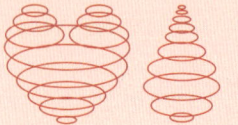

- ● C0 M0 Y0 K100 / R0 G0 B0
- ○ C0 M0 Y0 K0 / R255 G255 B255
- ● C10 M80 Y50 K0 / R219 G83 B94
- ● C95 M30 Y35 K0 / R0 G131 B197

SANZUI'S SELF-INITIATED PROJECT

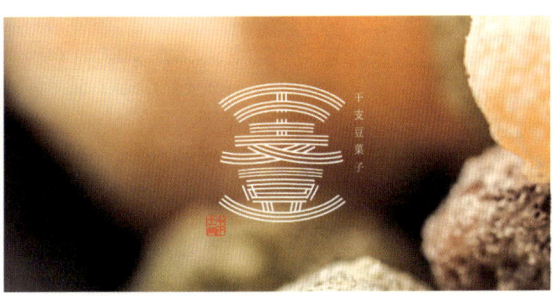

Designer sanzui is dedicated to creating works that highlight the intrinsic character and uniqueness of each motif. Through careful analysis, sanzui translates these elements into visuals that deeply resonate with viewers.

D. sanzui

◇ **Why Line?**

Designer sanzui used lines to effectively convey the essence of the logo—both eye-catching and easy to be recognized.

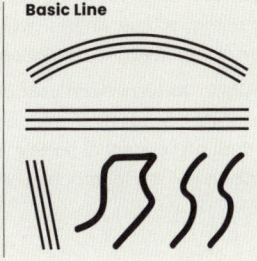

Basic Line

● C0 M0 Y0 K100 / R0 G0 B0
○ C0 M0 Y0 K0 / R255 G255 B255

KANO POSTER FOR 上陆许可 TRAVELING & HUGGING

◇ Why Line?

When the designer chose *KANO* as the inspiration for this poster, the initial plan was to faithfully replicate the comic's frame layout. However, simply copying the original structure clearly failed to capture the essence of the work in a new way. Therefore, the designer boldly removed the frames and used lines as the basic elements to present the image. In terms of content, the designer used baseball players in action and sport-specific onomatopoeia as the main elements, to deliver a visual reinterpretation of *KANO*.

Basic Line

● C0 M100 Y0 K0 / R228 G0 B127
● C0 M0 Y100 K0 / R255 G241 B0

This poster was featured in the 上陆许可 *Traveling & Hugging* Exhibition in 2022. The exhibition showcased works created during the COVID-19 pandemic, a time when travel was impossible. During this period, designers from Japan and Taiwan, China exchanged souvenirs remotely and used them as inspiration for their designs, fostering creative dialogue across borders.

For this piece, designer Tadashi Ueda collaborated with Ms. Sentian Dazi, who shared a selection of meaningful souvenirs. Among them was *KANO*, a baseball-themed manga, which became the central inspiration for the poster. While manga typically unfolds through sequential panels, the designer reinterpreted this format by merging multiple frames into a single composition. Additionally, the characters were intentionally rendered with simplified shapes, emphasizing a bold and graphic aesthetic.

D. Tadashi Ueda
CL. Zhong Dao GLAb

THE HAIR HAS DISAPPEARED

This is a poster depicting body hair vanishing of its own accord—yet removed against the person's will. The concept emerged while the designer was working on *Kami no g* (see page 301). If unrealistic hairstyles could be visualized, why not explore a phenomenon as well? Like *Kami no g*, this work uses "hair" as a central motif. However, the key difference lies in the contrast between body hair and the human form. Is the hair escaping, or is it merely standing still? What happens when body hair gains consciousness—how does it affect the human body? The designer leaves the interpretation open to the viewer.

D. Tadashi Ueda

◇ Why Line?

The designer used random vector lines of varying thickness to represent the hair in the image, adding a touch of fun.

Basic Line

- C100 M95 Y0 K0 / R23 G40 B139
- C0 M85 Y80 K0 / R233 G72 B49

"WE" AND "I"

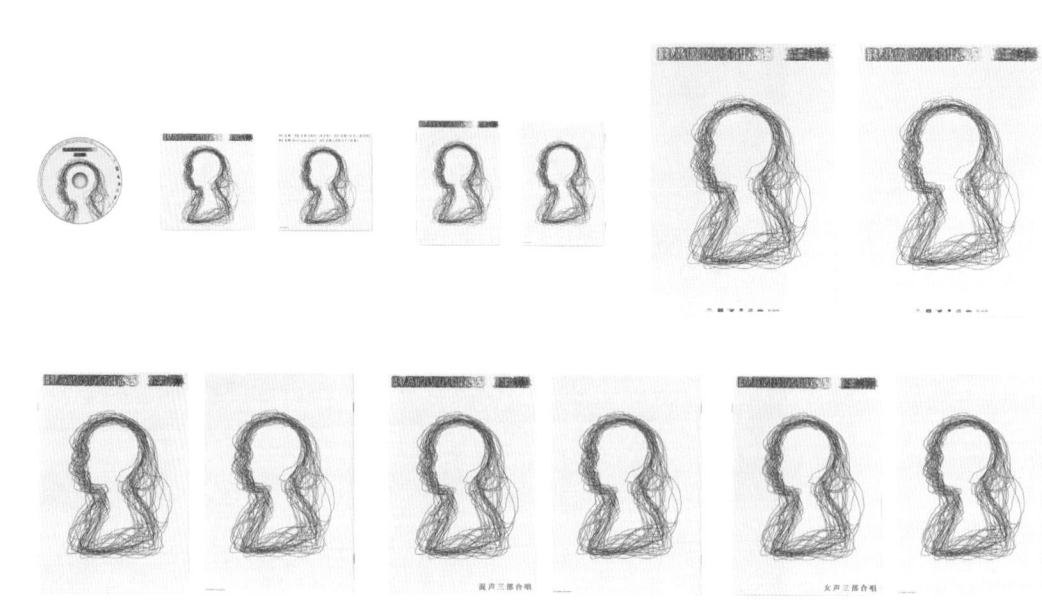

In Japanese high schools, choral performances are a key part of graduation ceremonies. The chosen song typically carries lyrics that reflect on shared memories and offer encouragement as students embark on their separate journeys. This tradition is so significant that many popular musical acts compose original graduation songs.

When the rock band RADWIMPS decided to write one, designer Taichi Tamaki was tasked with creating its visual identity. Given RADWIMPS' strong connection with young audiences and the song's deep resonance with everyday high school life, the designer sought an approach that would feel equally authentic to students.

Taichi Tamaki used a high school chorus as a metaphor. In a chorus, each singer has a distinct voice, yet together they create a harmonious and layered melody. Similarly, in high school, every student is an individual, but their experiences intertwine to form something dynamic and meaningful. To visualize this idea, the designer created a series of overlapping line silhouettes, and also introduced a hidden element—a solitary silhouette—that could only be revealed using a common study tool familiar to high school students, adding an interactive and personal touch to the design.

DA. DENTSU INC.
D. Taichi Tamaki
CL. Universal Music Group

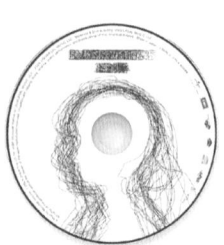

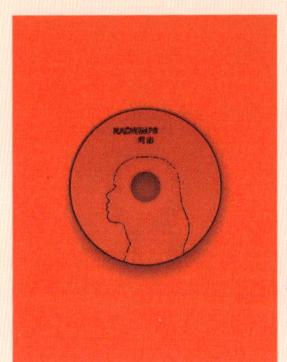 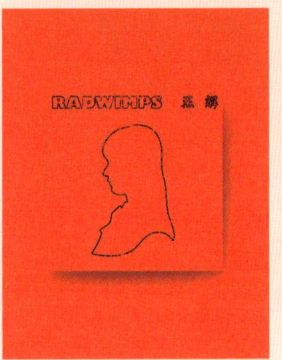  

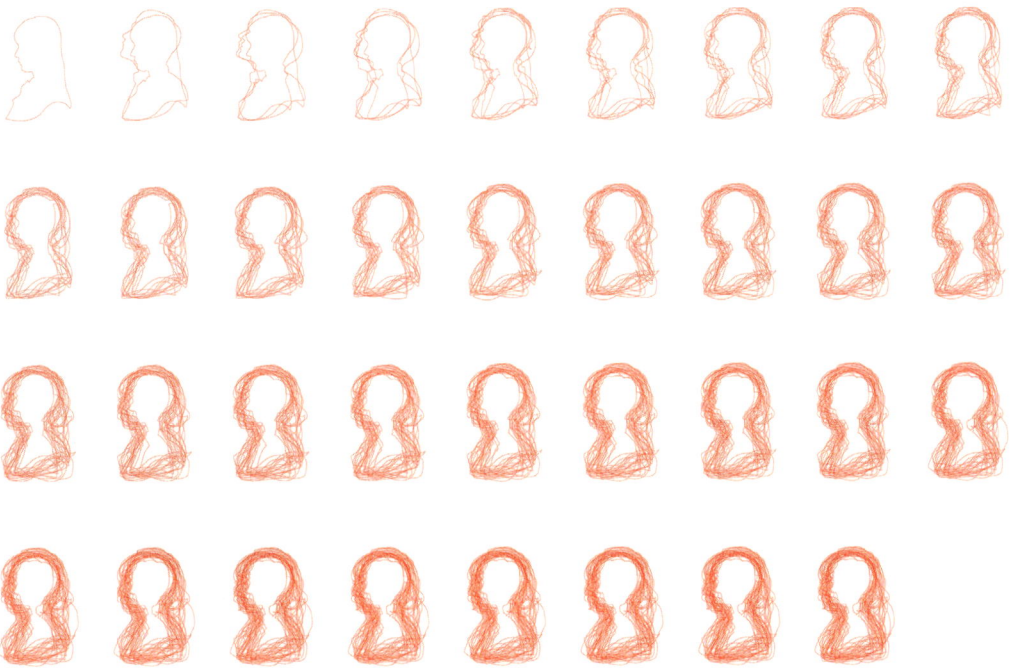

◇ Why Line?

To visually represent a choral piece in a simple yet meaningful way, the designer used human silhouettes. The overlapping silhouettes of 35 students symbolize the average class size in a Japanese high school. As these lines intersect, they evoke the emergence of sound—just like harmony in a choir. The designer believes that lines are more than just a means of shaping forms; they hold infinite possibilities for expression.

Basic Line   **Combine**

● C0 M95 Y90 K0 / R231 G36 B32
● C0 M0 Y0 K100 / R0 G0 B0
○ C0 M0 Y0 K0 / R255 G255 B255

🖋 WHAT'S HIDING?

Leveraging the unique property of yellow ink becoming invisible when covered by red paper, the designer created an interactive question-and-answer graphic poster. Viewers are invited to imagine what is depicted in the geometric shapes and then flip them over to reveal the answer, adding an element of surprise and playfulness to the experience.

D. Tasuku Matsuo

◇ Why Line?

Lines serve as clues to the content of the image. When the red paper is flipped over, the creatures emerge on a yellow shape, completing the picture. These lines not only function as elements of the quiz but also play a dual role in the design; as the paper is turned, they transform into a pattern of creatures, seamlessly blending form and function.

Basic Line

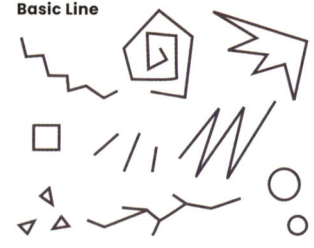

- C5 M10 Y80 K0 / R247 G224 B65
- C20 M95 Y100 K0 / R201 G42 B29
- C0 M0 Y0 K0 / R255 G255 B255
- C65 M85 Y55 K25 / R97 G52 B75

"1K GOOD NEIGHBORS" JAM & PASTE & POTATO & CAFE VISUAL IDENTITY & TOOLS

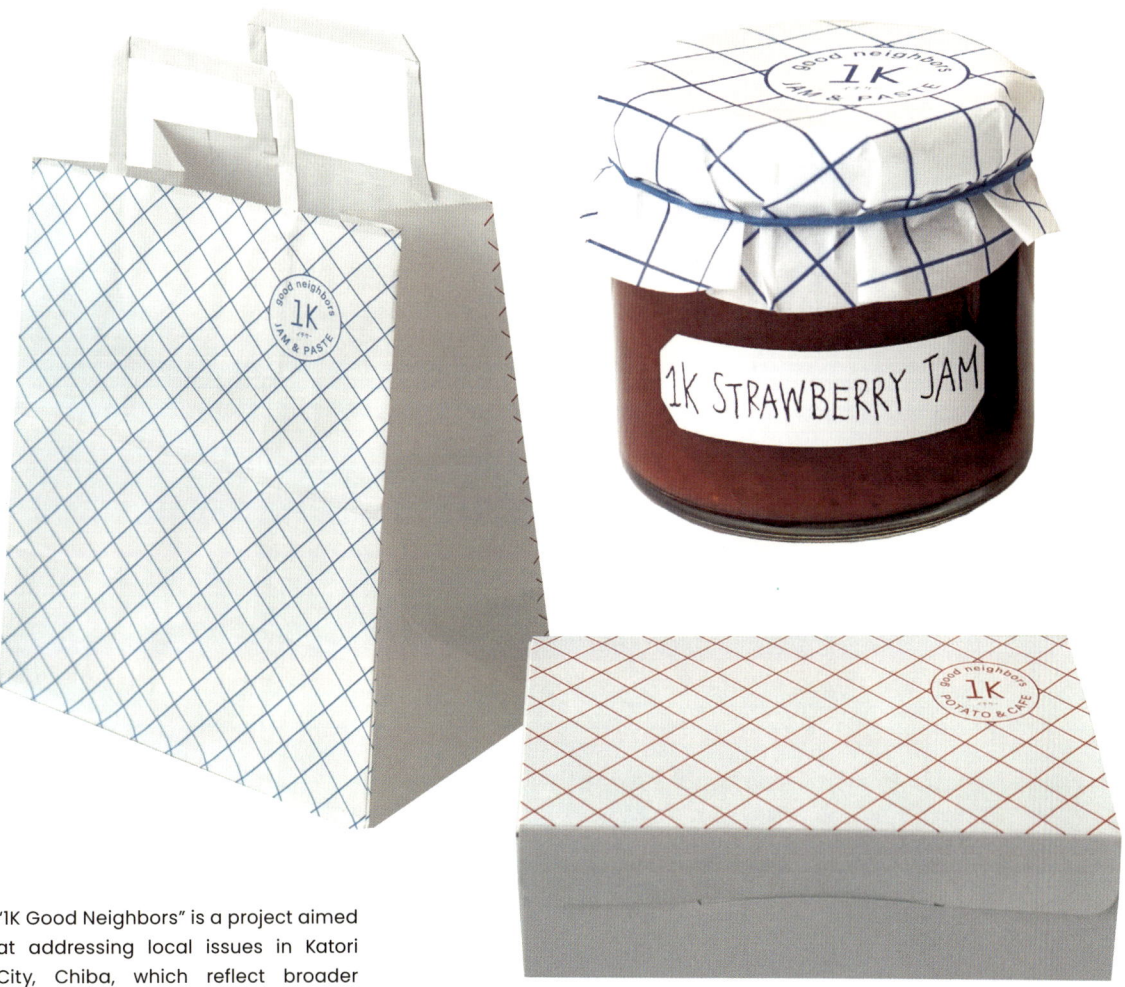

"1K Good Neighbors" is a project aimed at addressing local issues in Katori City, Chiba, which reflect broader challenges faced by rural Japan, such as abandoned farmland, neglected forests, and employment difficulties.

To create a cohesive visual identity while organizing multiple initiatives under a unified framework, the designer developed a system that fosters both clarity and connection. Having closely observed the project's evolution, the designer found the combination of a wrapping pattern and a label to be a practical and effective solution.

DA. woolen Co., Ltd.
D. Naoko Fukuoka

Why Line?

The designer prioritized simplicity, using simple elements such as lines to ensure that this visual style would be easy to implement in a variety of applications.

Basic Line **Combine**

- C100 M50 Y0 K0 / R0 G104 B183
- C0 M100 Y100 K0 / R230 G0 B18
- C0 M0 Y0 K100 / R0 G0 B0
- C0 M0 Y0 K0 / R255 G255 B255

LIVING KANJI

The *Living Kanji* initiative modernizes kanji—the Chinese characters used in Japan and China—by addressing gender bias and introducing inclusive symbols for LGBTQ+ terms. This groundbreaking project creates 17 new kanji to challenge stereotypes and promote gender equality.

The initiative debuted in Tokyo with the poster exhibition *Living Kanji: Modernizing Script for a Changing Japan*, sparking global media attention and dialogue. Collaborations with schools, such as a pilot program in Yokohama, integrate these concepts into education, helping children identify and challenge bias. With ongoing success, *Living Kanji* is proving that modernizing language can shape a more equal and inclusive world.

D. Miharu Matsunaga (Hami)
CL. Living Kanji

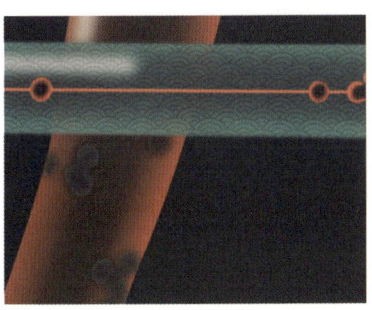
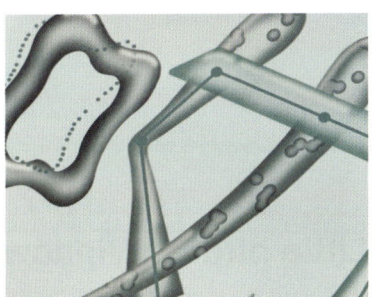

◇ Why Line?

Kanji is a living, integral part of our daily lives, much like the cells in our bodies. This inspired the designer to incorporate biological shapes, using fine dots and lines. The diverse team, with members from Japan, Switzerland, and the U.S., sought to blend cultures by combining Western 3D visual effects with the flat, traditional aesthetics of Japanese design. The result is a unique fusion that leaves a lasting and intriguing impression on viewers.

Basic Line

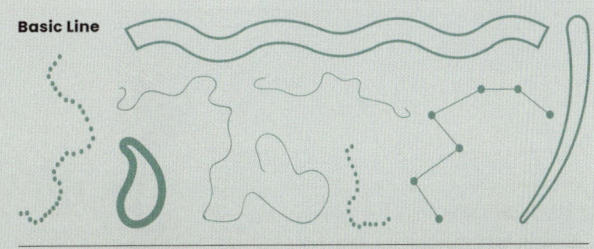

- C70 M65 Y20 K0 / R98 G96 B147
- C0 M0 Y0 K0 / R255 G255 B255
- C90 M85 Y40 K0 / R51 G63 B110
- C20 M10 Y15 K0 / R212 G220 B216
- C65 M20 Y45 K0 / R94 G163 B149
- C80 M65 Y75 K35 / R52 G68 B58
- C45 M90 Y95 K10 / R149 G54 B40
- C0 M65 Y65 K0 / R238 G121 B81
- C45 M65 Y20 K0 / R156 G106 B148
- C75 M45 Y0 K0 / R66 G123 B191
- C55 M35 Y0 K0 / R125 G152 B206
- C95 M70 Y0 K0 / R0 G79 B162

NATURAL ✳ ARTIFACT

Butterfly — Bug catching net —

Fire — Match to candle —

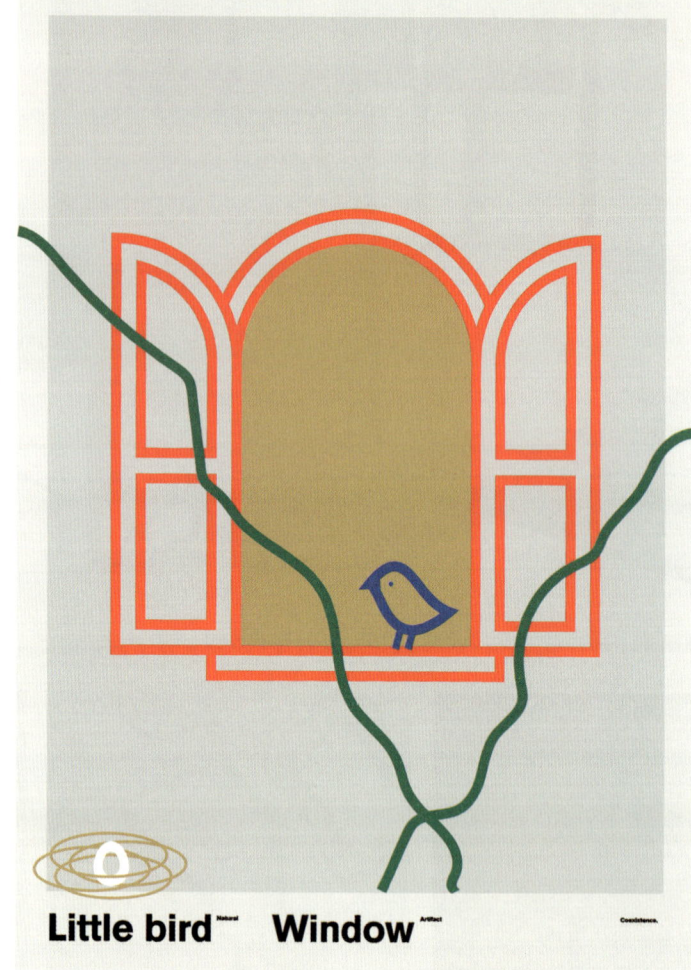

Little bird — Window —

Flower — Vase —

Smoke — Chimney —

The designer used lines and planes to express the moment when natural and human-made elements overlap. Rather than assigning a specific role to each—such as which should be represented by lines—he portrayed them as an intersecting and harmonious landscape.

D. Shimizu Kango

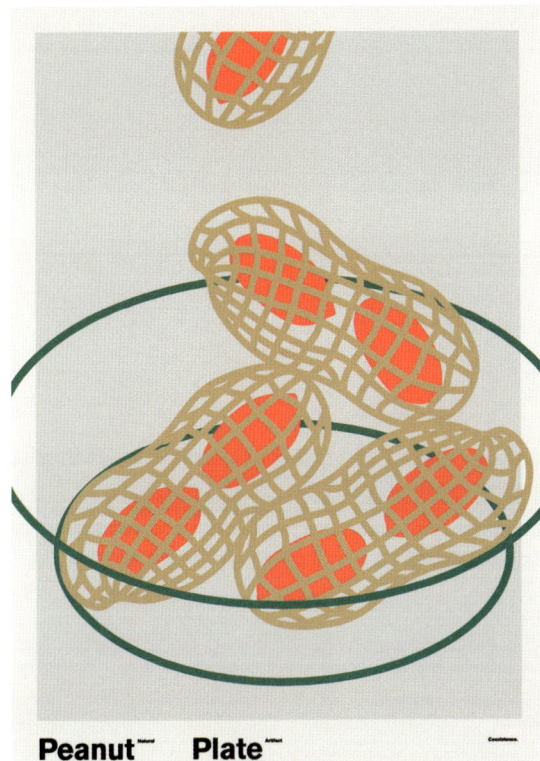

Peanut / Plate

Flame / Yaki-mochi

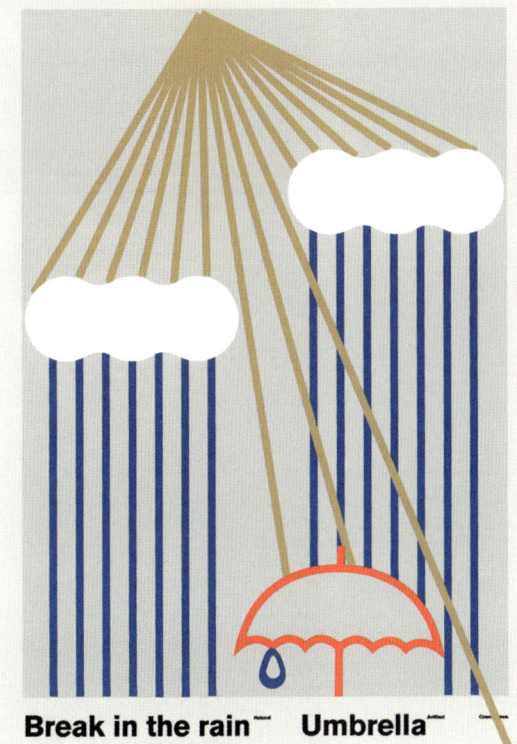

Break in the rain / Umbrella

◇ Why Line?

The design used lines with subtle inflections to avoid monotony. The same approach was applied to the inside of the card, incorporating varied shapes while maintaining a consistent overall design.

Basic Line

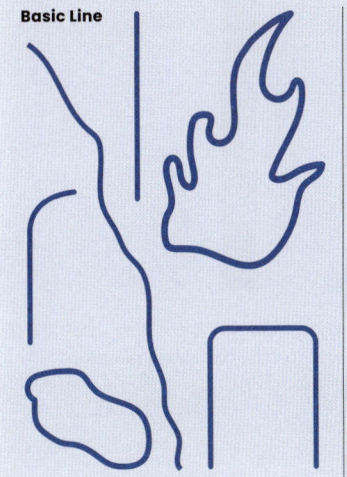

- C20 M30 Y65 K0 / R212 G181 B103
- C0 M80 Y80 K0 / R234 G85 B90
- C85 M65 Y0 K0 / R46 G89 B167
- C85 M35 Y100 K0 / R8 G128 B60
- C0 M0 Y0 K20 / R220 G221 B221
- C0 M0 Y0 K0 / R255 G255 B255
- C0 M0 Y0 K100 / R0 G0 B0

ꝑ my CLINIC

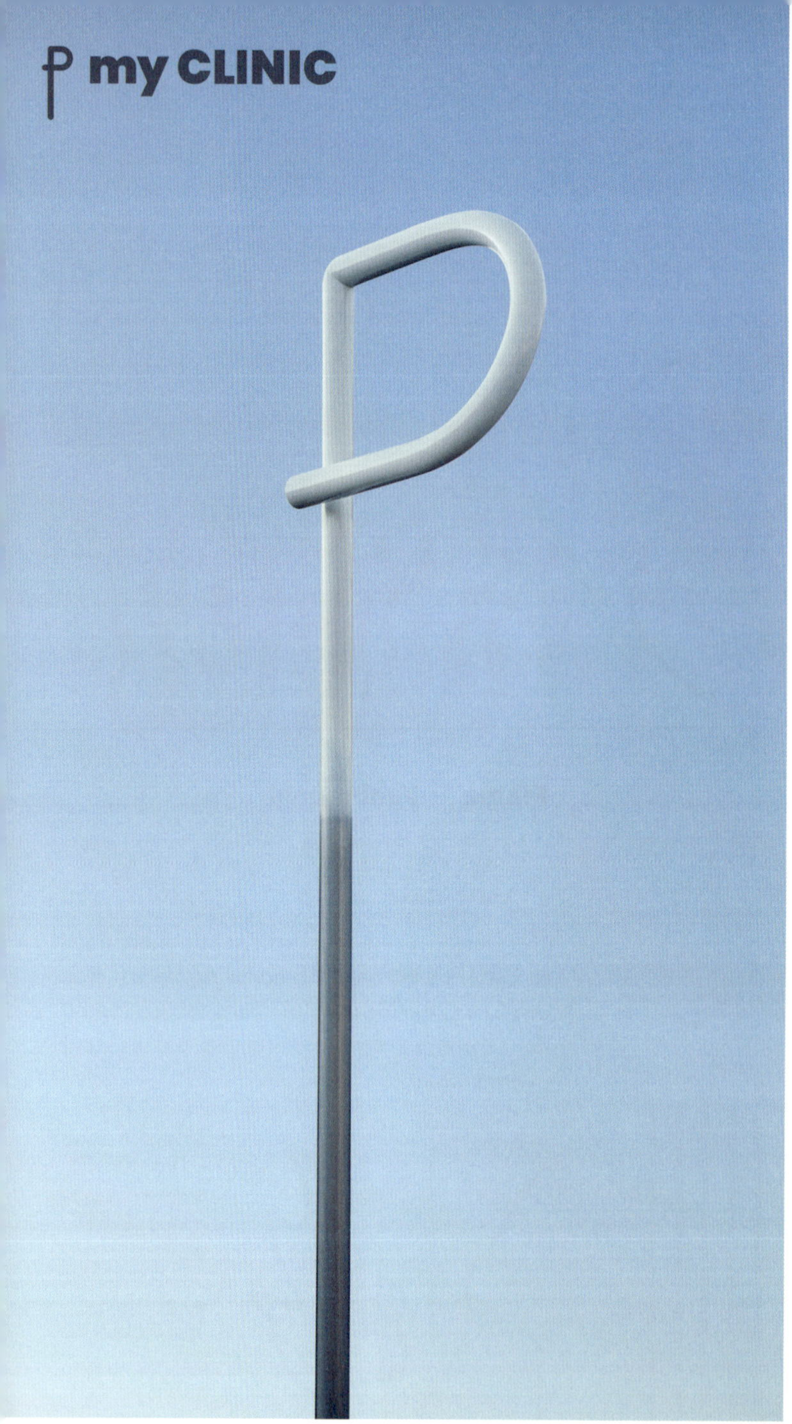

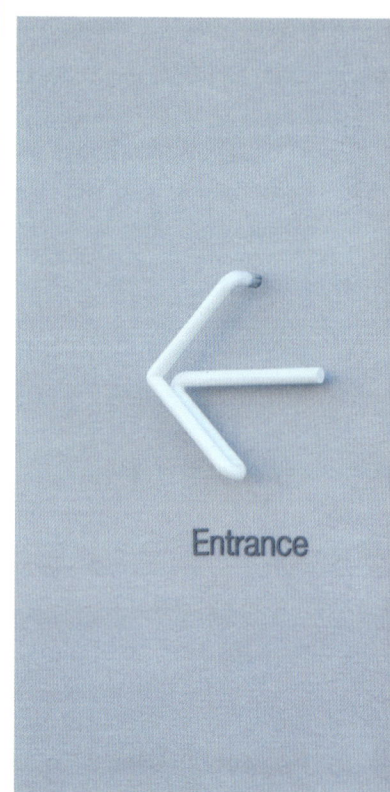

Entrance

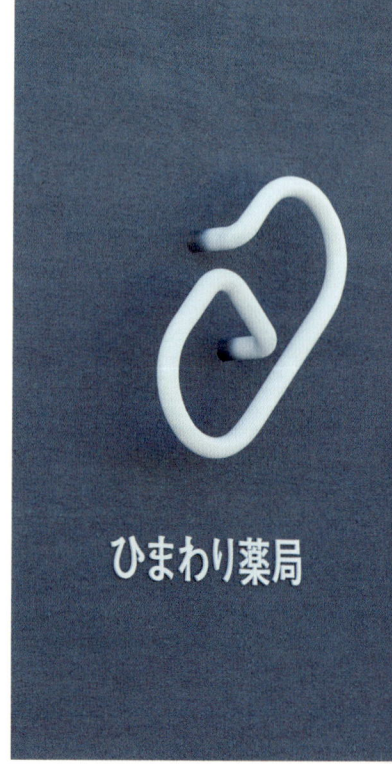

ひまわり薬局

The designer was responsible for the visual identity of the hospital titled my CLINIC, located in Kitamoto City, Saitama Prefecture.

DA. 6D
AD. D. Shogo Kishino
SD. Soichiro Yagi
PT. Shingo Fujimoto
CL. my CLINIC

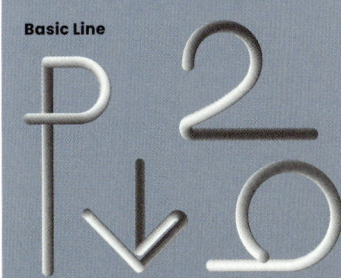

◇ Why Line?

All signage is crafted from bent metal tubing, representing the application of the three-dimensional "line" within everyday life.

Basic Line

- C80 M70 Y45 K5 / R71 G83 B110
- C55 M25 Y0 K0 / R121 G167 B217
- C65 M40 Y20 K0 / R101 G137 B172
- ○ C45 M25 Y15 K0 / R152 G175 B157
- ● C0 M0 Y0 K100 / R0 G0 B0
- ○ C0 M0 Y0 K0 / R255 G255 B255

LINE TO PLANE

The Concept of Line to Plane

● "Line to Plane" refers to the movement or arrangement of lines in space, resulting in planar forms with width and structure. This concept is widely applied in art, design, and architectural construction, where the extension and combination of lines create visual surfaces rich in depth and spatiality, guiding perception from the two-dimensional to the three-dimensional.

Various Kinds of Line to Plane

- **Parallel Arrangement:**

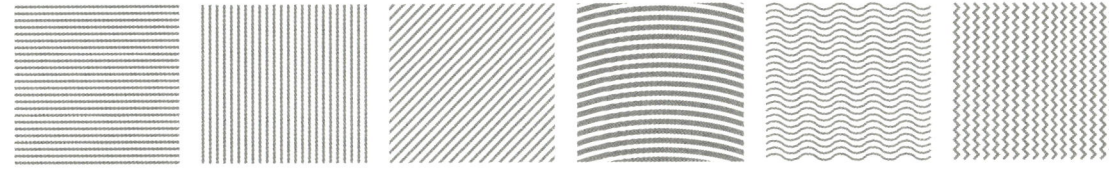

- **Rotational Arrangement:**

- **Encircling Arrangement:**

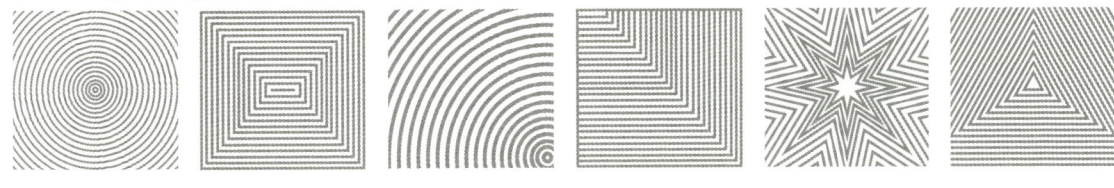

- **Intersecting Arrangement:**

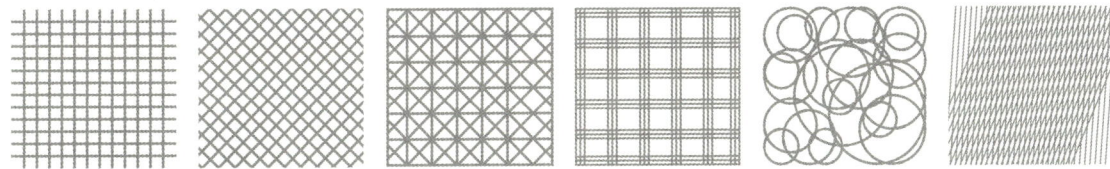

- **Overlapping Arrangement:**

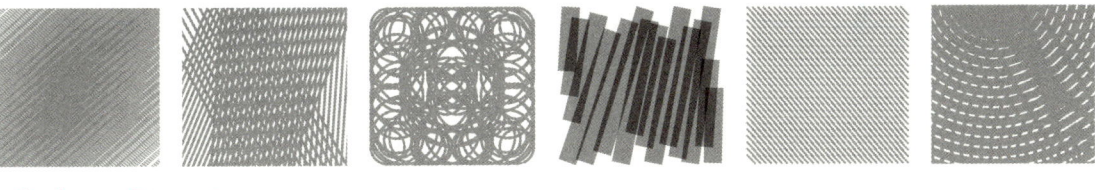

- **Thin Lines Thickened:**

- **Lines of Varying Thickness:**

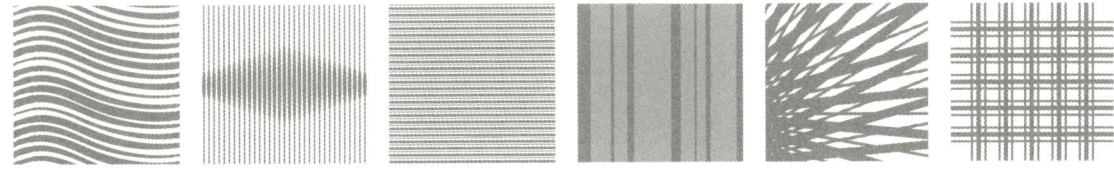

CHAIRS

This piece was created by the designer after recognizing the phenomenon that Japanese people sit for an average of 7 hours a day. His goal was to create a unique chair that could help alleviate the issues associated with prolonged sitting. The chair not only offers comfort but also provides visual enjoyment through its aesthetic design. During the creative process, he drew inspiration from numerous existing chair designs, ultimately creating a one-of-a-kind original piece. The design process began with the designer sketching the concept using colored pencils and ballpoint pens to visually present the idea. Then, using the illustration as a blueprint, he employed laser cutting to produce the wooden components, and finally assembled the chair.

D. SAKIE

Why Line to Plane?

The designer originally focused on creating flat illustrations primarily based on straight lines. In this design, he approached the project with an experimental mindset, attempting to transform his flat work into a three-dimensional piece, exploring new visual effects in three-dimensional space. At the same time, he pondered how an illustration that does not rely on perspective would present itself as a three-dimensional object.

Basic Line

Line to Plane

- C0 M50 Y0 K0 / R241 G158 B194
- C20 M10 Y5 K0 / R211 G221 B233
- C80 M55 Y0 K0 / R55 G106 B179
- C0 M95 Y75 K0 / R231 G35 B52
- C50 M0 Y95 K0 / R143 G196 B47
- C0 M0 Y0 K0 / R255 G255 B255

URBAN SCIENCES SYMPOSIUM: THINKING ABOUT NATURE FROM THE CITY AND THE CITY FROM NATURE

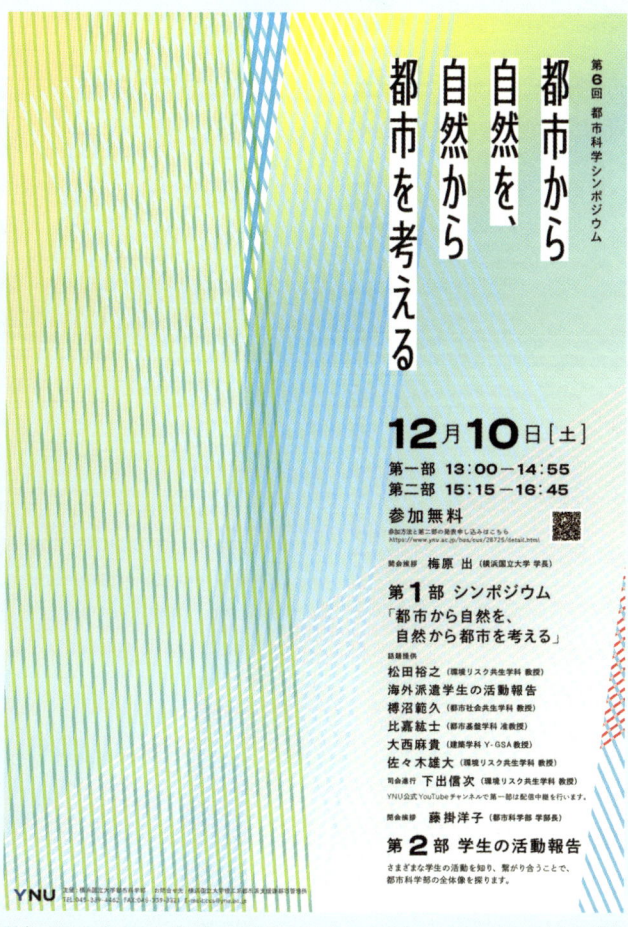

Why Line to Plane?

Elements such as light, air, and water circulation, which fall equally on cities and nature, are constantly filling our surroundings and are familiar to us, but at the same time it is difficult to confirm them with our eyes. In visualizing these elements, the designer first imagined a pattern of stripes from the image of rays of light, and as they folded together, the gradation of colors changed organically. The stripe pattern of repeating "there" and "not there" places was effective in depicting an elusive presence that is both visible and invisible.

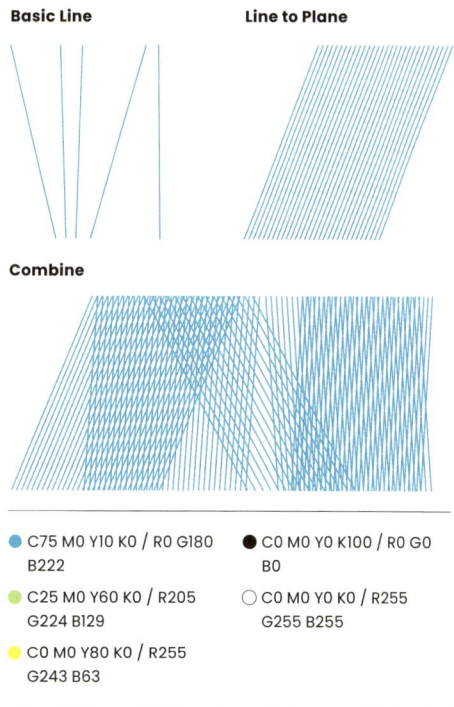

This poster was designed for a symposium sponsored by the university's urban science lab, centered on the theme "Thinking about Nature from the City and the City from Nature." The design team considered two possible approaches: one that contrasts the elements of "nature" and "city," and the other that unifies them. The team rejected the former, seeing it as a 20th-century perspective that viewed human activity and the global environment as separate and incompatible. In contrast, modern discourse emphasizes that human activities, like those of all living creatures, must be sustainable, supporting both human survival and environmental balance. Therefore, the design team chose to depict the environment—represented by the circulation of light, air, and water—as the foundational element, with both the city and nature existing within it, interconnected and interdependent.

DA. PINHOLE
D. Minako Izumi
CL. Yokohama National University

LOFTWORK YEAR END PARTY 2022

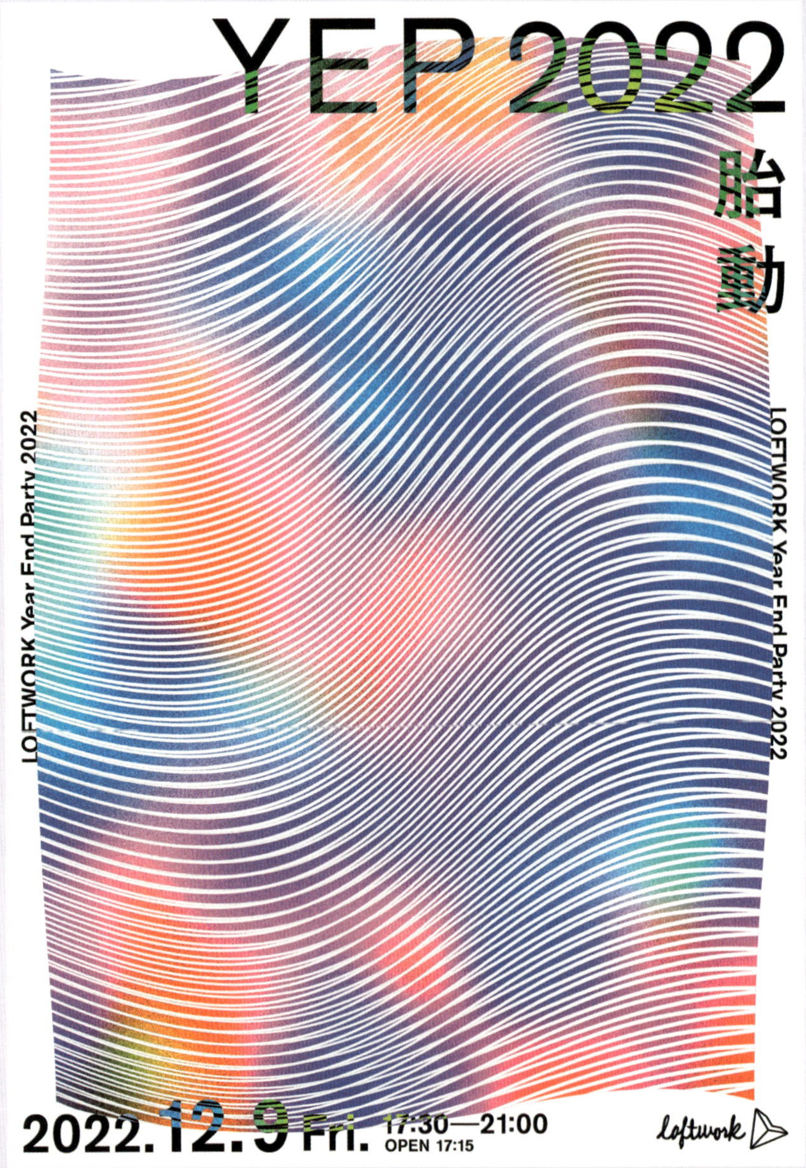

Why Line to Plane?

The staggered curves are used to create the desired visual effect, enhancing the sense of gentle, organic motion.

Basic Line

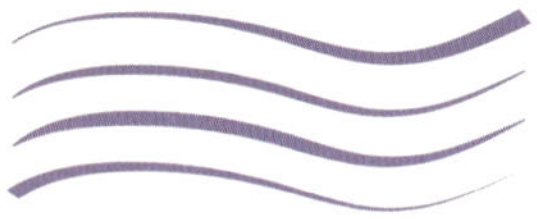

Line to Plane

Centered on the theme of "fetal movement," the design incorporates optical illusions to make it look as if the fetus is wriggling.

DA. Yuuri Mikami Design Office
D. Yuuri Mikami
CL. Loftwork Inc.

- ● C0 M95 Y95 K0 / R231 G36 B24
- ● C0 M80 Y70 K0 / R234 G85 B65
- ● C0 M25 Y85 K0 / R252 G201 B44
- ● C100 M15 Y100 K0 / R0 G141 B67
- ● C80 M0 Y25 K0 / R0 G174 B196
- ● C90 M70 Y0 K0 / R29 G80 B162
- ● C55 M60 Y0 K0 / R133 G109 B175
- ● C0 M0 Y0 K100 / R0 G0 B0
- ○ C0 M0 Y0 K0 / R255 G255 B255

✳ MASUDA TEA STORE

▨ Why Line to Plane?

The designer used parallel line segments to represent the rows of tea trees in the tea garden, then combined them together to form a layered field of tea leaves. The packaging pattern made in this way is traditional and elegant.

Basic Line

Line to Plane

- ● C45 M60 Y65 K0 / R158 G114 B90
- ● C20 M25 Y35 K0 / R212 G193 B166
- ○ C20 M15 Y15 K0 / R211 G212 B211
- ○ C0 M0 Y0 K0 / R255 G255 B255

This is the branding of a Uji tea specialty store located in front of Byodo-in Phoenix Hall. The design elegantly captures the essence of Uji with its simple, flowing lines that center around the phoenix, symbolizing the rich cultural heritage of the region.

D. Masunaga Akiko
CL. Masuda Tea Store

⌗ PANASONIC DESIGN KYOTO

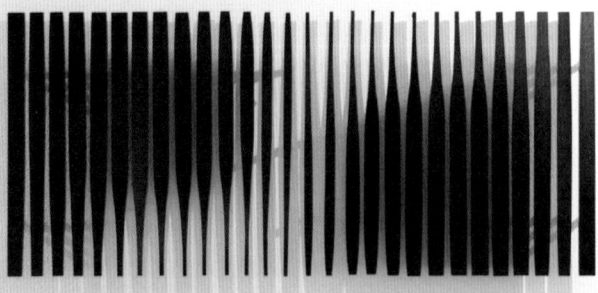

This is the Visual Identity for Panasonic Design Kyoto, the headquarters of Panasonic's product design. The company aims to engineer future lifestyles through its products.

DA. Econosys Design Inc.
AD. Mitsutaka Nakao
D. Takayuki Isomi / Takashi Kuroyanagi
CL. Panasonic Design Kyoto

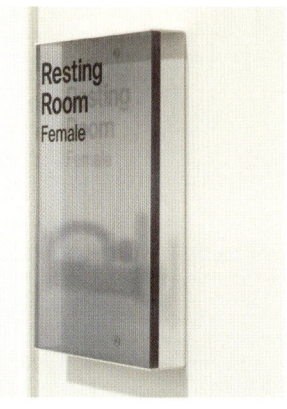

Why Line to Plane?

The designer developed a dynamic, three-dimensional symbol that shifts in appearance depending on the viewer's perspective. Composed of offset elements installed on the office wall, the tactile logo creates an undulating effect when seen in motion. Viewed head-on, the letters "P" and "D" appear when the line is transformed into a surface, symbolizing the fusion of creativity and technology at Panasonic Design Kyoto.

Basic Line

Line to Plane

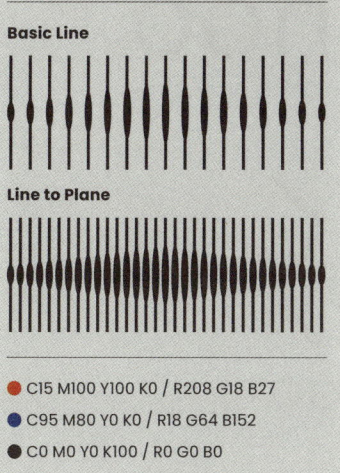

- C15 M100 Y100 K0 / R208 G18 B27
- C95 M80 Y0 K0 / R18 G64 B152
- C0 M0 Y0 K100 / R0 G0 B0
- C0 M0 Y0 K0 / R255 G255 B255

Daigo Daikoku developed a visual iden-tity system for Schoo, a company that operates online video learning services. Arrows deriving from the missing "L" in the name Schoo symbolize the company's goal of "innovating humanity through internet learning," which ultimately contributes to individuals' growth and leads to a dynamic, connected world.

DA. Nippon Design Center
AD. Daigo Daikoku
D. Naoko Sasaki
CL. Schoo

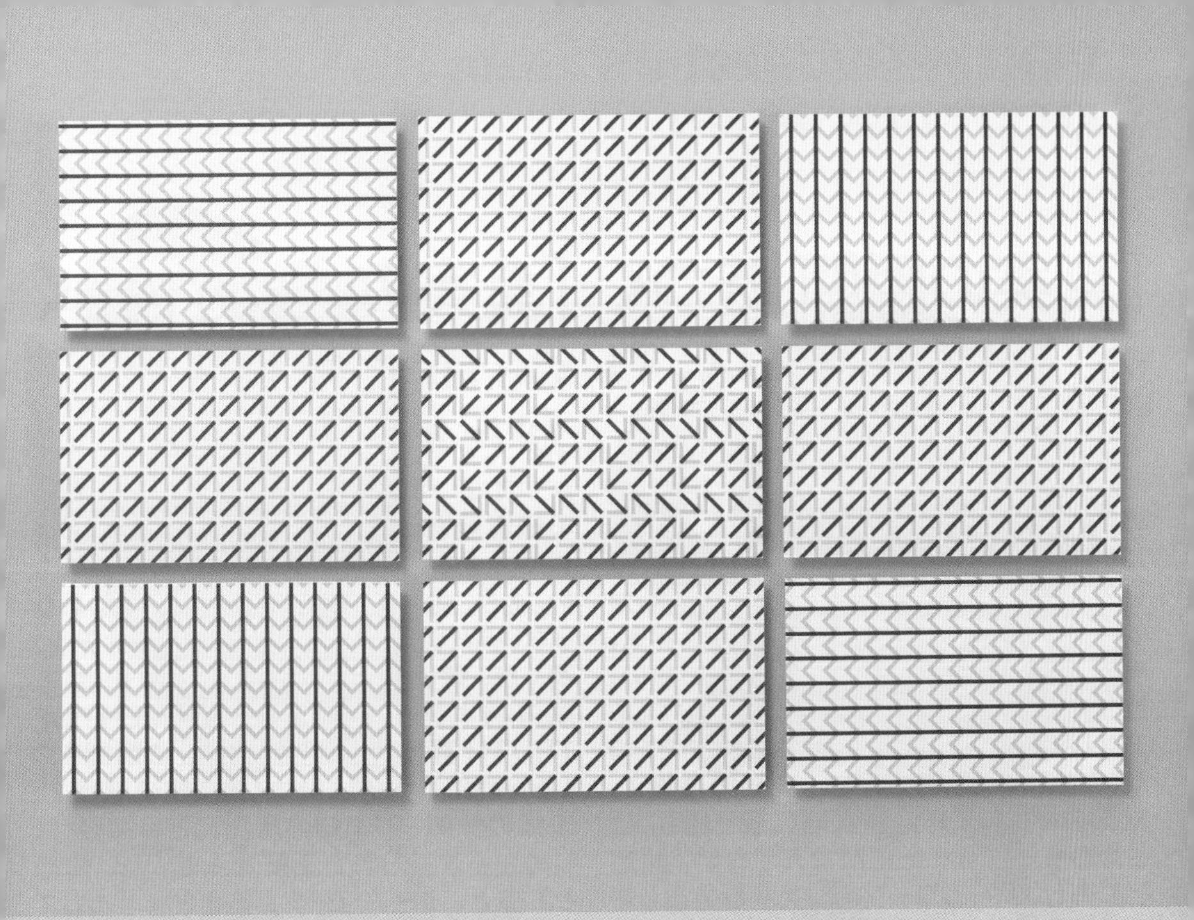

Why Line to Plane?

Schoo is an online learning platform. The mark represents an arrow, symbolizing the individual's freedom to move toward their areas of interest. The designer created multiple dynamic graphic patterns of arrows coming together, reflecting how the gathering of many people and the sharing of knowledge leads to change and growth.

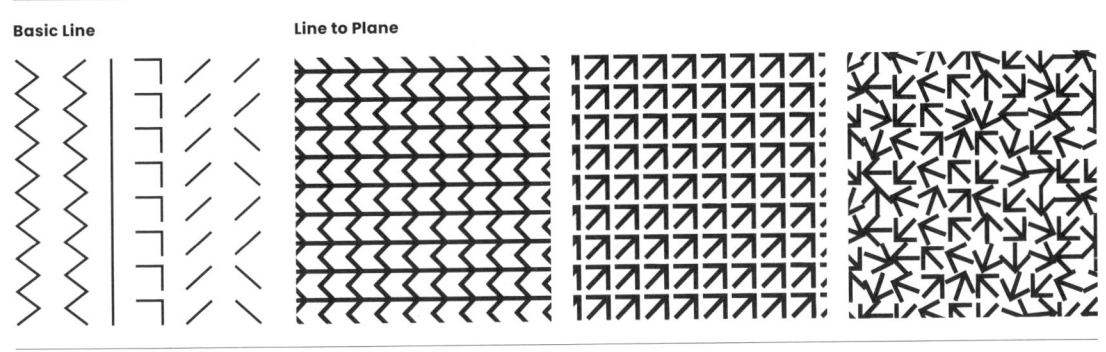

Basic Line **Line to Plane**

● C20 M15 Y15 K0 / R211 G212 B211 ● C0 M0 Y0 K100 / R0 G0 B0 ○ C0 M0 Y0 K0 / R255 G255 B255

DENTSU LIVE RECRUIT 2020:
ENJOY UNKNOWN

This is the promotional graphic for Dentsu Live's 2020 recruitment campaign, an event and space production company. In an era of uncertainty, the company sought individuals who embrace curiosity and are ready to move forward, rather than freeze in fear. With the slogan "ENJOY UNKNOWN," the designer used the question mark ("?") as a symbol of the unknown. The continuously evolving and interwoven question marks are crafted to evoke a sense of excitement and anticipation toward the unfamiliar.

DA. TM INC.
D. Yuto Tamura
CL. Dentsu Live Inc.

Why Line to Plane?

Punctuation marks are a powerful communication tool because they enable people to recognize things collectively. Since punctuation marks are composed of dots and lines, the designer retained the dot at the bottom of the question mark while allowing the line above it to undergo irregular changes, using thicker lines to achieve a sense of surface and effect. This method preserves the symbol's recognizability while introducing new conceptual possibilities, offering a fresh perspective on familiar objects.

Basic Line Line to Plane

○ C0 M0 Y100 K0 / R255 G241 B0
● C0 M0 Y0 K100 / R0 G0 B0
○ C0 M0 Y0 K0 / R255 G255 B255

POSTERS BY TAICHI TAMAKI

1-Second Graphics

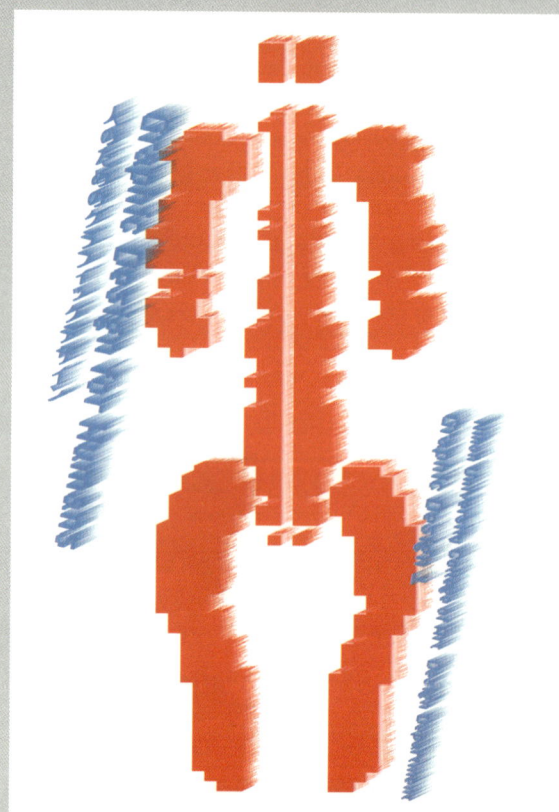

These posters were created for the Graphic Design Exercise class at the Department of Design, Nihon University College of Art.

1-Second Graphics: It defines graphic design as a visual language capable of conveying messages in just one second. Two variations were developed, both depicting dynamic imagery that instinctively draws the viewer's eye. The designs feature an eye moving within a face silhouette, while strong color contrasts create a striking, flashing effect.

Graphic Design for People: The yellow and blue human silhouettes are open to interpretation—they might suggest gender, digital imagery, or movement. However, no definitive answer is provided. This intentional ambiguity encourages viewers to reflect on a fundamental question: What does it mean to be human?

DA. DENTSU INC.
D. Taichi Tamaki
CL. Nihon University College of Art

Graphic Design for People

Why Line to Plane?

What unites these two posters is the use of fine lines that converge to create the illusion of movement within the composition.

The density and quantity of these lines make it nearly impossible to perceive every detail with absolute clarity. Instead, viewers experience the graphics as an impression rather than a sharply defined image.

This is precisely the intention behind the design—presenting ambiguity and leaving the interpretation up to the audience. Since these are posters for a university exercise, they are designed to respect the unique perspectives of each student.

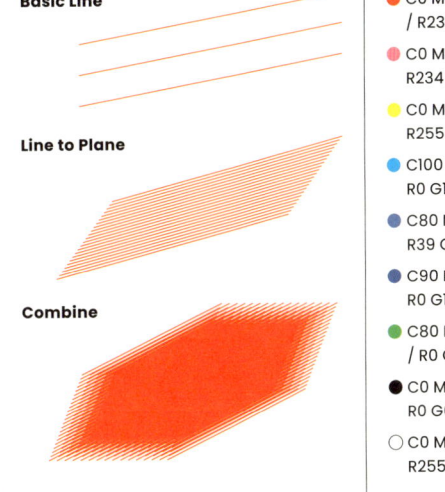

Basic Line

Line to Plane

Combine

- ● C0 M100 Y100 K0 / R230 G0 B18
- ● C0 M75 Y0 K0 / R234 G96 B158
- ● C0 M0 Y100 K0 / R255 G241 B0
- ● C100 M0 Y0 K0 / R0 G160 B233
- ● C80 M45 Y0 K0 / R39 G120 B190
- ● C90 M55 Y0 K0 / R0 G101 B178
- ● C80 M0 Y85 K0 / R0 G168 B86
- ● C0 M0 Y0 K100 / R0 G0 B0
- ○ C0 M0 Y0 K0 / R255 G255 B255

DENTSU LIVE 23

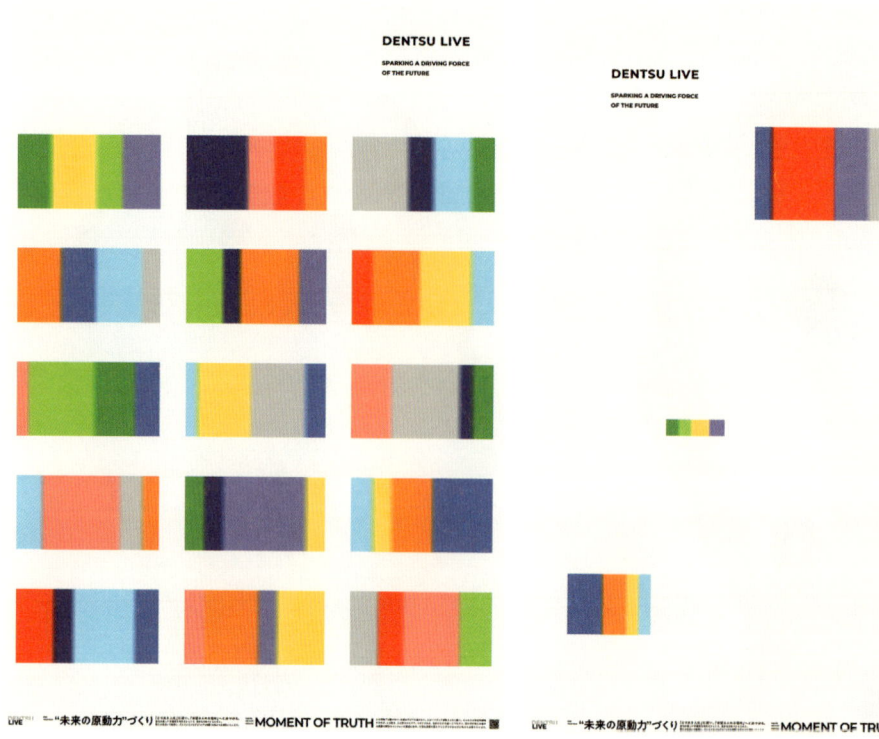

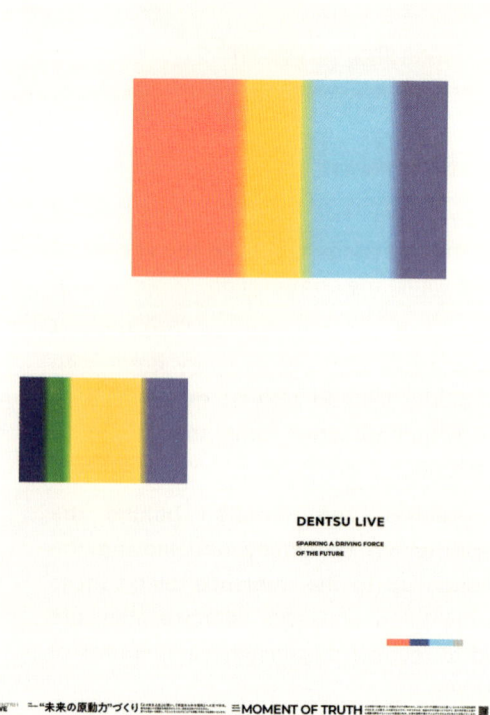

This graphic design was created for Dentsu Live's 2023 corporate advertisement. To represent the diversity of its business domains and the wealth of talent that drives them, the designer utilized dots, lines, and planes. The colors are drawn from the company's established palette, which is used to represent its various fields and industries. The combination of colors and shapes symbolizes how different areas of expertise and team members come together in dynamic, ever-evolving formations to craft tailored solutions for each project.

DA. TM INC.
D. Yuto Tamura
CL. Dentsu Live Inc.

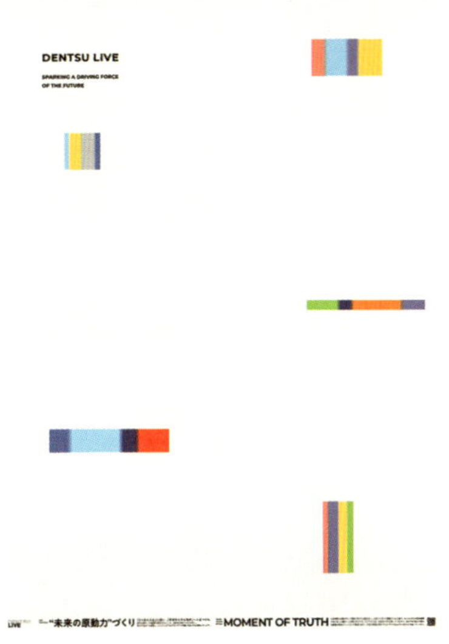

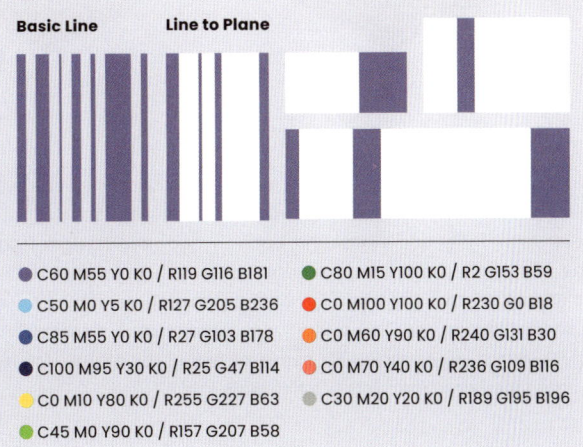

Why Line to Plane?

The design does not depict specific cases or individuals, but rather abstractly expresses the company's signature colors through rectangular shapes. When the shape is shrunk, it becomes a dot, and when stretched, it becomes a line; or these rectangles can be combined to form faces of different colors. By freely combining these elements, the design achieves flexibility and scalability, reflecting the dynamic collaboration between company members.

Basic Line   **Line to Plane**

- C60 M55 Y0 K0 / R119 G116 B181
- C50 M0 Y5 K0 / R127 G205 B236
- C85 M55 Y0 K0 / R27 G103 B178
- C100 M95 Y30 K0 / R25 G47 B114
- C0 M10 Y80 K0 / R255 G227 B63
- C45 M0 Y90 K0 / R157 G207 B58
- C80 M15 Y100 K0 / R2 G153 B59
- C0 M100 Y100 K0 / R230 G0 B18
- C0 M60 Y90 K0 / R240 G131 B30
- C0 M70 Y40 K0 / R236 G109 B116
- C30 M20 Y20 K0 / R189 G195 B196

NICE BALANCE

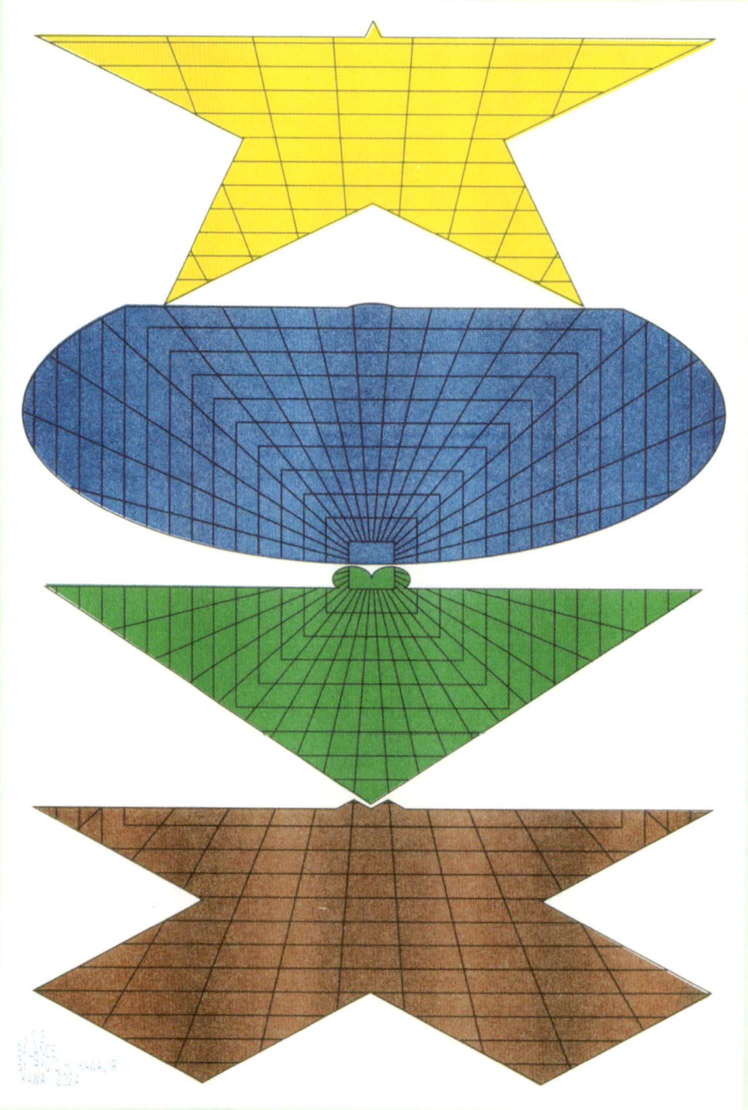

Why Line to Plane?

To capture the viewer's attention and encourage them to linger on the work longer, the designer incorporated intriguing elements into the design. By arranging the four shapes side by side and adding a grid element with a sense of depth, the designer achieved this effect, drawing the viewer's gaze into the composition.

Basic Line

Line to Plane

Combine

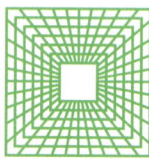

- C70 M0 Y70 K0 / R62 G179 B122
- C80 M40 Y0 K0 / R24 G127 B96
- C10 M5 Y100 K0 / R239 G226 B0
- C40 M55 Y80 K5 / R165 G121 B66

During the creative process, the designer focused on four basic shapes: star, circle, heart, and cross, aiming to imbue them with "anthropomorphic" qualities. After thoroughly deconstructing each symbol, the designer carefully identified the part most suitable to represent the "head" and scaled it down to one-tenth of its original size. This transformation reshaped the abstract symbols into visual representations with the perfect proportions of a "ten-head" figure, instantly conveying a supermodel-like sense of height. Ultimately, these unique designs came together to form this graphic work.

DA. Kawa
D. Ryuichi Kawajiri

TAKURAMITEN—MAKING NEAR FUTURE

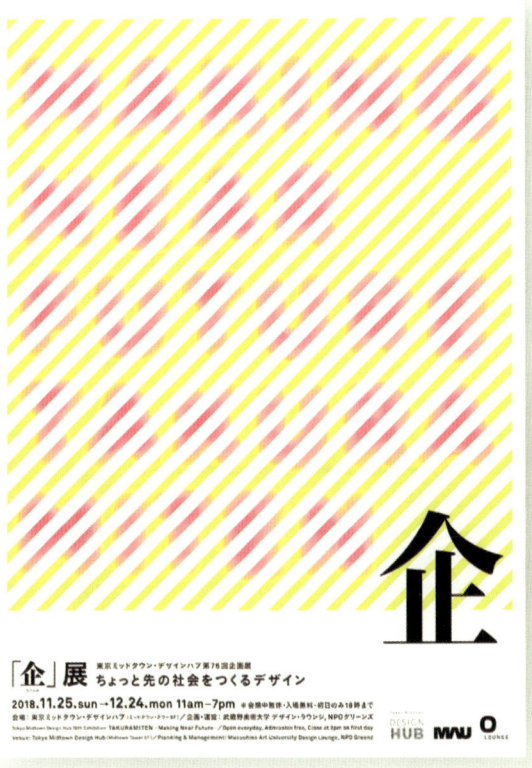

This poster conceals the phrase "Making Near Future" along with the exhibition title—illegible at close range but gradually revealed from a distance. This visual effect symbolizes the ambiguity of the near future, revealed through a shift in perspective.

DA. Yuuri Mikami Design Office
D. Yuuri Mikami
CL. Musashino Art University, NPO greenz

Why Line to Plane?

The designer drew inspiration from the diagonal stripes commonly seen on "under construction" signs, using two colors to divide the interior areas and make the letters on the poster stand out. The designer's goal was to create the greatest possible visual phenomenon.

Basic Line

Line to Plane

- C0 M50 Y0 K0 / R241 G158 B194
- C5 M0 Y60 K0 / R249 G242 B127
- C0 M0 Y0 K100 / R0 G0 B0
- C0 M0 Y0 K0 / R255 G255 B255

 POND

COPY CORNER by KOKUYO is a Risograph-printed product brand featuring a range of projects, including CAMPUS notebooks, clocks, and puzzles. Many creators have participated in this showcase. One of the featured designs is the Pond series, created for the brand.

The designer's inspiration for the Pond series comes from childhood memories of an elementary schoolyard pond. Fed by snowmelt from Mount Fuji, the water was exceptionally clear and beautiful, surrounded by a diverse and thriving ecosystem. This series captures the essence of that landscape. The design mimics the effect of highlighter painting, with the distinctive highlighter texture carefully crafted digitally.

D. Naonori Yago
CL. COPY CORNER by KOKUYO Co.,Ltd.

pond

pond

pond

pond

Why Line to Plane?

The designer explored how to use digital tools to showcase the organic hand-drawn texture of a highlighter pen. By tiling lines so that they partially overlap, the designer expressed the unevenness of color and the sense of movement created by lines converging into a surface.

Basic Line

Line to Plane

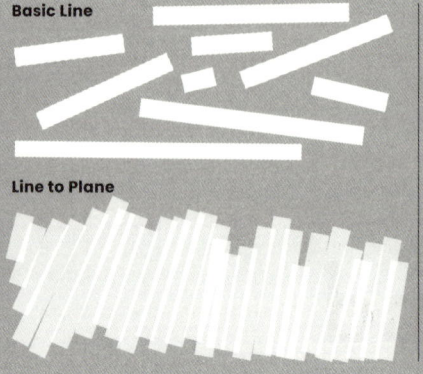

- C0 M85 Y95 K0 / R233 G72 B22
- C0 M55 Y85 K0 / R241 G142 B44
- C5 M5 Y95 K0 / R249 G230 B0
- C60 M0 Y70 K0 / R107 G188 B110
- C65 M0 Y5 K0 / R59 G190 B232
- C15 M60 Y0 K0 / R213 G128 B178
- C10 M10 Y10 K0 / R234 G229 B227
- C30 M40 Y50 K0 / R190 G158 B127
- C0 M0 Y0 K100 / R0 G0 B0
- C0 M0 Y0 K0 / R255 G255 B255

CIRCLE ANIMALS

This is a New Year's greeting card design inspired by the twelve zodiac signs. The designer built the composition using circular forms, incorporating subtle nuances reminiscent of Japanese calligraphy.

DA. SUKEDACHI DESIGN
D. Daisuke Kobayashi

Why Line to Plane?

The designer drew inspiration from one of the elements of his company's logo—the circle. By systematically arranging these circular lines according to specific rules, he formed various parts of animal bodies. This transformation from line to plane evokes a sense of depth and structure, resulting in a greeting card that embodies the brand's core philosophy.

Basic Line

Line to Plane

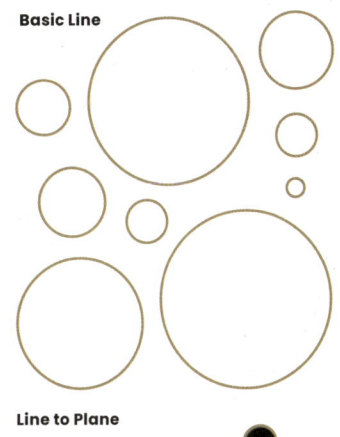
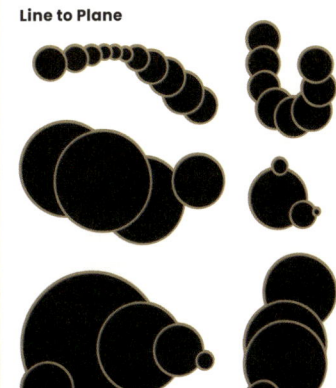

● C40 M50 Y70 K0 / R169 G134 B87
● C80 M85 Y90 K70 / R30 G16 B10
○ C0 M0 Y0 K0 / R255 G255 B255

🐘 MUSASHINO ART UNIVERSITY

Fusion (2014)

From 2011 to 2014, Daigo Daikoku held multiple roles, including art director, for Musashino Art University's course catalog (in both Japanese and English), exhibition catalogs, entrance exams, scholarship information, and various other marketing materials.

Each year featured a distinct theme, such as Expansion/Diffusion, Condensation, Fusion, the Five Senses, and Personality. He created posters and university guides for Musashino Art University based on these themes. The graphic designs were crafted with an imaginative and expressive worldview, aiming to engage the students' sensitivities. His goal was to create something that would inspire their creativity and encourage them in their artistic endeavors.

This is the Musashino Art University poster and university guide for 2014 and 2013. The annual themes were *Fusion* (2014) and *Condensation* (2013).

DA. Nippon Design Center
AD. Daigo Daikoku
CL. Musashino Art University

Condensation (2013)

Why Line to Plane?

Fusion (2014): The designer used lines with variations in thickness as the basic elements, and then combined them to form different graphic and textural effects on a square surface.

Condensation (2013): The designer thickened the lines of the base and the lines blended into each other to form the effect of a surface.

- C20 M100 Y100 K0 / R200 G22 B29
- C95 M60 Y0 K0 / R0 G93 B172
- C0 M0 Y0 K100 / R0 G0 B0
- C0 M0 Y0 K0 / R255 G255 B255

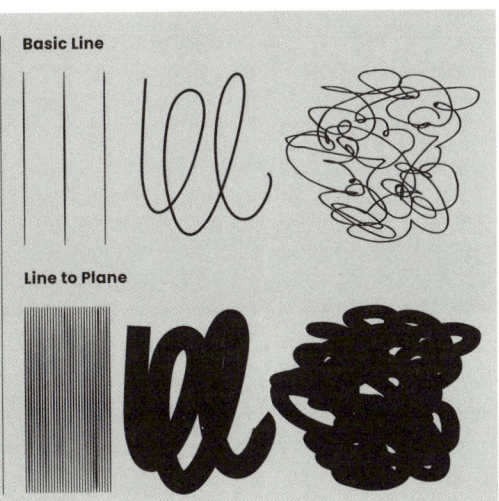

KITOKITO

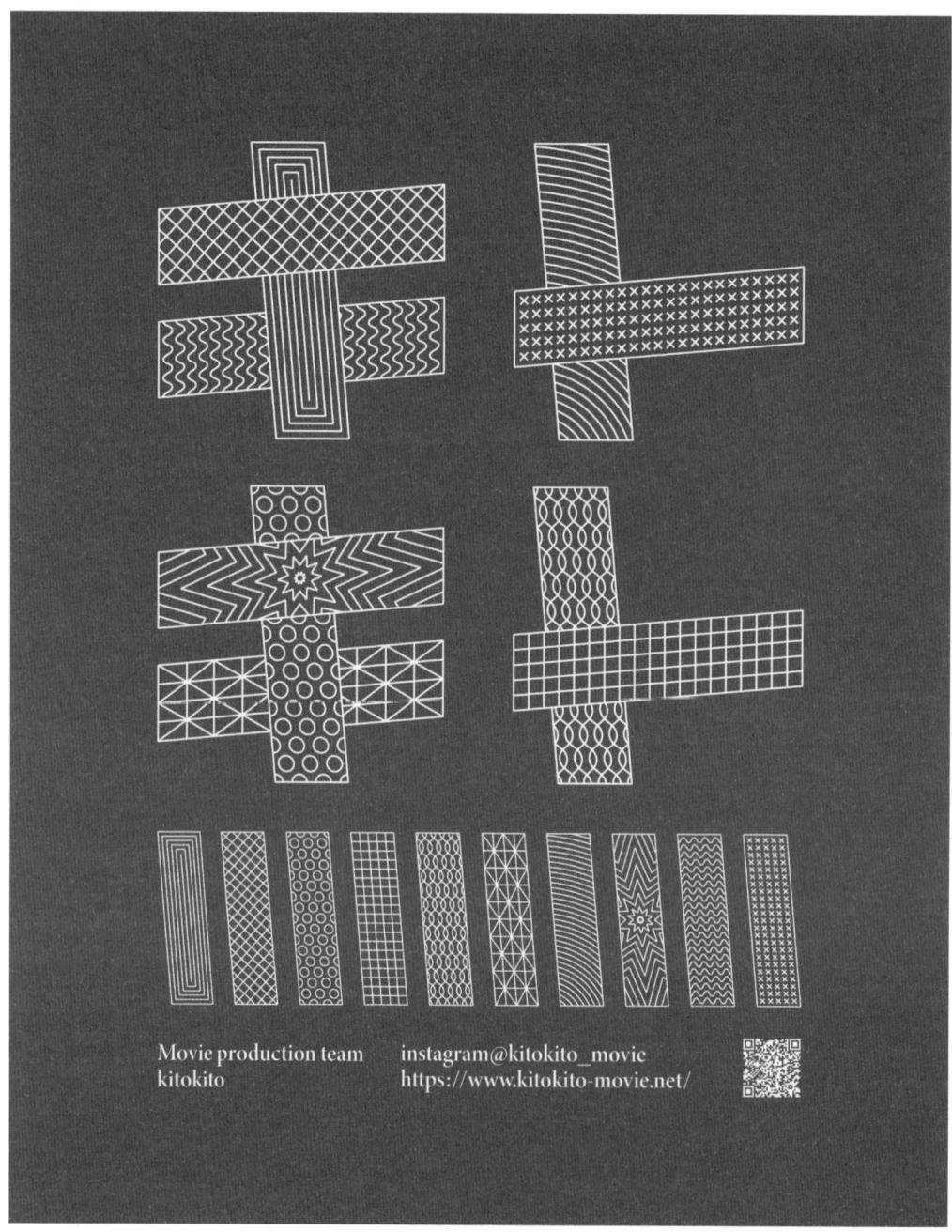

The designer was in charge of the design of the video production team "Kitokito." The logo features overlapping columns of patterns, each representing different emotions and memories. The designer intended to symbolize the couple capturing and preserving a wide range of memories through images.

D. Shimizu Kango
CL. Kitokito

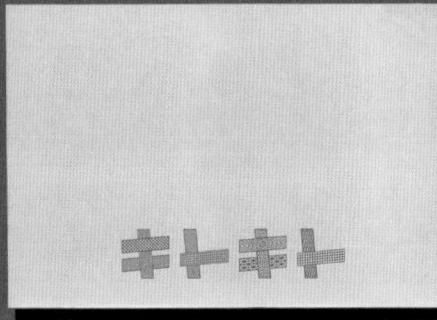

Why Line to Plane?

In order to create a popular and refined image, the designer chose a design based on lines, using various different lines in different ways to form blocks. The designer used a variety of elements, striving to create a sense of unity while maintaining variety.

Basic Line

Line to Plane

● C90 M70 Y0 K0 / R29 G80 B162   ○ C0 M0 Y0 K0 / R255 G255 B255

PLANE

What's a plane?

- A plane is a two-dimensional form with distinct attributes, such as shape, size, and properties. It can either exist in isolation, or combine with others to build a more complex structure via different arrangements, rendering depth and hierarchy to the design.

- Planes are fundamental in graphic design. By skillfully combining planes of different shapes and sizes, designers can create various compositional elements that bring life and variety to the design and make the overall presentation more affluent and engaging. The attributes of planes, such as color, texture, and transparency, are key to shaping the visual impact of a design. By altering the properties of planes, designers can create impressive and layered designs. Planes provide designers with infinite possibilities of graphic creativity, presenting viewers with an opulent visual feast.

The Compositional Aesthetics of Planes

- **As a basic element of graphic design, planes, thanks to their diverse forms, serve as a wonderful design language.** In this context, creation is not simply a stack of geometric shapes; it has become a verbal articulation shaped by the interplay of planes with varied forms and structures. Whether it is a simple geometric one or an organic curved one, designers express their deep understanding of visual art and aesthetic pursuit through mastery of planes.

- **Planes come in a wide variety of forms, from geometric ones to organic curved ones, all of which can form a unique design language.** Through combinations and variations, designers give their works different visual effects rather than just a simple stack of shapes.

- **Planes serve splitting and organizing functions in design.** The size and layout of the planes determine the structure of the picture, and a reasonable combination can balance the visual relationship, avoid visual monotony or clutter, and render the composition clearer and more orderly.

- **Depending on the structural characteristics of the planes, designers can choose the most appropriate planes to express their core concept.** Organic planes are used to display the flow and complexity of life, natural planes to convey the connection with nature, and accidental planes to highlight unpredictability and surprise. By flexibly using planes of diverse forms, designers can infuse their creations with richer meaning and greater depth.

Various Planes in Design

- **SIZE OF PLANES:**
  Large Planes: **Small Planes:**

Pictograms: Graphics derived from the contour of a specific object, evoking direct visual associations.

- **SHAPE OF PLANES:**

Regular:
Basic Geometric Planes:

Composite Polygonal Planes:

Irregular:
Distorted Planes: Planes produced through design tools or freehand adjustments, resulting in unconventional graphics.

- **QUANTITY OF PLANES:**
  Single Plane: A standalone plane that dominates the composition is the main visual center.

Multiple Planes: A combination of several planes that together forms the principal visual structure.

BLOCK BY BLOCK: SHAPING A GRAPHIC VOICE

AKI KANAI & TAKU SASAKI

Aki KANAI
Art Director

Born in Tokyo, Japan, Aki Kania joined KOKUYO in 2008 after receiving a master's degree in design from Tokyo University of the Arts. Currently, while working at Kokuyo YOHAK DESIGN STUDIO, she also works on various designs as KANAISASAKI. Awards received include JAGDA New Designer Award 2018, ADC Award 2018, 2020-2021, Good Design Award Gold Prize, Red Dot Design Award, Jury Recommended Work at Japan Media Arts Festival, and Kokuyo Design Award 2014 In-house Special Award.

TAKU SASAKI
Art Director / Product Designer

Born in Tokyo, Taku Sasaki graduated from Tama Art University in 2008 with a degree in Product Design, and joined KOKUYO. Currently, while belonging to Kokuyo YOHAK DESIGN STUDIO, he also works on various designs as KANAISASAKI. Awards received include JAGDA New Designer Award 2022, ADC Award 2020-2021, Good Design Award Gold Prize & Best 100, Red Dot Design Award, Jury Recommended Work at the Japan Media Arts Festival, Kokuyo Design Award 2005 Excellence Award, and Kokuyo Design Award 2014 Company Special Award.

◯ In graphic design, dots, lines, and planes are the essential building blocks of visual communication. For designers Aki Kanai and Taku Sasaki, these seemingly simple geometric elements have long transcended their technical function to become foundational principles guiding their creative process.

In this interview, the duo shares how they draw from abstract graphic forms, tactile craftsmanship, and the cultural heritage of Japanese design to transform basic geometry into expressive, rhythmically composed visuals. By thoughtfully combining these elements, they create works that are not only visually striking but also resonate with audiences on both cultural and emotional levels.

PLANE IN PUBLIC SPACE DESIGN

● **In their works—particularly in designs intended for public spaces—large areas of graphic color blocks often take center stage.** These abstract forms do more than shape the atmosphere of a space; they effectively draw attention from diverse audiences. Compared to representational graphics, abstraction offers broader interpretive possibilities and integrates more naturally with architecture and the surrounding landscape. This high level of adaptability is a key reason why such forms are a preferred choice in public projects. Kanai and Sasaki frequently collaborate with spatial designers to ensure that their graphics not only deliver visual interest but also align with the structure and rhythm of the space itself.

● **Designing graphics for public environments requires a careful balance between visual impact and functionality.** Unlike advertisements, which aim for immediate attention, large-scale public visuals tend to prioritize long-term engagement and experience. Even when certain spaces call for quick and clear communication, the two designers favor creating visuals that seamlessly blend into the community's context.

● **Their approach begins with close observation of the site's unique characteristics.** By introducing subtle visual "disruptions," they add intrigue without compromising harmony. Simple planar forms, built from basic elements, are brought to life through layering, three-dimensional structures, deconstruction, and strategic placement. Lighting effects and other transformative treatments further enhance the works' ability to guide the viewer's gaze, evoke emotion, and enrich the spatial experience.

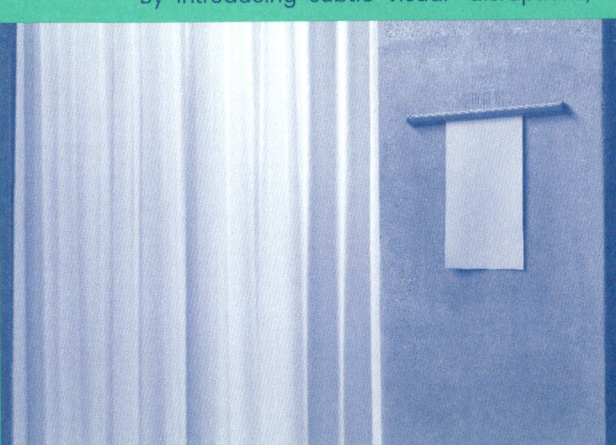

Fig. 1 The Campus Flats, designed by KANAISASAKI, 2023.

TEXTURE AND CRAFT: SURFACES WITH SOUL

● **Their works often transcend the traditional boundaries of graphic design, skillfully incorporating texture and handcrafted elements to enrich visual depth and enhance tactile engagement.** When integrating texture, Kanai and Sasaki tend to extract key elements from the project's context and integrate them into the graphic language in meaningful ways. This process is iterative: if texture compromises the overall impact at any stage, the idea is decisively discarded. However, if it enhances the works, they continue to test and refine it. For now, texture and craft primarily serve to reinforce existing concepts rather than transform or reconstruct the core ideas—but they are eager to explore this potential more deeply in the future.

● **A recent example of this integration is their corporate identity (CI) design for COPY CORNER, which opened in April 2024.** As part of Kokuyo's printing facility and label business, COPY CORNER operates a RISOGRAPH printing service in the heart of Harajuku. While RISOGRAPH is beloved by creators, its unique textural output and highly saturated colors remain unfamiliar to many. The designers' visual strategy for COPY CORNER was to harness these distinctive qualities to create a brand identity that resonates with both seasoned creators and curious newcomers. By highlighting the tactile richness and vibrant visual appeal of RISOGRAPH printing, the project successfully elevated public awareness and appreciation of this expressive, energetic print medium.

Fig. 2 COPY CORNER Brand Visual, designed by KANAISASAKI, 2024.

TYPOGRAPHY: BRIDGING GRAPHICS AND MESSAGE

● **Typography plays a vital role in their works, but it is always in service of the larger graphic composition.** Kanai and Sasaki treat typography and graphic design as a unified form rather than separate entities. Graphics set the tone and create visual identity, while typography is tasked with delivering information clearly and effectively.

● **Their design philosophy prioritizes legibility, but never at the expense of creativity.** Type is often seamlessly integrated into the broader graphic structure, with each element reinforcing the other to form a cohesive visual message. They continually strive for balance: letting graphics amplify the impact of the content, while ensuring that typography remains a bridge for communication—making information accessible, precise, and engaging.

DESIGN IN MOTION

● **From brand identities to editorial design, Aki Kanai and Taku Sasaki have cultivated a rich body of works across a wide range of media and environments.** Whether working on digital platforms or physical formats, their design approach remains consistent. Even when designing for static mediums like printed posters, they often explore the potential for motion within stillness.

● While much of their works are rooted in traditional graphic design forms—posters, signage, and print materials—they continuously challenge the boundaries of the static image. They imagine how these designs might exist in dynamic contexts—through animation, projection, or interactive installations. Even when confined to the printed page, their compositions evoke a sense of something unfolding through visual rhythm, graphic variation, and deliberate pacing, inviting audiences to engage on multiple sensory levels.

● This ongoing investigation of motion reflects a core tenet of their design philosophy: **that even the most fundamental elements—dots, lines, and planes—can generate endless visual possibilities through thoughtful arrangement and transformation.** Bringing a sense of movement into static design is more than a formal experiment— it's a way of building fresh, unexpected connections with viewers and driving their creative practice forward.

Fig. 3 n.5. Shimokitazawa, designed by KANAISASAKI, 2022.

CULTURAL CONTEXT: MINIMALISM AND ABSTRACTION

● **Kanai and Sasaki's design practice is deeply rooted in Japanese cultural traditions.** The minimalist and abstract visual language that defines much of their works draws directly from Japan's long-standing aesthetic history—an influence that continues to shape their creative outlook in meaningful ways. One of their key inspirations lies in the ancient system of kamon, or family crests—traditional graphic emblems used to communicate identity and meaning through pared-down, symbolic forms.

● Dating back to the 8th century, kamon are characterized by highly distilled geometric designs. These emblems were used for quick and clear identification, often on the battlefield, where their simplicity and directness made them immediately recognizable. This clarity of expression—abstract yet powerful—resonates strongly with Kanai and Sasaki. They channel this centuries-old visual wisdom into their contemporary design language, using elemental forms like dots, lines, and planes as a starting point to create compositions that are both visually striking and culturally resonant.

Fig. 4 HOW WE LIVE Pop-up, designed by KANAISASAKI, 2024.

THE FUTURE OF BASICS

● **Looking ahead, the foundational role of dots, lines, and planes in design remains as vital as ever.** For Kanai and Sasaki, these elements are not just building blocks of visual composition—they are a universal language that transcends nations, mediums, and eras. Though seemingly simple and ubiquitous, their strength lies in boundless potential and endless variation, offering designers a limitless playground for creativity.

● With even the slightest shift in form or arrangement, these basic elements can create entirely new rhythms and spatial experiences, capturing attention and evoking emotional resonance. By continually exploring the expressive capacity of these forms, design maintains a familiar structural clarity while evolving into fresh, compelling visual languages. In the works of the future, these core elements will remain essential—serving as bridges between beauty, function, and meaning, and sustaining their irreplaceable role in the creative process.

✸ SHEEP CANDLE PACKAGING

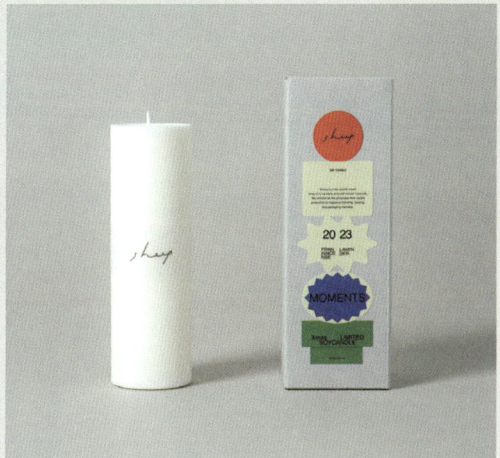

🟩 Why Plane?

Simple shapes are adorned with letters and jagged lines, reminiscent of special offer stickers. Arranged in a vertical row to resemble a tree, the stickers evoke a festive and joyful Christmas atmosphere.

Basic Plane

This packaging design was created for the Christmas candles of the SHEEP candle brand. The design incorporates multiple promotional stickers, each representing a different element, while preserving the original rustic grey packaging.

AD. D. Aki Kanai / Taku Sasaki
CL. SHEEP DESIGN Inc.

- C 89 M70 Y0 K0 / R34 G60 B249
- C 0 M80 Y67 K0 / R221 G84 B71
- C7 M4 Y31 K0 / R245 G242 B196
- C 82 M27 Y100 K0 / R81 G143 B67
- C0 M0 Y0 K100 / R0 G0 B0

n.5 SHIMOKITAZAWA

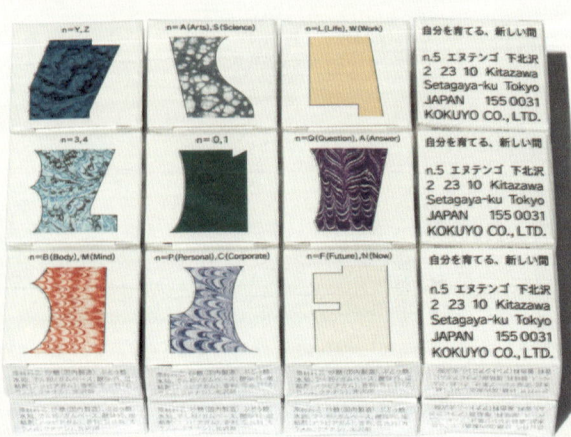

The visual identity for n.5, a satellite-based multi-purpose space for employees launched in 2022, is built around the concept of "A new ma (間) to nurture yourself." The theme draws from the symbolism of diverse options and infinite possibilities that exist in the "ma" of things by cutting out the letter symbol "ma" and the initial letters of words that express the idea of the facility, such as Life and Work, Personal and Corporate, and bringing them into relief using lines.

AD. D. Aki Kanai / Taku Sasaki
CL. KOKUYO Co.,Ltd.

n = P (Personal), C (Corporate)

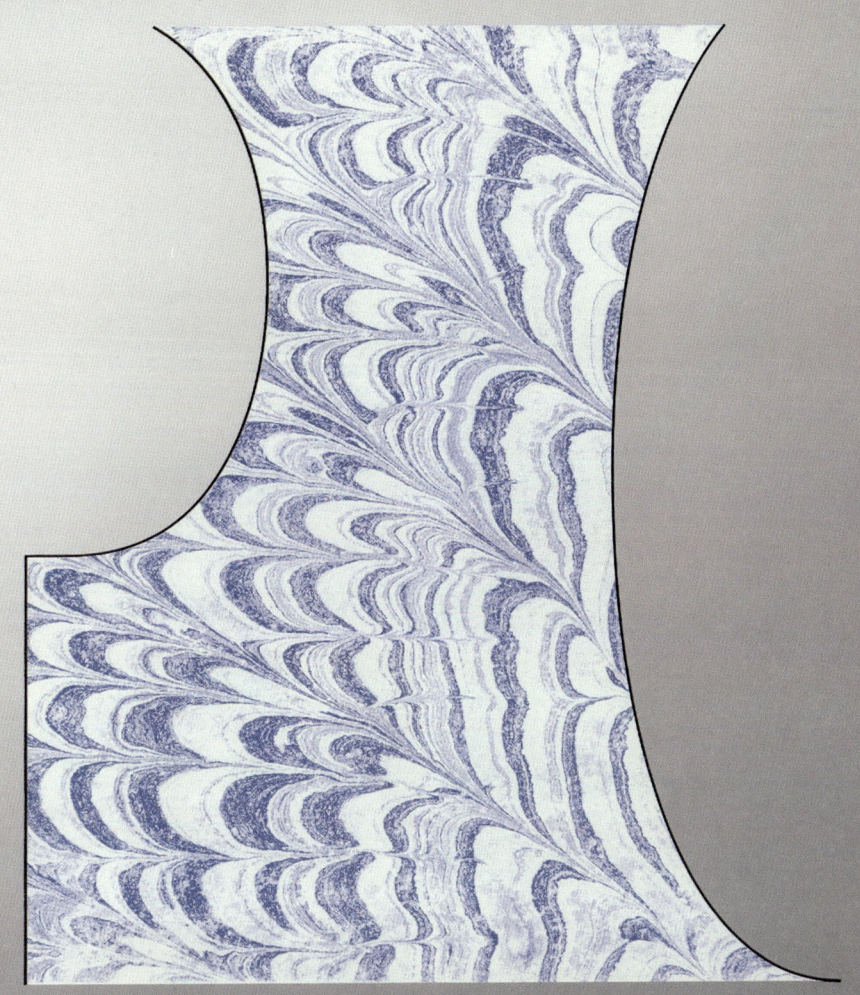

08 Aug 2022 OPEN

1st プレイス＝家、2nd プレイス＝オフィス、3rd プレイス＝カフェ、コワーキング……。さまざまに呼び名が変われど、場所は常に人の行動を規定してきた。言い換えれば、私たちは「そこで何をしたいか」よりも「そこで何をすべきか どうふるまうべきか」というコードに無意識に縛られながら、その時々で行くべき場所を選んでいる。これはなかなか窮屈だ。ワークとライフのスタイルが混ざる未来に向けて、「場」はもっと人のアイデアや行動を解放できるような存在になった方がいい。そのためにはまず、場そのものがステレオタイプな枠組から外れた自由なものであってほしい。目的を縛ることのない、自在な場所を。目盛りに規定されない、自分らしい物差しを。ものごとの間を埋める、あたらしい概念を。「私」を単位にしてみたら、無限の「間」が見えてきた。

n.5 下北沢　　2 23 10 Kitazawa Setagaya-ku Tokyo JAPAN 1550031　　KOKUYO CO.,LTD.

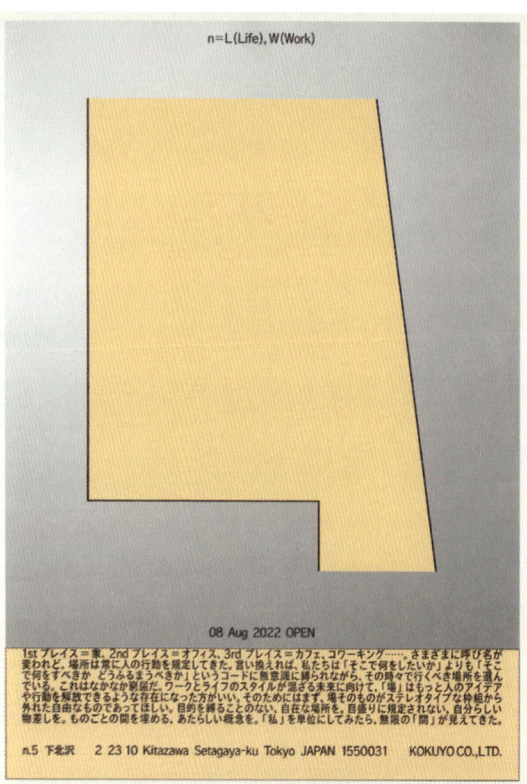
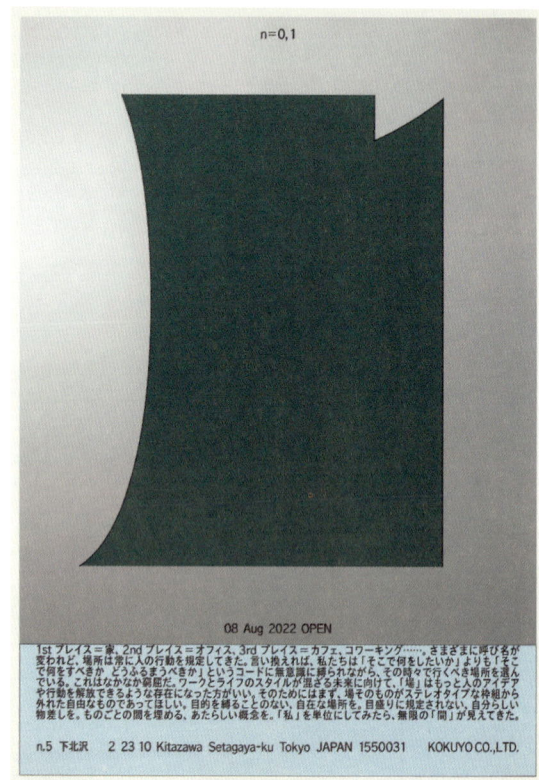
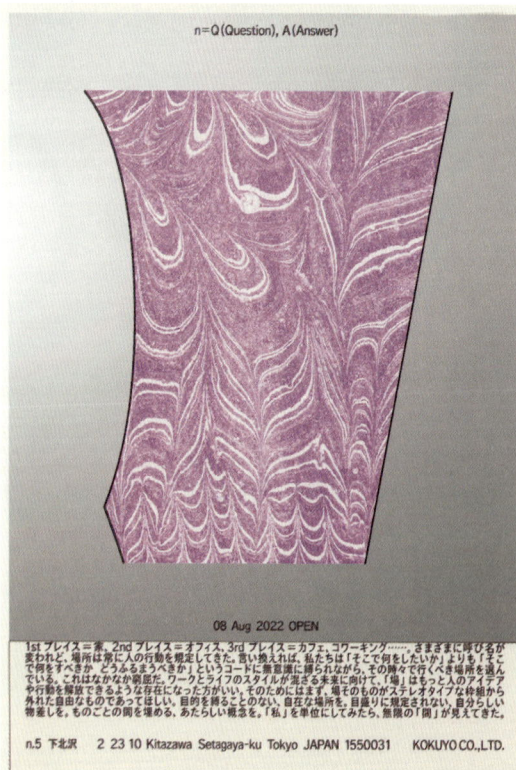

Why Plane?

The designers deepened the concept of "ma" by connecting the edges of two letters or numbers, constructing new shapes, and then giving them different material and texture effects.

Basic Plane

- C75 M45 Y70 K5 / R75 G118 B92
- C20 M15 Y15 K0 / R211 G212 B211
- C0 M20 Y60 K0 / R252 G212 B117
- C25 M0 Y0 K0 / R199 G232 B250
- C75 M95 Y25 K0 / R96 G44 B117
- C15 M70 Y60 K0 / R213 G105 B88
- C75 M70 Y20 K0 / R87 G86 B143
- C25 M15 Y0 K0 / R199 G209 B234
- C5 M10 Y10 K0 / R244 G234 B228
- C0 M0 Y0 K0 / R255 G255 B255
- C0 M0 Y0 K100 / R0 G0 B0

HOW WE LIVE

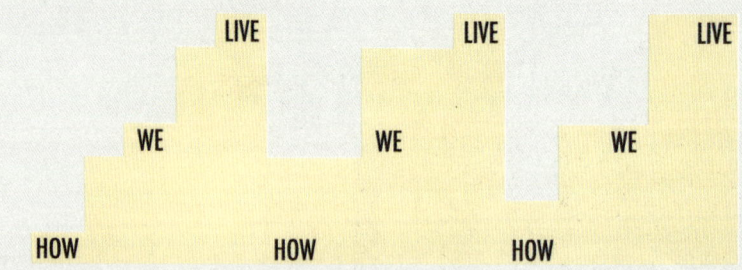

HOW WE LIVE

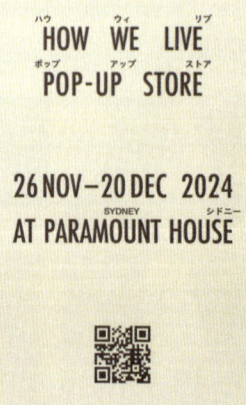

HOW WE LIVE is the global lifestyle brand of Actus, an interior retail business, and Kokuyo. This graphic series was created for the pop-up store held in Sydney, Australia.

AD. D. Aki Kanai / Taku Sasaki
CL. KOKUYO Co.,Ltd.

Why Plane?

The motifs and colors draw inspiration from Sydney's iconic brick buildings and the earthy tones of the Australian landscape. Letters are framed by square lines and surfaces, stacked like building blocks to form a visual identity that resonates with the local environment.

Basic Plane

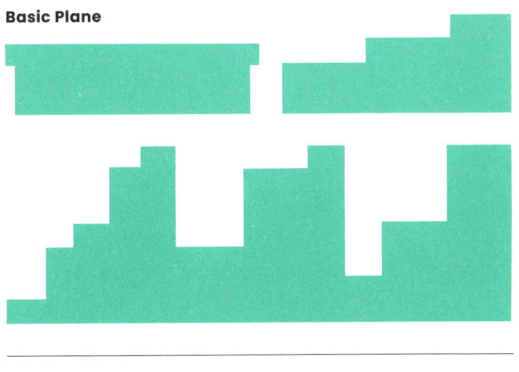

● Dulux S05G6　　● Dulux S30H7
● Dulux S18G1H　　● C0 M0 Y0 K100 / R0 G0 B0

COPY CORNER

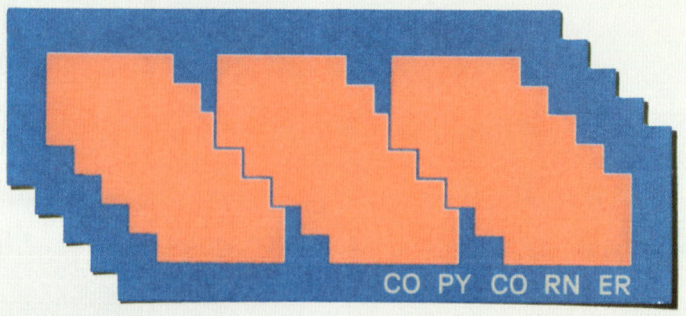
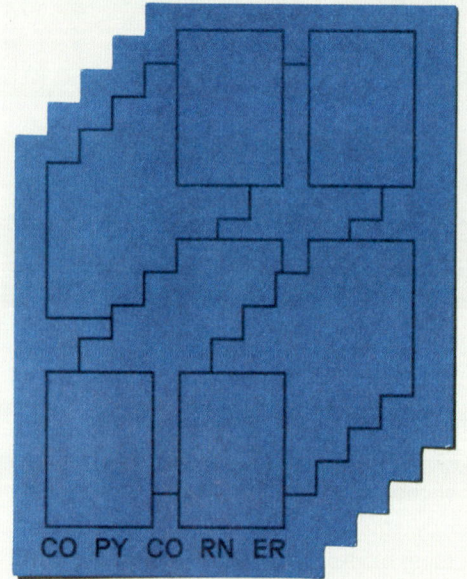
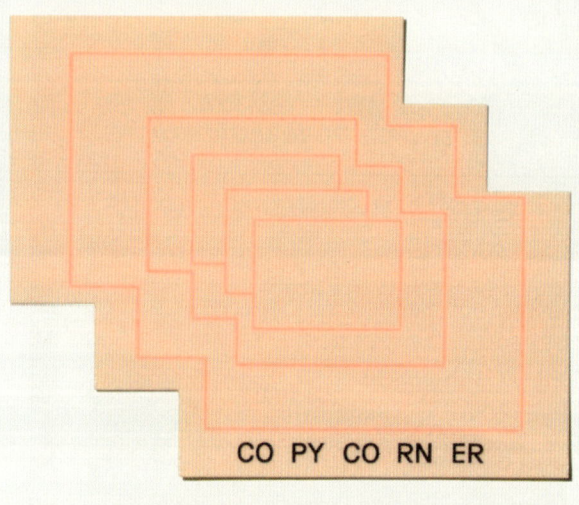
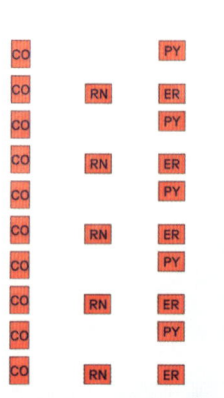

This visual identity was created for the 5.5-tsubo factory and printing label, COPY CORNER. Based on A-standard paper-sized squares, the design features decomposed letterforms arranged in various alignments. The composition maximizes the rectangular format, creating dynamic color fields that accentuate the vibrancy of lithographic ink.

AD. D. Aki Kanai / Taku Sasaki
CL. KOKUYO Co.,Ltd.

COPY CORNER
OPENING HOURS 11:00-21:00
TOKYU PLAZA HARAJUKU BLDG. 3TH FLOOR
6-31-21, JINGUMAE, SHIBUYA-KU, TOKYO, 150-0001, JAPAN
東急プラザ原宿「ハラカド」3階　営業時間：11時-21時
東京都渋谷区神宮前6丁目31番21号
コピー・コーナー

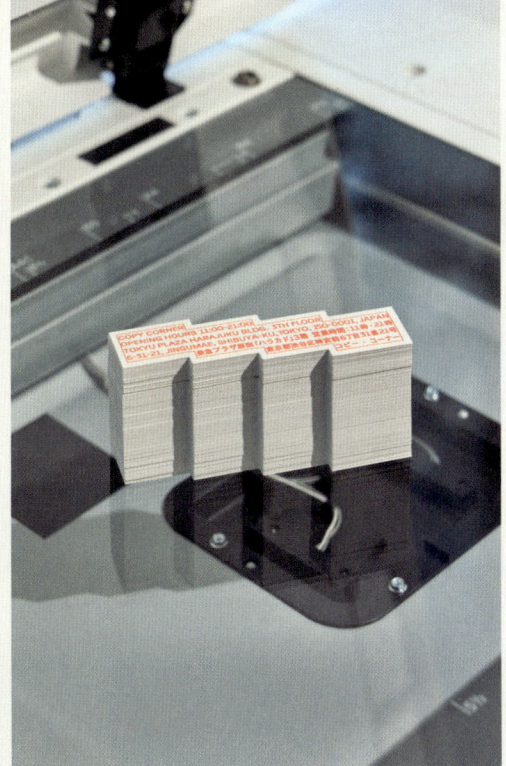

Why Plane?

The designers copied the basic graphics and combined them to create a "replica" feel and a new recognizable brand identity.

Basic Plane

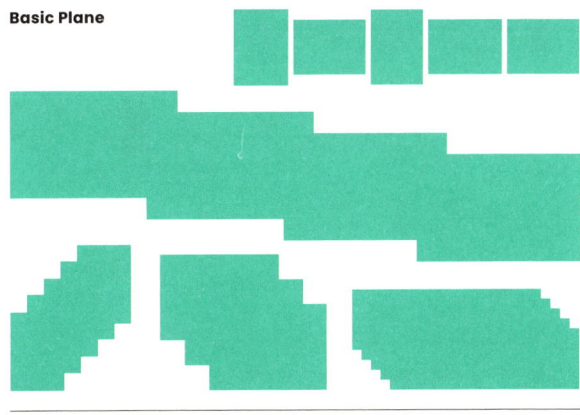

- RISO INK BLUE / R152 G206 B151
- RISO INK FLUORESCENT ORANGE / R238 G238 B140
- RISO INK FLUORESCENT ORANGE / R237 G121 B113
- C0 M0 Y0 K0 / R255 G255 B255
- C0 M0 Y0 K100 / R0 G0 B0

201

◾ NATURAGRAPH

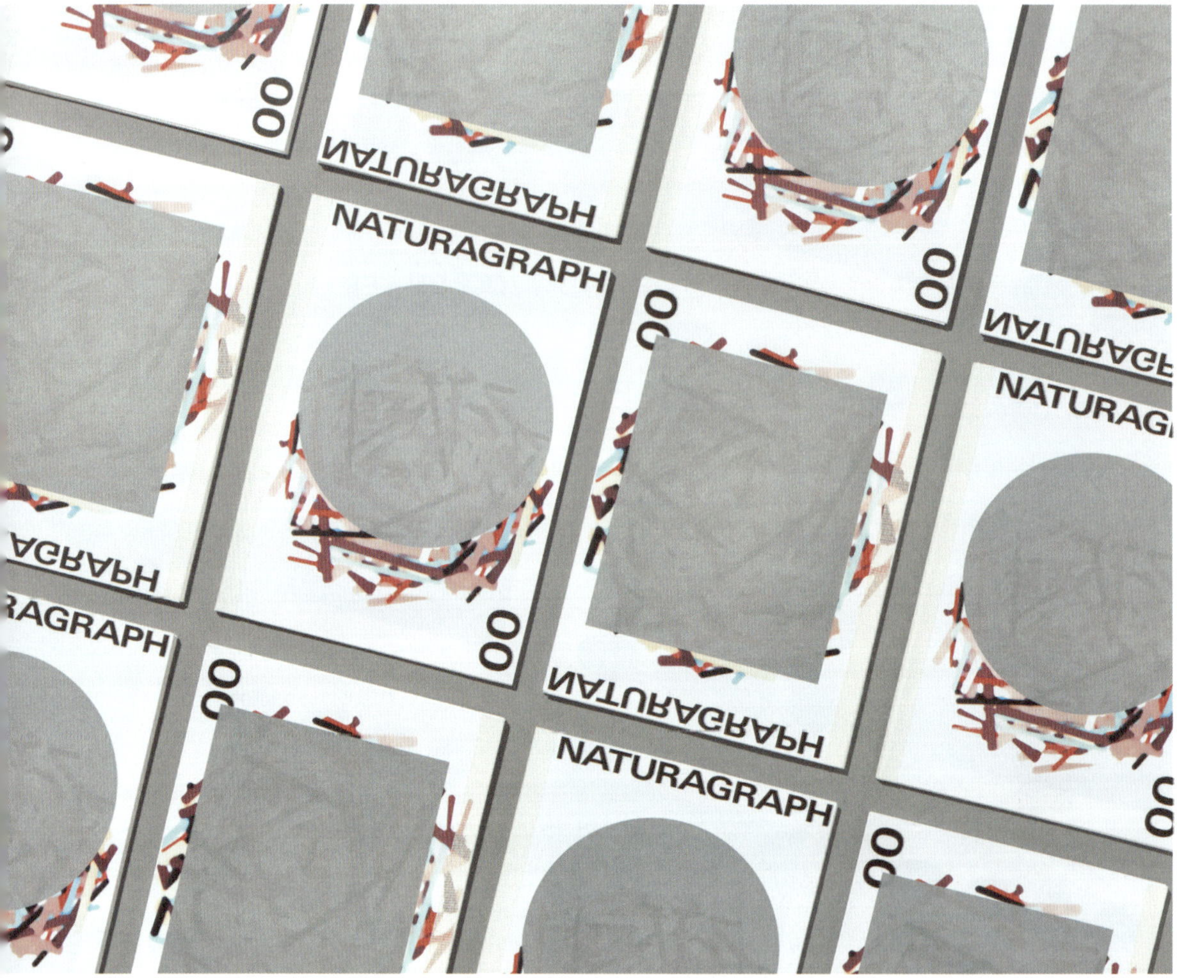

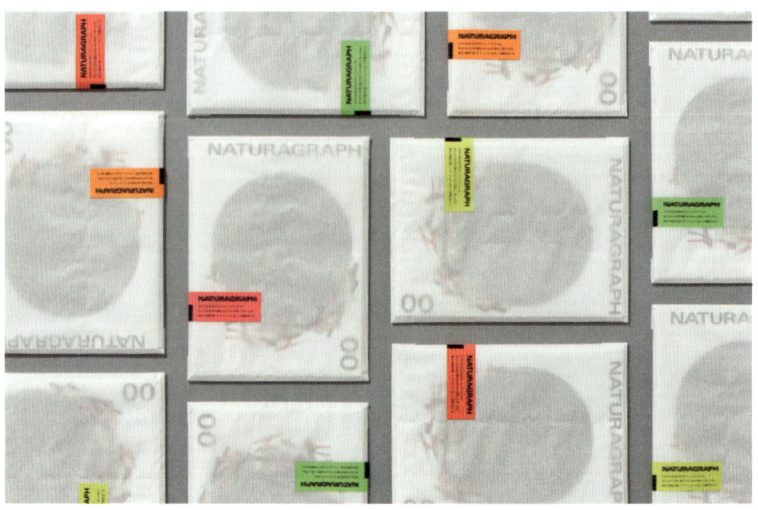

NATURAGRAPH is an experimental publication that explores nature's hidden charms from every conceivable angle, visualizing them through a distinctive creative lens. The design team investigated captivating natural elements—such as color, form, and harmony—through the lens of art and design, rendering them visible through new interpretation.

DA. Nippon Design Center
AD. Daigo Daikoku
D. Hana Yazaki

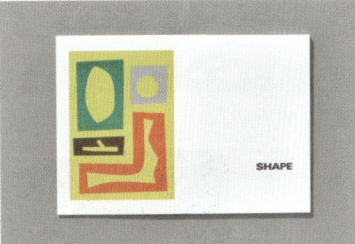
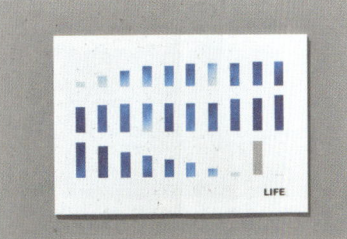
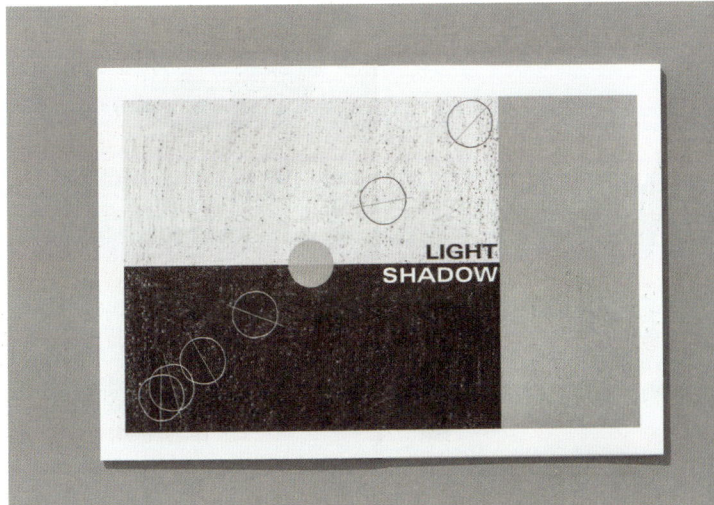
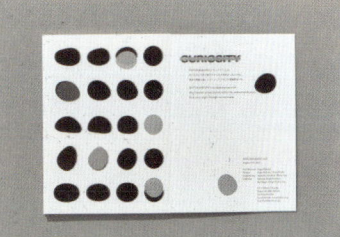

Why Plane?

The visual book design, centered on the theme of "nature," reflects the designer's enduring source of creative inspiration. By focusing on mountains and natural landscapes as primary motifs, the designer developed a graphic collection that examines the forms, shadows, and movements found in the natural world. This approach aims to convey the raw energy and vitality that nature inherently embodies.

- C0 M0 Y0 K45 / R170 G171 B171
- C0 M0 Y0 K100 / R0 G0 B0
- C0 M0 Y0 K0 / R255 G255 B255

◼ ONE IS NOT BORN, BUT RATHER BECOMES, A WOMAN.

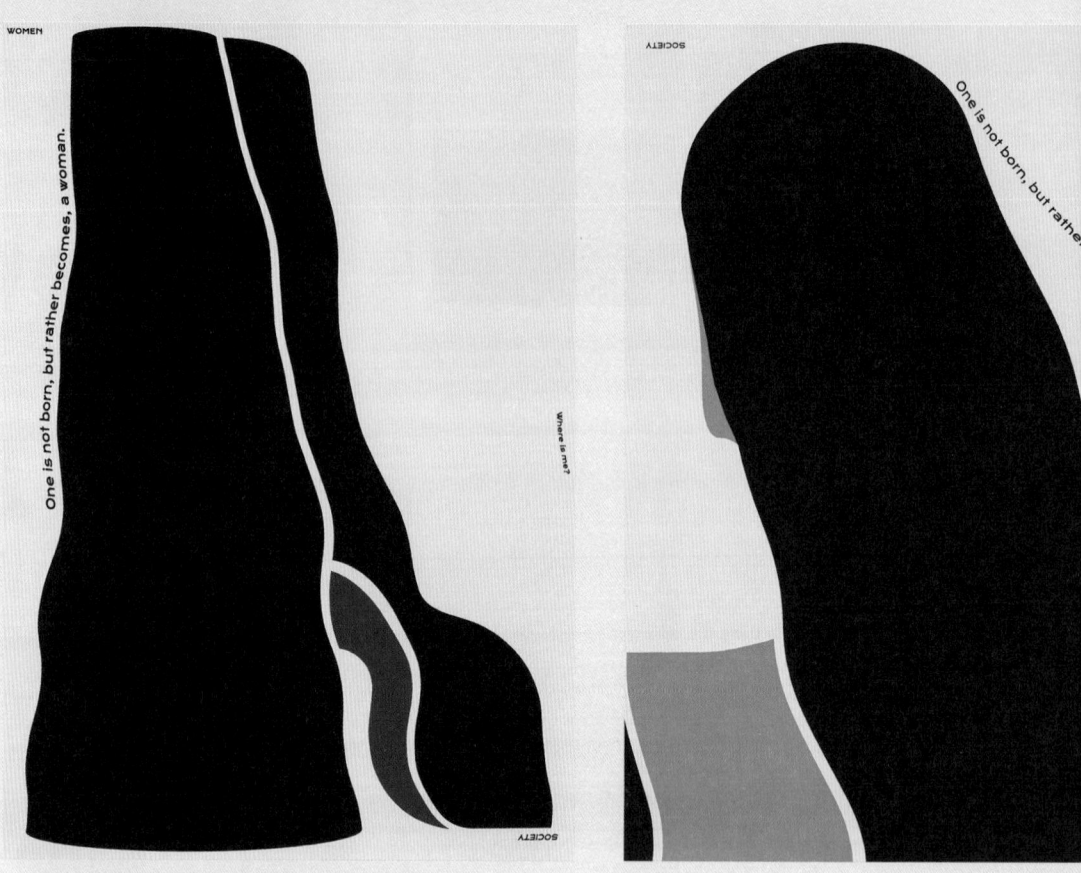

This image was inspired by Simone de Beauvoir's famous quote from *The Second Sex*: "One is not born, but rather becomes, a woman." Beauvoir, a key figure in second-wave feminism, influenced the design's message.

According to the *2024 Global Gender Gap Report* by the World Economic Forum (WEF), Japan ranks 118th out of 146 countries, showing a significant gender gap. Despite growing awareness of feminism in Japan, progress remains slow. This image was created by the designer to inspire women to challenge societal expectations.

The designer reflects on a time when she, too, mistakenly believed that hair, nails, and high heels defined femininity. This self-consciousness mirrored her own misconceptions about the image of women, which she now seeks to address through this work.

D. Miharu Matsunaga (Hami)
CL. One is not born, but rather becomes, a woman.

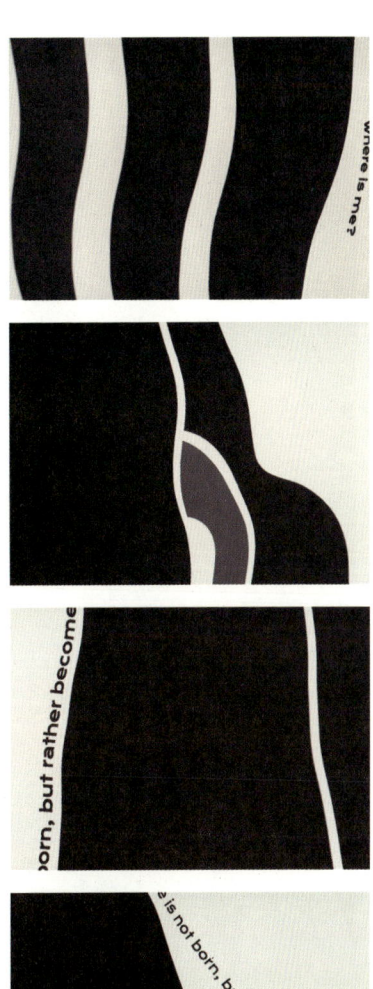

Why Plane?

Feminist graphics are not widely recognized in Japan, and it's rare to see designers creating works in this genre. However, during her time in Scandinavia, the designer came to understand the significant role feminism plays in society and felt empowered to address it openly. The piece itself is simple and stark, using only two colors—black and grey. Texture is added by scanning hand-drawn illustrations, enhancing the piece's raw, minimalistic feel.

Basic Plane

- C15 M10 Y15 K0 / R223 G224 B217
- C20 M10 Y15 K0 / R212 G220 B216
- C15 M15 Y15 K0 / R222 G216 B212
- C45 M40 Y40 K0 / R156 G149 B143
- C75 M70 Y65 K25 / R73 G71 B73
- C0 M0 Y0 K100 / R0 G0 B0
- C0 M0 Y0 K0 / R255 G255 B255

▲ LITTLE FUTURE

Why Plane?

The designer chose extinct animals as the theme and sought out an illustrator to collaborate with, hoping to convey the complex topic of regenerative medicine in an interesting way. It is clear that the illustrator is skilled at filling the page with large blocks of color, creating a strong visual impact, as if the extinct dinosaurs were about to be reborn on the page!

Basic Plane

Regenerative medicine is often described as a cutting-edge medical technology that can "bring the departed back to life." Driven by the continuous advancement of science, this technology may one day become a reality. To fully capture the immense potential of regenerative medicine, the designer turned to dinosaurs, using a dreamlike visual language to incorporate dinosaur elements into the design, aiming to ignite public anticipation for the future of regenerative medicine. A bold scientific hypothesis predicts that once regenerative medicine reaches maturity, even the resurrection of Neanderthals may no longer be considered a fantasy. This hypothesis deeply moved the designer, inspiring her to center the design around "monsters," hoping to convey the vast potential and promising future of regenerative medicine to the public.

D. Miharu Matsunaga (Hami)
CL. Little Future

- C0 M0 Y0 K100 / R0 G0 B0
- C75 M65 Y65 K20 / R75 G81 B79
- C40 M35 Y35 K0 / R168 G161 B156
- ○ C20 M15 Y15 K0 / R211 G212 B211
- C0 M0 Y0 K0 / R255 G255 B255

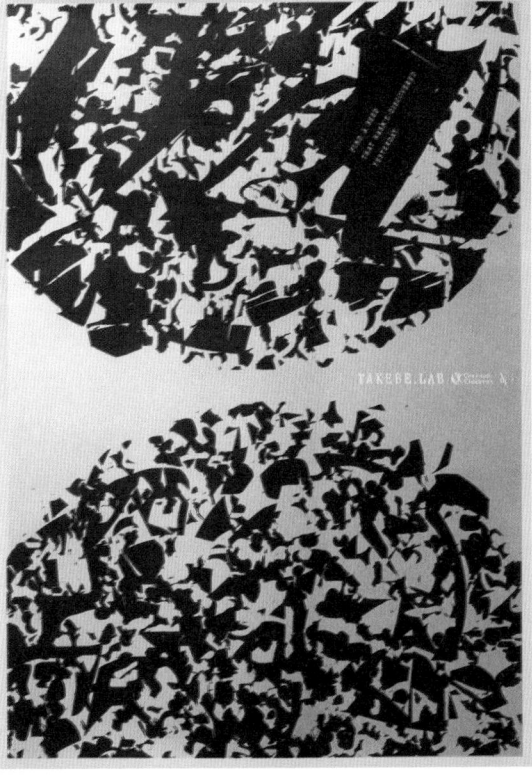

KURONEKOAN

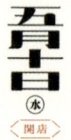

This is the Corporate Identity for "Kuroneko-an," a soba restaurant located in Kuramae, Japan.

DA. CYAN
D. Yukari Okada
CL. Ryo Hasegawa

■ Why Plane?

The designer first created the logo inspired by the three key elements of soba making: "soba flour," "flour for dusting," and "water." She then deconstructed the logo into 34 individual components, which were applied to various items such as noren (curtains at the entrance of shops), paper bags, and soba packaging. The logo's texture is brought to life through woodblock printing, with each element individually cut using a laser cutter to create the printing plates.

Basic Plane

- C0 M0 Y0 K100 / R0 G0 B0
- C5 M5 Y5 K0 / R245 G243 B242
- C0 M0 Y0 K0 / R255 G255 B255

🌸 FREE&PEACE

🌸 Why Plane?

These letters were created for the new collection of the Hong Kong fashion brand GrowthRing & Supply. The character for "自由" (free) is designed with a bird, symbolizing freedom, while the character for "和平" (peace) incorporates an olive tree, symbolizing peace, along with a girl holding a flag. The design of "自由 & 和平" in this way communicates the same message to those who may not read Chinese characters, making it more universally accessible.

In this design, the designer aimed to prioritize the motif, which led to some modifications of the characters. For instance, the four holes in the character "由" were connected to form a notch, and the single hole in the character "和" was completely removed. While these changes significantly alter the original shapes, the designer carefully considered how to retain readability while maintaining the integrity of the design's concept.

D. Yu Miyama
CL. GrowthRing & Supply

Basic Plane

● C10 M85 Y65 K0 / R218 G71 B71
○ C10 M15 Y20 K0 / R233 G219 B204

CHINESE CHARACTER "装"

This is one of the Chinese characters created as part of an independent project. The character "装" (to dress) is depicted by three clothed figures. The clothing has been stylized to a more primitive form in order to align with the structure of the character, merging the visual representation with the essence of the design.

D. Yu Miyama

Why Plane?

This design was inspired by the resemblance between the parts "士" and "衣" in the character "装" and stick figures. Just as one would dress a stick figure, the designer transformed the lines of the character into the planes of clothing, shaping the design to reflect this concept.

Basic Plane

- C0 M0 Y0 K100 / R0 G0 B0
- C0 M0 Y0 K0 / R255 G255 B255

🏠 MA-CHI

Why Plane?

This font uses a 2.5D effect, which creates a three-dimensional illusion using ordinary flat graphics.

Basic Plane

- 🟥 C0 M90 Y70 K0 / R232 G56 B61
- ⬛ C0 M0 Y0 K100 / R0 G0 B0
- ⬜ C0 M5 Y35 K0 / R255 G143 B184
- 🟩 C95 M15 Y100 K0 / R0 G143 B65
- 🟪 C0 M40 Y0 K0 / R244 G180 B208
- 🟢 C25 M10 Y20 K0 / R201 G215 B206
- 🔵 C80 M0 Y20 K0 / R0 G175 B204
- 🔷 C100 M90 Y10 K0 / R12 G51 B136

The font is called "MA-CHI," and as you type the letters, a town gradually takes shape. The symbolic characters within the font are inspired by a person, a bird, a cat, and a dog walker. This design was created for Featured Projects 2024 in Tokyo, centered around the event's theme, "Works that will Open Up Tomorrow." The designer's intention was to evoke a sense of peace and harmony in everyone's life.

AD. TD. D. Zin Nagao

THE TOWN IS ALIVE.
PAST, PRESENT,
AND FUTURE.
THE STORIES WOVEN
BY IT'S PEOPLE, SHAPE THE HEART OF THE TOWN.
WALKING ON THE
COBBLESTONE PATH,
YESTERDAY'S FOOT-
PRINTS REMAIN.
A NEW DAY BEGINS,
ALONG WITH THE
SMILES OF PEOPLE.

DAY
TO
DAY
LIFE

MUSASHINO ART UNIVERSITY

Five Senses (2015)

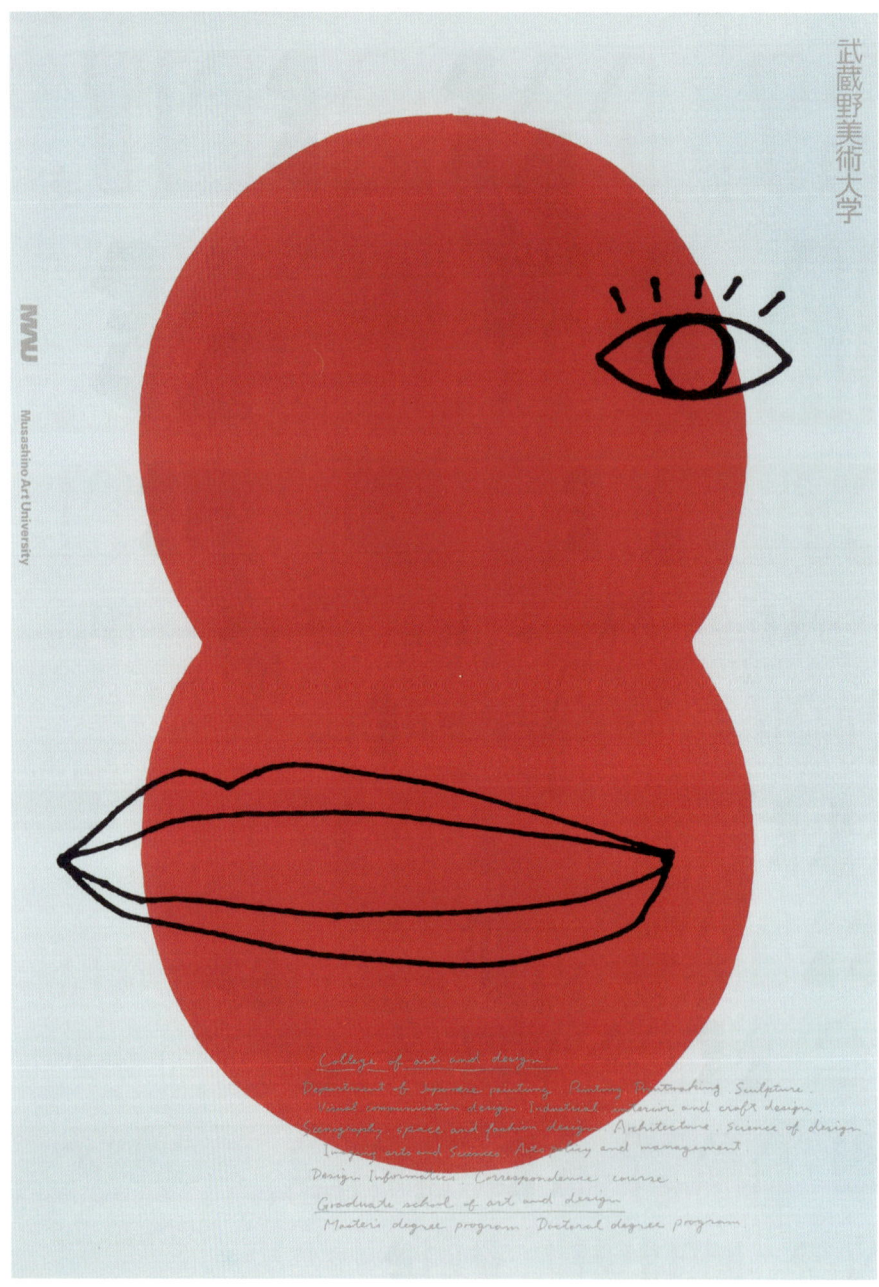

This is the Musashino Art University poster and university guide for 2015. The annual theme is *Five Senses*.

DA. Nippon Design Center
AD. Daigo Daikoku
CL. Musashino Art University

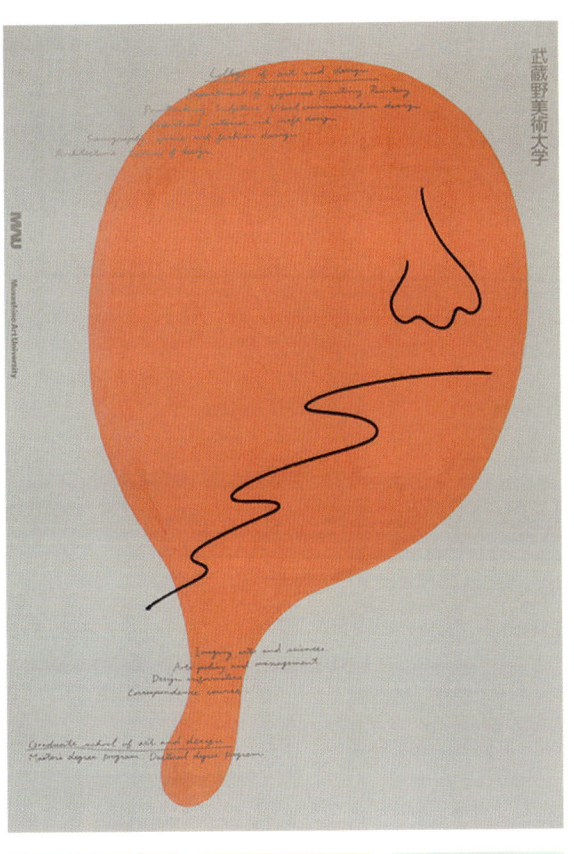

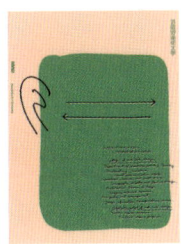 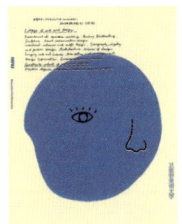 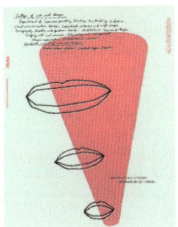   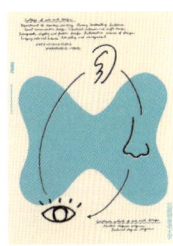

Why Plane?

The designer combined organs representing hearing, sight, smell, taste, and touch with irregular shapes to create this series of posters.

Basic Plane

- C15 M95 Y65 K0 / R209 G38 B67
- C20 M5 Y5 K0 / R212 G229 B239
- C5 M60 Y65 K0 / R232 G130 B84
- C0 M0 Y0 K30 / R201 G202 B202
- C75 M85 Y15 K0 / R92 G61 B135
- C80 M15 Y85 K0 / R0 G154 B83
- C0 M25 Y25 K0 / R249 G208 B186
- C80 M50 Y0 K0 / R48 G113 B185
- C0 M5 Y25 K0 / R255 G244 B205
- C10 M65 Y20 K0 / R221 G118 B148
- C15 M0 Y10 K0 / R224 G240 B235
- C0 M30 Y90 K0 / R250 G191 B19
- C12 M12 Y12 K0 / R229 G224 B221
- C40 M0 Y70 K0 / R169 G208 B107
- C60 M0 Y20 K0 / R93 G164 B208

♪ POROPORO, NI

Why Plane?

The designer created an abstract representation of a person using geometric shapes, as the combination of simple elements can effectively form an image that resonates with the audience.

Basic Plane

○ C15 M10 Y5 K30 / R175 G178 B186
● C0 M35 Y15 K0 / R246 G189 B192
● C5 M30 Y50 K0 / R240 G192 B133
● C80 M85 Y90 K0 / R81 G67 B59
● C75 M40 Y45 K0 / R70 G129 B135
● C25 M0 Y50 K0 / R205 G225 B152
● C75 M50 Y10 K0 / R72 G116 B174
● C0 M0 Y0 K100 / R0 G0 B0
○ C0 M0 Y0 K0 / R255 G255 B255

This is the flyer for a theater performance by the company Horobite. The story revolves around a person whose emotions spill uncontrollably from his mouth, while the main character observes him in silence. To reflect the complexity of the protagonist, the designer used geometric shapes, symbolizing the many facets of his personality. Inspired by cubism, the design allows the figure to be seen from multiple angles, embodying the multifaceted nature of his emotional journey.

DA. coton design
D. Hiroko Sakai
CL. Horobite

JAGDA SCHOOL 2019

Why Plane?

The designer created 5 specially designed graphics as the main elements of this series of posters, and then randomly combined them to form 4 different posters.

Basic Plane

○ C40 M5 Y60 K0 / R168 G203 B128
○ C50 M15 Y5 K0 / R134 G186 B222
○ C5 M30 Y10 K0 / R239 G196 B206
○ C5 M10 Y25 K0 / R245 G232 B220
● C0 M0 Y0 K100 / R0 G0 B0

JAGDA SCHOOL is a one-day workshop organized and led by a professional graphic designer to review the portfolios of students aspiring to graphic design. During the portfolio review in 2019, the concept of "my ruler" was introduced. To illustrate this idea, the designer created the motif featuring various ruler silhouettes.

D. Masunaga Akiko
CL. JAGDA SCHOOL KANSAI

🌱 SPRING & SUMMER GRAPHICS

Spring Graphics

These postcards were created with the theme of the four seasons, inspired by spring and summer. The designer incorporated elements that sparked his interest, blending visual appeal with ideas that become intriguing once their meaning is understood.

DA. SOBOKU DESIGN
D. Yusei Oi

Summer Graphics

■ Why Plane?

The designer used basic geometric shapes to create his designs. These shapes are combined to depict events related to the theme, producing many interesting effects.

Basic Plane

- ○ C0 M50 Y90 K0 / R243 G152 B28
- ● C100 M0 Y100 K0 / R0 G153 B68
- ● C0 M0 Y100 K0 / R255 G240 B0
- ● C80 M0 Y0 K0 / R0 G175 B236
- ● C0 M100 Y100 K0 / R230 G0 B18
- ● C20 M70 Y80 K10 / R192 G97 B54
- ● C0 M0 Y0 K100 / R0 G0 B0
- ○ C0 M0 Y0 K0 / R255 G255 B255

◮ ORIGINAL WORKS BY YOU KOJIMA

The designer resides in a small town called Obuse in Japan, where he works as a graphic designer while also managing a bookstore. There, interactions with books, colleagues, collaborators, and customers serve as a constant source of design inspiration. During his creative residencies, the unique cultural and environmental contexts of different regions also open new windows for inspiration. Additionally, his daily morning football training at a nearby field plays another significant role in fueling his creativity.

DA. YOU
D. You Kojima

Why Plane?

The designer has been fascinated by minimalist shape drawings since childhood. While his peers depicted dinosaurs with intricate, realistic details, he, being unable to master such techniques, could only outline the basic shapes with simple lines. However, he became deeply captivated by this minimalist style, which continues to influence his work today. During a graphic design course in his student years, he submitted a business card design composed entirely of simple lines. When the teacher asked, "Why not add more design elements?" it profoundly impacted him. This experience sparked a deeper exploration of the expressive power of shapes and minimalist aesthetics.

Basic Plane

- C0 M80 Y95 K0 / R234 G85 B20
- C0 M0 Y0 K50 / R159 G160 B160
- C0 M0 Y0 K100 / R0 G0 B0
- C0 M0 Y0 K0 / R255 G255 B255

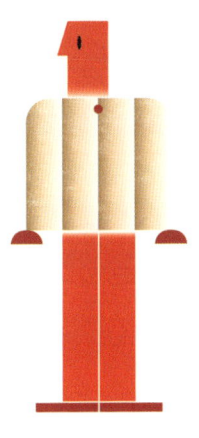

WOKU (をく)

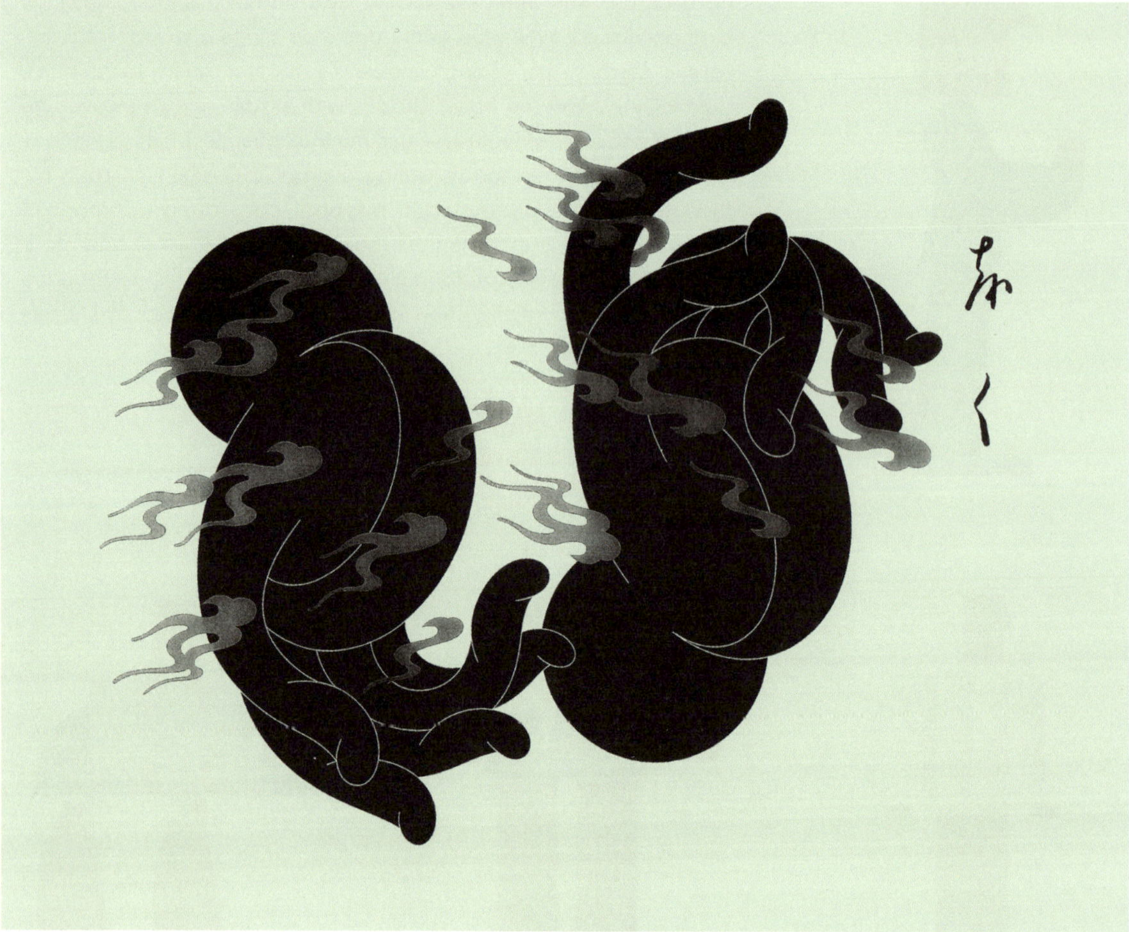

This logo represents a restaurant located in a quiet corner of Kyoto's historic Kawaramachi district. The establishment is discreet and hard to find without guidance. To address this, the designer crafted the logo in the shape of a hand, subtly leading customers into the restaurant. Drawing inspiration from the hand gestures of clergy and monks, the design creates a sense of mystery and intrigue.

DA. Ito Kashiwagi Design Office Inc.
D. Mitsuki Kashiwagi
CL. DAY inc.

Why Plane?

For this logo design, the designer aimed for it to be "unobtrusive yet easy to find." To achieve this, a minimalist all-black design was chosen, paired with a unique shape to ensure the logo stands out among Kyoto's many shops, creating a truly distinctive brand identity.

Basic Plane

- C10 M0 Y10 K50 / R146 G153 B148
- C0 M0 Y0 K100 / R0 G0 B0
- C0 M0 Y0 K0 / R255 G255 B255

KUKONOMI & SHIOKOMBU

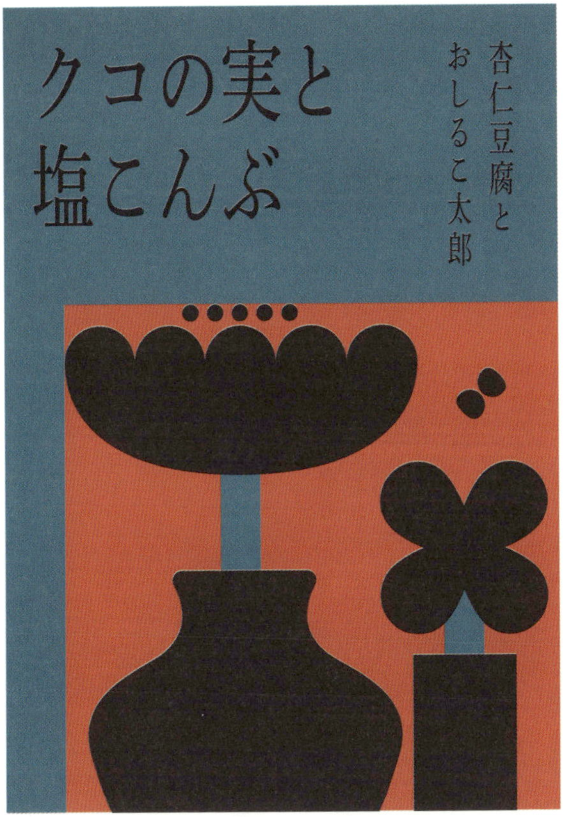

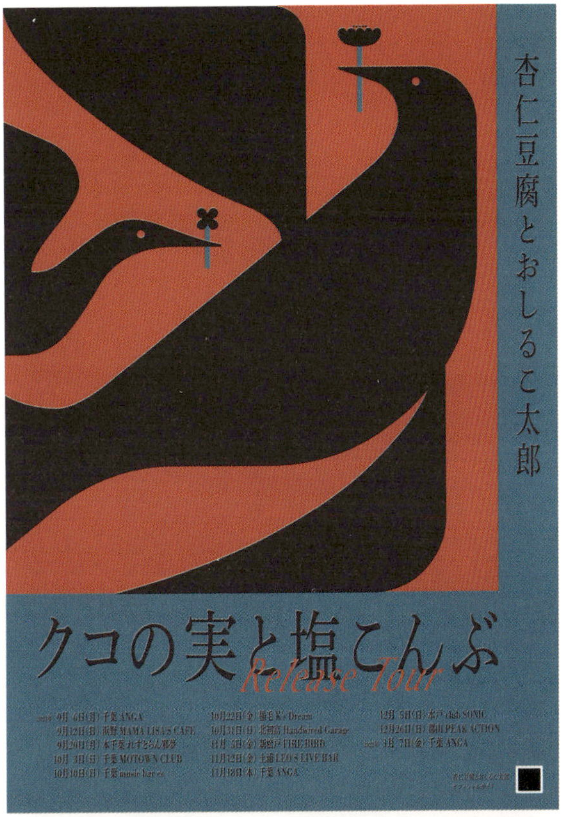

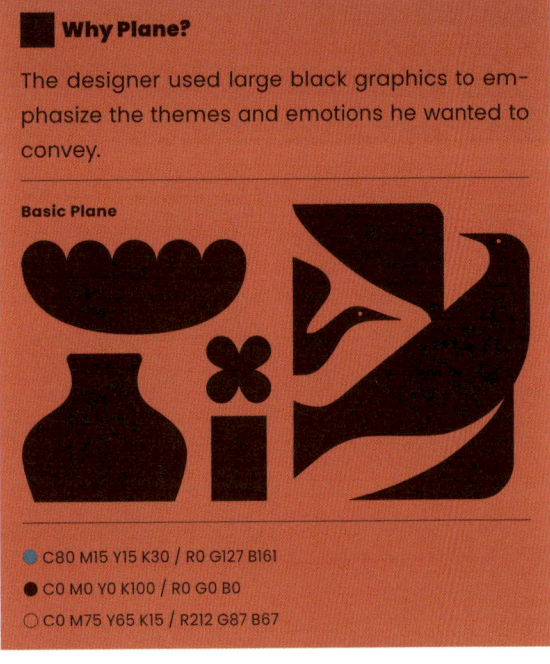

Why Plane?

The designer used large black graphics to emphasize the themes and emotions he wanted to convey.

Basic Plane

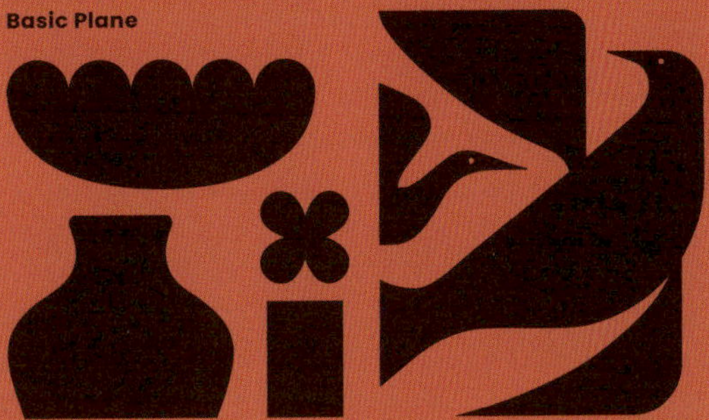

- C80 M15 Y15 K30 / R0 G127 B161
- C0 M0 Y0 K100 / R0 G0 B0
- C0 M75 Y65 K15 / R212 G87 B67

This artwork is for an acoustic duo's song, released during a time when people were restricted from going outside. The song was described as a "flowery" melody, brightening life indoors. For the subsequent live tour, the imagery of freedom and escape was symbolized by two birds in flight, representing the desire to break free and soar beyond the confines.

DA. TARO inc.
D. Hiroyuki Masuda
CL. Annindofu & Oshirukotaro

IKEBANA RYUSEI EXHIBITION: *ASPECTS OF PLANTS*

2020

2022

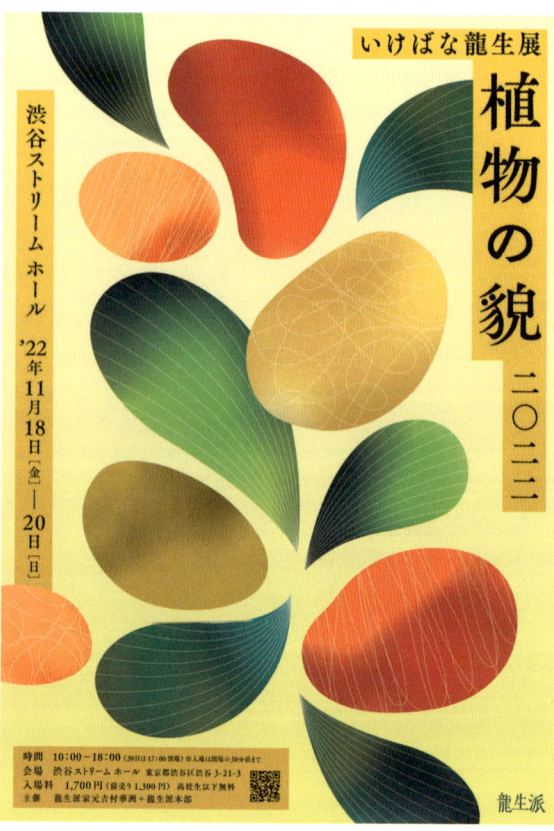

The Ikebana Ryusei Exhibition—*Aspects of Plants* is an annual showcase by Ikebana Ryuseiha, celebrating the dynamic beauty and expressive potential of floral arrangement. Each year, the exhibition's visual identity evolves to reflect a unique interpretation of ikebana, blending traditional artistry with contemporary design techniques.

The 2020 design featured a plant composed of vigorous brushstroke-like elements, symbolizing the powerful and graceful nature of Ikebana Ryuseiha's floral artistry. Organic color gradations, achieved by blurring photographs of plants, added depth and movement to the composition.

In 2022, the concept centered around discovering "ikebana gemstones," represented by a plant motif with flower-like stones. Free-form curves express the fluidity and organic nature of Japanese flower arrangement. Since the exhibition is held in Shibuya, the color scheme was carefully selected to stand out within the urban landscape.

For 2023, the design emphasizes the vitality of plants through three large, cutout-style motifs arranged in a row to create a striking visual impact. A sand grain screen effect is applied to the cut-outs, merging modern and classic aesthetics.

DA. coton design
D. Hiroko Sakai
CL. Ikebana Ryuseiha

2023

Why Plane?

The designer simplified the shapes of plants into graphic combinations and placed them prominently in the composition to create a powerful visual impact, aiming to strike a balance between strength and delicacy.

Basic Plane

- C0 M85 Y40 K0 / R232 G69 B102
- C60 M100 Y0 K0 / R127 G16 B132
- C35 M10 Y5 K0 / R175 G207 B230
- C0 M35 Y100 K0 / R248 G181 B0
- C80 M25 Y80 K0 / R29 G143 B89
- C0 M30 Y15 K0 / R247 G199 B198
- C5 M5 Y60 K0 / R248 G235 B125
- C15 M90 Y90 K0 / R210 G58 B39
- C0 M50 Y80 K0 / R243 G153 B57
- C65 M60 Y10 K0 / R109 G105 B164
- C0 M0 Y0 K100 / R0 G0 B0
- C0 M0 Y0 K0 / R255 G255 B255

ODDITIA BY CHIIO

This music sleeve design was created for the Japanese alternative rock band Chiio. Inspired by the album's lyrics, which incorporate quotes from Kurt Vonnegut Jr. and others, the design reflects a sci-fi worldview that blends the primitive with the near-future. To visually convey this theme, the designer depicted figures emerging from and dissolving into an abstract haze, evoking a sense of movement between reality and illusion.

D. I. Hirokazu Matsuda

Why Plane?

In order to capture this unique musicality, the designer sought to blend modernity and futurism with universality. Light blue and purple were chosen as the main colors, and irregular, fluid shapes were used to evoke a mysterious and transcendent atmosphere.

Basic Plane

- C65 M0 Y0 K0 / R55 G190 B240
- C85 M50 Y5 K0 / R7 G111 B179
- C55 M50 Y0 K0 / R130 G127 B187
- C35 M35 Y0 K0 / R176 G167 B209
- C0 M0 Y0 K0 / R255 G255 B255

● WEB GREETING CARD 2022

■ Why Plane?

The theme of this project is sunrise. The designer captured the ever-changing surface of the water as the sun rises above the sea, simplifying it into abstract graphics to offer a fresh, modern interpretation of sunrise in the design.

Basic Plane

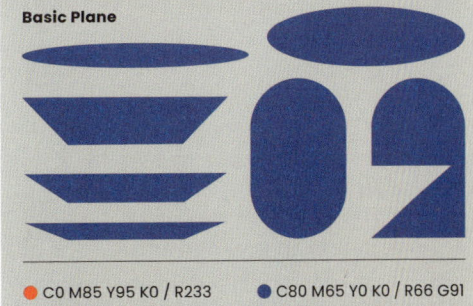

- ● C0 M85 Y95 K0 / R233 G72 B22
- ● C70 M0 Y65 K0 / R60 G179 B122
- ○ C20 M15 Y15 K0 / R211 G212 B211
- ● C80 M65 Y0 K0 / R66 G91 B168
- ● C0 M0 Y0 K100 / R0 G0 B0
- ○ C0 M0 Y0 K0 / R255 G255 B255

This is the New Year's card from CYAN for 2022. The design team created two variations, blending traditional Japanese color schemes with numbers and shapes.

DA. CYAN
D. Yukari Okada

SUPER PAPER MARKET

SUPER PAPER MARKET is an inaugural retail space directly managed by Fukunaga Print, specializing in an eclectic selection of paper products from both Japan and around the world. The visual identity was meticulously crafted to evoke the dynamic energy of a vibrant marketplace, bringing together a diverse array of paper materials in a lively and engaging environment.

DA. NEW Creators Club
D. Shunta Sakamoto
CL. Fukunaga Print Co., Ltd

SUPER PAPER MARKET

■ Why Plane?

To convey the unique physical properties of paper, such as its tension and texture, which distinguish it from materials like cloth, the designer paid meticulous attention to preserving the complexity of the modeling. Every detail was carefully considered to reflect paper's inherent characteristics, ensuring its distinctiveness was captured in the design.

Basic Plane

- ● C90 M70 Y0 K0 / R29 G80 B162
- ● C5 M85 Y85 K0 / R226 G71 B42
- ● C0 M0 Y0 K100 / R0 G0 B0
- ○ C0 M0 Y0 K0 / R255 G255 B255

ITOKAKU SHIP INTERIOR

The logo design aims to establish a high-recognition brand identity for a ship interior company founded by former octopus fishermen. The designer broke from tradition by not relying on the typical ship and ocean elements commonly seen in the shipbuilding industry, instead boldly using an octopus as the brand symbol. The octopus stands out as a unique visual symbol in the industry, creating a striking contrast that piques curiosity. The founder's background as an octopus fisherman is cleverly woven into the brand story, enhancing its memorability. Today, the company's employees are affectionately known as the "Octopus People."

DA. Ito Kashiwagi Design Office Inc.
D. Mitsuki Kashiwagi

■ Why Plane?

This design emphasizes "freedom" and discards all explanatory elements, leaving only visual graphics that strike a chord with the viewer—octopuses.

Basic Plane

- C10 M5 Y85 K0 / R239 G227 B49
- C0 M0 Y0 K5 / R247 G248 B248
- C0 M0 Y0 K100 / R0 G0 B0
- C0 M0 Y0 K0 / R255 G255 B255

CRAFT GIN "TERROIR A"

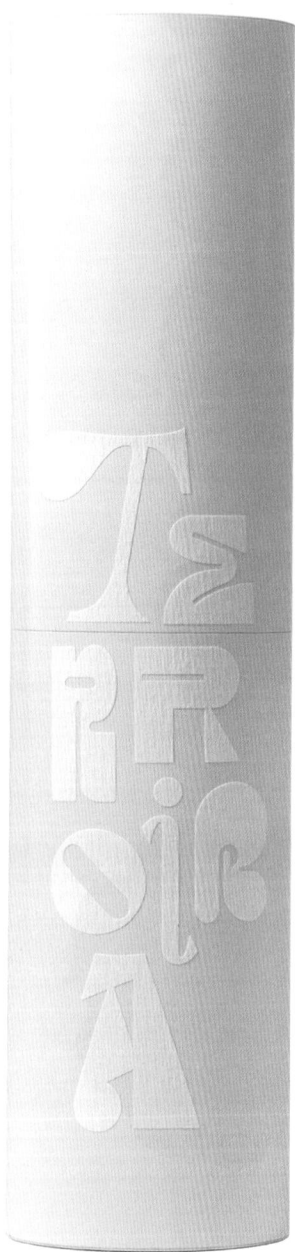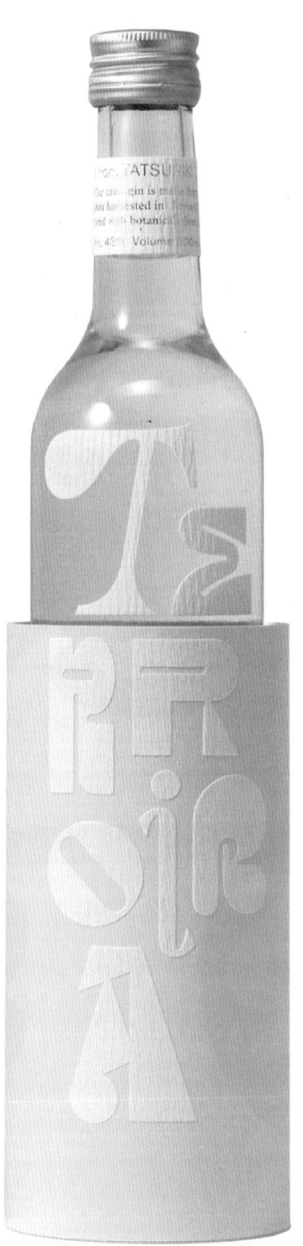

"Terroir A" is a new craft gin produced by Tatsuriki, a traditional Japanese sake brewery. The word "terroir" means "soil" in French, and the name Terroir A reflects the brewery's dedication to the land, overseeing every step from cultivation to production in-house.

DA. CYAN
D. Yukari Okada
CL. Honda Shoten

■ Why Plane?

While most craft gins on the market use inexpensive base spirits made from wheat, corn, or molasses, the base spirit for Terroir A, produced by Ryu-ryoku, is made from Yamadanishiki, one of the highest quality ingredients from the "Tokushu A" district.

To reflect this premium quality, the design team crafted the logo with a blend of bold and subtle typography, creating a strong impression of the name "Terroir A." The label is made from Japanese paper, featuring a die-cut process. It is punched out and affixed to a transparent bottle, adding an elegant touch to the overall design.

Basic Plane

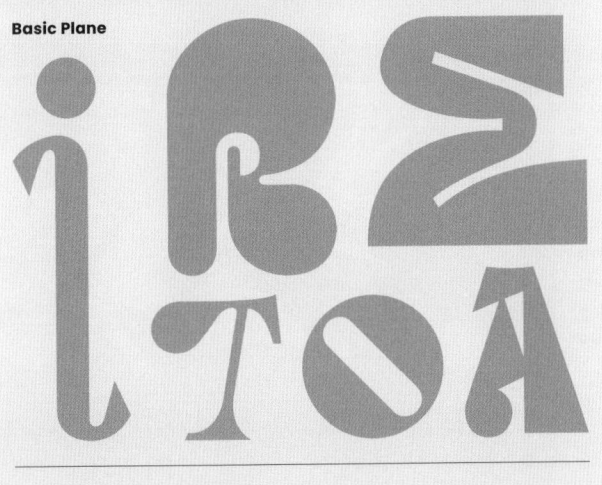

● C0 M0 Y0 K0 / R255 G255 B255

RF ORGANIC POWDER

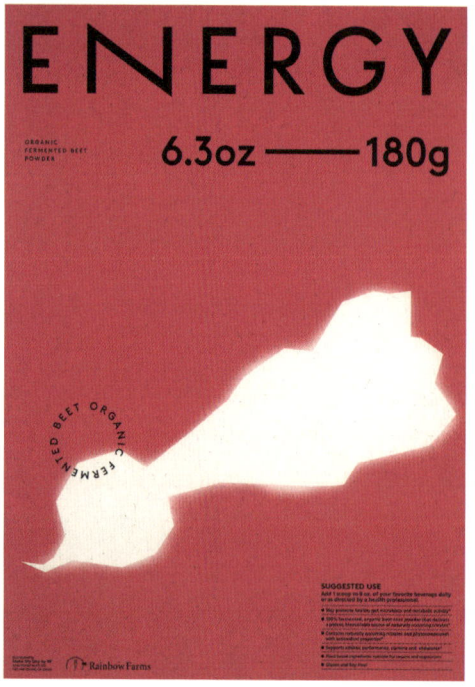

Why Plane?

By depicting the ingredient silhouettes with simple, paper-cut-like shapes, the design minimizes visual information, resulting in a clean and refined impression. This approach allows users to effortlessly imagine how the product can seamlessly integrate into their own lifestyle, reinforcing its natural and approachable qualities.

Basic Plane

- C35 M40 Y50 K0 / R180 G155 B127
- C0 M0 Y0 K100 / R0 G0 B0
- C20 M90 Y40 K0 / R201 G54 B100
- C5 M30 Y90 K0 / R241 G188 B26
- C45 M25 Y75 K0 / R158 G170 B89
- C15 M25 Y45 K0 / R222 G195 B147

This is a graphic design for RF Organic Powder, a product created to support a healthy diet. Made from pure organic ingredients, the powder boasts vibrant colors reminiscent of paint pigments. The composition centers on these distinctive colors, emphasizing their natural appeal. To enhance the visual impact, silhouettes of the ingredients are incorporated, serving as complementary elements that highlight the product's wholesome origins.

DA. TM INC.
D. Yuto Tamura
CL. Rainbow Farms

🔴 THE ROASTERS AND THE STAND

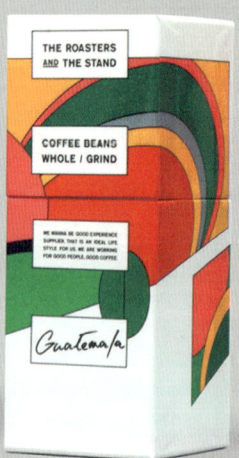

The Roasters is a coffee roastery and café located in Wakayama, Japan, a place rich in natural beauty. The roastery specialises in meticulously selected single origin coffee beans, roasted onsite.

Tokyo-based graphic design studio emuni created the packaging design for the single origin coffee beans, released in limited quantities.

DA. emuni
D. Masashi Murakami
CL. The Roasters

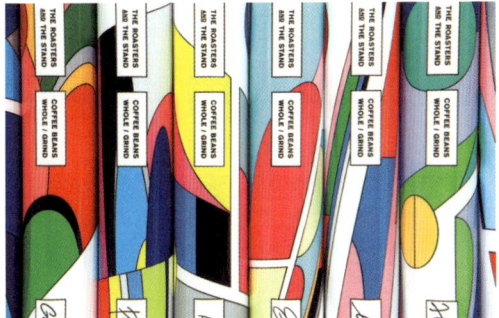

Why Plane?

The designer set an abstract graphic on this package, inspired by the flavors of coffee beans from each region of production, and then translated these taste experiences into a combination of colors and shapes that express the flavor variations of coffee, creating a coffee brand that is very different from traditional packaging.

Basic Plane

- C0 M95 Y45 K0 / R230 G30 B88
- C0 M85 Y10 K0 / R232 G67 B136
- C5 M45 Y0 K0 / R234 G166 B220
- C5 M95 Y100 K0 / R224 G38 B19
- C0 M45 Y100 K0 / R245 G162 B0
- C10 M0 Y95 K0 / R240 G233 B0
- C0 M0 Y0 K100 / R0 G0 B0
- C0 M0 Y0 K0 / R255 G255 B255
- C15 M0 Y60 K0 / R228 G233 B128
- C35 M0 Y100 K0 / R184 G210 B0
- C75 M10 Y100 K0 / R50 G162 B56
- C85 M40 Y100 K5 / R24 G118 B57
- C50 M0 Y10 K0 / R129 G205 B228
- C80 M10 Y5 K0 / R0 G165 B220
- C100 M90 Y0 K0 / R11 G49 B144
- C40 M90 Y0 K0 / R165 G48 B140

✱ EXPLORE NEW FORMS OF CHINESE CHARACTERS

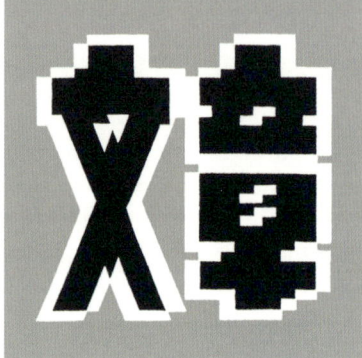

This poster was created as a summary of an independent project exploring new forms of Chinese characters for an exhibition held in Düsseldorf, Germany, in June 2024. In Chinese character culture, unique techniques for lettering have a long history, but few people are experimenting with them today. The designer has focused on this tradition, exploring new shapes while pushing the limits of readability. This process involves breaking down the outlines of Chinese characters, transforming them into symbolic images, and then reinterpreting them as characters. The designer began posting them on Instagram around 2021 and has since created over 100 characters. This poster features a selection of 80 of these works.

D. Yu Miyama

■ **Why Plane?**

Chinese characters are fundamentally composed of lines, but by widening these lines and treating them as planes, a variety of interpretations become possible. This collection represents a series of experiments in which lines are viewed as planes, with those planes further expanded into graphic forms, offering new perspectives on the structure and visual expression of Chinese characters.

Basic Plane

● C15 M100 Y100 K0 / R208 G18 B27
● C25 M45 Y65 K0 / R200 G151 B96
● C0 M15 Y90 K0 / R255 G218 B1
● C80 M15 Y100 K0 / R2 G153 B59
● C80 M0 Y0 K0 / R0 G175 B236
● C100 M85 Y0 K0 / R0 G56 B148
● C0 M50 Y0 K0 / R241 G158 B194
● C0 M0 Y0 K100 / R0 G0 B0
○ C0 M0 Y0 K0 / R255 G255 B255

▮ VOICE OF ART: ART PUBLISHING AND EVENTS

This poster was created for a company that organizes art-related events. Guided by the concept of "peering deep into the heart of art, opening door after door," the design invites viewers into a layered visual experience. Unlike typical posters printed in B1 or B0 sizes, this one was produced in a painterly format—F40.

DA. MU DESIGN ROOM
D. Muramatsu Takehiko
CL. VOICE OF ART

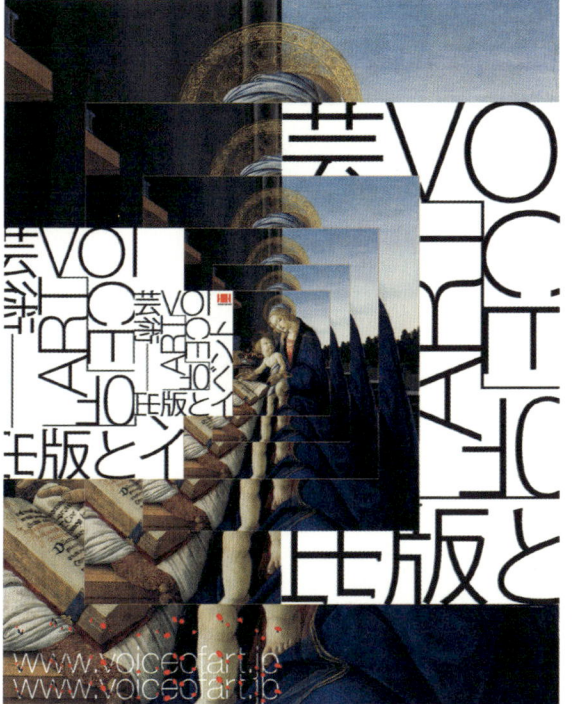

Why Plane?

The following artworks are referenced:
The Night Watch by Rembrandt van Rijn,
Madonna of the Book by Sandro Botticelli,
The Balcony by Édouard Manet, and
Portrait of Dr. Gachet by Vincent van Gogh.

If the referenced paintings are considered as "planes," then the depth created by layering these "planes" is intended to visually express and reinforce the concept above.

Basic Plane

- C60 M75 Y95 K40 / R90 G56 B29
- C0 M100 Y100 K0 / R230 G0 B18
- C5 M30 Y80 K0 / R241 G189 B63
- C15 M75 Y100 K0 / R213 G94 B18
- C60 M40 Y40 K100 / R0 G0 B0
- C0 M0 Y0 K0 / R255 G255 B255

PLANE TO DOT

Concept of Plane to Dot

● "Plane to Dot" is a way of viewing the whole through its smallest components, recognizing that every complete plane is ultimately composed of countless dots. When a plane is subdivided and broken down, each dot emerges as an indispensable unit that forms the graphic. The density and arrangement of these dots define the plane's shape and texture; when the number of dots is sufficiently large and closely packed, their boundaries blur into what we perceive as a plane. This concept reveals how complex forms are built layer by layer from the most fundamental visual elements.

Various Kinds of Plane to Dot

- **Regular Arrangements:**

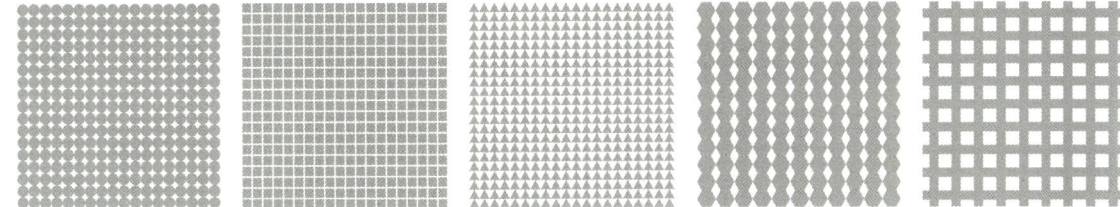

- **Overlapping Arrangements:**

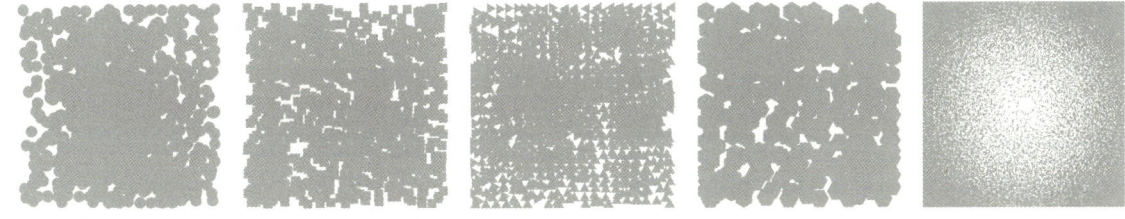

- **Irregular Combination:** A plane formed by dots of varying shapes.

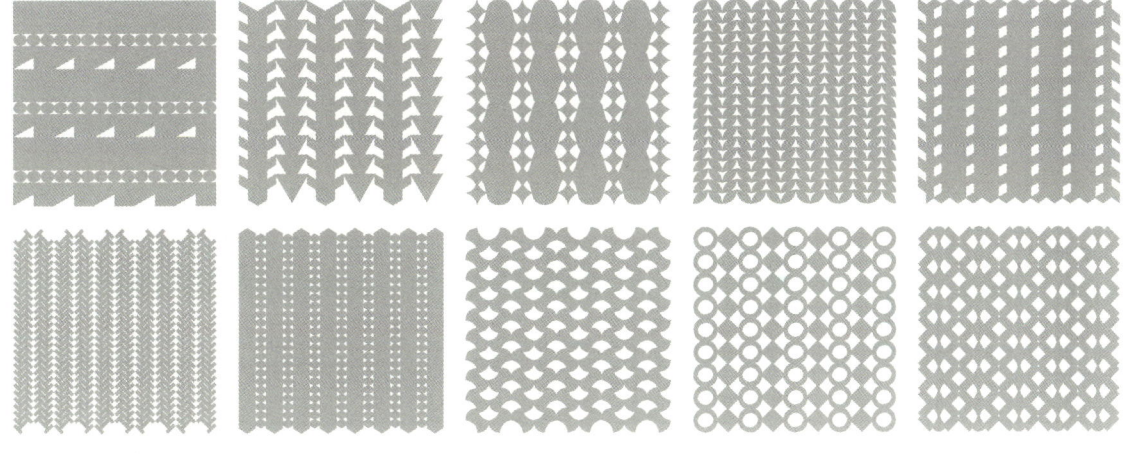

- **Scale Combination:** A plane formed by dots of different sizes.

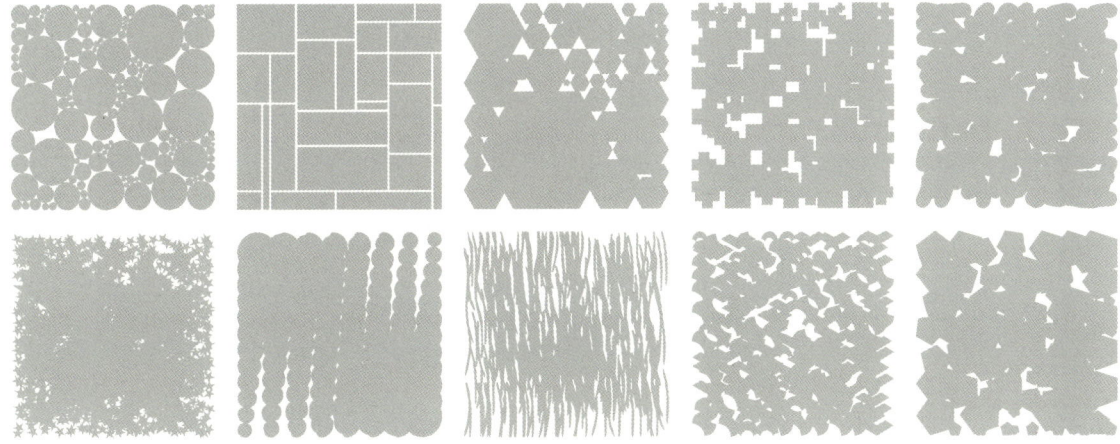

::: PERIOD PAIN

In Japan, discussing menstruation remains a sensitive and often avoided topic. This led the designer to question why such a natural and fundamental part of life is rarely spoken about, especially considering that half of the population is directly affected.

To bring awareness and start a conversation, the designer chose to express this subject through visual art. By incorporating the physical experience of menstruation—the pain, the stretching, and contracting of the uterus—into the graphic, the intention was to convey the often-overlooked discomfort and emotional complexity associated with it, encouraging a more open dialogue.

D. Miharu Matsunaga (Hami)
CL. Period Pain

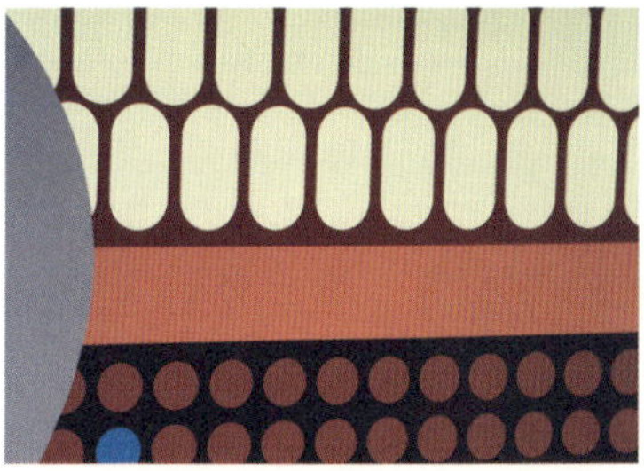

⟨ DEEP INTO THE THOUGHTS ⟩

▦ Why Plane to Dot?

The designer used basic shapes to create an abstract representation of uterine contractions and internal blood flow during menstrual cramps. The flowing curves represent the contractions of the uterus, while the dots represent blood.

The colors evoke a "pain" theme, yet are selected for their refined quality. The shapes are bold and vibrant, while the composition harmoniously blends soft tones, resulting in a visually balanced yet impactful experience.

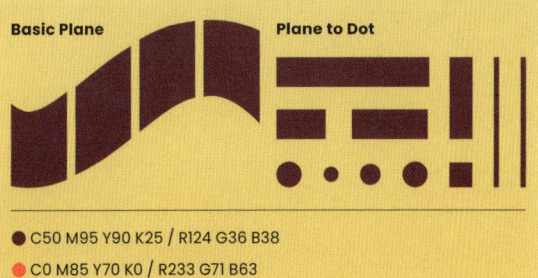

Basic Plane   **Plane to Dot**

- C50 M95 Y90 K25 / R124 G36 B38
- C0 M85 Y70 K0 / R233 G71 B63
- C10 M15 Y75 K0 / R236 G212 B82
- C15 M10 Y40 K0 / R225 G221 B168
- C40 M85 Y85 K5 / R163 G67 B52
- C75 M25 Y20 K0 / R41 G150 B185
- C45 M40 Y30 K0 / R156 G150 B160

● MUSASHINO ART UNIVERSITY

Expansion/Diffusion (2012)

This is the Musashino Art University poster and university guide for 2012. The annual theme is *Expansion/Diffusion*.

DA. Nippon Design Center
AD. Daigo Daikoku
CL. Musashino Art University

Why Plane to Dot?

The designer used thousands of extremely tiny dots and brought them together to form the central visual of the poster—a plane with blurred borders. This creates a main visual graphic that reflects the theme of "Expansion/Diffusion."

Basic Plane   **Plane to Dot**

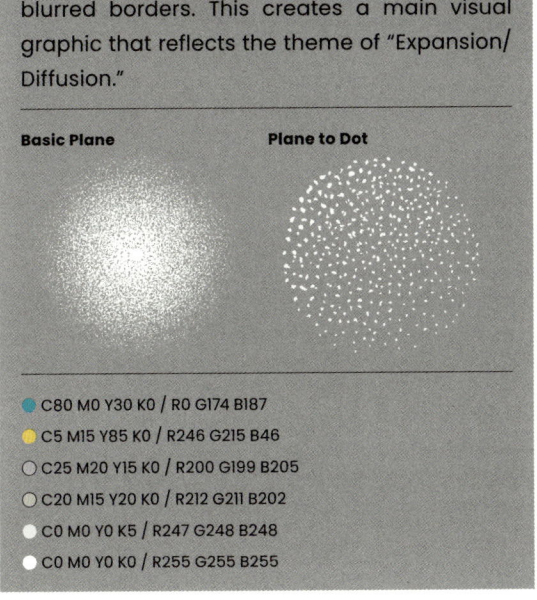

- C80 M0 Y30 K0 / R0 G174 B187
- C5 M15 Y85 K0 / R246 G215 B46
- C25 M20 Y15 K0 / R200 G199 B205
- C20 M15 Y20 K0 / R212 G211 B202
- C0 M0 Y0 K5 / R247 G248 B248
- C0 M0 Y0 K0 / R255 G255 B255

NEW DAY, NEW LIGHT. NIKKO

This symbol mark represents Nikko City, located in Tochigi Prefecture, Japan, a city rich in historical and cultural heritage, renowned for its tourist attractions. In recent years, however, the area has faced challenges, including a declining population and a lack of new industries, leading to a stagnation in its role as a tourist destination.

To address this, a project was launched to rediscover and reawaken the charm of the town. The logo mark captures the essence of "光" (light), symbolizing hope and renewal. The color palette draws from traditional Japanese hues, further reflecting the city's cultural legacy.

The designer simplified the town's name, Nikko (日光), into a minimalist form, with the intention of creating a design that anyone in the community could easily recreate, making it memorable and approachable. This versatile symbol is designed to be universally recognizable, whether displayed as an app icon or on town walls. Its simple, yet evocative shape offers potential for expansion and adaptation across a wide range of future projects.

D. Arata Kubota
CL. Nikko City, Tochigi Prefecture, Japan

Why Plane to Dot?

The designer broke down the strokes of Chinese characters and filled them with different colors, transforming the characters from complete graphics into several "stroke dots." This unique approach did not compromise readability and cleverly converted text characters into graphic symbols.

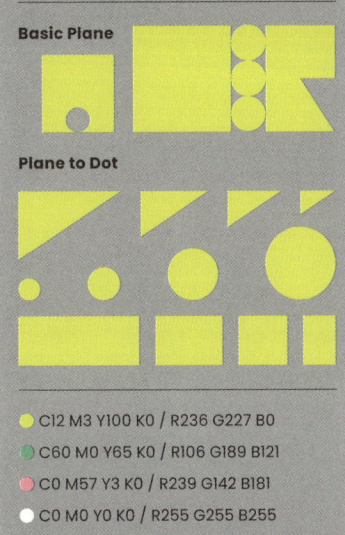

Basic Plane

Plane to Dot

- C12 M3 Y100 K0 / R236 G227 B0
- C60 M0 Y65 K0 / R106 G189 B121
- C0 M57 Y3 K0 / R239 G142 B181
- C0 M0 Y0 K0 / R255 G255 B255
- C0 M0 Y0 K80 / R89 G87 B87

✳ 2023 PLAY GRAPHIC

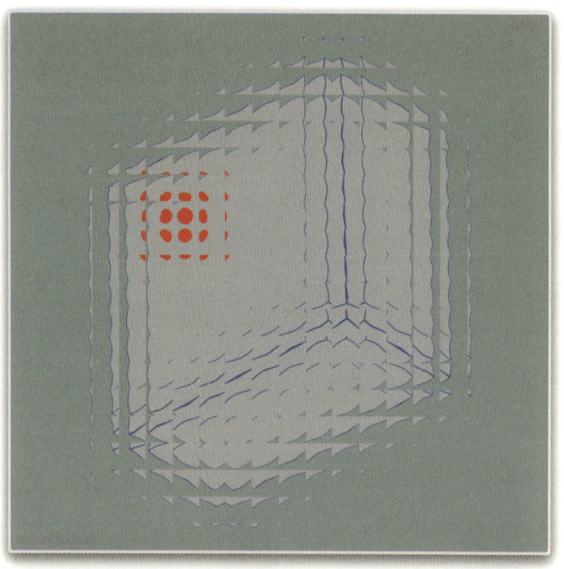

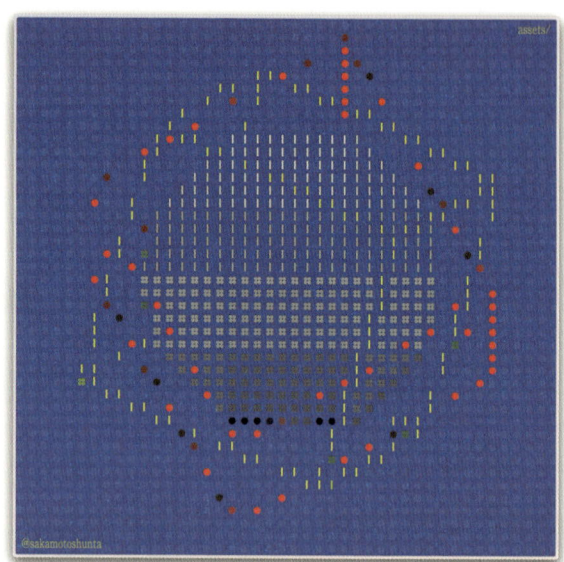

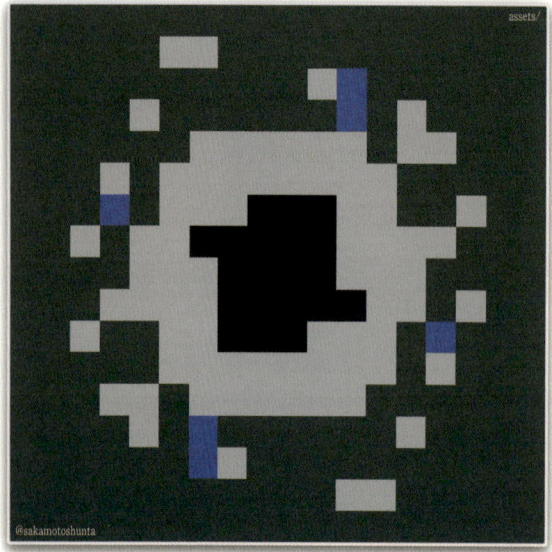

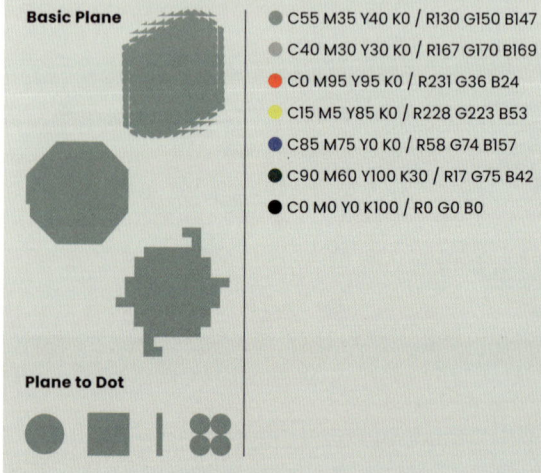

Why Plane to Dot?

The designer deliberately avoided using general graphic production software, instead focusing on controlling the planes and lines that naturally emerge in the process of programming, approaching the creation from a graphic design perspective.

These graphics, constructed from code, transition between the virtual and the real, and are essentially thousands of pieces of data.

Basic Plane

- C55 M35 Y40 K0 / R130 G150 B147
- C40 M30 Y30 K0 / R167 G170 B169
- C0 M95 Y95 K0 / R231 G36 B24
- C15 M5 Y85 K0 / R228 G223 B53
- C85 M75 Y0 K0 / R58 G74 B157
- C90 M60 Y100 K30 / R17 G75 B42
- C0 M0 Y0 K100 / R0 G0 B0

Plane to Dot

It was created as an excellent work, using the program as if it were a paintbrush.

DA. sakamoto app
D. Shunta Sakamoto

PLANT A SEEDLING

Why Plane to Dot?

The seedlings are depicted using a variety of techniques, including photography, pen drawings, and watercolor painting. Each method brings a unique texture and character to the composition. To unify these diverse elements, plane shapes are used to create a sense of balance and cohesion, ensuring harmony throughout the visual design.

Basic Plane

Plane to Dot

- C85 M15 Y85 K0 / R0 G150 B85
- C85 M25 Y100 K15 / R0 G126 B54
- C50 M20 Y95 K10 / R137 G161 B44
- C65 M15 Y85 K0 / R98 G166 B78
- C20 M5 Y60 K0 / R216 G222 B126
- C0 M0 Y0 K0 / R255 G255 B255

This is the story of a person whose hand one day transforms into a blade. Faced with the potential to harm, he instead chooses to plant seedlings and nurture their growth. To visualize this narrative, the designer illustrated a variety of seedlings, imbuing them with a sense of vitality and arranging them in a field-like composition. Reflecting the character's blade-like hand, the designer shaped the quadrilateral forms to appear as if they had been precisely cut, reinforcing the thematic interplay between creation and destruction.

DA. coton design
D. Hiroko Sakai

E UNIDOTS "-REWEAVE-"

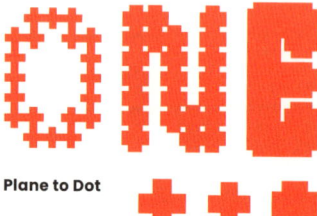

Why Plane to Dot?

The designer used basic "cross dots" to create fonts, and by translating and copying these dots, they form "planes" in the shape of letters.

Basic Plane

Plane to Dot

- C0 M90 Y100 K0 / R232 G56 B13
- C80 M35 Y5 K0 / R0 G134 B196
- C30 M35 Y60 K0 / R191 G166 B112
- C0 M0 Y0 K100 / R0 G0 B0
- ○ C0 M0 Y0 K0 / R255 G255 B255

This is the announcement visual for the one-man live performance "-reweave-" by Japanese music artist UNIDOTS, held in October 2023. Drawing inspiration from the title, the designer abstracted the letters to evoke the concept of stitches, transforming them into a graphic design.

AD. D. TD. Zin Nagao
CL. UNIDOTS

UNDERSTANDING ADHD[1]

Why Plane to Dot?

To express the restlessness and agitation associated with ADHD, the designer used dense, irregular dots to create a face without eyes, nose, or mouth. The absence of these features creates an unsettling feeling. Up close, the composition appears abstract, but from a distance, its form becomes more concrete—allowing the intended message to change depending on the viewer's perspective.

This poster was created to promote awareness and understanding of ADHD. To visually represent hyperactivity, a collection of bold lines comes together to form a single face. Aiming for a balance between abstraction and figuration, the design seeks to express the movement of the mind.

1. ADHD (Attention-Deficit/Hyperactivity Disorder) is a neurodevelopmental condition characterized by inattention, impulsivity, and hyperactivity, affecting focus and self-regulation.

DA. DENTSU INC.
D. Taichi Tamaki

Basic Plane / **Plane to Dot**

- C45 M45 Y5 K0 / R154 G142 B189
- C40 M65 Y40 K0 / R168 G108 B122
- C95 M75 Y45 K10 / R9 G70 B104
- C60 M30 Y25 K0 / R112 G155 B175
- C25 M5 Y90 K0 / R207 G214 B41
- C55 M90 Y80 K30 / R110 G43 B46
- C95 M80 Y10 K0 / R19 G66 B144
- C90 M50 Y90 K20 / R0 G94 B60
- C0 M0 Y0 K100 / R0 G0 B0
- C0 M0 Y0 K0 / R255 G255 B255

▤ AVANT GROUP

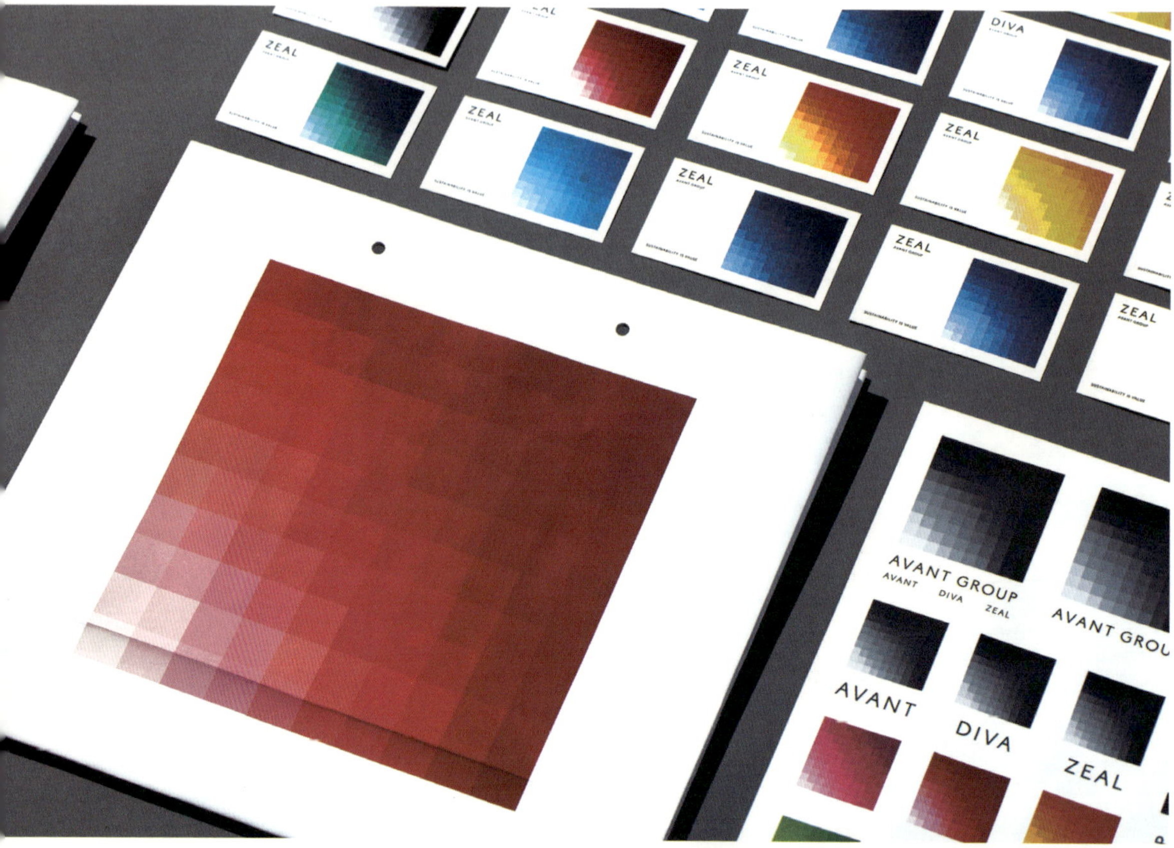

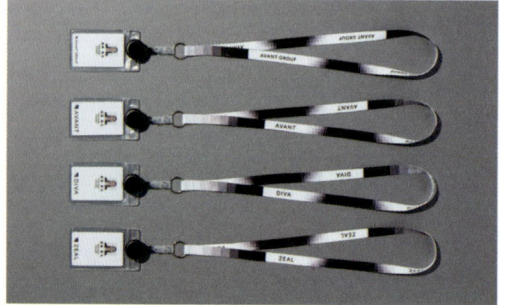

Avant Group is a company focused on promoting sustainable business management through the "popularization of business information" and the implementation of a company-wide management model powered by information technology. To accurately convey the company's vision of "creating a century-old enterprise," the designer crafted the logo using 100 grid squares, with a gradient bar chart effect representing the "popularization of business information." This new logo is not just a symbol, but a vivid representation of the company's core values through its design.

D. Miharu Matsunaga (Hami)
CL. Avant Group

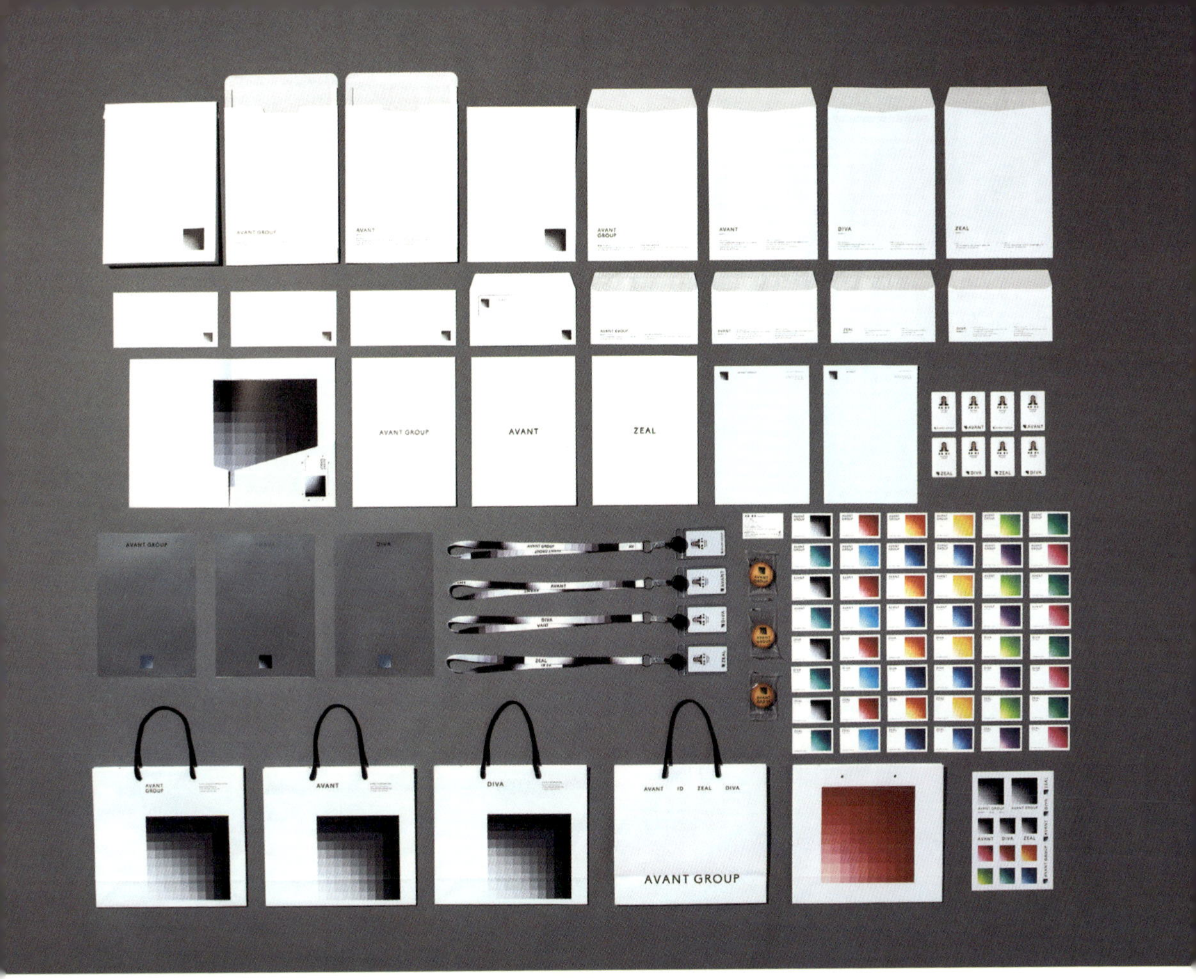

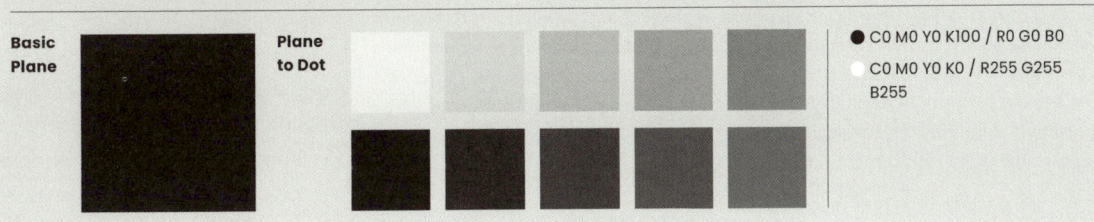

Why Plane to Dot?

This design focuses on using a simple visual language to precisely represent the company's philosophy. The logo employs a gradient bar chart effect to clearly illustrate the "popularization of business information." The bright colors extending from the bottom-left corner symbolize the company's commitment to serving society. Given that the company's operations rely on diverse team collaboration, the design incorporates the primary colors of both pigment and light, blending into black and white, symbolizing the complementary and harmonious unity of team members' personalities.

While the logo itself is designed in black and white, the business cards feature a colorful version, allowing employees to showcase their individuality through card colors, creating an organic fusion of corporate identity and personal expression.

- C0 M0 Y0 K100 / R0 G0 B0
- C0 M0 Y0 K0 / R255 G255 B255

Basic Plane

Plane to Dot

GENDER ISSUES FACING MEN IN JAPAN 2023

The "Gender Map" is a thinking tool released by Dentsu in *Gender Issues Facing Men in Japan 2023 (Vol. 2)*, aimed at addressing gender disparity. With Japan's gender equality still ranked low globally, the designer created this map to integrate data on the social challenges faced by men.

As a core concept of DEI, gender equality seeks to eliminate gender-based inequality and discrimination. Traditionally, gender issues have been seen as affecting only women, but masculinity studies show that "traditional masculinity" is creating struggles for men and, in some cases, contributing to women's challenges. In Nordic countries, where gender equality is strong, the focus has shifted from "women's economic independence" to the effects of traditional masculinity. Similarly, in English-speaking countries, men's gender issues are gaining significant academic and social attention.

D. Miharu Matsunaga (Hami)
CL. Gender Issues Facing Men in Japan 2023

Why Plane to Dot?

To create a soft visual perception, this project introduces circular elements and uses circles to construct human figures. Focusing on reshaping men's gender perception, it begins with the concept of "dialogue and reflection," using the "mirror" as a central motif. Gender identity is deeply influenced by one's

ジェンダー課題チャート vol.2 男性版

upbringing and nationality, and understanding social roles requires profound self-reflection, which the design aims to convey. Additionally, to address issues arising from "toxic masculinity" in a gentler way, the design moves away from the stereotypical "blue = male" color scheme, opting instead for more soothing and inclusive colors.

- C10 M10 Y15 K0 / R234 G229 B218
- C50 M30 Y55 K0 / R144 G160 B125
- C0 M35 Y70 K0 / R248 G184 B86
- C0 M25 Y25 K0 / R249 G208 B186
- C0 M55 Y90 K0 / R241 G142 B29
- C70 M30 Y50 K0 / R83 G146 B134
- C23 M13 Y22 K0 / R206 G212 B200

9TH INTERNATIONAL ORGAN COMPETITION MUSASHINO-TOKYO

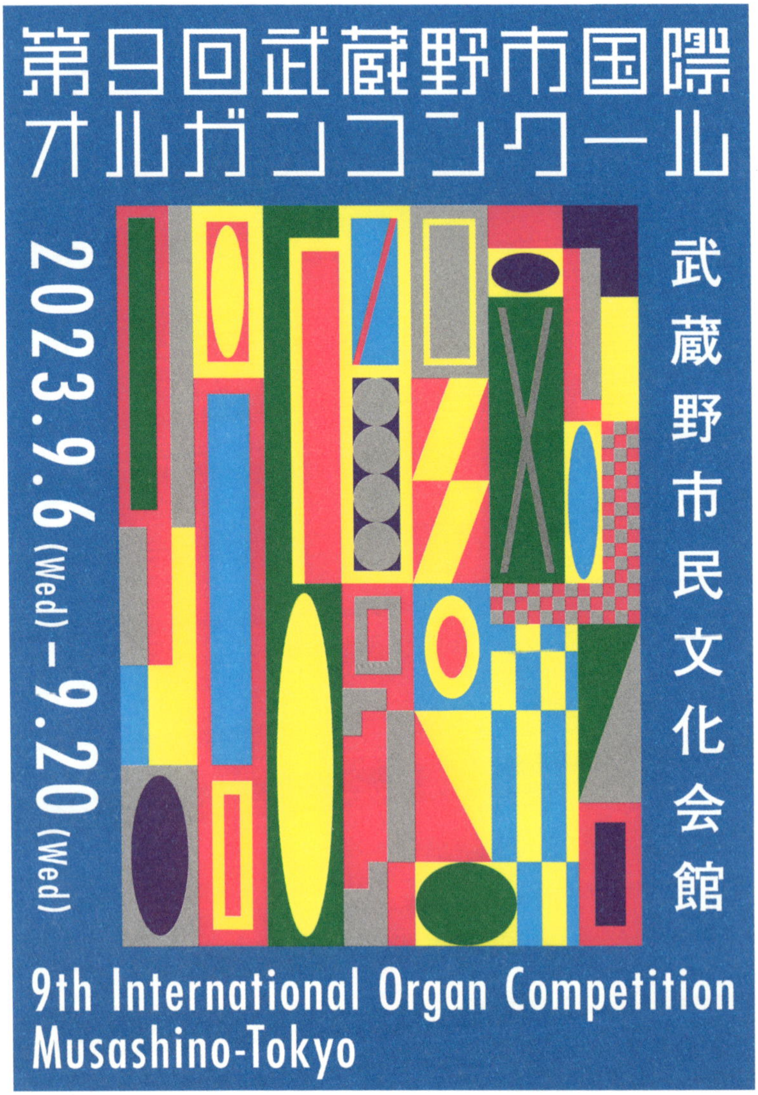

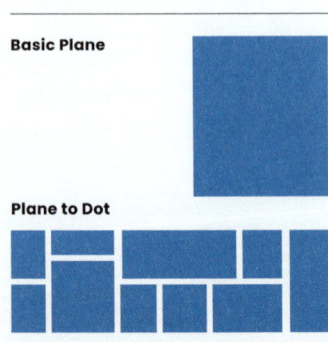

Why Plane to Dot?

The concept is to represent various tones through diverse geometric shapes. Achieving a sense of unity was essential. For instance, the designer felt that mixing hand-drawn elements with geometric forms could weaken the overall impact. To maintain clarity and strength, a flat, two-dimensional composition was chosen. The main visual graphics are composed of fragmented images, expressing cultural diversity. Additionally, the placement of Japanese and English text in contrasting positions creates a sense of rhythm, further enhancing the design's visual harmony.

Basic Plane

Plane to Dot

- C0 M100 Y0 K0 / R228 G0 B127
- C75 M100 Y0 K0 / R96 G25 B134
- C90 M40 Y0 K0 / R0 G121 B195
- C90 M0 Y100 K0 / R0 G144 B58
- C85 M0 Y0 K0 / R0 G171 B235
- C0 M0 Y0 K30 / R201 G202 B202
- C0 M0 Y100 K0 / R255 G241 B0
- C0 M0 Y0 K100 / R0 G0 B0
- C0 M0 Y0 K0 / R255 G255 B255

The designer oversaw the overall design for the 9th International Organ Competition Musashino-Tokyo, a world-renowned event celebrating pipe organ music. He vividly recalled being overwhelmed by the sheer power of the instrument upon hearing it for the first time.

To translate that emotional experience into design, he crafted the main visual using geometric forms to represent the organ's rich and varied tones. Additionally, as an international competition, the design also symbolizes the coming together of diverse individuals from around the world.

D. Tadashi Ueda
CL. The Musashino Foundation for Culture and Lifelong Learning

SELECTED WORKS FROM MUSASHINO ART UNIVERSITY DEGREE SHOW 2019

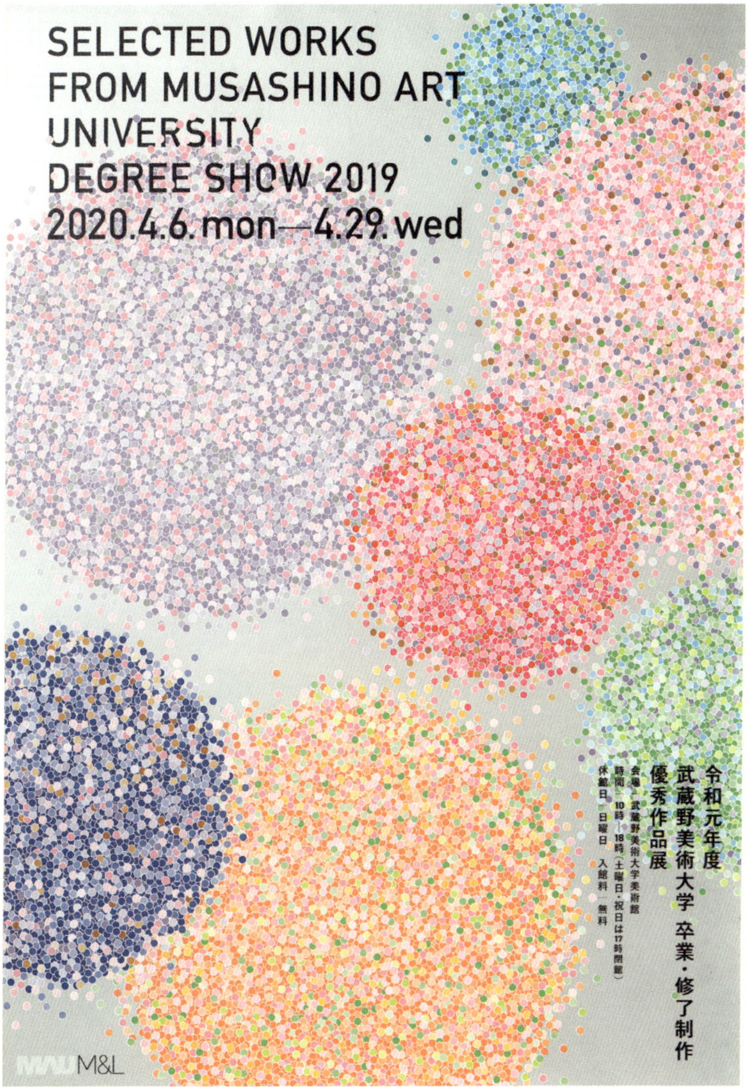

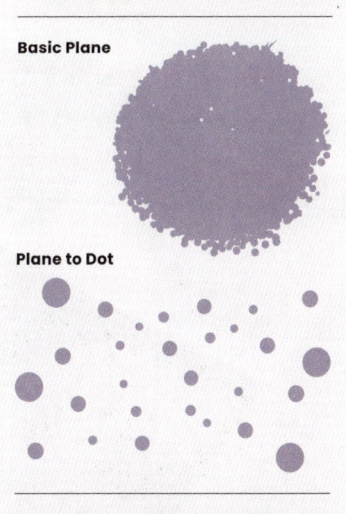

Why Plane to Dot?

The dots represent individual students, coming together to form a circle—an expression of how individuals unite to shape groups and society. The circle, a flawless and ideal form, symbolizes the inherent value and uniqueness of each individual life.

Basic Plane

Plane to Dot

- C45 M45 Y5 K0 / R154 G142 B189
- C0 M25 Y0 K0 / R249 G211 B227
- C0 M65 Y5 K0 / R236 G122 B167
- C90 M65 Y0 K0 / R13 G87 B167
- C0 M60 Y75 K0 / R240 G132 B65
- C65 M5 Y85 K0 / R93 G177 B80
- C0 M0 Y0 K100 / R0 G0 B0
- C20 M10 Y10 K0 / R212 G221 B225
- C0 M0 Y0 K0 / R255 G255 B255

This is the visual design for Musashino Art University's 2019 Selected Works.

DA. Yuuri Mikami Design Office
D. Yuuri Mikami
CL. Musashino Art University

ALPHABET KNOT

This work presents alphabets inspired by traditional Japanese patterns that have been used for centuries, with the goal of blending cultural harmony into a modern, graphical expression. To create the six distinct patterns, the designer selected a symbol from each of twelve classic patterns and paired two matching shapes together. The resulting installation was then exhibited at "TDSNBXDXD" (DICE&DICE, supported by TOKYO DESIGN STUDIO New Balance) in Fukuoka.

AD. D. TD. MD. Zin Nagao
PT. Daisuke Akashi
CL. Dice&Dice "TDSNBXDXD"

1."Bundou Tsunagi" + "Seigaiha"

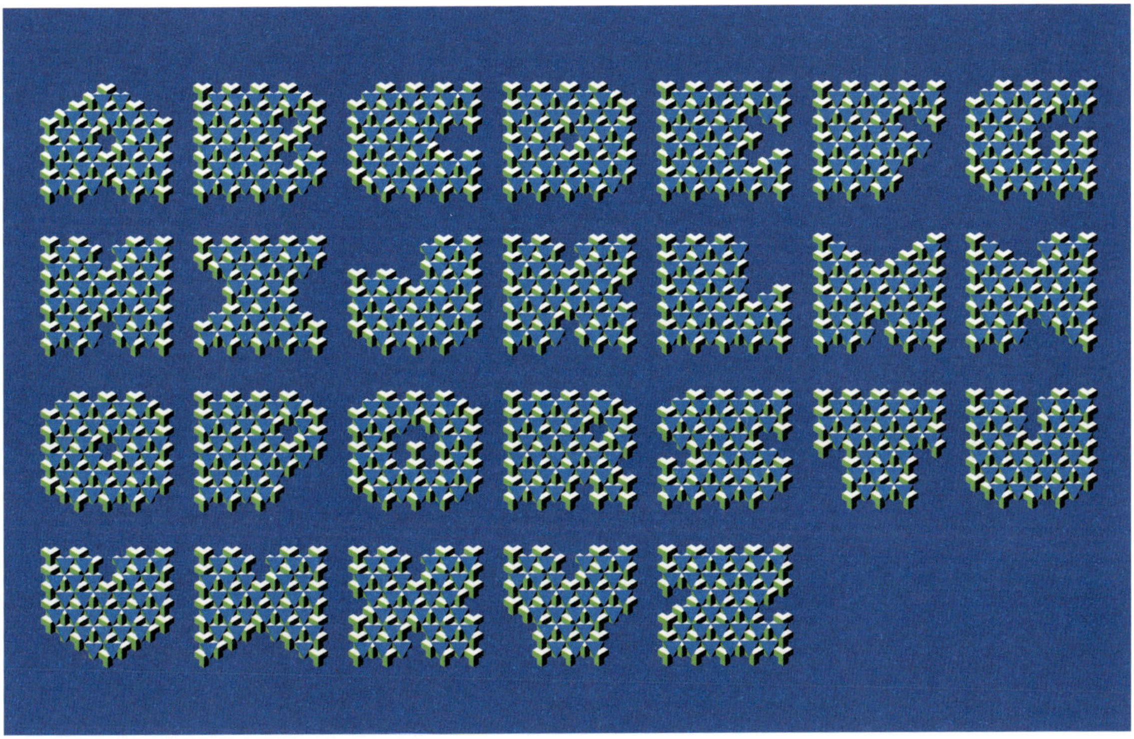

2."Higaki" + "Kouji Tsunagi"

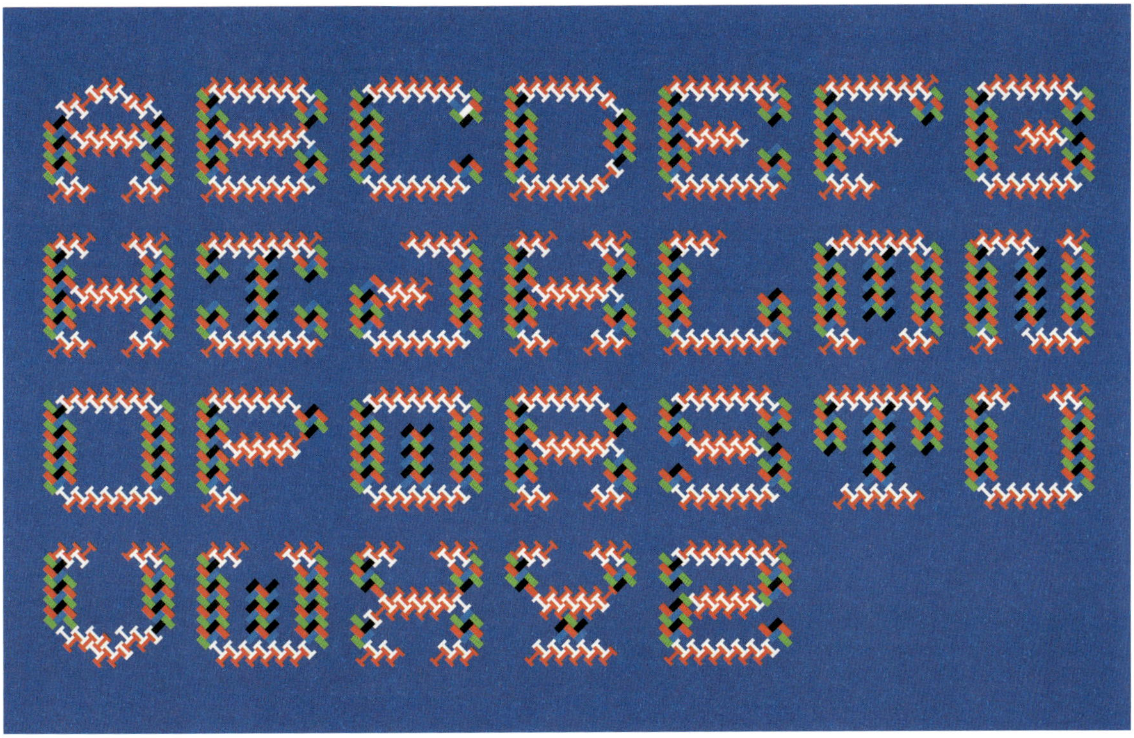

3."Shippou" + "Amimemon"

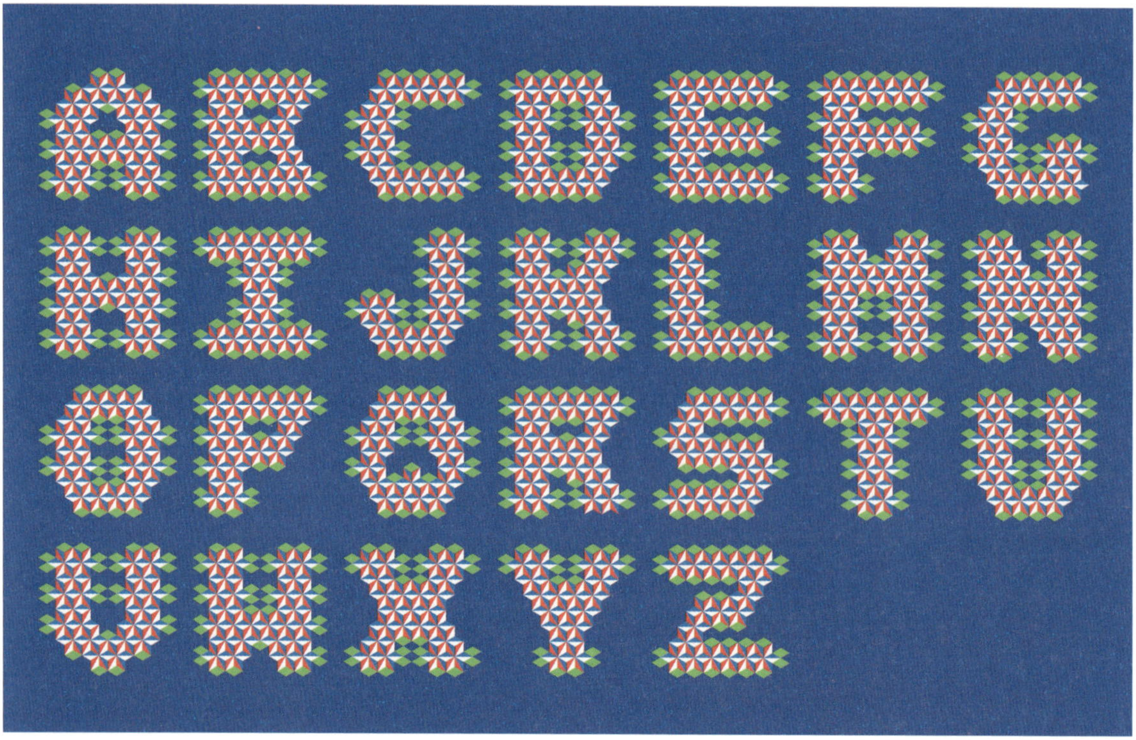

4."Asanoha" + "Hishi"

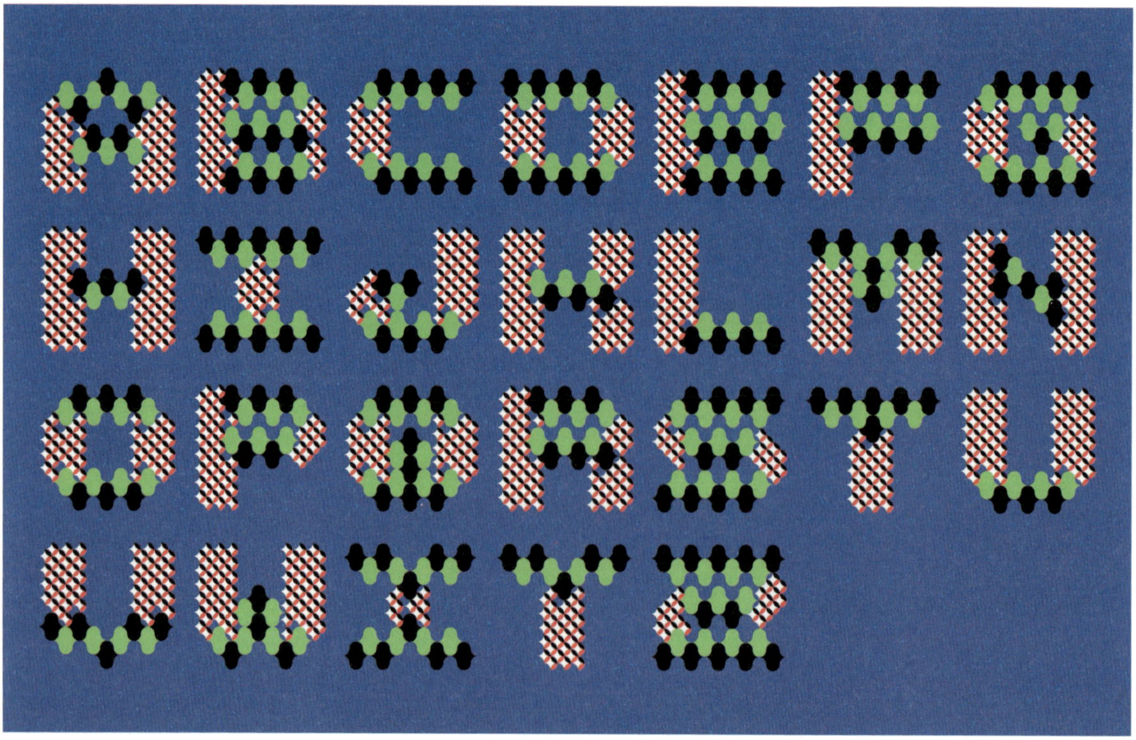

5. "Bishamon Kikkou" + "Uroko"

6. "Mutsude Manji" + "Kikkou"

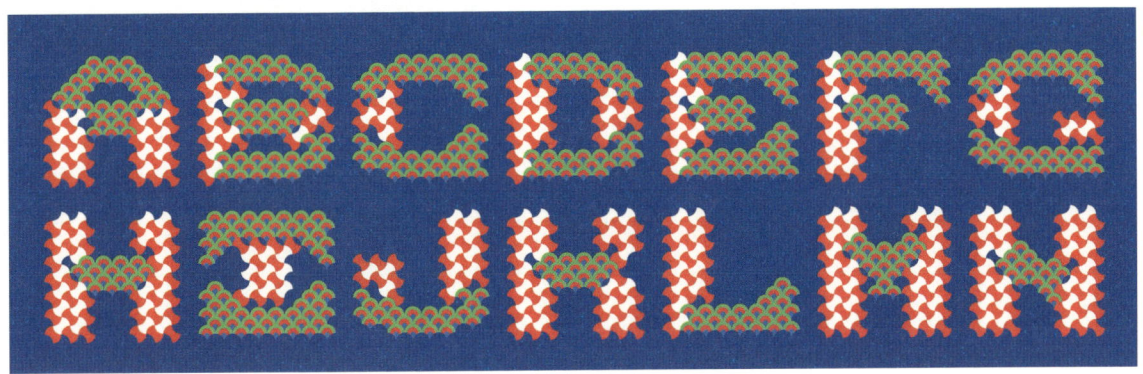

Why Plane to Dot?

The designer cleverly incorporated traditional Japanese patterns into the font design, achieving a perfect blend of traditional patterns and modern technology. The small graphics that make up traditional Japanese patterns are woven together to form a unique and interesting text system.

Basic Plane

Plane to Dot

- C0 M100 Y100 K0 / R230 G0 B18
- C60 M5 Y100 K0 / R112 G181 B44
- C95 M40 Y0 K0 / R0 G119 B194
- C100 M75 Y0 K0 / R0 G71 B157
- C0 M0 Y0 K100 / R0 G0 B0
- C0 M0 Y0 K0 / R255 G255 B255

DOT, LINE, AND PLANE

● **Stringing and Extension:** Dots, lines, and planes are connected to each other, which can form a continuous combination of images. This extended relationship not only strengthens the integrity of the picture but also creates a sense of flow and vitality.

● **Surrounding and Encircling:** Dots, lines, and planes surround and enclose each other and can form closed paths or forms, such as circles or other geometric structures. This enclosure brings a visual sense of stability and cohesion.

● **Scattering and Clustering:** Dots, lines, and planes can either exist independently in the picture in a dispersed manner, showing an open and light posture; or they can be gathered together to form a difference in density, thus presenting a rich visual hierarchy and tension.

● **Connection and Breakage:** Dots, lines, and planes can be connected together to form an organic network structure. Through the treatment of deliberate breaks and gaps, a sense of distance and tension can be created, bringing visual impact.

● **Repetition and Rhythm:** Repeated arrangement of dots, lines, and planes can show a sense of rhythm in the picture, making the visual experience more orderly and musical.

EXPLORING GEOMETRIC EXPRESSION IN TYPE DESIGN

ZIN NAGAO

Type Designer
Graphic Designer

Zin Nagao, born in Japan and currently based in Fukuoka, is a designer specializing in typeface design, graphic design, and motion graphics. His works explore new expressions and possibilities of letters through experimental typefaces and letter-based graphics. With a focus on conveying the joy and playfulness of typography, Nagao aims to engage viewers with the visual and emotional potential of letters. He has been recognized with the TDC Ascenders 2023 and Young Guns 21 awards.

○ If we treat letters as graphic elements, can typography open up new possibilities? For designer Zin Nagao, basic elements like dots, lines, and planes form the foundation of his creative process. Through their combination, he reimagines the boundaries of letterforms. In this interview, Nagao shares his playful and experimental approach to using dots, lines, and planes, challenging the legibility of traditional letterforms and transforming each character into an expressive graphic element. He also reflects on his design journey, noting how his past fascination with Japanese retro video games has shaped his works. Looking ahead, he envisions new intersections between type, motion, and sound— exploring fresh possibilities for type in multi-sensory environments.

REDEFINING TYPOGRAPHY THROUGH GEOMETRIC EXPRESSION

● **In the world of type design, where legibility often takes precedence, however, Zin Nagao brings a fresh and unconventional approach by focusing on the artistic potential of basic geometric elements: dots, lines, and planes.** His approach proposes a new, unconventional method that breaks away from the norms of traditional typography, opening up fresh avenues for creative expression.

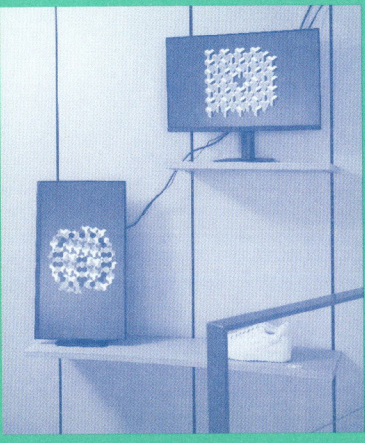

Fig. 1 Alphabet Knot, designed by Zin Nagao, 2023.

● **Nagao's approach to type design stands apart from the creation of standard fonts.** He openly states, "I've never wanted to design a standard typeface." Instead, he aims to push the boundaries of typography, elevating letters from purely functional forms into dynamic, expressive characters. Recently, he has been experimenting with the font creation software Glyphs, incorporating color data directly into the font itself. This exploration brings a unique personality and artistic flair to his works, turning each letter into a bold graphic statement. Merging graphic and type design, his works use geometric construction and an avant-garde visual language to prompt viewers to reconsider the role of typography in visual communication.

A PROCESS OF REPETITION AND DISCOVERY

● In his creative process, Zin Nagao avoids overthinking in the initial stages. "I don't typically start with rough sketches. Instead, I jump straight into the computer and begin creating shapes using basic forms like circles, squares, and triangles," he explains. **He describes his design process as a continuous cycle of trial and error—constantly creating and refining until he arrives at a visual outcome that resonates with him.** "Sometimes, it works with a simple composition, but other times it doesn't. When that happens, I break the rules and search for new visual values. It's a process of repetition and discovery."

● These geometric elements in type design do more than just create visually interesting shapes. According to Nagao, the purpose is to blur the lines between typefaces and graphic design. Letters, he believes, are not merely carriers of

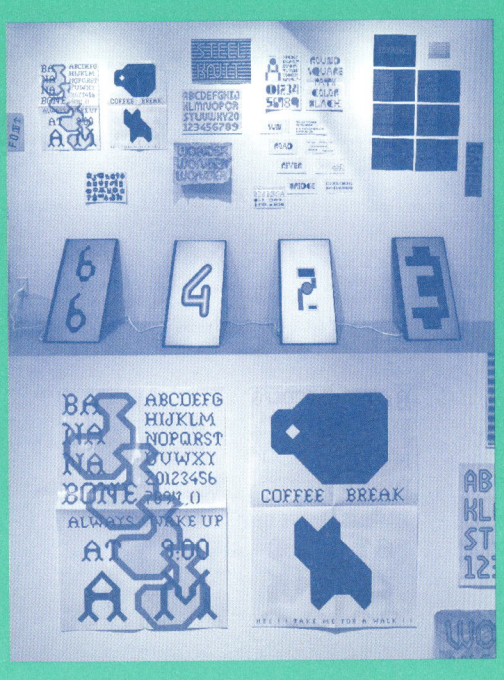

Fig. 2 Exhibition "Lucky Letter" at Ao-Hata Bookstore, 2023.

information—they can also be graphic elements that communicate through color and form. By approaching type from the perspective of dots, lines, and planes, designers can create typographic forms that open up new possibilities. While legibility still matters, this approach allows for a broader range of creative expression. Nagao is convinced that typography has the potential to go beyond its traditional function and become a powerful graphic tool.

INSPIRATION AND PERSONAL EXPRESSION

● Zin Nagao's design approach is shaped by a wide range of influences, from iconic figures in design history to personal life experiences. One key influence in his early years was Dutch designer Wim Crouwel. "I remember finding Crouwel's books in a secondhand bookshop during my student days," he recalls. "I was fascinated by his works, unsure if it was letters or graphic design." While Crouwel had a significant impact on him, his deep love for retro video games plays a central role in his creative process. "Playing games fostered my habit of creating objects like puzzles and instilled a deep sense of color," he says. This playful, puzzle-like approach is a core aspect of his design philosophy.

● **While Nagao is a Japanese designer, his cultural background subtly informs his works, even though he doesn't deliberately pursue a distinctively "Japanese style."** He acknowledges that elements of Japanese culture, particularly retro video games, have influenced his design sensibilities to a large extent. However, he feels less connected to certain contemporary trends in Japanese design, such as an emphasis on negative space or the use of surreal illustrations. In contrast, Nagao leans more toward typographic practices, often

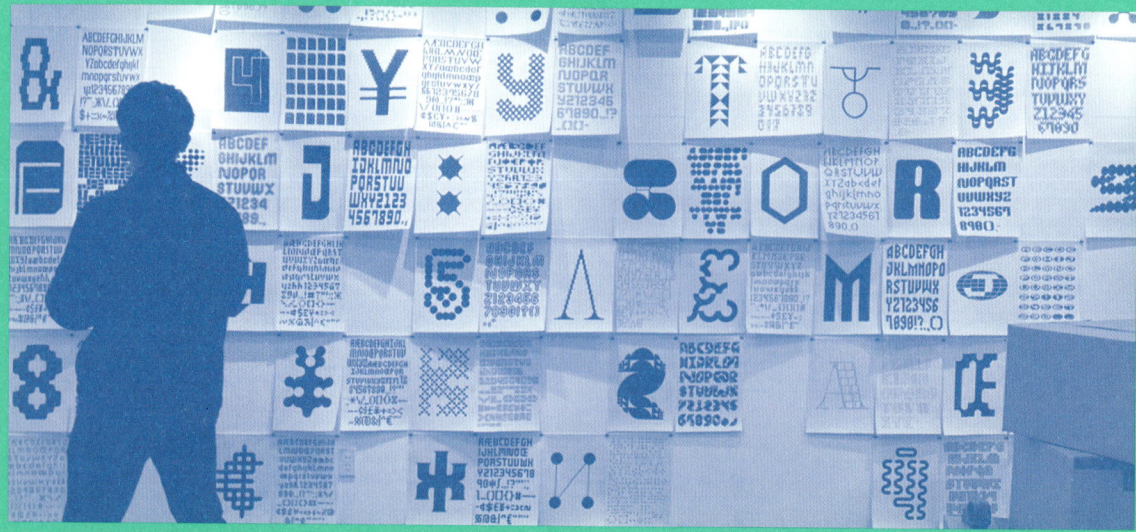

Fig. 3 Zin Nagao Exhibition *POLTERTYPE*, 2023.

"cramming everything in," leaving little to no white space—a method he considers more traditional, or even old-school, in the context of Japanese design.

EVOLUTION AND FUTURE DIRECTIONS

● Reflecting on his development as a designer, Zin Nagao recalls his early student days, when type design felt both daunting and highly specialized. "There were no teachers who could guide me, so I taught myself by creating letters as geometric puzzles," he says. This self-directed learning approach paid off when he showcased his works at a typography conference in Tokyo. While some Japanese designers critiqued his rapid typeface experiments, international attendees were more receptive. They told him, "It's interesting, and there are surprisingly few people who make typefaces like this. You should do more of this." That encouragement gave him the confidence to embrace and develop his unique style.

Fig. 4 Zin Nagao Exhibition *POLTERTYPE*, 2023.

● **Looking ahead, Nagao is eager to expand his work further into new realms.** "I want to create typefaces that integrate more with music and motion graphics," he says. His goal is to push the boundaries of type design, exploring new intersections with digital art forms and expanding the possibilities of how type can be experienced in a multi-sensory context.

269

COLOR TYPE DIARY

When Zin Nagao is walking outside, he always takes notes, observing things like grass, flowers, ground, fences, and signs, thinking, "It would be interesting to create something like this, using these colors and shapes as inspiration." He often pulls out his computer to experiment with these ideas on the spot. Additionally, his long-time love for retro games has had a strong influence on his graphics and color choices.

AD. TD. D. Zin Nagao

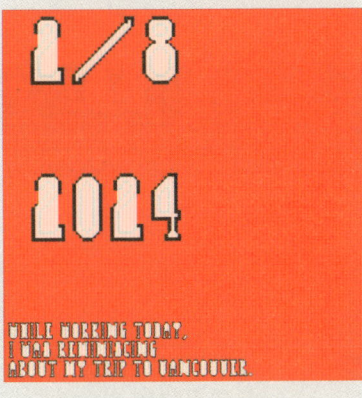
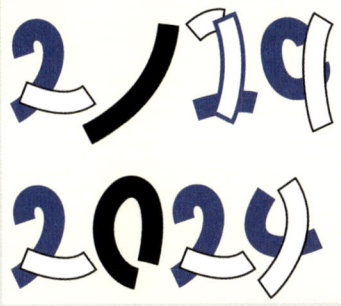

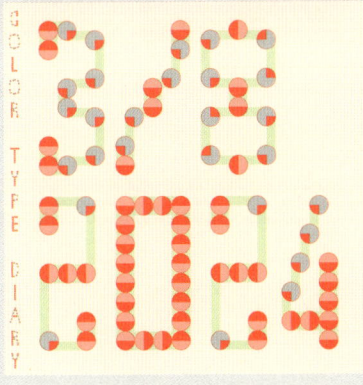

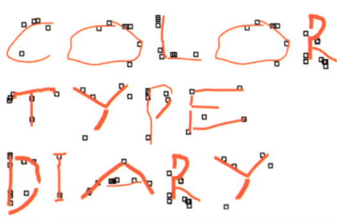

● ◆ ■ Why Dot, Line, and Plane?

The designer used different design techniques, combining various dot, line, and plane elements, forming many different styles and fonts. He practices his type design skills using this method, which ultimately leads him to develop his own unique type design style.

- ● C0 M0 Y0 K60 / R137 G137 B137
- ● C0 M100 Y100 K0 / R230 G0 B18
- ● C75 M55 Y0 K0 / R75 G108 B179
- ● C75 M0 Y75 K0 / R19 G174 B103
- ● C25 M80 Y0 K0 / R192 G77 B191
- ● C0 M0 Y0 K100 / R0 G0 B0
- ● C65 M35 Y70 K0 / R105 G141 B98
- ● C25 M0 Y50 K0 / R204 G225 B152
- ● C80 M55 Y100 K30 / R52 G43 B40
- ● C65 M65 Y95 K35 / R86 G72 B36
- ● C10 M0 Y50 K0 / R238 G239 B153
- ● C0 M10 Y10 K0 / R253 G237 B228
- ● C0 M50 Y30 K0 / R242 G156 B151
- ● C0 M95 Y100 K0 / R231 G36 B16
- ● C30 M25 Y20 K0 / R189 G187 B191

Basic Dot, Line, and Plane

ᴮ UNIDENTIFIED FLYING ALPHABET

Why Dot, Line, and Plane?

This alphabet is composed of intriguing shapes made from colored lines and graphic objects. By combining lines and planes, complex forms are created, adding depth and visual interest.

These alphabet stickers were designed for the "STICKER STAND" event, a sticker project organized by the Tokyo shop and café THINK OF THINGS. The designer wanted to create something people could enjoy visually, not just for reading, so he designed them to blur the line between "alphabet" and "shape."

D. Zin Nagao
CL. THINK OF THINGS

- C0 M5 Y95 K0 / R255 G234 B0
- C0 M90 Y100 K0 / R232 G56 B13
- C80 M10 Y20 K0 / R0 G164 B197
- C0 M0 Y0 K100 / R0 G0 B0

COPY CORNER COLLABORATION

These are collaborations with the COPY CORNER printing label. Recently, the designer has become interested in creating "color fonts"—typefaces that incorporate two or more colors into the font data. To explore this concept, the designer decided to experiment with separating the letters into colors for lithograph printing. The result includes a clock that lets you experience the fun of letters and printing, a notebook for designing typefaces, and a puzzle that can never be completed, as the words are always misspelled.

AD. D. Zin Nagao
PRT. COPY CORNER
CL. COPY CORNER

◉ ◇ ■ Why Dot, Line, and Plane?

The designer is good at using the elements of dots, lines, and planes in typeface design, and emphasizing the graphic structure with color.

Basic Dot, Line, and Plane

- C0 M75 Y80 K0 / R235 G97 B51
- C0 M25 Y5 K0 / R249 G210 B220
- C65 M0 Y75 K0 / R88 G183 B101
- C40 M0 Y5 K0 / R160 G216 B239
- C75 M25 Y0 K0 / R26 G150 B213

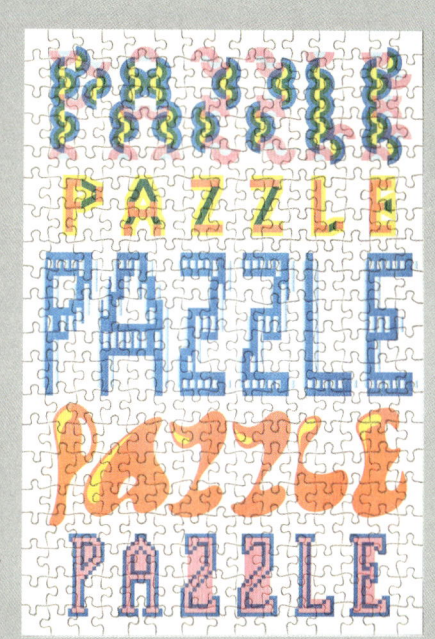

WWW MONTHLY SCHEDULE ANIMATION 2022–2023

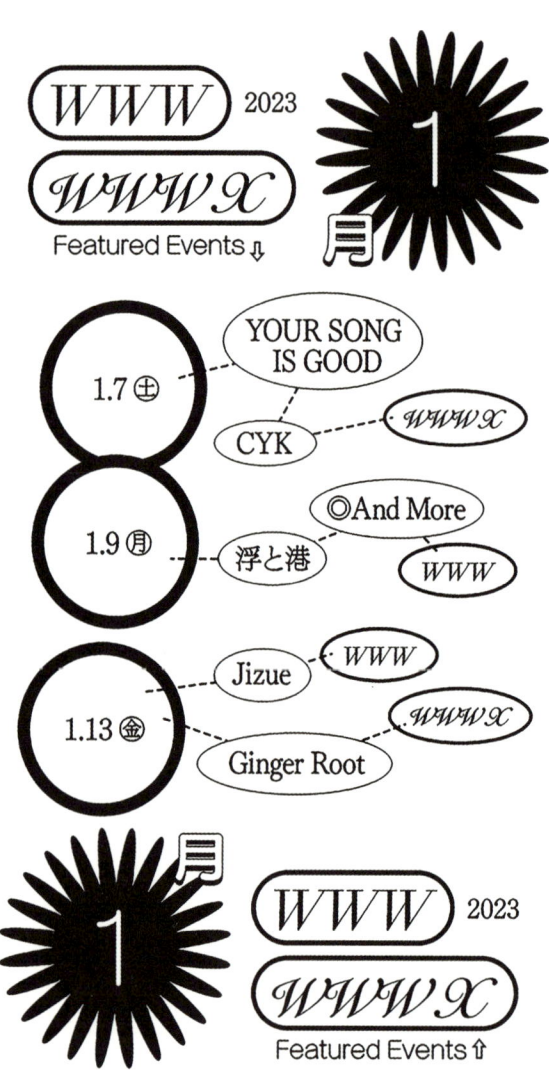

This project involved the design and animation of the monthly schedule for WWW, a live house in Shibuya, covering one year from November 2022 to October 2023. The design was completely reimagined from the previous version, introducing a new format where each artist is listed with motion graphics in a vertical layout. The central symbol combines the sensory experience of music with the monthly numeral design, serving as the monthly key visual.

AD. MD. D. Zin Nagao
CL. WWW

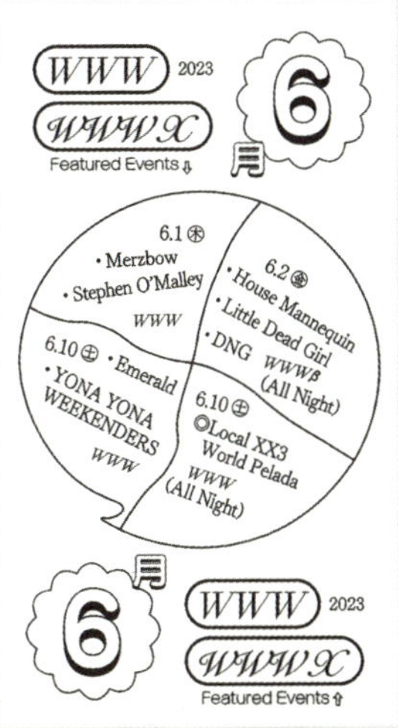

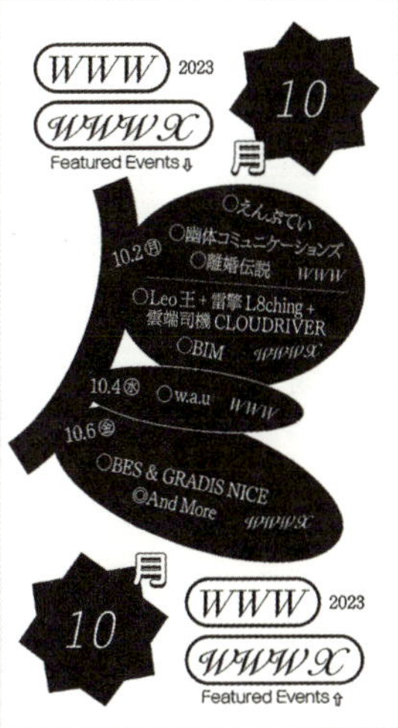

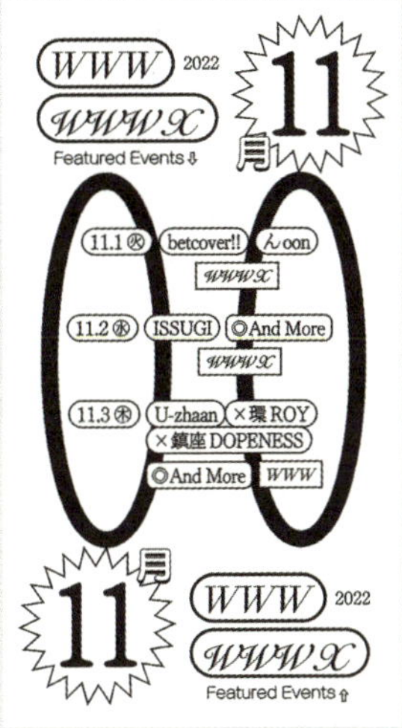

🟢 🔷 🟩 Why Dot, Line, and Plane?

The designer used the most basic elements of dots, lines, and planes to create the main visual, and was able to provide a rich visual experience using only black and white colors. Furthermore, since the project was displayed on an online platform, the designer also created an animation to enhance its dissemination.

Basic Dot, Line, and Plane

○ C0 M0 Y0 K0 / R255 G255 B255

● C0 M0 Y0 K100 / R0 G0 B0

YON YON

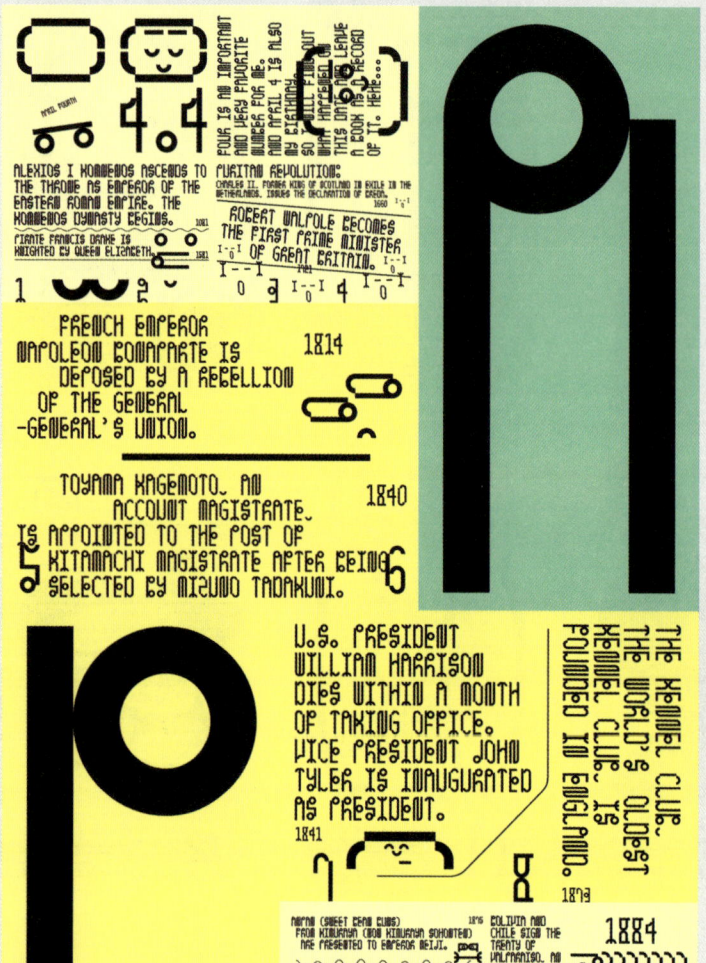
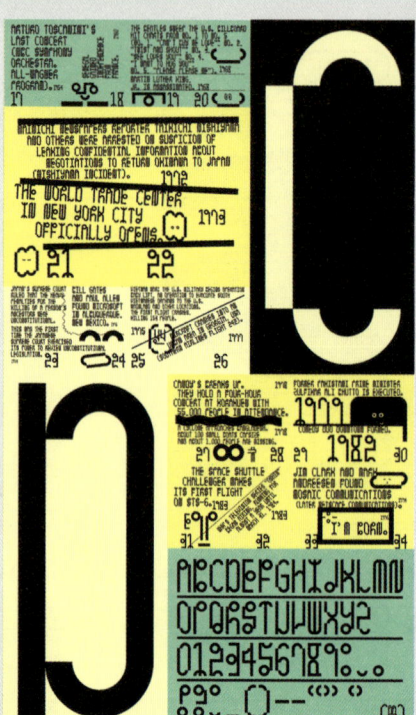

Why Dot, Line, and Plane?

The strokes of Korean characters can be broken down into basic shapes. Designers extracted the strokes of the characters and recombined them to form this unique set of English letters.

Basic Dot, Line, and Plane

- C5 M0 Y40 K0 / R248 G245 B176
- C5 M0 Y75 K0 / R250 G240 B84
- C55 M0 Y50 K0 / R120 G196 B191
- C0 M0 Y0 K100 / R0 G0 B0

Inspired by Korean characters, the designer created this typeface by dividing it into four parts and incorporating the mysterious and charming geometric shapes of Hangeul into European text. He named it "YON YON" (4/4 in Japanese) as a personal reward for himself on April 4, his birthday. A type specimen booklet was also produced to showcase the design.

AD. TD. D. Zin Nagao

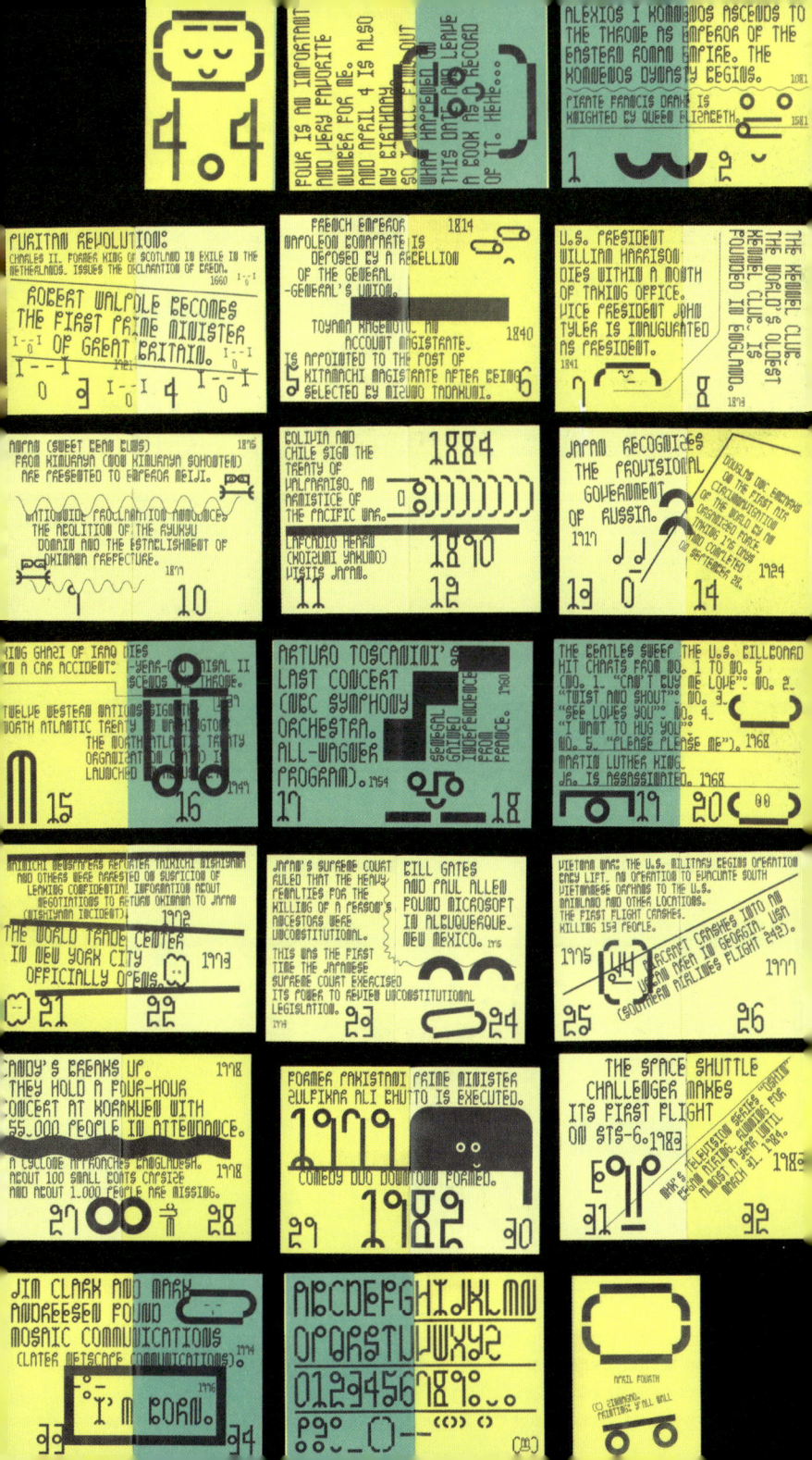

🅐 THE THREE LANGUAGES

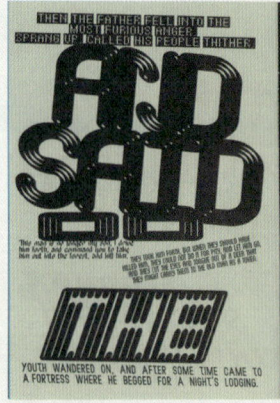
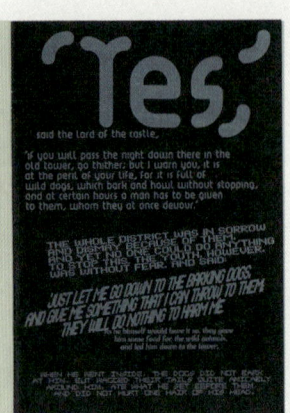

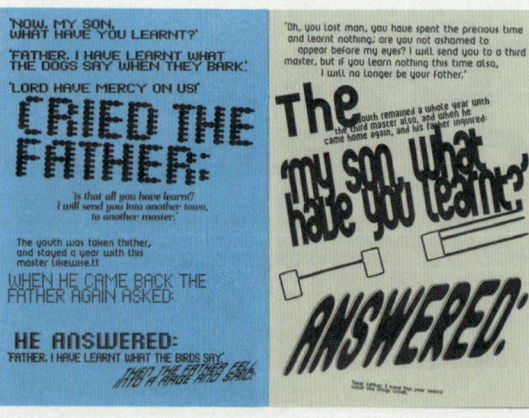

The designer created a book using his own typeface for Grimm's Fairy Tales: *The Three Languages*. It's a short yet dynamic story, full of twists and a sense of speed, about a young man who learns to understand the languages of animals. To capture the story's lively tempo, the designer used only letters to express this energy, changing the typeface for each sentence and word. He also laid out the pages in an unformatted, free-flowing style based entirely on his creative ideas.

AD. TD. D. Zin Nagao

Why Dot, Line, and Plane?

The designer used multiple unique fonts of his own design to typeset this book, perfectly interpreting the theme of "Three Languages." The typesetting method also abandoned tradition. Opening each page, one can intuitively feel the dots formed by letters, the lines formed by sentences, and planes formed by paragraphs from a visual perspective. It is very novel and experimental.

Basic Dot, Line, and Plane

- C70 M20 Y10 K0 / R61 G161 B205
- C30 M20 Y30 K0 / R190 G194 B179
- C75 M60 Y50 K5 / R82 G98 B111
- C0 M0 Y0 K100 / R0 G0 B0

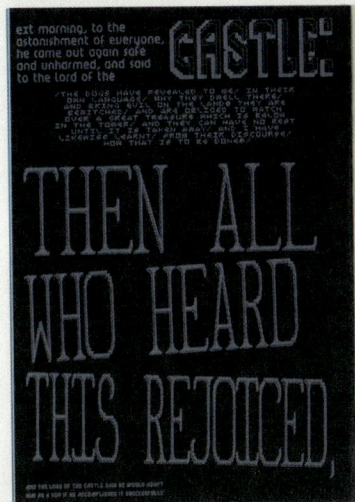

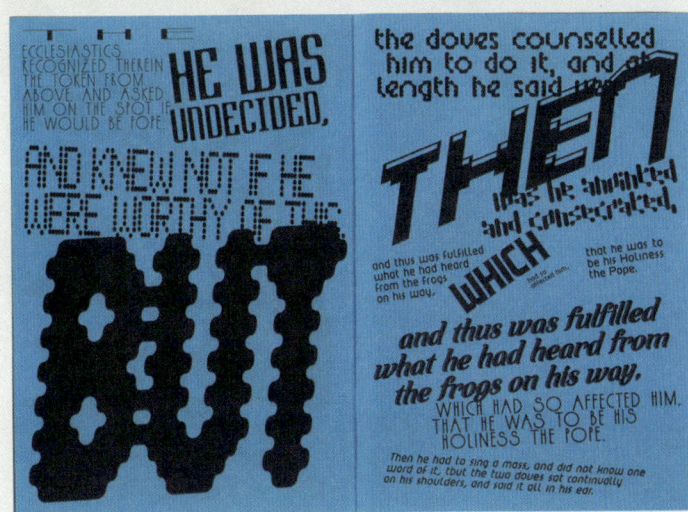

NEW JAPAN PHILHARMONIC CHAMBER MUSIC SERIES

A series of brochure designs for the chamber orchestra performances of the New Japan Philharmonic.

DA. Nippon Design Center
AD. Daigo Daikoku
CL. New Japan Philharmonic

Why Dot, Line, and Plane?

By combining simple geometric shapes and text, the designer created a monochrome graphic that evokes a sense of "sound."

Basic Dot, Line, and Plane

● C0 M0 Y0 K100 / R0 G0 B0
○ C0 M0 Y0 K0 / R255 G255 B255

■ SUPER PLANTS

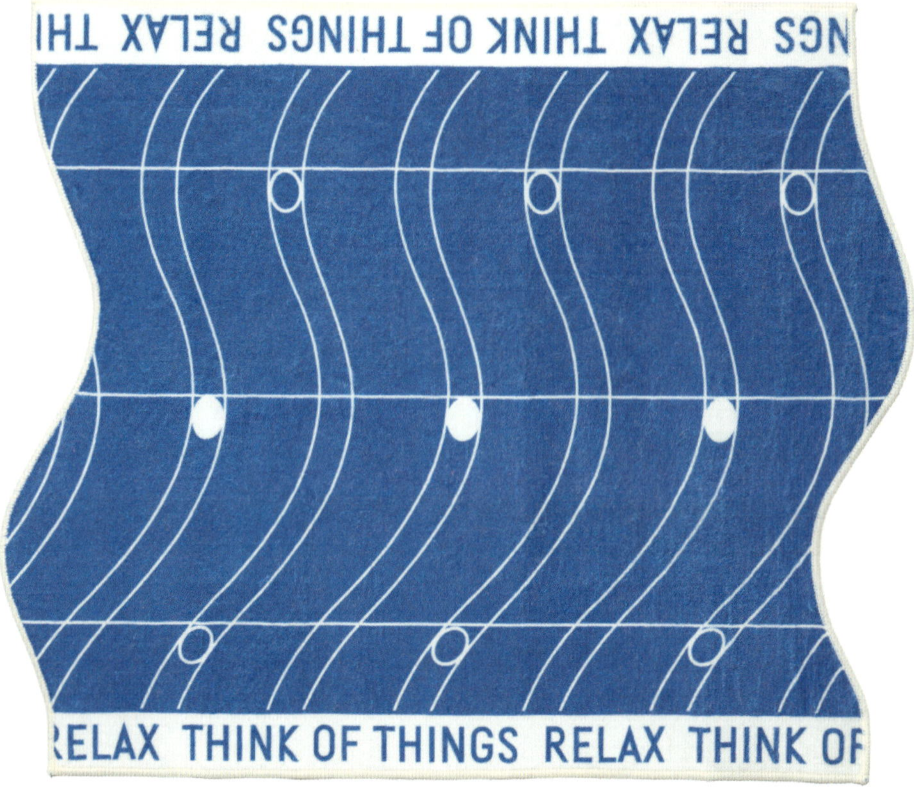

This product is a collaboration between Kokuyo's THINK OF THINGS and SUPER PLANTS, a Beijing-based brand that promotes plant care as a form of self-relaxation. SUPER PLANTS emphasizes a fun and simple approach to foster a relaxing environment.

AD. D. Aki Kanai / Taku Sasaki
D. Xiaojun Shi
CL. KOKUYO Co.,Ltd. & SUPER PLANTS

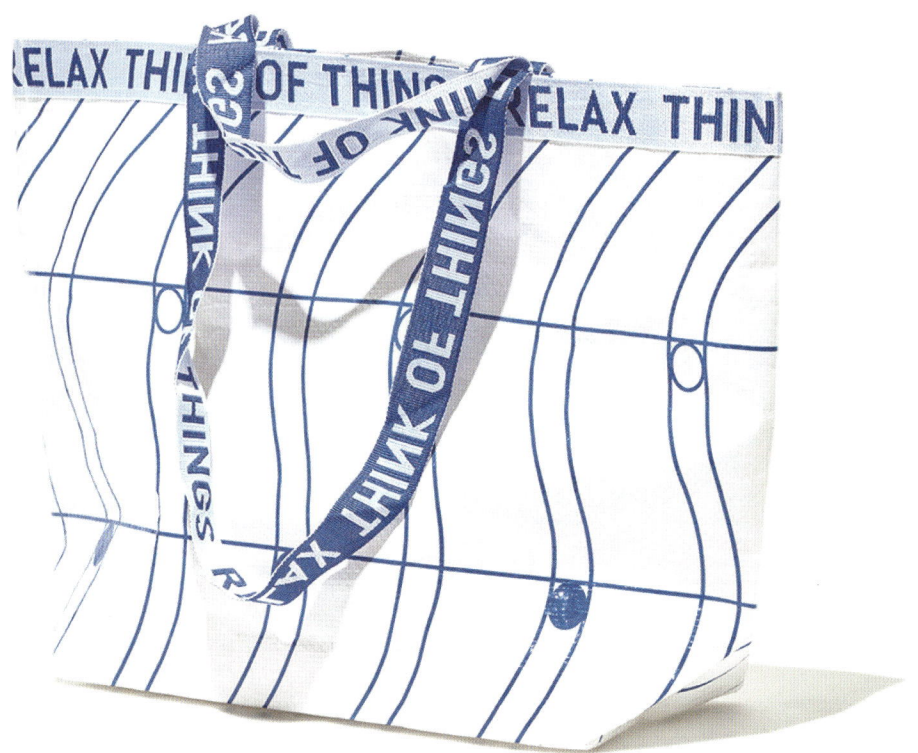

 **Why Dot, Line, and Plane?**

The graphics, inspired by THINK OF THINGS' signature use of compact lines and planes, are reinterpreted with wavy distortions and organic shapes to harmonize with the soothing atmosphere of the collaboration.

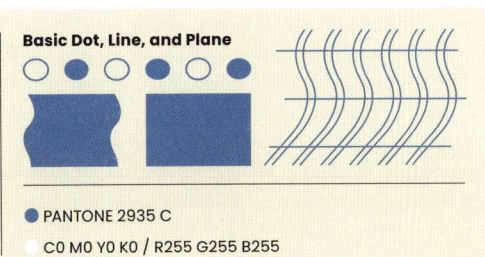

Basic Dot, Line, and Plane

● PANTONE 2935 C
○ C0 M0 Y0 K0 / R255 G255 B255

🌷 VASE OF FLOWERS

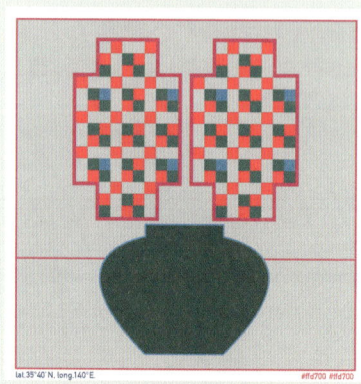

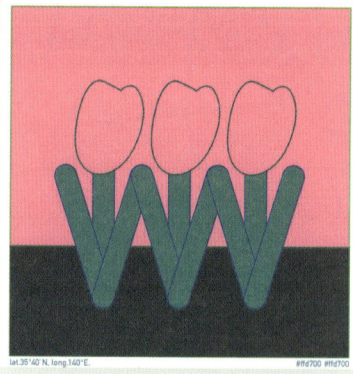

These graphics of flowers and vases, created in 2021, were designed for sale on an NFT platform. Featuring motifs commonly found in interior spaces, the artwork was expressed through static movement and sold as digital paintings for monitor display. The aim was to create a subtle, rhythmic movement that integrates seamlessly into interior design. By continuously recombining and shifting colored dots, lines, and planes, the piece evokes a vivid sense of playfulness while capturing idyllic activities through its minimal yet dynamic composition.

AD. D. Aki Kanai

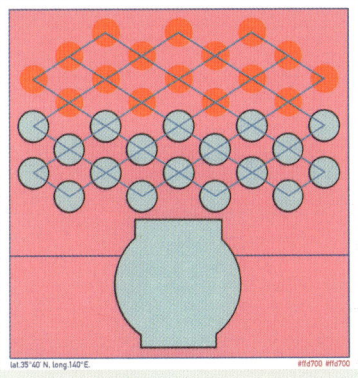
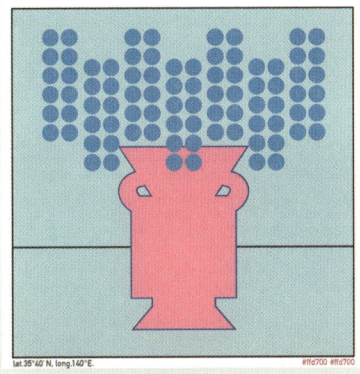
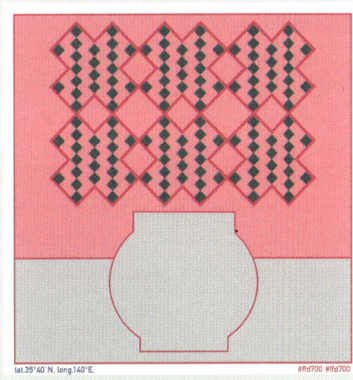

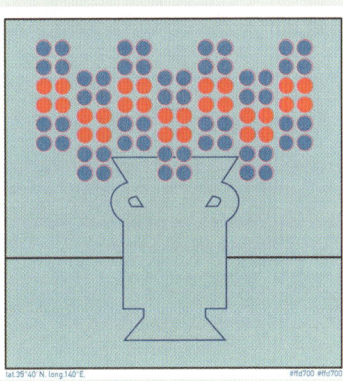
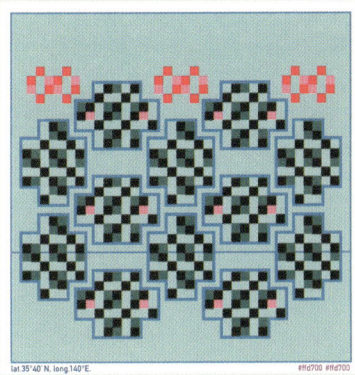

 **Why Dot, Line, and Plane?**

Under the same theme and the same composition, the designer used different shapes to replace different parts of the picture, forming a set of vase illustrations with the designer's personal characteristics.

Basic Dot, Line, and Plane

MUSASHINO ART UNIVERSITY

Personality (2016)

This is the Musashino Art University poster and university guide for 2016. The annual theme is *Personality*.

DA. Nippon Design Center
AD. Daigo Daikoku
CL. Musashino Art University

 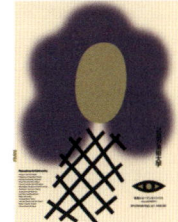 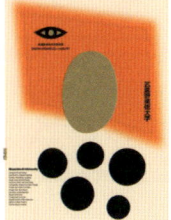  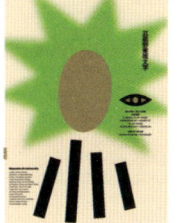 

Why Dot, Line, and Plane?

The designer used basic elements of dots and lines to construct abstract figures with different hairstyles and outfits as a way of highlighting the theme of the year—personality.

Basic Dot, Line, and Plane

- C10 M80 Y40 K0 / R219 G83 B107
- C90 M45 Y70 K5 / R0 G111 B94
- C5 M25 Y95 K0 / R243 G197 B0
- C20 M75 Y5 K0 / R202 G91 B153
- C50 M0 Y100 K0 / R143 G195 B31
- C100 M75 Y35 K0 / R0 G74 B122
- C70 M5 Y40 K0 / R54 G177 B167
- C80 M100 Y45 K10 / R80 G36 B89
- C5 M70 Y100 K0 / R230 G107 B0
- C30 M40 Y60 K0 / R191 G157 B109
- C5 M15 Y20 K0 / R243 G223 B204
- C0 M0 Y0 K100 / R0 G0 B0
- C0 M0 Y0 K0 / R255 G255 B255

GOOD GOOD GOOD COLLÉ POSTER

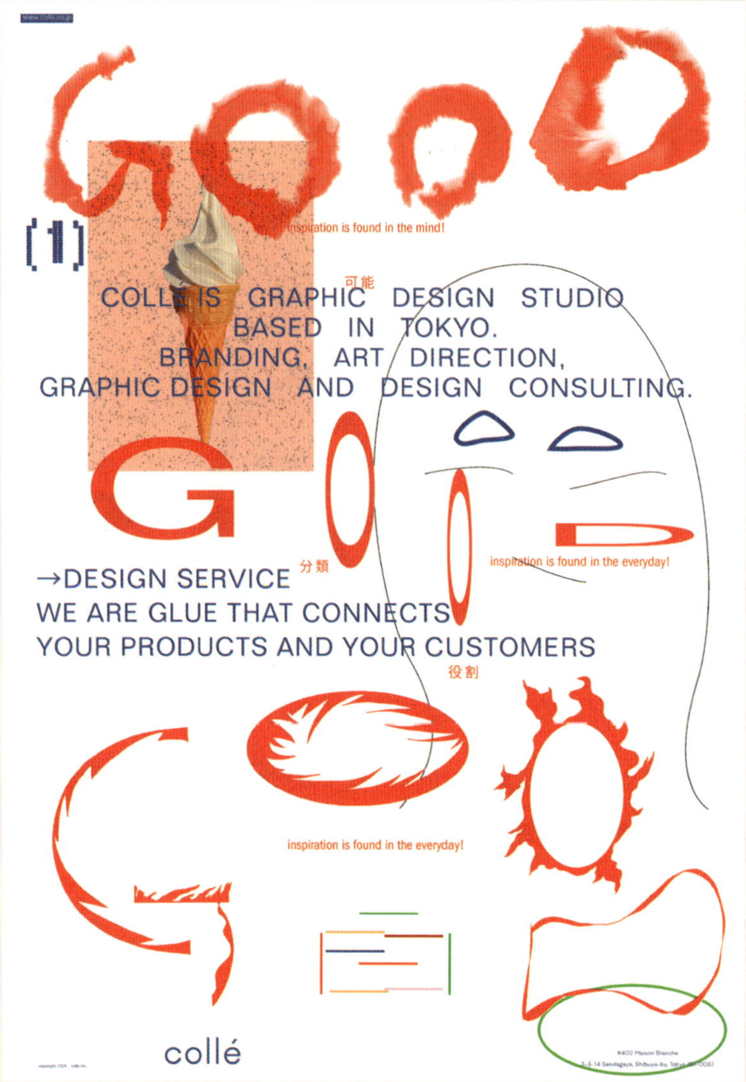

Why Dot, Line, and Plane?

The designer believes that the most emotional aspect of this work lies in the hand-written elements. The bright, positive feelings it evokes are not intended to be "uplifting" or "omnipotent," but rather a more relaxed, grounded sense of "it's good." To neutralize the emotional intensity of the lettering, the design incorporates various elements—such as lines that make it difficult to read emotions—creating a more subtle and balanced visual experience.

Basic Dot, Line, and Plane

This is a promotional poster for collé, a design studio where Yamaguchi serves as the representative. The theme of collé is "cheerful graphic design"—one that embodies a positive and uplifting approach. "Cheerful" reflects not only a state of positivity but also an intentional effort to convey optimism through graphic design. The goal is to transform everyday or unexpected situations—whether encountered on the street or in daily life—into engaging and intriguing experiences, shifting perceptions from "creepy" to "interesting."

DA. collé
D. Agata Yamaguchi
CL. collé

- C0 M80 Y65 K0 / R234 G85 B72
- C90 M60 Y0 K0 / R0 G94 B173
- C70 M0 Y95 K0 / R68 G177 B63
- C45 M15 Y0 K0 / R148 G191 B230
- C45 M95 Y100 K15 / R143 G41 B34
- C0 M0 Y0 K0 / R255 G255 B255

GRAPHIC REPORT VOL.2

From 2023 to 2024, Yamaguchi experienced a wide range of emotions and moments that deeply influenced his creative process. Whether at work, on the train, in a café, or in the quiet of his bedroom, he captured the essence of his daily life by jotting down his thoughts, observations, and fleeting impressions in a notepad. These notes included vivid scenes, faces, and words that came to mind throughout the day. He then imported these collected materials into his computer, blending images and words with intuitive connections, sharing them on social media.

In the summer of 2024, he selected ten of his most compelling creations from this ongoing collection, printing them on poster- or flyer-sized sheets. He compiled these into a single work, which he calls a "graphic report." Traditionally, a report serves to accurately convey events and details, but Yamaguchi's version departs from this expectation. Rather than offering event summaries or diary-like entries, his graphic report is an art book that invites readers to engage with glimpses of his daily life through a thoughtful combination of color, form, and text.

DA. collé
D. Agata Yamaguchi

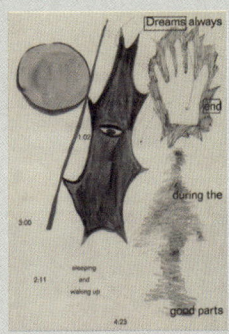

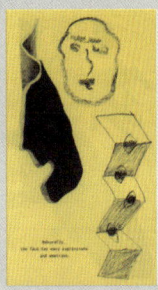

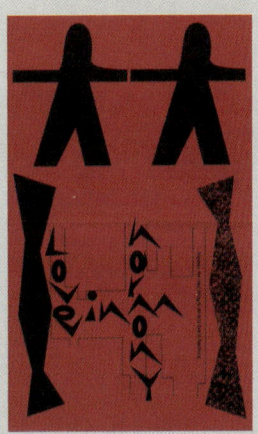

● ◆ ■ Why Dot, Line, and Plane?

To reflect his daily emotions and thoughts directly in his drawings and letters, the designer often chooses hand-drawn lines over computer-generated dots and lines. He frequently fills surfaces with pencil or brush strokes, imbuing his works with a tactile, personal quality. The intensity of the emotions he wishes to convey is expressed through darker, thicker lines, while lighter, more subdued areas feature thinner lines and gentle curves.

With the abundance of hand-drawn elements, the designer finds that introducing inorganic elements creates a natural contrast. For instance, in the piece *Dialogue*, the sharp lines produced by cutting a sheet of paper in two and the resulting triangular shapes effectively communicate the dynamic of a conversation between two people. In many of his other works, he combines hand-drawn elements with randomly arranged typewritten characters. The designer believes this combination is effective because it allows for a balance of contrast and harmony, reinforcing the emotional resonance of each piece.

Basic Dot, Line, and Plane

- 🟡 C0 M5 Y75 K0 / R255 G236 B81
- 🔴 C0 M80 Y70 K0 / R234 G85 B65
- 🔵 C90 M55 Y0 K0 / R0 G101 B178
- 🟢 C70 M5 Y80 K0 / R69 G173 B92
- ⚫ C0 M0 Y0 K100 / R0 G0 B0
- ⚪ C0 M0 Y0 K0 / R255 G255 B255

JAPANESE ILLUSTRATION

When the designer was tasked with this project, the inspiration seemed to stem from his previous work, *Face Myself*. This two-piece series portrays a figure standing in front of a mirror, where the reflection is distorted and elusive. The unusual pose and the shifting image create a sense of movement when viewed alternately. For this book, which allowed for different designs for the cover and the jacket, the designer was asked to create a similar two-piece composition that would evoke movement when removed. Although the work is a still image rather than a video, the designer intentionally avoided smooth motion. Instead, he used arrows to suggest direction and crafted visuals that blur the passage of time, with the connection between the two pieces slightly defying imagination.

DA. collé
D. Agata Yamaguchi
CL. SendPoints Publishing Co., Ltd.

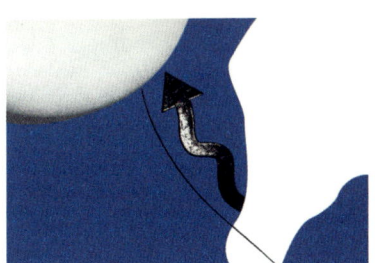
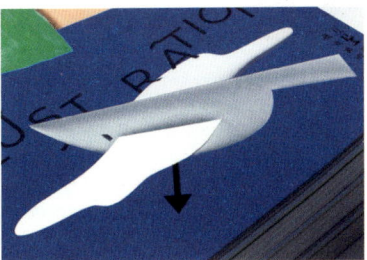

 **Why Dot, Line, and Plane?**

Given that the cover was to be printed in full color and the front jacket using silk screen printing, the designer aimed to ensure that the attention to detail was effectively conveyed through both techniques. Full-color printing allowed for the intricate textures of the hand-drawn artwork to come through, while silk screen printing, being a one-color process with limited use of gradation, required a focus on silhouette and flatness. To prevent a stark contrast between the cover and jacket that might disrupt the sense of "movement," the designer sought to create a balance between the simple lines and unique silhouette shapes. This 1:1 balance helped align the visual impressions, guiding the eye naturally toward the movement within the design.

Basic Dot, Line, and Plane

- C90 M65 Y0 K0 / R13 G87 B167
- C30 M25 Y20 K0 / R189 G187 B191
- C0 M0 Y0 K100 / R0 G0 B0
- C0 M0 Y0 K0 / R255 G255 B255

📦 UNBOX 2ND | BETWEEN BOX AND BAG

This is the second website for Fukunaga Print's UNBOX project. The illustrations, inspired by still life paintings from the Louvre Museum, blend physical interactions with digital elements, allowing users to engage with the artwork through a mouse or other means. The materiality of the box is further reimagined in the digital realm.

DA. NEW Creators Club
D. Shunta Sakamoto
CL. Fukunaga Print Co., Ltd

Why Dot, Line, and Plane?

Dots, lines, and planes are effectively used as graphic elements to express the structure of paper.

Basic Dot, Line, and Plane

- C85 M85 Y0 K0 / R65 G57 B147
- C30 M15 Y20 K0 / R189 G203 B201
- C5 M25 Y85 K0 / R243 G198 B47
- C60 M0 Y100 K0 / R111 G186 B44
- C70 M45 Y30 K0 / R89 G126 B153
- C35 M25 Y20 K0 / R178 G183 B191
- C15 M40 Y20 K0 / R218 G169 B177
- C40 M50 Y80 K0 / R170 G133 B70
- C50 M45 Y15 K0 / R143 G139 B176
- C0 M0 Y0 K100 / R0 G0 B0
- C0 M0 Y0 K0 / R255 G255 B255

WHERE DID I COME FROM?

Through experimenting with various lettering practices and methods of expression, the designer discovered the captivating qualities of woodblock prints and conceived the idea of using woodblocks to create printing types for her original Chinese characters. Woodblock printing, widely used in social movements across Asia, aligns perfectly with her works, as folk art influences her Chinese characters designs. However, given the vast number of Chinese characters, she decided to begin with a single Chinese poem as the subject for the typesetting. "我生何處來" (Where Did I Come From?) is a poem written by the Japanese monk Ryokan during the Edo period. The designer chose this poem because she felt that a work written by a Japanese poet, like herself, would be the ideal choice for her first poem in this project.

D. Yu Miyama

● ◆ ■ **Why Dot, Line, and Plane?**

This work is an adaptation of the "Explore New Forms of Chinese Characters" project, but here the designer did not treat all elements of the characters as planes. Instead, she designed with a focus on the relationship between lines and planes. For Chinese characters with abstract meanings, the designer sought to express them through the interplay of lines and white space, or by pursuing aesthetically beautiful shapes that function as abstract figures.

Basic Dot, Line, and Plane

○ C12 M12 Y16 K0 / R229 G223 B214
● C0 M0 Y0 K100 / R0 G0 B0

◉ UENO STOREHOUSE UPCOMING LINEUP (2 VERSIONS)

This is a poster-sized backing sheet designed for a Tokyo theater, intended to highlight upcoming performances.

Although the theater is equipped with poster frames, many theater companies today no longer produce posters. As a result, only a single flyer is often posted in the center of the frame, making the display feel sparse and somewhat lonely. To address this, a backing sheet was created to hold the flyer at the center while enhancing the overall presentation—drawing more attention to upcoming performances without making the display feel empty.

The sheet is printed on paper from a 100-yen shop, printed with a home monochrome printer, and then assembled. This makes it easy to repair if damaged, as individual sections can be replaced without redoing the whole piece. Initially, yellow paper was used, but it drew too much attention away from the central flyer. In the updated version, the paper was changed to a more subdued, low-saturation brown to better support the overall balance.

DA. MU DESIGN ROOM
D. Muramatsu Takehiko
CL. Ueno Storehouse

● ◆ ■ Why Dot, Line, and Plane?

The flyer placed at the center serves as the "plane." To avoid clashing with it visually, the design intentionally avoids using additional plane-like elements. Instead, directional lines are used to draw attention toward the central flyer.

There was an issue where the word "観劇" (meaning "watching theater") appeared too large, leading to the next revised version of the design. In the updated version, the word "観劇" was removed. In its place, more linear elements were added.

The goal was to use lines to liven up the space around the flyer, drawing the viewer's attention and evoking the vibrant energy of theater.

The design takes inspiration from karakusa (arabesque) patterns, which were introduced to Japan from China via the Silk Road.

Basic Dot, Line, and Plane

● C0 M8 Y85 K0 / R255 G230 B40 (color paper)
● C42 M53 Y72 K0 / R166 G128 B82 (color paper)
● C60 M40 Y40 K100 / R0 G0 B0

COTON DESIGN NEW YEAR'S CARD FOR 2022

Why Dot, Line, and Plane?

The designer used geometric shapes to balance the tiger's majestic presence with a playful, cute aesthetics, making it both striking and approachable.

Basic Dot, Line, and Plane

- C10 M10 Y100 K0 / R238 G218 B0
- C15 M0 Y80 K0 / R229 G230 B71
- C5 M100 Y100 K0 / R223 G6 B21
- C0 M0 Y0 K100 / R0 G0 B0
- C0 M0 Y0 K0 / R255 G255 B255

This is coton design's New Year's card for 2022, featuring a tiger rendered with geometric shapes. The designer used four colors, including fluorescent yellow, to create a vibrant print. The design was crafted to represent the tiger using the fewest elements possible, ensuring immediate recognition.

DA. coton design
D. Hiroko Sakai

💡 IMAGINATION & TECHNOLOGY

This design was created for the Japanese advertising and creative magazine *BRAIN*, with the theme "AI x Creativity: Expanding Creativity that Moves People's Hearts." The designer crafted the characters for "技術" (technology) and "発想" (imagination) using motifs that reflect their respective meanings. The character for "技術" was designed with elements inspired by flow charts and diagrams used to explain deep learning, while the character for "発想" incorporated visual elements from the human brain, body, and natural objects, symbolizing the process of creative thinking.

D. Yu Miyama
CL. *BRAIN*

● ◇ ■ Why Dot, Line, and Plane?

This time, the designer chose to work with lines as the primary design element. However, there was a challenge in differentiating between two distinct planes for coloring. Simply using colors or textures didn't seem engaging enough. In an effort to add depth and meaning, the designer decided to replace the dots with letters. At first glance, these might appear to be simple dots, but upon closer inspection, they are actually English words that convey the meaning of each Chinese character, or they serve as credits for the design.

Basic Dot, Line, and Plane

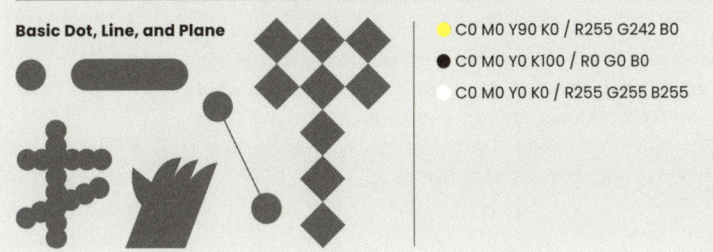

- C0 M0 Y90 K0 / R255 G242 B0
- C0 M0 Y0 K100 / R0 G0 B0
- C0 M0 Y0 K0 / R255 G255 B255

THEATRICAL COMPANY TOEN RECRUITMENT FLYER

 **Why Dot, Line, and Plane?**

Common:

The designer sought to use contour lines to evoke the feel of manga and illustration. He believed this style would resonate with younger audiences, offering a clear expression without feeling too overly serious or heavy-handed.

Energetic Body:

He used white areas as both "figure" and "ground," symbolizing not only light but also the purity and innocence associated with youth.

Think and Imagine:

Starting with an A4-sized flyer design, he transformed and layered it like a collage, using it as a kind of surface material. The piece reflects the spirit of experimentation—embracing the process of trying new things and learning through a process of trial and error.

Basic Dot, Line, and Plane

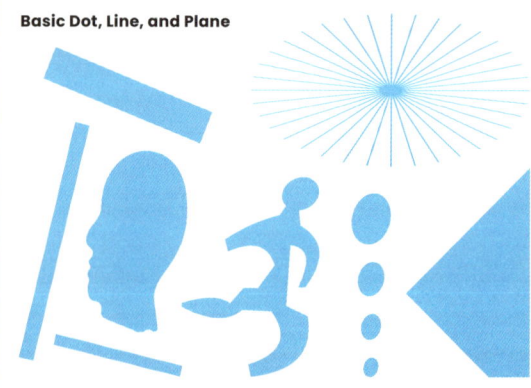

- C55 M0 Y0 K0 / R107 G200 B242
- C0 M45 Y0 K0 / R243 G169 B201
- C0 M0 Y90 K0 / R255 G242 B0
- C80 M0 Y100 K0 / R0 G167 B60
- C80 M100 Y0 K0 / R84 G27 B134
- C0 M85 Y85 K0 / R233 G72 B41
- C60 M40 Y40 K100 / R0 G0 B0
- C0 M0 Y0 K0 / R255 G255 B255

This is a recruitment flyer for a theater company—intended to inspire a sense of "future" and "hope" among young people. The designer created two distinct versions: "Energetic Body" and "Think and Imagine," each reflecting a different aspect of youthful potential.

DA. MU DESIGN ROOM
D. Muramatsu Takehiko
CL. Theatrical Company TOEN

未来の演劇人たちへ

劇団東演 新人募集

あなたの可能性を舞台へ 二〇二四年度新人募集！

築地小劇場開場100周年・劇団東演創立65周年　劇団東演　info@t-toen.com (Eメール)　http://www.t-toen.com (WEB)

♣ CHOCOLATE WITH FRUITS

A limited-edition Valentine's Day package design created for a chocolate brand, showcasing a new chocolate that highlights the unique characteristics of both chocolate and fruit.

*Note: The package is currently unavailable.

D. Eriko Kawakami
CL. Mary Chocolate Co.,Ltd.

● ◇ ■ Why Dot, Line, and Plane?

The confectionery market is saturated, with packaging overwhelmed by logos, photos, and illustrations all competing for attention. During Valentine's season, when countless gift-seekers are browsing for something special, it becomes even harder to stand out. To break through, the design required a bold visual impact—something memorable at a single glance.

By returning to the basics of dots, lines, and planes, the package achieved a striking and distinctive presence.

- ● C90 M60 Y85 K25 / R17 G79 B59
- ● C20 M100 Y100 K0 / R200 G22 B29
- ● C25 M35 Y100 K0 / R203 G166 B0
- ○ C0 M0 Y0 K0 / R255 G255 B255
- ● C0 M75 Y100 K0 / R235 G97 B0
- ● C20 M15 Y95 K0 / R216 G203 B0
- ● C10 M55 Y5 K0 / R223 G141 B180
- ● C85 M100 Y50 K5 / R71 G40 B88
- ● C45 M25 Y25 K0 / R153 G174 B181
- ● C40 M30 Y40 K0 / R168 G169 B152

Basic Dot, Line, and Plane

FACE AND MEANING

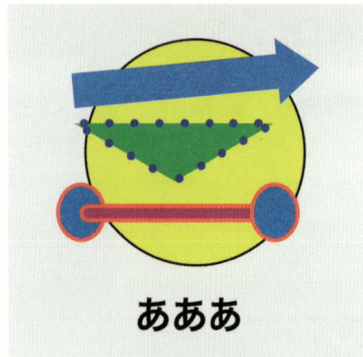
ааа

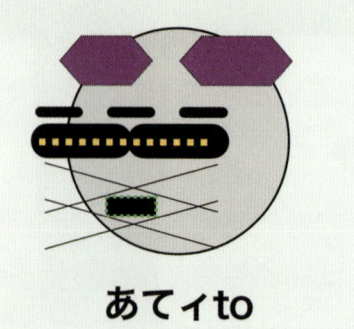
あてィto

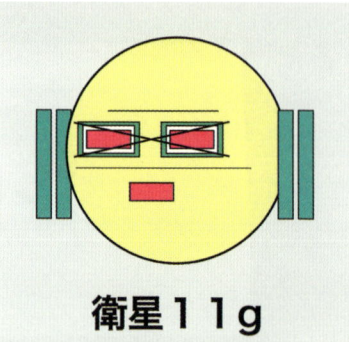
衛星11g

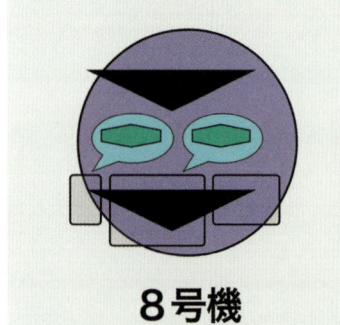
8号機

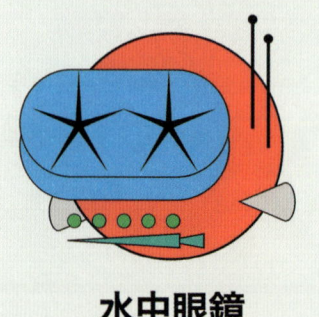
水中眼鏡

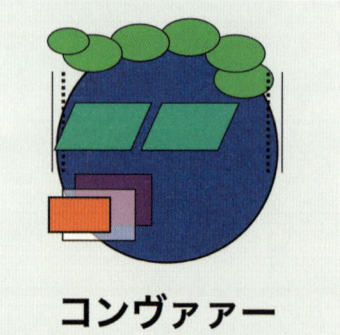
コンヴァァー

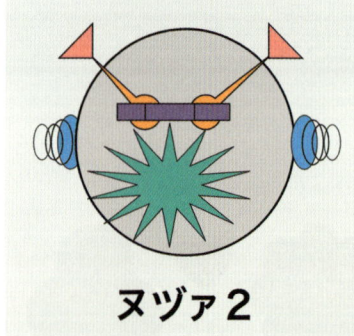
ヌヅァ2

nyんギェ

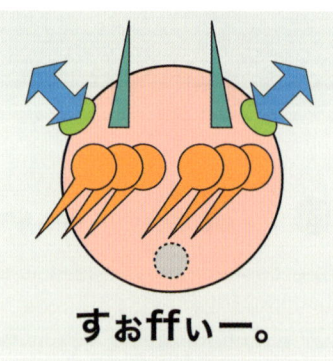
すぉffぃー。

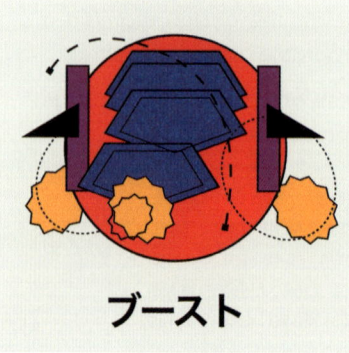
ブースト

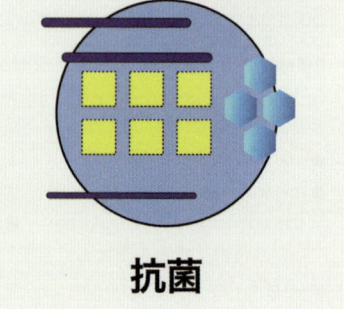
抗菌

This series explores the theme of "figures that subtly resemble faces." The designer aimed to deconstruct the face—a motif rich with meaning—and liberate it from its traditional meaning.

D. Ryohei Miyata

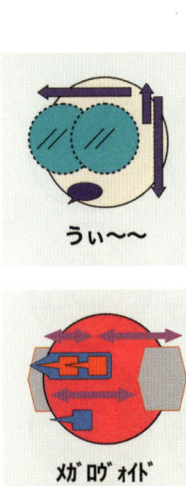
うぃ〜〜

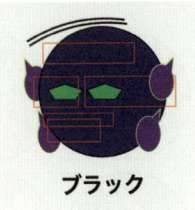
ブラック

掃除機

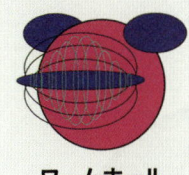
ワームホール

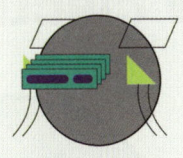
スペック_wf

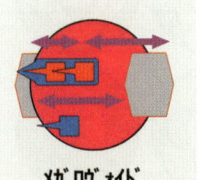
メガロヴォイド

ヲ〜をを

ネックレス

グルーヴ

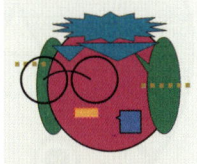
さっぱチョ?

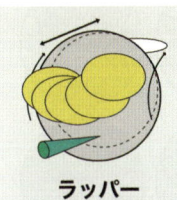
ラッパー

c00-X

ガム

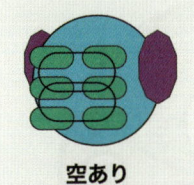
空あり

カレーパン

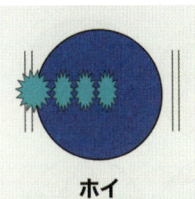
ホイ

かぜ・花粉

氷菓

65枚入り

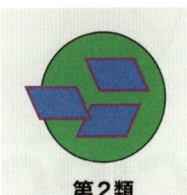
第2類

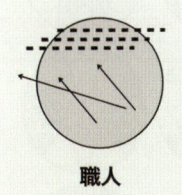
職人

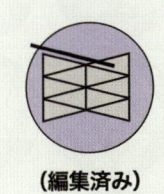
(編集済み)

タンパク質

磁石ボーイ

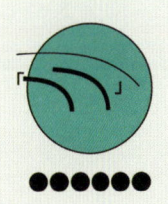
●●●●●●

Why Dot, Line, and Plane?

The designer employed the simplest possible elements to explore the essence of a face.

Basic Dot, Line, and Plane

- C85 M0 Y100 K0 / R0 G163 B62
- C75 M0 Y40 K0 / R0 G177 B169
- C75 M5 Y0 K0 / R0 G175 B233
- C0 M25 Y15 K0 / R249 G209 B203
- C10 M5 Y60 K0 / R238 G230 B126
- C70 M90 Y0 K0 / R105 G49 B142
- C0 M100 Y25 K0 / R229 G0 B106
- C30 M25 Y0 K0 / R187 G188 B222
- C20 M15 Y15 K0 / R211 G212 B211
- C0 M90 Y95 K0 / R232 G56 B23
- C0 M40 Y90 K0 / R246 G172 B25

★ CIRCLES

These posters are a compilation of creatures that live inside the circle—one for each day over a span of 100 days. The designer initiated this project as a way to create an icon for his social networking site.

D. Shimizu Kango

Why Dot, Line, and Plane?

The designer's goal was to create appealing characters using humorous, bold lines and basic circles, combined with popular colors, striving for vividness and power that would stand out even in a small space.

Basic Dot, Line, and Plane

- C85 M40 Y100 K0 / R25 G122 B59
- C85 M55 Y10 K0 / R29 G104 B168
- C10 M0 Y70 K0 / R239 G236 B100
- C0 M85 Y50 K0 / R232 G70 B90
- C0 M0 Y0 K100 / R0 G0 B0
- C0 M0 Y0 K0 / R255 G255 B255

CIRCLES

◉ HIMAWARI

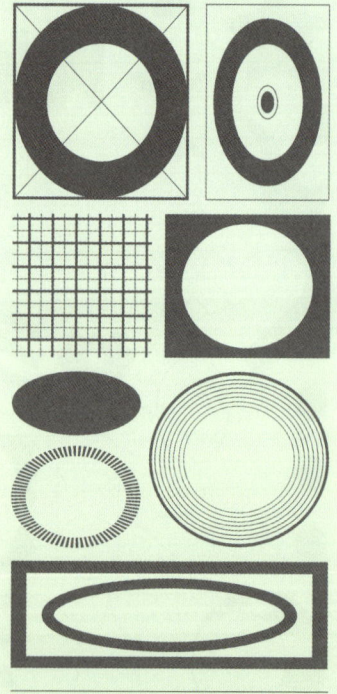

HIMAWARI / NEON / #0201
[LES TOURNESOLS]   向 日 葵

Why Dot, Line, and Plane?

By reconstructing the well-known masterpiece using the fundamental visual elements of dots, lines, and planes, the designer sought to uncover the structural framework that underpins the painting. This approach reveals the foundational aspects of the artwork, offering a fresh perspective on its composition.

Basic Dot, Line, and Plane

- C5 M0 Y35 K0 / R248 G246 B187
- C0 M20 Y5 K0 / R250 G220 B226
- C20 M20 Y25 K0 / R212 G202 B189
- C30 M0 Y5 K0 / R187 G226 B241
- C30 M0 Y40 K0 / R191 G222 B174
- C0 M0 Y0 K5 / R247 G248 B248
- C0 M0 Y0 K100 / R0 G0 B0
- C0 M0 Y0 K0 / R255 G255 B255

This poster and its series were created for Tung Fang Design University. This experimental work reinterprets the boundary between fine art and graphic design by sampling the composition of Van Gogh's *Sunflowers*, blending artistic elements with contemporary design to create a unique visual experience.

DA. TM INC.
D. Yuto Tamura
CL. Tung Fang Design University

HIMAWARI / NEON / #0203
[LES TOURNESOLS]　　　　　　向　日　葵

HIMAWARI / PAPER / #0810
[LES TOURNESOLS]　　　向　日　葵

HIMAWARI / LIGHT / #0903
[LES TOURNESOLS]　　　向　日　葵

HIMAWARI / LIGHT / #0908
[LES TOURNESOLS]　　　向　日　葵

HIMAWARI / PAPER / #0805
[LES TOURNESOLS]　　　向　日　葵

HIMAWARI / LIGHT / #0909
[LES TOURNESOLS]　　　向　日　葵

AMBIDEX 2024 SPRING EXHIBITION

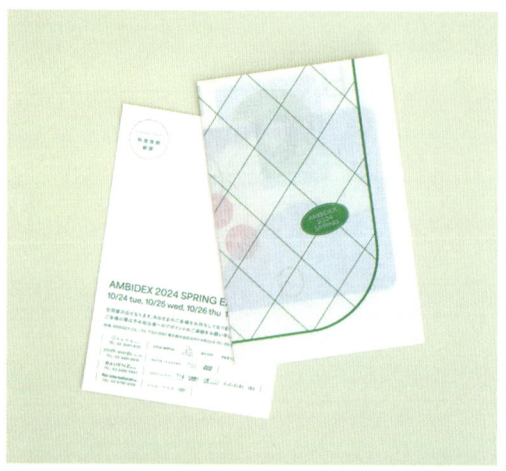

● ◇ ■ Why Dot, Line, and Plane?

The design incorporates seasonal spring fruits along with stickers and mesh wraps commonly used for fruit packaging. Enclosed is a mini folded poster printed on translucent paper—when the mesh-patterned poster is opened, the fruit appears underneath. The design expresses the charm and playfulness that can be felt in the clothing created by AMBIDEX.

Basic Dot, Line, and Plane

- ● C40 M5 Y85 K0 / R170 G201 B69
- ○ C15 M5 Y20 K0 / R224 G232 B212
- ● C75 M20 Y0 K0 / R0 G157 B218
- ● C75 M50 Y0 K0 / R71 G116 B185
- ● C0 M70 Y20 K0 / R235 G109 B142
- ● C0 M85 Y80 K0 / R233 G72 B49
- ● C5 M30 Y85 K0 / R241 G189 B47
- ● C5 M10 Y55 K0 / R246 G227 B135

This is the DM for AMBIDEX, an apparel manufacturing and retail company, for their Spring 2024 exhibition.

D. Sakura Kashiwazaki
CL. AMBIDEX

● CIRCLE & RECTANGLE RISOGRAPH POSTER

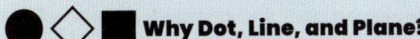

This poster was created using risograph printing, featuring selected illustrations from a previously produced zine titled "Circle & Rectangle." The zine compiled curious compositions—seemingly meaningful, yet ambiguous—that emerged from exploring combinations of circles and rectangles. To express a sense of visual ambiguity, risograph printing was used with complex layering of colors, including white and transparent tones.

D. Sakura Kashiwazaki

● ◇ ■ Why Dot, Line, and Plane?

The designer believes that working within limitations can help draw out unexpected forms from her own mind. This piece began as an exploration of creating compelling visuals using only the limited shapes of circles and rectangles.

Basic Dot, Line, and Plane

- ● C0 M0 Y0 K100 / R0 G0 B0
- ○ C0 M0 Y0 K0 / R255 G255 B255
- ○ C20 M5 Y5 K0 / R212 G229 B239
- ● C40 M10 Y5 K0 / R162 G203 B229
- ● C95 M75 Y0 K0 / R0 G72 B157

⁜ AFFECTS POSTER

The *Affects* project by Masashi Murakami—a private exhibition held at TAKEO Co., Ltd., a Japanese paper distributor, explored the intersection of graphic design and art. Murakami created a series of posters for each exhibition booth, transforming them through environmental influences and presenting them as installations.

The project was grounded in the idea that form itself can transcend borders and languages. By freeing letters from their semantic meanings and reinterpreting them as pure visual elements, Murakami sought to demonstrate how graphic design can be a universal language. In contrast to the digital and interactive art dominating contemporary scenes, *Affects* reimagined familiar digital motifs through analog techniques, imbuing them with materiality and offering a fresh perspective on digital expression.

DA. emuni
D. Masashi Murakami
CL. TAKEO Co., Ltd.

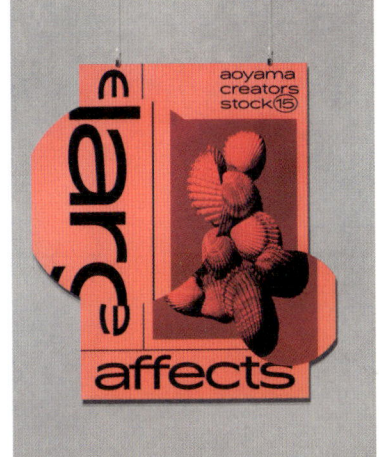

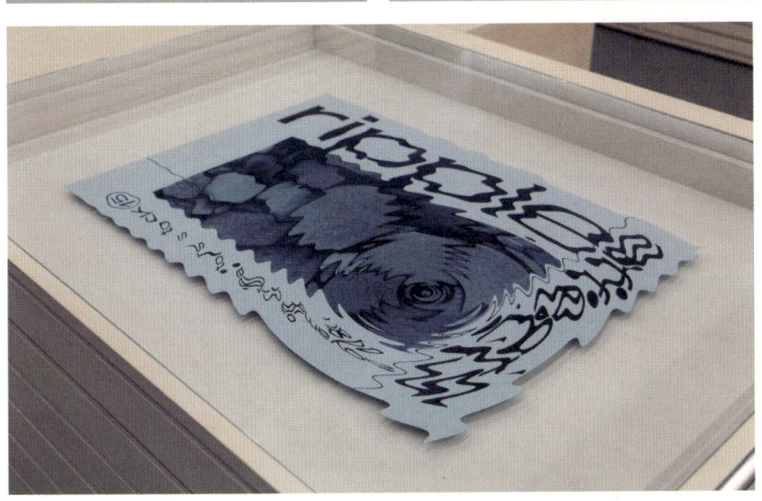
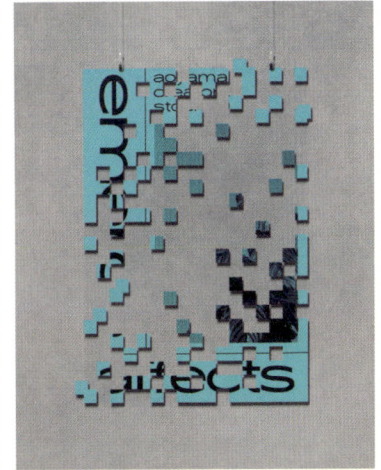

Why Dot, Line, and Plane?

The designer used technology to process traditional digital images, producing distorted and liquefied effects that abstract the graphic visuals of dots, lines, and planes.

Basic Dot, Line, and Plane

- ○ C45 M0 Y15 K0 / R146 G210 B220
- C10 M60 Y0 K0 / R222 G130 B178
- C5 M80 Y55 K0 / R227 G84 B87
- C20 M10 Y10 K0 / R212 G221 B225
- C40 M20 Y15 K0 / R165 G187 B203
- C65 M0 Y25 K0 / R71 G188 B198
- C80 M55 Y35 K0 / R61 G107 B138
- C0 M0 Y0 K100 / R0 G0 B0
- C0 M0 Y0 K0 / R255 G255 B255

✻ TWO-FACED CIRCUS

The exhibition space employs a circus motif to represent the front and back of the world, as well as the exterior and interior. The surface layer is depicted as a digital texture in white, while the inner reality is conveyed through black hand-drawing and graffiti. By positioning the emotions of joy and anger, embodied by the animals, on opposing sides—left and right, front and back—within the seemingly cheerful circus setting, the work juxtaposes contrasting atmospheres. This interplay serves as a visual critique of societal structures, presented through the medium of graphic art.

D. Tasuku Matsuo

● ◆ ■ Why Dot, Line, and Plane?

The unique shapes of the animals are captured as planes. Dots and lines create accents and rhythms as decorative elements that represent the circus and complement the animals. The bold placement of these elements creates a design with a sense of dynamism and visual impact.

Basic Dot, Line, and Plane

- C20 M95 Y100 K0 / R201 G42 B29
- C0 M100 Y15 K0 / R229 G0 B115
- C5 M0 Y90 K0 / R250 G238 B0
- C5 M70 Y70 K0 / R229 G108 B70
- C70 M0 Y100 K0 / R69 G176 B53
- C85 M10 Y85 K0 / R0 G155 B86
- C80 M10 Y5 K0 / R0 G165 B220
- C100 M80 Y0 K0 / R0 G164 B152
- C0 M0 Y0 K100 / R0 G0 B0

POSTER FOR SHINGEKI EXCHANGE PROJECT
LEGEND OF THE BEAUTIFUL THINGS

This production is one of the representative works of Shingeki[1], and also a group drama that portrays the era in which Shingeki was born. This visual design serves as a promotional poster for an exchange project among seven Shingeki troupes. Conceptually, it pays homage to a past flyer designed by Kiyoshi Awazu, centering on photographs of the characters as its primary visual element.

While honoring this classic approach, the design also aims to convey a sense of historical depth, reflecting both the era in which the story is set and the legacy of Shingeki. The female figure in the image is drawn from *Woman Combing Her Hair*, a work by the Taishō period artist Goyō Hashiguchi.

1. Shingeki is a theatrical genre that originated during the Meiji period. The name, meaning "new drama," was coined to distinguish it from Kabuki, which was considered "old drama." In its early stages, Shingeki focused primarily on staging translated Western plays. Today, its various troupes have grown into established institutions, and while they have shifted toward creating original works, the genre's non-commercial, artistic spirit continues to this day.

DA. MU DESIGN ROOM
D. Muramatsu Takehiko
CL. Shingeki Exchange Project (Seven Theater Companies Exchange Project)

● ◆ ■ **Why Dot, Line, and Plane?**

In the concept development, the female portrait is treated as a "plane" element. Through the continuity of this plane, the design conveys a layered set of visual meanings: a sense of history that bridges past and future, the unstable social atmosphere of the era in which the play is set, and a striking new visual impact. The linear arrangement of these planes also creates a sense of visual flow and motion.

Interspersed character portraits highlight the ensemble nature of the drama, expressing the strength, passion, and vulnerability of youth, as well as the charged atmosphere of anticipation before the dawn of something new. The title information is placed against a black background to ensure visual clarity and legibility.

Basic Dot, Line, and Plane

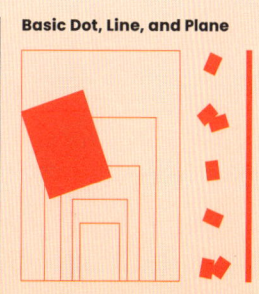

● C0 M100 Y100 K0 / R231 G0 B18
● C60 M40 Y40 K100 / R0 G0 B0
○ C0 M0 Y0 K0 / R255 G255 B255

▲ MASU

Why Dot, Line, and Plane?

The designer reinterpreted the traditional *shōchikubai* (pine, bamboo, plum) motif in a symbolic and lighthearted way. By employing dots, lines, and planes, the design achieves a sense of lightness. Combined with subtle textures, such as faint or broken lines, these elements convey warmth while maintaining simplicity.

Basic Dot, Line, and Plane

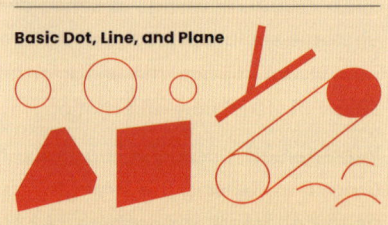

● C5 M95 Y85 K0 / R224 G38 B41
○ C5 M15 Y25 K0 / R243 G223 B195

This work was created for an exhibition featuring *hinoki masu* (Japanese cypress measuring cups), crafted by 160 creators in collaboration with artisans from Ōgaki. Proceeds from sales are donated to Save the Children as part of a charitable initiative.

The *masu*, meaning "to increase" or "to prosper," is considered an auspicious item. The design draws inspiration from pine, bamboo, and plum, plants known for their resilience even in harsh winter conditions and traditionally regarded as symbols of good fortune. These motifs are often used to celebrate joyful occasions, such as weddings or New Year's decorations like *kadomatsu*.

D. Eriko Kawakami
CL. Recruit Holdings Co., Ltd.

◀ KAMI NO G

This zine is designed as a fictional hairstyle catalog, created after the designer shaved his head for the first time in 17 or 18 years. Inspired by the experience, he imagined a series of nearly impossible hairstyles.

Printed using Risograph with a three-color rule, the zine features a silk-screen-printed cover. The designer first developed the graphics for each hairstyle and then assigned them names that reflected their unique characteristics. Adding to its distinctiveness, the zine's handmade binding—crafted by KARIYA®STORE—uses an accordion fold, further enhancing its unconventional presentation.

DA. KAMI NO G
D. Tadashi Ueda / KARIYA®STORE

● ◇ ■ Why Dot, Line, and Plane?

The designer aimed to keep the graphics simple. This approach applies to all of his works, but in this case, he deliberately reduced the shapes to their most basic forms. Since the zine features a variety of imaginary hairstyles, it takes time for viewers to fully grasp them. Overcomplicating the visuals would risk overwhelming the viewers with too much information.

Basic Dot, Line, and Plane

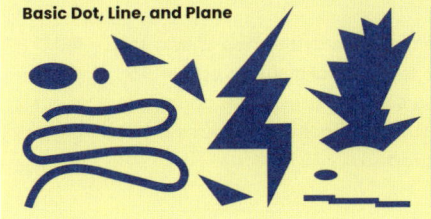

- C10 M5 Y85 K0 / R239 G227 B49
- C85 M75 Y0 K0 / R58 G74 B157
- C0 M65 Y55 K0 / R238 G121 B97
- C0 M0 Y0 K0 / R255 G255 B255

PARADE & DREAMING OF THE FUTURE BY TAKESHI NAKATSUKA

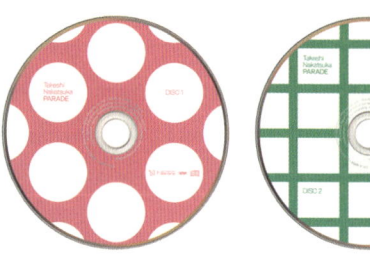

The music sleeve design was created for vibrant, pop music to celebrate the 20th anniversary of Takeshi Nakatsuka's career. To reflect his straightforward, uplifting sound—an essence captured in the "parade" theme of the title—the designer envisioned it as a flag waving at the forefront of a parade.

D. Hirokazu Matsuda
I. Shunsuke Imai

 **Why Dot, Line, and Plane?**

Nakatsuka told the designer, "Music is meant to be easy to understand and enjoyable." To capture this spirit, the design needed to remain simple, avoiding complex figures and expressions. The designer turned to Shunsuke Imai, whose paintings blend primitive shapes and vibrant colors—perfectly aligning with Nakatsuka's kaleidoscopic music.

Basic Dot, Line, and Plane

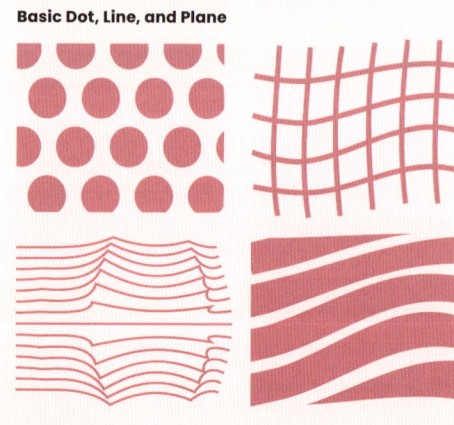

● C10 M65 Y10 K0 / R221 G118 B160
● C75 M10 Y100 K0 / R50 G162 B56
● C90 M65 Y5 K0 / R15 G88 B163
● C55 M90 Y5 K0 / R137 G50 B138
● C0 M45 Y80 K0 / R245 G163 B59
● C70 M10 Y30 K0 / R56 G172 B181
● C0 M0 Y0 K100 / R0 G0 B0
　C0 M0 Y0 K0 / R255 G255 B255

G8 CAFE

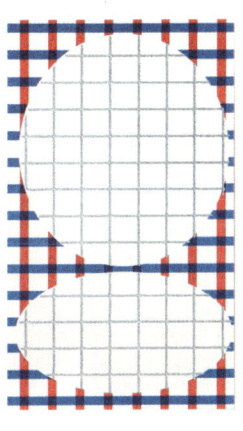
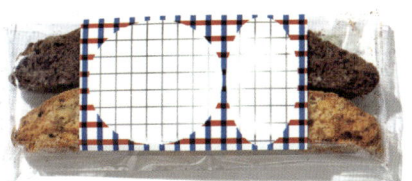

Why Dot, Line, and Plane?

Designed as a transforming café, a mysterious "BOX" was created to suddenly appear within the space. The logo was developed with a flexible concept, adapting its form based on size and location. By utilizing dots, lines, and planes, the design allows for extensive variation, producing versatile graphics suitable for applications such as the web.

A coffee stand–style café with an attached gallery, designed to make creative use of vacant lobby space. The café's exterior and ambient music are regularly renewed through collaborations with various creators, ensuring a dynamic and evolving experience.

Note: This café is currently closed.

D. Eriko Kawakami
CL. Recruit Holdings Co., Ltd.

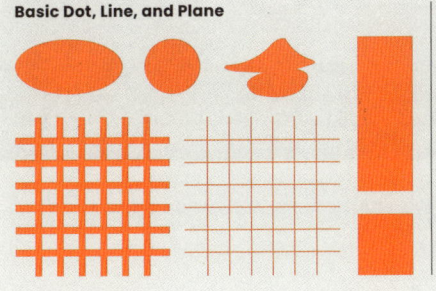

Basic Dot, Line, and Plane

- C0 M65 Y85 K0 / R238 G120 B43
- C90 M65 Y0 K0 / R13 G87 B167
- C25 M95 Y100 K0 / R193 G44 B31
- C0 M0 Y0 K100 / R0 G0 B0
- C0 M0 Y0 K0 / R255 G255 B255

PAPER BREAKS LP

This is a design tool that creates music using stickers on paper records.

DA. NEW Creators Club
D. Shunta Sakamoto
CL. Living Motif

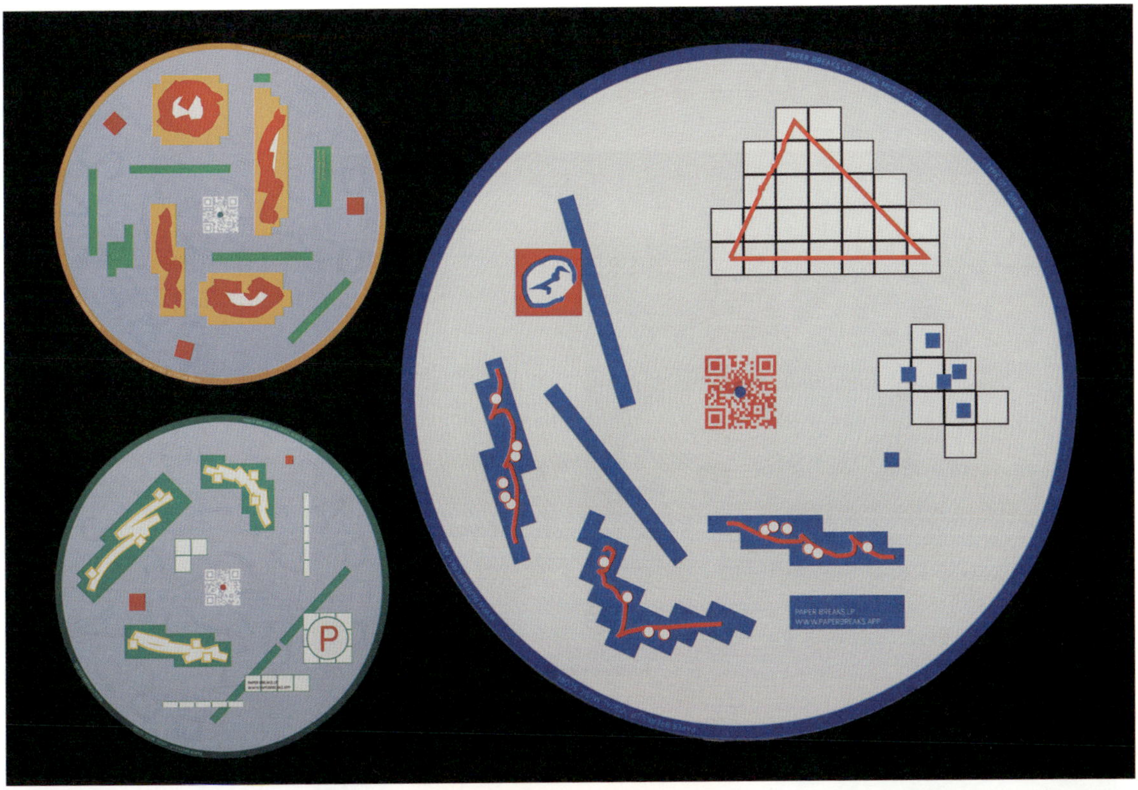

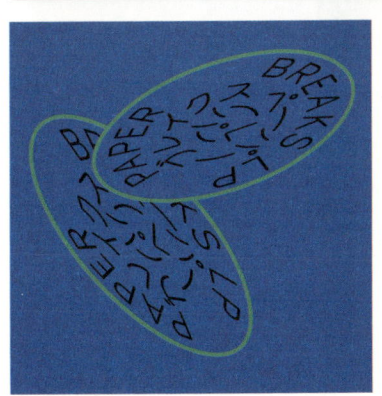

◉ ◆ ■ Why Dot, Line, and Plane?

The designer used dots, lines, and planes to express the dynamism of music and the sense of this technology.

Basic Dot, Line, and Plane

- ● C95 M55 Y0 K0 / R0 G99 B178
- ● C85 M15 Y85 K0 / R0 G150 B85
- ● C15 M85 Y80 K0 / R211 G71 B53
- ○ C5 M30 Y75 K0 / R241 G190 B77
- ● C0 M0 Y0 K100 / R0 G0 B0
- ○ C20 M15 Y15 K0 / R211 G212 B211

🌸 **TOKYO ZOKEI UNIVERSITY OPEN CAMPUS 2022**

This is the art direction for the Tokyo Zokei University Open Campus 2022. The design incorporates a diverse range of characters, fostering an environment where students can easily connect with one another. It invites them to view their university experience as an exciting adventure, one in which they, alongside their peers, step beyond the ordinary and explore new possibilities.

D. Tasuku Matsuo
CL. Tokyo Zokei University

Why Dot, Line, and Plane?

In this work, the elements of dot, line, and plane are integral to the geometric structure of the characters and the overall composition. The use of lines and planes as patterns and effects adds a sense of dynamic movement, capturing the excitement and energy of the adventure. Additionally, the vibrant color schemes and harmonious shapes create a striking visual impact, amplifying the design's lively and engaging atmosphere.

Basic Dot, Line, and Plane

- C0 M65 Y100 0 / R238 G120 B0
- C0 M85 Y100 K5 / R72 G30 B131
- C80 M5 Y65 K0 / R0 G166 B121
- C40 M30 Y20 K0 / R166 G171 B185
- C0 M0 Y0 K100 / R0 G0 B0
- C0 M0 Y0 K0 / R255 G255 B255

🔴 RECOLLETION

Fuzzy and fragmented memories are graphically represented and reconstructed on screen, intertwined with drawings and photographs from the designer's childhood. The designer connected the misalignment of memory with the displacement of stereoscopic photographic plates, creating a visual dialogue between past and present.

D. Tasuku Matsuo

 **Why Dot, Line, and Plane?**

A large oval at the center serves as a symbol of memory, surrounded by childhood drawings of tigers and fish. Elements like dots, lines, and planes are replaced with various objects, each reconstructing fragmented memories in a visual collage.

Basic Dot, Line, and Plane

- C85 M15 Y90 K0 / R0 G150 B77
- C15 M100 Y100 K0 / R208 G18 B27
- C95 M65 Y0 K0 / R0 G86 B167
- C0 M30 Y90 K0 / R250 G191 B19
- C90 M100 Y40 K5 / R58 G39 B98
- C35 M40 Y25 K0 / R178 G157 B168
- C0 M0 Y0 K70 / R114 G113 B113
- C0 M0 Y0 K100 / R0 G0 B0
- C0 M0 Y0 K0 / R255 G255 B255

USUAL ARTWORKS BY TOMOMI MIZUKOSHI

These artworks reflect the designer's usual approach—deforming everyday objects to create new compositions. Like a word association game, her drawings gradually reveal an imagined and ideal world—one she deeply loves.

I. Tomomi Mizukoshi

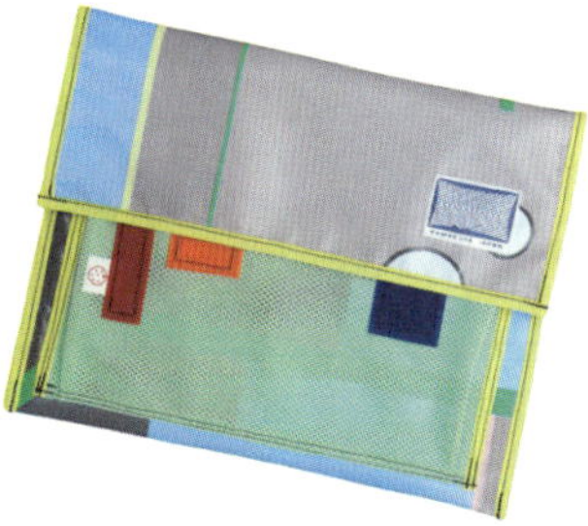

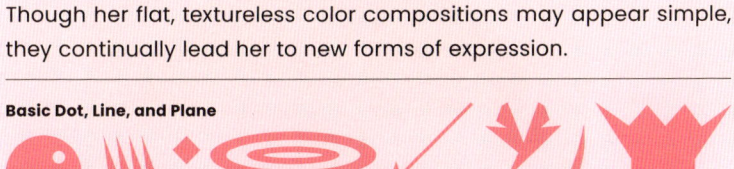

● ◇ ■ Why Dot, Line, and Plane?

When creating her artworks, she treats dots and lines as planes. Though her flat, textureless color compositions may appear simple, they continually lead her to new forms of expression.

Basic Dot, Line, and Plane

- ● C0 M90 Y100 K0 / R232 G56 B13
- ● C0 M70 Y0 K0 / R230 G110 B165
- ● C0 M0 Y70 K0 / R255 G244 B98
- ● C0 M20 Y50 K0 / R252 G214 B140
- ● C0 M40 Y75 K0 / R246 G173 B72
- ● C100 M0 Y100 K0 / R0 G153 B68
- ● C50 M0 Y80 K0 / R141 G197 B86
- ● C65 M0 Y65 K0 / R86 G184 B121
- ● C30 M0 Y0 K0 / R186 G227 B249
- ● C90 M0 Y0 K0 / R0 G167 B234
- ● C100 M30 Y0 K0 / R0 G129 B204
- ● C0 M0 Y0 K100 / R0 G0 B0
- ○ C0 M0 Y0 K0 / R255 G255 B255

❋ IMAGINARY FLOWERS

Since February 2022, the designer has been creating *Imaginary Flowers*, an exploration of several visualizing flowers in a unique and personal way.

Imaginary Flowers delves into how flowers live within our memories. From childhood to adulthood, flowers are always near us. Whether we're playing in the park, observing insects drawn to blossoms, visiting a local florist, or exchanging flowers for celebrations, they are a constant presence. We develop a deep affinity for floral patterns, which appear on the things we wear, carry, or encounter in stores. This connection extends to both ourselves and others.

The visual memory of flowers remains ever-present in our minds. We come to realize that "flowers are deeply embedded in people's memories." Even if we don't consciously think about it, the image of flowers is continuously stored in our minds. *Imaginary Flowers* represent this subconscious recollection through our everyday visual experiences. Though these flowers do not physically exist, the memory of them persists, and as long as that memory is within us, we continue to see them as flowers.

D. UESATSU

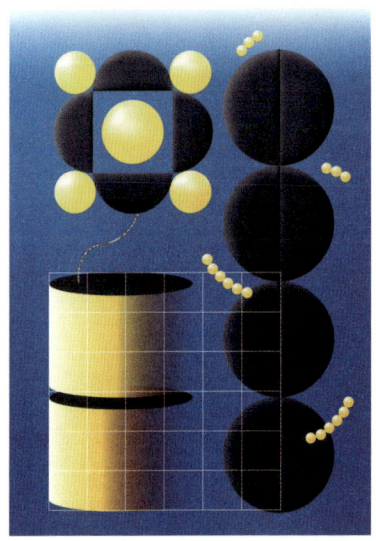

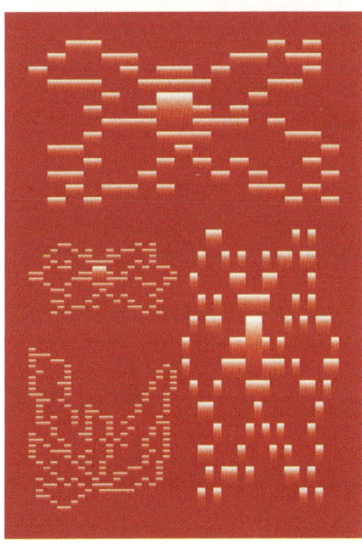

Why Dot, Line, and Plane?

In this series of works, the elements of flowers are abstractly deconstructed and reimagined. When viewed at an extremely low resolution, the concept of flowers is reduced to dots, lines, and planes. By utilizing these fundamental elements, the designer aimed to evoke the essence of flowers that people unconsciously remember through their visual experiences.

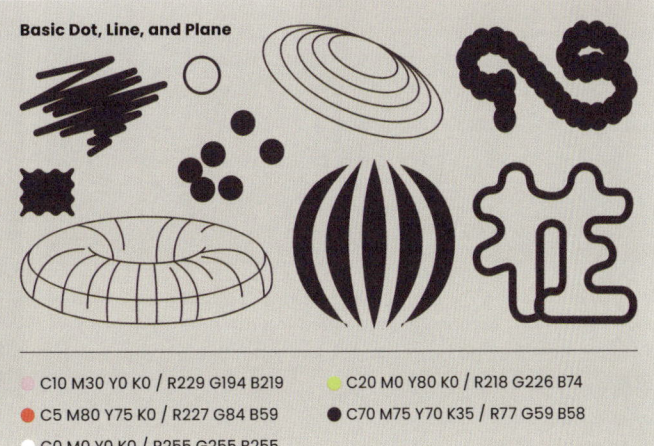

Basic Dot, Line, and Plane

- C10 M30 Y0 K0 / R229 G194 B219
- C5 M80 Y75 K0 / R227 G84 B59
- C0 M0 Y0 K0 / R255 G255 B255
- C20 M0 Y80 K0 / R218 G226 B74
- C70 M75 Y70 K35 / R77 G59 B58

THE CAMPUS FLATS

"Prototypical Living" is the concept behind Kokuyo's first shared house initiative, launched in 2023. Mirroring the approach used for Kokuyo's THE CAMPUS graphics, the key visual is built around the facility's initial letter.

AD. D. Aki Kanai / Taku Sasaki
CL. KOKUYO Co.,Ltd.

 **Why Dot, Line, and Plane?**

By replacing the letter "F" with lines and dots, and freely expanding and distorting its surfaces, the design evolves into a dynamic form. This visual representation captures the organic growth of the community, reinforced through repeated logotypes.

Basic Dot, Line, and Plane

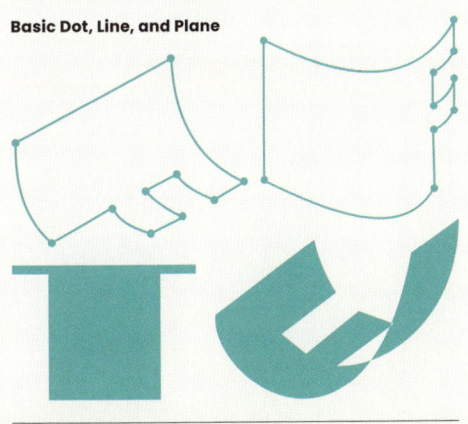

- PANTONE 929 C / R43 G183 B175
- C85 M50 Y0 K0 / R3 G110 B184
- C0 M0 Y0 K100 / R0 G0 B0

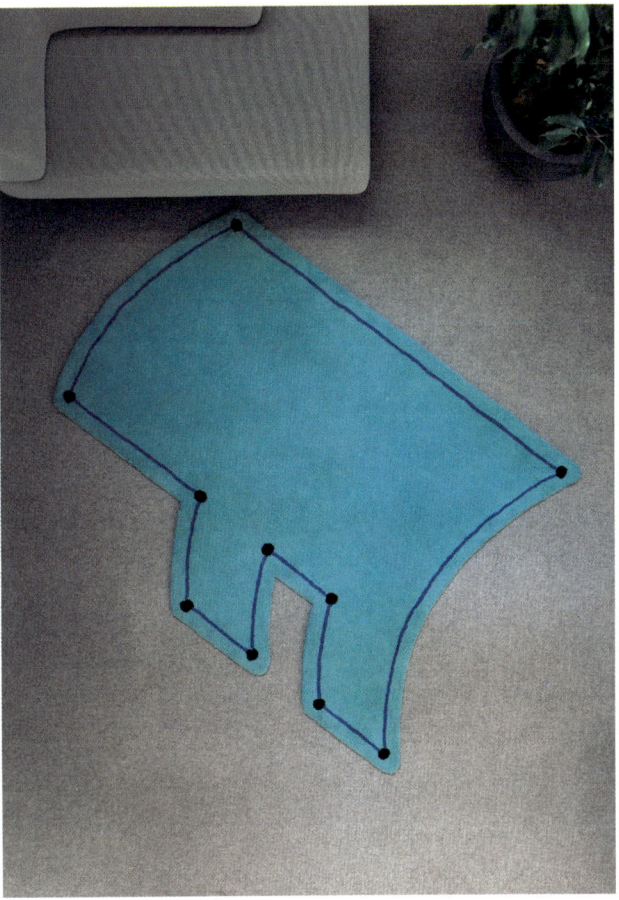

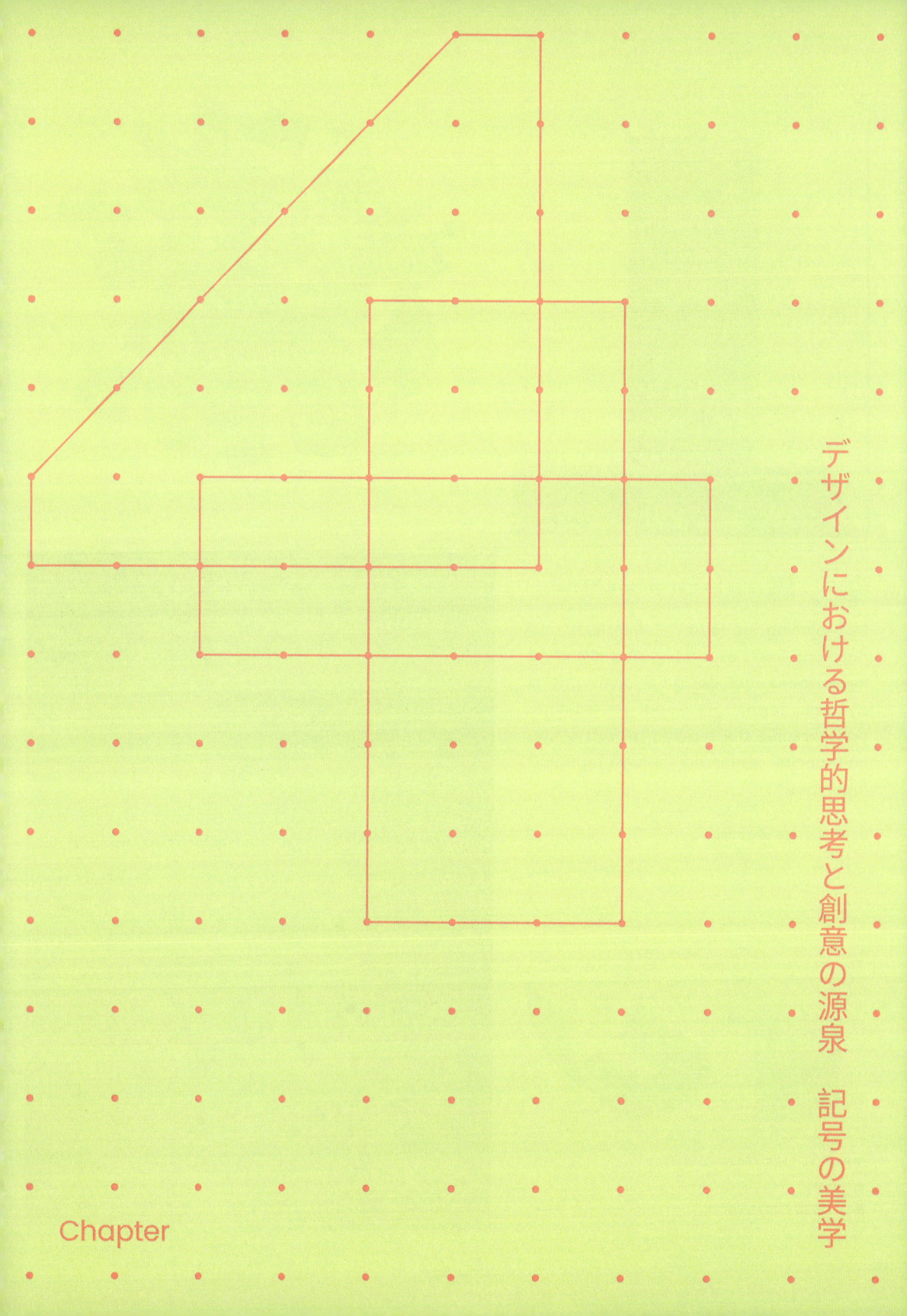

Chapter

デザインにおける哲学的思考と創意の源泉　記号の美学

PHILOSOPHY IN DESIGN AND THE SOURCE OF CREATIVITY: SYMBOLIC AESTHETICS

● Design is not merely about beauty in form but a profound pursuit of philosophical ideas. In design, dots, lines, and planes transcend simple geometric elements, becoming mediums for designers to express aesthetic choices and philosophical thoughts. Through the creative use of these basic elements, design not only conveys visual beauty but also embodies deep reflections on life, time, and existence.

● **In design, the dot holds profound symbolic meaning. It represents both the origin of creation and an independent existence, symbolizing infinite possibilities.** As the source of creativity, the dot is the foundation of design. By manipulating the dot's position and size, designers can guide the viewer's gaze, giving the works focus and depth. The dot carries boundless creativity, leading the viewer to the eternal beauty of the design.

● **The line symbolizes creativity, suggesting growth and evolution through its infinite extension and layering.** As a symbol of connection, journey, and the flow of life, the line gives the design movement and structure. It is not merely a tool for linking elements but for structuring the narrative and guiding the visual reading. Through the rhythm of the line, designers depict the flow of life and the endless extension of creativity.

● **The expansion of the plane represents the balance of self, nature, and wisdom.** As the main body of the shape, the plane displays the beauty of stability, wholeness, and balance. It is not only a medium for conveying information but also a vessel for designers to convey this harmony. Through the precise use of the plane, designers create visual depth and layers, echoing the balance of beauty in the "permanence in impermanence."

● **The collaboration of dots, lines, and planes is essential to constructing graphic design.** A dot becomes a line, a line transforms into a plane, and a plane is broken down into dots—these elements influence and transform one another, creating a design language rich in layers and depth. This arrangement allows simple elements to unfold into meaningful visual content, highlighting the profound philosophical pursuit embedded in the design.

● **Aesthetic choices and the use of symbols in design serve as mediums for expressing philosophical thoughts and ideas, offering a unique artistic interpretation of "permanence in impermanence."** Through a deep exploration of dots, lines, and planes, the philosophical pursuit in design resonates with the core principles of Japanese graphic design, seeking beauty in the eternal amidst the transient. Designers are not merely creators of art; they are bearers of philosophical thought, using the organic combination of dots, lines, and planes to present a philosophical beauty that profoundly reflects on life, time, and existence. This fusion of aesthetics and philosophy transcends visual perception, guiding the viewer toward a deeper contemplation of "the permanent beauty in impermanence."

● In this chapter, we will delve into the philosophical reflections and symbolic aesthetics behind the use of these fundamental elements, exploring the creative applications and potential of dots, lines, and planes by designers.

CREATIVE APPLICATION OF FUNDAMENTAL ELEMENTS

○ During the transformation process of dots, lines, and planes in design, have you consciously sought or discovered innovative ways to apply these basic elements? How do these creative transformations inject new vitality into the design language?

BLURRING THE BOUNDARIES BETWEEN DOTS, LINES, AND PLANES

● At first glance, dots, lines, and planes may appear to be distinct, independent entities, each serving a specific role in the composition. A dot is the most basic design element, marking a position in space. A line adds length and direction, guiding the eye and defining rhythm or space. And a plane establishes boundaries and forms the surface for shapes, colors, and composition. However, in the eyes of Japanese designers, these boundaries are not fixed; they are fluid and can constantly interact with one another.

● Designers often push the conventional boundaries of dot, line, or plane, allowing these elements to flow into one another. A dot can transform into a line, a line can evolve into a plane, and a plane can split back into dots. By "blurring" these boundaries, designers invite viewers to reconsider their perceptions of space, form, and meaning. This creates a visual language that is both minimalist and complex, reimagining the most basic shapes to evoke more profound meanings and conceptual depth. Ultimately, this approach breaks the limits of design, enabling greater creative expression through fluid, interconnected forms.

EXPLORING NEW POSSIBILITIES WITH LIMITED ELEMENTS

● **Using the most basic modeling elements—dots, lines, and planes—provides a powerful approach for exploring the "geometrization" of things in design.** These fundamental elements may seem simple or minimalist, yet they possess boundless potential for transformation and abstraction. By distilling the complex world around us into basic geometric forms, designers can build new visual expressions. The process of geometrizing objects or concepts helps break them down into their core components, deepening our understanding of their structure and meaning. This abstraction not only simplifies the design process but also opens space for innovative visual language that resonates clearly with viewers.

● **Through iterative prototyping and refinement, designers explore more possibilities within limited elements.** The iterative process allows for gradual improvement, uncovering new forms and relationships within the design. Each prototype becomes a stepping stone, bringing us closer to discovering the ideal combination of elements that conveys the desired message or aesthetic. Designing within a limited set of shapes, this simple approach stimulates the designers' creativity by challenging them to express within a confined framework. Even slight adjustments to these basic shapes can produce unexpected effects. Thus, limitations become not constraints, but gateways to new expressions and visual languages.

● **Even with the most mundane elements—dots, lines, and planes—designers can make their works unique by infusing their personal ideas and aesthetic consciousness.** The beauty of these simple elements lies in the flexibility they offer. What may begin as a basic geometric shape can transform into something entirely unique by incorporating a creative approach. Adding color, texture, proportion, and rhythm allows designers to breathe life into the simplest forms. Even under seemingly uniform constraints, the ability to inject individuality into minimalism makes each design truly one-of-a-kind.

DIVERSE APPROACHES: ANALOG AND DIGITAL CREATION

● **Artists have explored and contrasted analog and digital methods of creation throughout their process.** Analog techniques are often rooted in the tactile interaction with materials, while digital methods offer precision and flexibility. Both approaches can inspire unexpected creative sparks. Some designers are passionate about hand-drawing, as it allows them to form an intuitive connection with their works. Hand-drawing encourages the free flow of creativity, with imperfect, spontaneous marks and the organic feel of a pen on paper becoming an integral part of the creative process. These "imperfections" often result in unexpected forms or structures, providing inspiration that might not arise in a purely digitally controlled environment. Analog techniques are not just a method of creation but a way of discovery, often sparking new directions for design.

● **Digital tools and applications, on the other hand, offer precision and flexibility, making it easier to create clean lines, smooth planes, and precise geometric compositions.** Digital design allows designers to realize their ideas with a level of control and accuracy that traditional media can rarely achieve. However, even within the digital space, there are surprising moments. When designers manipulate elements—whether through algorithms, digital strokes, or program-generated patterns—unexpected forms or structures can emerge, adding an element of unpredictability to the design process. These surprises can lead to innovative solutions, much like the "serendipity" found in analog design.

● **Designers note that switching between these two creative modes can also spark new ideas and inspiration.** Each medium provides unique insights and interpretations, enriching the possibilities of the other. Whether through the imperfect touch of hand-drawing or the precise rendering of digital tools, designers continuously transform these basic elements, creating distinct and meaningful expressions. Blurring boundaries, embracing limitations, and leveraging both analog and digital techniques ensure that the design language remains vibrant, dynamic, and ever-evolving.

THE DESIGNER'S RESPONSE

● **Agata Yamaguchi:** Placing elements, such as dots, lines, and planes, within the margins is a fundamental principle of graphic design, crucial for creating a harmonious composition of static elements. When designing, I also pay attention to the proportion between the elements and the margins. I study how much space the main elements and the edges of the paper should occupy on a square sheet to achieve an aesthetic balance, drawing inspiration from outstanding examples of past graphic design. In my own work, I don't aim for absolute beauty; instead, I intentionally break away from it, seeking innovative visual expression. ○ When others see my designs, they might ask: "Why place this element here?" or "Why this specific position?" Many might be skeptical. However, I don't intend to make people feel like I've deliberately chosen an odd placement. While my designs are guided by intuition, I hold traditional aesthetics in high regard. At the same time, sometimes I prioritize my own sense of harmony and layout over conventional aesthetics.

● **Aki Kanai & Taku Sasaki:** We are now more concerned with making new discoveries through simple applications rather than pursuing innovation through dots, lines, and planes. We believe design emerges from activities that engage with the everyday, so we strive to create visuals that subtly refine our perception—introducing small changes that we may not even notice. We believe this is because moving the viewer's mind is challenging unless we push the boundaries of what lies just beyond their tolerance.

● **Arata Kubota:** Designing with dots, lines, and planes allows for the creation of designs that can communicate non-verbally to anyone. I place great importance on taking time to think through creative ideas, seeing if I can craft a design that accurately conveys information within a limited set of elements.

● **Daisuke Kobayashi:** In design, I believe that dots, lines, and planes are ways to simplify visual information, offering the clearest interpretation to the viewer. While simplifying the design as much as possible, I continuously explore the limits of expression to achieve the intended purpose.

● **Eriko Kawakami:** I believe that by varying the position of dots, lines, and planes, information can be organized, and the focal point becomes clearer. I also think that designing within limited elements provides an opportunity to explore new forms of expression.

● **Hirokazu Matsuda:** The process of discovery through hand-drawing is essential. It's not about creating something entirely new, but rather engaging with the ongoing history of design and the foundational roots of the world.

● **Hiroko Sakai:** I often make special use of flat elements. By incorporating photographic elements and hand-drawn fills, I can create designs with more depth. At times, I combine analog techniques like handwriting and paper cutting with digital expression. I believe this enhances the expressive power and impact of flat elements, boosting their originality.

● **Josephine Grenier:** Rather than seeing it purely as a pursuit of innovation, I view it as an opportunity to reveal the underlying structure of my designs to the viewer, essentially inviting them backstage. For example, in the *Wurface* project, I intentionally left my grid visible, much like the architectural plans for tiling, as a nod to the tile design distributor's aesthetic. While it may not be a groundbreaking innovation, it adds a layer of transparency and authenticity to the design, imbuing it with depth and context. Similarly, in *Cacao Haven*, dynamic movement is conveyed through the strategic use of dots and lines, infusing energy into what could otherwise feel static. By embracing the fundamental elements of dots, lines, and planes in design and making them visible to the viewers, I aim to introduce a new design language that goes beyond aesthetics. It's about creating a deeper connection between the viewers and the design process, encouraging them to appreciate the thoughtfulness and intricacies behind every creative decision.

● **Maehara Shoichi:** Using applications for design is incredibly convenient. It makes creating clean lines and smooth planes much easier. However, in exchange for this convenience, we sometimes lose the subtle fluctuations of new expressive possibilities, like the habits of drawing shapes or the blurring of lines caused by breath. I don't think applications are bad—I use them often because they're so practical. However, I believe it's important to recognize that we are losing these fluctuations of possibility. In fact, just being aware of this is already an exploration of new forms of expression.

● **Miharu Matsunaga:** For me, the desire to create something unprecedented, whether in client work or personal projects, is a driving force. Often, the simplest elements—dots, lines, and planes—are enough to convey powerful ideas. Simplifying things requires courage, but true craftsmanship is born in the process of subtraction.

● **Minako Izumi:** When I begin designing, I start by trying the simplest approach. In other words, I look for ways to achieve the design using dots, lines, planes, and typography combinations. Illustration and photography are suitable and effective for commercial and cultural projects, but they are often not ideal for academic or architectural design. The most creative and satisfying moments come when we can transform abstract and complex information into a design that, in a sense, "says nothing" yet "feels like something." It's also important for us not to strip away the viewers' imagination and creativity.

● **Mitsuki Kashiwagi:** I don't really care whether something is novel; what matters more to me is whether the shape is beautiful and comfortable. However, sometimes things created with this mindset end up feeling fresh and new. If you deliberately chase novelty, it becomes difficult to create something interesting, so I try to avoid being constrained by that.

● **Mitsutaka Nakao:** My idea is to create a shape in the simplest way possible. It could be a line, a plane, or even a dot. I want the shape to be as simple as possible, yet unique for various reasons.

● **Muramatsu Takehiko:** I am dedicated to creating fresh and unprecedented designs. While I am not proficient in new technologies such as programming or artificial intelligence, I excel at subtly adjusting design principles or referencing and integrating past materials to construct entirely new visual effects. ○ I have always aimed to achieve the following three goals: ① To explore cross-disciplinary expressions between image and text, design and illustration; ② To inject emotion and wildness into vector graphics; ③ To incorporate elements that deviate from modern design ideals—such as kitsch, indigeneity, and absurdity—into my works, turning them into mediums for dialogue across Asian cultures. ○ To this end, I often step outside the geometric framework of dot, line, and plane, and instead adopt a visual language that carries a sense of distortion, hesitation, or awkwardness. However, I do not intend to adopt the hand-drawn aesthetic often described as "tasteful" in the Japanese design context. Rather, I aim to use textureless vector graphics as my primary mode of design expression.

● **Naoko Fukuoka:** Even if you choose the "right" idea, it will still take effort and exploration to make it visually appealing. In other words, before you begin, you need to carefully consider whether you have found a theme or concept that is truly appropriate for the work you are about to create. ○ Even novel expressions can lack impact if they appear in the wrong context, while well-known expressions can feel fresh depending on their placement. Popular expressions and trends often introduce unintended contexts that may diverge from your intended message. To break free from these constraints, it can be helpful to return to fundamental elements such as dots, lines, and planes.

● **Naonori Yago:** I discovered this approach while drawing with my elder daughter. Her lines were very captivating, and I observed them closely as she drew. They had distinct qualities—some were controlled, others uncontrolled; some were strong, others weak. I wanted to create something using these lines. That led me to explore how to express handwritten texture through dots in graphic design. ○ Before this, I struggled to create individual expressions using fundamental geometric shapes on a computer. This discovery was a breakthrough in my design process. Graphic design is fundamentally about simplifying expression. However, this can sometimes contradict the need to establish a designer's identity. Moreover, graphic design often plays a supporting role to other elements like photography, text, or illustration, making it even harder to build a distinct identity. ○ In the industry, we often use the term "scrape off" to describe simplifying the design process. However, I prefer to think of it as "compression." Scraping away risks losing unique essence, whereas compression allows it to be preserved in a refined yet lightweight form. With this philosophy of compression, I strive to create distinctive designs using fundamental elements.

● **Ryohei Miyata:** To break free from my hand-drawing habits, I use document applications like Keynote on my MacBook. I believe that the limitation of using only simple shapes expands the range of impressions and interpretations I can derive from the picture.

● **Ryuichi Kawajiri:** In graphic design, dots, lines, and planes are fundamental elements. To me, they are preset tools that anyone can easily handle. In other words, I don't believe that simply arranging uniform materials as they are will make them look the same. So, when using these elements for design expression, I always try to add some ideas and aesthetic value. For example, when I look at an oil painting, I ask myself: Why can I gaze at this painting for so long? I try to bring the insights I gain from this into my graphic design work. I strive to create designs with elements that are worth appreciating.

● **Shunta Sakamoto:** If there's anything that sets me apart from other designers, it's my approach to using software. I try to embrace the unintended forms that arise during the coding process and incorporate them into my designs in an "aikido-like" manner. I feel this is similar to human work, as humans have always found meaning in natural phenomena.

● **SAKIE:** Lines are the expressive technique in my work, characterized by mechanical repetition and intersection. My creative concept is that when the expressiveness of ordered lines is combined with the warmth of colored pencils in an illustration, a new impression emerges.

● **Sakura Kashiwazaki:** Ever since a long time ago, I have focused on basic shapes like circles (which can also be seen as dots) and rectangles in my independent creations. I've found that repeatedly designing and modifying prototypes under simple rules is more fascinating than freely choosing from an infinite number of options. It also makes it easier to discover unexpected shapes.

● **sanzui:** In my design process, I focus on observing the inherent beauty and characteristics of the elements themselves. I often draw inspiration from studying nature and architecture, observing the balance between the natural world and man-made structures. This allows me to imagine how specific shapes, lines, and dots can come together in a unique and meaningful way. By combining these observations with my creative ideas, I aim to create designs that reflect the essence of the subject and transform basic elements into something innovative.

● **Shimizu Kango:** Each time I design, I explore new possibilities. When inspiration strikes, it often feels like I've discovered an entirely new form of expression—but looking back, it frequently turns out to be something strangely familiar. Although I strive to break new ground in my visual language, it's not an easy task. That's why I try to combine design with a concept or a system, using this approach to search for a sense of originality that is uniquely mine.

● **studio wonder:** In my works, steam is generated by arranging small dots into circles that anyone can handle, then placing them in strips. These graphics are also placed in the illustration to represent the sizzle of freshly baked croissants and freshly ground coffee, which is the main appeal of the Shirokuma Mikazuki Coffee (See Page 89).

● **Tadashi Ueda:** I don't think about it too much. For me, distorting basic shapes is a way to introduce a sense of playfulness.

● **Taichi Tamaki:** I believe dots, lines, and planes are fundamental elements of design. What matters is how well they are composed in balance. Equally important is embedding a story within these elements—when a story is present, dots, lines, and planes transform into new forms of expression.

● **Tasuku Matsuo:** In my design process, I focus on both analog and digital iterations. Digital tools themselves limit the expression of shapes, so I first use a pencil to explore shapes and discover interesting forms intuitively. I then refine the shapes with digital tools, followed by further modifications and texturing using analog techniques. We believe that by repeating this process, we can create a new form of expression that combines classical beauty with modern vitality.

● **Tomomi Mizukoshi:** Using basic shapes like circles, triangles, and squares in artworks abstracts the motif. For example, circles can resemble eyeballs, apples, or snowmen, while triangles can become trees or umbrellas. I always enjoy how different shapes and color combinations can transform a piece into something entirely new.

● **UESATSU:** I've always sought interesting ways of observation and creation. First, the dots, lines, and planes in my digital works are the core elements, all built on a foundation of constraint. By "constraint," I mean the forms that exist within the limitations of software, where anyone can create standardized forms of beauty. As creators integrate their own rules, the originality of the work gradually emerges. In this context, there is no unstable "fluctuation" from hand-drawing, but rather life forms completed in software, where unpredictable coincidences give birth to a new utopia.

● **You Kojima:** We are currently exploring a new technique. However, it's a very simple one. It's similar to stencil techniques, but I'm trying to make it faster and more graphic in design. Here's a brief explanation about "Feeling the Painting." ① First, use a craft knife to carefully cut a shape into a piece of paper to create the stencil. ② Lay a new piece of architectural paper underneath and use a roller to apply paint. ③ Try to complete the process within three minutes. ○ "Affordable, fast, and simple" are the key principles of my design work. Through this method, I maintain and nurture my sensitivity.

● **Yukari Okada:** During the design process, I consciously establish rules and limitations. Each design concept is different, so the rules and limitations vary each time. I think that's where the fun lies. The clearer the concept, the more defined the rules and limitations become, and the more I can play with the combination of dots, lines, and planes. I question, break, and reconstruct the rules and limitations I set for myself in pursuit of interesting and unexpected graphic observations.

● **Yu Miyama:** I'd like to answer this question using my expertise in letter design. People usually think of letters as made up of lines, but lines always have width. In the process of designing letters, I expand the width of these lines into planes, then transform these expanded planes into various shapes, allowing for free letter forms. The same goes for dots. The way of thinking that blurs the boundaries between dots, lines, and planes is crucial. Lines in letters also have different qualities. Imagine what material is used to draw the lines and how they are drawn—it changes how the line is expressed. For example, it's difficult to draw uniform lines with a brush (like the kind used in calligraphy), as the lines will always have fluctuations. But with a hard-bristled or flat brush, you can create slightly more uniform lines. I believe that by expanding lines into planes and imagining the process of drawing lines in this way, new letterforms can be created.

● **Yusei Oi:** By paying attention to the shapes of objects in everyday life, I began to realize their aesthetic qualities. For example, constellations are also made up of dots, lines, and planes. I believe that the ideas and perspectives involved in transforming things into geometric forms can inspire new creativity.

● **Yuto Tamura:** I don't see dots, lines, and planes as mere tools for constructing a design. Instead, I uncover and capture them as they naturally exist within all things. To me, designing with these elements is like taking an X-ray, revealing the structural essence of an object. In the process, unexpected visuals sometimes emerge—images I never could have imagined. It's in those moments of small but profound discovery that I find joy, especially when I can share them with others.

● **Yuuri Mikami:** When designing, rather than consciously focusing on transforming dots, lines, and planes, I start with words or concepts and deeply research the subject. Through this process, I reinterpret basic elements like dots, lines, and planes from new perspectives, incorporating unconventional arrangements or movements to inject fresh vitality into the design language.

● **Zin Nagao:** Whatever I'm doing, I always have the urge to create. Even when I'm out for a walk, I record things I find interesting, like grass, flowers, the ground, road fences, and signs, etc. If I get inspired while reading a book or watching a video at home, I'll immediately pull out my computer and try it out. I also love Dutch and French design. Since my student days, I've been collecting art books and font samples. Looking at these designs I admire, I feel that my desire to create a lot of interesting things has led me to create fascinating characters. I've also loved retro video games, and I think my use of graphics and color may have been influenced by them.

PHILOSOPHICAL PURSUITS IN DESIGN

Q2

◯ In your design work, how do you convey and present philosophical ideas and concepts through aesthetic choices and the use of symbols?

TARGETING INFORMATION DELIVERY

● **In design rooted in dots, lines, and planes, designers commonly use these basic elements as tools for conveying information. True skill lies not in presenting information in exhaustive detail, but in cleverly controlling the content, method, and extent of communication.** Effective design does not tell everything directly; rather, it manages the amount of information shared, emphasizes key aspects, and leaves space for the audience to actively engage in interpretation. This meticulous approach embodies design thinking—where communication is purposeful and dynamic, invites the audience to participate, rather than overwhelming them with excessive detail.

● **At the heart of this process is the drive to clarify ideas and concepts.** Designers should distill complex thoughts into their simplest form, ensuring the essence of the message is conveyed without being overshadowed by unnecessary embellishments. By controlling the flow of information and focusing on what truly matters, designers can make complex concepts more digestible, understandable, and accessible. This balance between clarity and simplicity is central to design, allowing it to engage the audience directly without sacrificing depth or meaning.

● **Moreover, creating visuals in a way that is acces-sible and understandable to everyone is key to ensuring the effectiveness of a design language.** By utilizing basic geometric shapes, straightforward structures, and legible typography, designers can create powerful and easily understandable information. This minimalist approach makes the design intuitive and clear, enabling anyone to grasp the essential information at a glance. When executed well, such designs not only deliver information effectively but also create a visually engaging experience that attracts the audience and encourages deeper interaction.

CREATING A WORLDVIEW

● **Not all designers have a clear or strong concept when creating; some focus more on expressing their inner feelings, allowing their designs to emerge organically.** For these designers, elements like dots, lines, and planes transcend basic communication—they become mediums for expressing personal and philosophical ideas. In their hands, simple forms convey a worldview that is both warm and inviting, yet subtly dissonant. The tension between warmth and discord reflects deeper emotional complexities, where the design speaks not only to the intellect of the audience but also resonates with their emotions, creating a visual narrative that both challenges tradition and maintains openness. Through this approach, design becomes a powerful, introspective expression of the designers' worldview.

THE DESIGNER'S RESPONSE

● **Agata Yamaguchi:** I often use hand-drawn lines, shapes, dots, and illustrations, but I've found that they can come across as somewhat heavy. By "heavy," I mean they can be overly emotional or take time for viewers to fully understand their meaning. In contrast, digital lines have a light, adaptable, and somewhat inexpensive quality that blends well with my hand-drawn elements. It's like the experience of occasionally having fast food while mostly cooking at home. When you cook every day, you might get tired of the taste of your own food, and suddenly having to serve it to friends can feel awkward. But when you eat fast food, it often surprises you with its good taste, and sharing it with friends is a more relaxing choice.
○ Relying too much on hand-drawn elements can sometimes create a sense of distance for the viewer, even causing them to stop engaging with the works before fully grasping the concept I want to express. While digital lines and shapes are more universally accepted, I strive to find a balance between them and my hand-drawn elements. Through this way, I can create expressions that are more accessible to a wider audience and encourage more people to engage with my works.

● **Aki Kanai & Taku Sasaki:** When working on a design, our first priority is how to fit in with the given location and brand. We assemble and present ideas that fit in with the existing backgrounds but also form an identity. So our philosophy is of secondary importance. We find the challenges in front of us, how we can break through, and what new ways of thinking and seeing can be presented through design.

● **Arata Kubota:** First and foremost, design should be easy to remember, ideally simple enough for anyone to draw. Building on that, I then create novel and appealing shapes.

● **Daisuke Kobayashi:** My goal is to provide people with new insights and express them in a way that is easy for them to understand and absorb. Therefore, I prioritize controlling the amount of information included in the expression.

● **Eriko Kawakami:** I am committed to creating a balance between warmth and discord. Dots, lines, and planes can have different effects depending on their color, texture, and other factors. To evoke a sense of warmth, I might use blurriness or hand-drawn elements. And to create a sense of discord, I might remove certain elements from the final piece, creating a blank space or atmosphere.

● **Hirokazu Matsuda:** Abstract and simple character designs, if not carefully crafted, can end up being just images of people and may not convey any meaningful information. I believe what's important is that the images I create should make the viewer feel that there is "something" in them.

● **Hiroko Sakai:** The main visual effect I aim to create is to convey philosophical ideas and abstract concepts to the audience. In stage design, I focus on designing around the concept of the story to enhance the audience's imagination. For the flower arrangement exhibition, I transformed the philosophy of "Ikebana Ryuseiha" into a powerful visual presentation. The choice of colors, shapes, and elements will be crucial.

● **Josephine Grenier:** In my design, I prioritize simplicity to effectively convey philosophical ideas.

I've learned that simplicity often has the greatest impact by distilling complex concepts into accessible visuals. For instance, in a recent project on Earth's regeneration, we used a simple circular hole in the packaging to symbolize returning to our roots and embracing the life cycle. Ultimately, my approach centers on selecting meaningful symbols and aesthetic elements with inherent resonance.

● **Maehara Shoichi:** In selecting products and creating symbols, technique and knowledge are important, but I don't believe they alone lead to good design. I think it's more about not being confined by existing methods, like "this will look good" or "this will work well," but rather valuing the feelings that arise from within—those I may not fully understand but sense could be right. Pushing into the unknown is what I find most exciting.

● **Miharu Matsunaga:** I believe it's important to reduce the number of things that must be done. It's about clarifying thoughts and defining concepts, rather than being stingy with details.

● **Minako Izumi:** My clients often have innovative ideas in the academic field, so I use the simplest elements and basic, readable typography to convey their messages powerfully, quickly, and accurately. Even simple elements, through their combination and structure, can create an invisible appearance. When they magically align with the theme, the information is deeply understood by the audience and communicated more effectively.

● **Mitsuki Kashiwagi:** It's important for design to move away from descriptive language and leave space for the viewer's imagination. It should avoid being too preachy or forceful.

● **Mitsutaka Nakao:** The approach varies depending on the client and concept. There's no one-size-fits-all method, as the way we communicate and present ideas changes each time. I believe the key to design is sharing the client's vision of the world and the future, and visualizing it. Visualization is a crucial part of the design process, and we will always seek and consider the best way to convey it.

● **Muramatsu Takehiko:** I do not deliberately convey philosophical ideas. My focus lies in achieving the goals of a project and creating visually pleasing results.

● **Naoko Fukuoka:** Even when I'm not doing design work, visual images can sometimes help me understand philosophical ideas and concepts. When I am asked to visually represent an abstract concept, I first read texts and do research to better understand it. ○ As I do so, some fragmented images pop into my head. In addition to that, I often think about what kind of picture I would draw if I were to explain the concept to someone. I can't use those images as they are, but I look at them objectively and consider whether there are any ethical issues. I try not to worry even if the resulting image is something you haven't seen before or isn't a trendy expression. Rather than that, I care about whether the connection is made with the concept.

● **Naonori Yago:** One of my core philosophical themes in graphic design is "Humane Error"—embracing mistakes and celebrating humanity. I express this through noise, freehand strokes, and rough cut-ups on the surface of my designs. However, not all projects are centered around graphic design. Some, like photo direction, book design for photographers, or branding for large clients, require a different approach. In these cases, where I can't rely on surface treatments, I integrate my philosophy into the production process itself. ○ Rather than enforcing a rigid, perfected idea, I create a foundation—like the base of a house—through creative direction. Team members then build upon it, shaping each section in their own way. By allowing room for diverse opinions and suggestions, this process leads to unique outcomes that go beyond our initial vision.

● **Ryohei Miyata:** I intentionally avoid conveying the concept of facial patterns, as they inherently carry meaning. When I create, it's like collecting shapes I happen upon by chance.

● **Ryuichi Kawajiri:** I don't aim for entirely new forms that no one has seen before; instead, I focus on familiar objects as creative subjects. For such topics, we can easily imagine a standard prototype, and I hope people will compare it, understand how it's shaped, how it transforms, and why it's this way, allowing them to interpret the message the design conveys in their own way. I want people to enjoy it, because I believe that beautiful or interesting things always have meaning behind them.

● **Shunta Sakamoto:** What I value is not creating a form based on concepts or philosophy, but rather extracting the beauty hidden within the form and letting the process naturally reveal itself through the form.

● **SAKIE:** For some time, an important element in my work has been creating colorful planes with lines. I believe solid colors can feel oppressive, so I aim to create color through layers of straight lines, bringing a sense of airiness and lightness. By using the rigid element of straight lines, I try to create a gentle worldview.

● **Sakura Kashiwazaki:** I find design interesting because you can subtly control the content, method, and degree of what's conveyed, rather than simply stating everything outright. So, in any project, I constantly think about what to keep and what to remove. Is each element truly essential to the design, or can it be discarded? Or can seemingly unnecessary elements actually make the design more engaging?

● **sanzui:** I aim to create designs that allow viewers to feel comfort and enjoyment. In doing so, I focus on making the design easily recognizable and memorable for third parties. Through this, I strive for the design to have a positive impact on many people, becoming a helpful presence and bringing a sense of happiness.

● **Shimizu Kango:** I always aim to present my design ideas in the most honest way possible. But in the process of giving form to those ideas, I often face practical limitations where "meeting the requirements" becomes the main priority. As a result, I frequently have to rely on subjective judgment. ○ Although I wouldn't call this a "philosophy," these decisions inevitably carry my personal style. Sometimes I wonder whether designers should assert their individuality when working with client demands. But then again, since every piece is created by a human hand, pure objectivity is impossible—and with that in mind, I continue designing with a sense of acceptance and ease.

● **studio wonder:** Originality and creativity arise from creating visual effects and identities in a way that anyone can use and understand, but with a twist—through a sense of discordance, something strange yet clearly visible.

● **Tadashi Ueda:** While it's important for a message to be conveyed even without words, I also want to leave just enough ambiguity to make the viewer pause and think.

● **Taichi Tamaki:** I believe the answer lies within the audience. Rather than merely creating the shapes I want, it's more important to explore forms that are unfamiliar to the viewer. By doing so, I can craft graphics that leave a lasting impression.

● **Tasuku Matsuo:** In my design, I place great emphasis on the spirit of play. Much like when I was a child, freely playing with paper and clay, I enjoy the process of creating shapes and color combinations, finding joy in crafting forms that satisfy me. I aim to use bold, unique shapes and vibrant colors to create designs that delight the viewer.

● **Tomomi Mizukoshi:** By rendering all motifs flat and abstract, they appear to coexist equally and vibrantly within the artwork.

● **UESATSU:** My design work typically revolves around a single theme, such as flowers, hearts, or eyes. These patterns carry knowledge that people have accumulated through experience. The depth of this knowledge may vary from person to person, but everyone goes through the process of engaging with established concepts. Based on this, in the *Imaginary Flowers* series, we explored how to communicate with people through flowers; and in the *Love and Emotion* series, we looked at how to confront love. These two themes are essential to life, and my aim is to encourage the audience to question and reflect through universal concepts. By adding my own interpretation to existing symbols and patterns, I aim to present new perspectives and ideas, leaving intentional ambiguity and space for viewers to freely feel and think.

● **You Kojima:** Let me give you an example from my past work that left a lasting impression on me. When I designed the cover for my musician friend XTAL's second album *Aburelu*, I was reflecting on this very question (the cover was a photographic design, so it might not align directly with the concept of this book). I believe that when designing for music, the role of a graphic designer is to feel the music created by the artist and translate it into visual form. ○ To return to the original question, my concept and approach are centered around this: when I use symbols and other graphic representations, I shape them by distorting the discomfort, comfort, and improved environments I experience in everyday life. Rather than simply presenting these feelings, I just focus on making them exist.

● **Yukari Okada:** When I incorporate philosophical ideas and concepts into graphic design, I strive to make them simple and easy to understand. During the process, I come up with a few design narratives and attempt to visualize them through design. However, if too much content is crammed into the design, it no longer qualifies as good design. I focus on extracting the core essence of the story and symbolizing it, reducing it to its most minimal form.

● **Yu Miyama:** In my design, I strive to convey more with fewer elements. I often incorporate Chinese characters into my works because they are almost the only existing written symbols that are both text and pictorial in nature. Of course, modern Chinese characters no longer contain many pictographic elements, but I reinterpret their forms in a contemporary way, so they can function as both images and text (Ideally, even if one doesn't understand Chinese characters, they should still be able to interpret the picture). I believe this approach allows the characters to convey additional visual information beyond their linguistic function, thus making my intended message clearer. Furthermore, I see the overlap of meaning and function as a form of information in itself, which can enhance the design.

● **Yusei Oi:** I make subtle adjustments to color and shape to effectively communicate ideas to others. I also showcase the design process to clients and present the work, helping them gain a deeper understanding of the design.

● **Yuto Tamura:** I believe the world should be simple. An excess of information and choices often obscures what truly matters. In my design work, I always strive to capture the essence, clarify priorities, and deliver the message in its simplest form.

● **Yuuri Mikami:** I believe that understanding human cognition is just as important as deeply understanding the subject of the design. As a theoretical foundation for designers, I think it's necessary to broadly study semiotics, cognitive psychology, and phenomenology, as well as sociology, ethics, and contemporary philosophy. When it comes to symbols, we must consider social and cultural differences in their use, so understanding different cultures is also crucial. Additionally, I work with the premise that it's impossible for the intended message to be 100% conveyed to the audience, and misunderstandings are inevitable. With these principles in mind, I aim to create expressions that allow for positive misunderstandings—designs that leave room for varied interpretations. For this reason, rather than using concrete motifs, I often opt for abstract expressions that allow for interpretive flexibility.

● **Zin Nagao:** I mainly focus on experimental type design, but I don't prioritize concepts or ideas—rather, I aim to create something unseen before, something that surprises people. I also design things that I personally enjoy, finding comfort in the process of creating new forms and characters. I believe that the inspiration and emotions I experience during this process are directly conveyed to the audience. By combining shapes and animation, I can express things more concretely and directly.

CONTINUOUS ITERATION OF DESIGN PHILOSOPHY

Q3

O The mutual transformation and fusion of dots, lines, and planes create graphics that seem to perpetually evolve. Design is an iterative process. How do you stay sensitive to new ideas and technologies, and integrate different philosophical considerations into your design practices?

PERCEIVING THE CHANGING WORLD

● **In the group interview, many Japanese designers emphasized the importance of being sensitive to new ideas and technologies, as design must constantly adapt to an ever-evolving world.** Their sensitivity to change stems from the belief that design is not static but a dynamic force that must reflect shifts in society, culture, and technology.

● **Equally important is the process of observation and experience.** Designers often highlight that the key to perceiving the changes in the world lies in direct engagement—whether through participatory courses, exhibitions, or observing daily life around them. This active involvement allows them to discover new forms of "beauty," as they are constantly exposed to fresh ideas, perspectives, and visual stimuli.

● **Interestingly, some designers shared the concept of "tuning"—stepping away from continuous design work to reconnect with broader cultural and sensory experiences.** This intentional detachment from design enables them to refresh their perspectives, draw inspiration from new sources of influence, and remain open to unconventional creative ideas. By embracing both the familiar and the unknown, designers can keep their works innovative and responsive to the ongoing changes in the world.

"NEW" DESIGN

● In design, what is often considered "new" is not entirely novel; rather, it is a fusion of existing ideas and elements with something "new." **The concept of "new design" frequently relies on reimagining and remixing influences from the past, blending old concepts with new technologies, techniques, or perspectives.** In many cases, the boundaries between the old and the new are blurred because contemporary design evolves from historical styles, cultural trends, and traditional techniques. Modern design concepts do not emerge from nothing; they are based on a reinterpretation and adjustment of what already exists to suit the current environment.

● In fact, some artists suggest integrating their usual techniques into a new work, and this "freshness" itself evokes a sense of novelty, as designers explore new ways to express their established practices. The interplay of familiarity and novelty creates a dynamic space where innovation thrives, fueling creativity through a reassessment and recreation of the past.

● Ultimately, the goal of design is not merely to capture a moment, but to create works that stand the test of time—what we previously referred to as seeking permanent beauty in impermanence. By drawing from both the past and the present, designers can create works with real significance and impact, ensuring their value and resonance extend far beyond current trends.

THE ROLE OF THE DESIGNER

● **In this era of constant emergence of new ideas and technologies, the role of the designer has never been more significant.** Some designers suggest that they are not just followers of trends; driven by a unique aesthetic awareness and the ability to envision new possibilities, they have the potential to create trends themselves. By blending innovation with a strong personal style, designers shape the way we perceive the world around us. Their works not only respond to current trends but also anticipates and defines the future. Truly influential designers are those who seamlessly integrate new ideas and technologies into their creations while staying true to their distinct aesthetic sense, ultimately leading the way in both trends and aesthetics.

THE DESIGNER'S RESPONSE

● **Agata Yamaguchi:** I believe that around 80% of universal aesthetics and graphic design principles remain constant. While my work is firmly grounded in these enduring fundamentals, I am constantly learning and deepening my understanding of emerging trends and technologies. I draw inspiration from design books, award-winning works, popular projects, and social media to stay informed about the latest developments. As trends evolve, I've noticed shifts in the balance between hand-drawn elements and inorganic lines and dots in design. I strive to remain flexible and adaptable, never settling for the status quo.

● **Aki Kanai & Taku Sasaki:** We believe that it is mainly acquired through our work. New projects and new client collaborations allow us to see the contours of our design thinking clearly in form, and exposure to new people and products continuously challenges us to revisit and evolve our ideas. The use of flexible and universal motifs is also an important part of our activities. By keeping that basic point in mind and repeating the process many times in an iterative way, fresh ideas become visible.

● **Arata Kubota:** I believe my design evolves through various projects and experiences. From the traditional craftsmanship to latest technologies, my works continuously develop through interactions with diverse ideas. There is much to learn from things seemingly unrelated to design, which is why I believe it's essential to closely observe our daily lives and the events unfolding in the world around us.

● **Daisuke Kobayashi:** In our daily lives, I believe that perceiving the changes of the times provides valuable cues for continuous creativity and design. Through newly emerging perspectives, I am confident that the expression of dots, lines, and planes will once again offer us fresh inspiration.

● **Eriko Kawakami:** Continuously improving my design is extremely important to me. Throughout the design process, I carefully observe the details of everyday life and take note of my impressions when encountering new things.

● **Hirokazu Matsuda:** I feel somewhat distanced from new ideas and technologies. What I do is observe the patterns of the world—while these discoveries may be new, my intention is not to seek out novelty.

● **Hiroko Sakai:** I strive to stay attuned to new technologies and current design trends by gathering information from museums, books, and social media. At the same time, there is much to learn from the great designs of the past. By maintaining sensitivity to trends while digesting these elements and integrating them into my works, I believe I can create new forms of expression.

● **Josephine Grenier:** As a graphic designer, I recognize that design must adapt to an ever-evolving world. To ensure my works remain innovative and relevant, I stay attuned to new ideas and technologies, continuously integrating them into my practice to stay ahead. For example, I am currently involved in a sustainability project focused on developing eco-friendly packaging using innovative materials such as food waste and sustainable seaweed. By actively participating in these initiatives, I keep my designs aligned with the latest advancements in sustainable technology while making a positive contribution to environmental conservation. ○ In addition, I strive to incorporate diverse philosophical perspectives into my design practice, with a strong emphasis on inclusive design. Recently, I utilized the Atkinson Hyperlegible typeface, developed in collaboration with a Braille research institute, to ensure that the medical product labeling I designed is accessible to individuals with low vision.

● **Maehara Shoichi:** What I cherish is embracing unnamed values in a state of ambiguity. Rather than trying to understand what I don't comprehend, I prefer to accept it and explore it with a sense of innocence rather than analysis. I aspire to be an extension of the drawings I once created with crayons as a child.

● **Miharu Matsunaga:** For me, this means stepping beyond Japan and into the world. I have especially lived between Japan and Sweden, where I see my works as a fusion of Japan's strong design identity and Scandinavian design. If design connects me to China, I hope to visit again.

● **Minako Izumi:** I love dots, lines, and planes—they are the fundamental elements of visual design, yet they hold no inherent meaning. Design often conveys unnecessary information, such as poorly executed images, clashing colors, overly decorative typography, or excessive text. These can be avoided through basic design principles and typography. If these fundamental elements can express my intended message, I am satisfied. I am not driven by innovation in imagery, but rather by how these elements can be used to communicate new ideas in future creations.

● **Mitsuki Kashiwagi:** I always try to approach my works as if I were crafting by hand. Sometimes, design elements I create for fun unexpectedly find their way into client projects. I value these moments and find joy in creating with this mindset.

● **Mitsutaka Nakao:** I believe it is important to closely observe things beyond design itself. Exposure to diverse experiences can often lead to new insights and creative outcomes.

● **Muramatsu Takehiko:** ① I often post sudden flashes of visual inspiration on Instagram, treating them as "bait" for self-inspiration from a bystander's perspective. These works are usually conceptual sketches, often presented in minimalist forms using dots, lines, and planes from geometry. ② I actively explore fields beyond design. I'm deeply interested in crafts, folklore, cultural anthropology, and multiculturalism around the world. ③ To generate ideas distinct from other designers, I once deliberately distanced myself from design trends and avoided contemporary works. However, this approach has many drawbacks, and I wouldn't recommend it to others.

● **Naoko Fukuoka:** Various complex conditions call for new expressions. For example, printing colors may be limited, the design might need to be adapted into a video, ethical considerations must be addressed, or it needs to be multilingual. Furthermore, concepts are constantly being recombined in the world—hidden problems are given names, and existing values are disrupted. ○ Recombining concepts demands new visual representations, and finding ways to meet that challenge is exciting. In any case, conflicts arise when you attempt to visually express the image in your mind. I believe that's when a designer's work truly begins. Concepts and visual representations never fully align, and that gap is what makes the process so compelling.

● **Naonori Yago:** I think almost all graphic designers' work is client-based, but as creators, we should have our own projects. Having a project means having a concept for oneself. A creator with a strong concept can influence other industries and people while also gaining access to the latest information and unique ideas from different fields, bringing fresh perspectives into their own works. ○ As graphic designers, we work with fundamental elements—dots, lines, and planes. To create something new, we must combine these basics with fresh ideas and evolving technologies.

● **Ryohei Miyata:** I aim to incorporate human perceptual phenomena into my designs, such as "illusory perception," where a stain on a wall appears to resemble a face, or "pareidolia," where three dots can be perceived as a face (see page 308–309).

● **Ryuichi Kawajiri:** I'm not very attuned to new ideas and technologies—I often ignore app updates, even when they introduce useful features, simply because I don't notice or know how to use them. It's a bit embarrassing. Of course, I have some interest in new forms of expression and current design trends, but when it comes to my own works, I'm less concerned with chasing novelty. I prefer function-driven design over superficial trends, and I try to practice this approach. I want my designs to transcend time and be genuinely appreciated. Personally, I have a deep love for historical clothing and antiques—I feel that graphic design resonates with them in the way both exist as mass-produced reproductions.

● **Shunta Sakamoto:** Every day, I realize that if we consciously seek beauty in things not yet widely considered beautiful, we will discover unseen forms and aesthetics—bringing them to life in our designs.

● **SAKIE:** I have been exploring the fresh possibilities that emerge when combining techniques of depicting and expressing straight lines within a single piece. The same lines, simply by varying their color and density, can create an infinite range of visual effects. In the future, I hope to push these possibilities even further.

● **Sakura Kashiwazaki:** Trendy designs may gain attention on social media, but they aren't necessarily the latest innovations since many people are already practicing them. I believe that creating something truly new requires a unique aesthetic sensibility. Beyond design itself, I think personal experiences play a key role in shaping this sensibility, which is why I strive to stay true to the things that genuinely interest me. When it comes to sharing my insights, I still have a lot to learn, but as I gain more experience through independent projects and client work, I'm gradually refining my approach.

● **sanzui:** To remain sensitive to new ideas and technologies, I focus on constantly finding elements that I find "interesting." For example, when combining two different elements, there are moments when I instinctively feel, "This could create a new expression." These realizations breathe new life into my designs. Moving in a direction that excites me personally also translates into my client work, where I aim to create designs that surprise and delight my clients. This creative evolution, I believe, forms philosophical elements within the design, leading to deeper and more meaningful expressions.

● **Shimizu Kango:** Social media is undeniably the fastest way to discover new ideas and technologies. However, the overwhelming flood of information can also blur one's aesthetic direction. ○ To counter this, I print out the works and materials that I like—or those I want to be consciously influenced by—and keep them nearby. At the same time, I make a point of regularly creating personal works, refining ideas through repetition until they can be applied to actual projects.

● **studio wonder:** We continuously follow both Japanese and international design. We believe that by incorporating the client's requirements and highlighting the differences between a product and its competitors, we can create truly unique and original designs.

● **Tadashi Ueda:** When generating ideas, I don't rely solely on graphic design for inspiration. I also don't believe it's necessary to constantly chase contemporary trends.

● **Taichi Tamaki:** Gaining insight into society is essential, as design should play an active role within it. With the diversification of media, I believe design must communicate a consistent message, regardless of time, place, or audience. This makes the design of fundamental and universal graphic elements—such as dots, lines, and planes—more important than ever.

● **Tasuku Matsuo:** We believe that exploring unexpected combinations based on our experiences and observations can lead to new forms of expression. To achieve this, we must stay attuned to technological advancements and trends while also stepping out into the world to reassess our lifestyles and gather diverse inspirations. Our goal is to create designs that stand the test of time and possess enduring beauty.

● **Tomomi Mizukoshi:** I enjoy taking paths I've never been on before and talking to people. It gives me a sense of familiarity with what I already know, while allowing me to experience the freshness of something new.

● **UESATSU:** I believe that modern ideas emerge from a fusion of existing and not entirely new elements. In my daily graphic design work, it is crucial to successfully integrate established techniques and ways of seeing with new technologies while incorporating them into my own creative framework.

● **You Kojima:** Sometimes, I make a habit of fine-tuning my daily routine—taking time to look at the mountains, walking through the forest, waking up early to observe how my body feels during movement—ensuring that my senses don't become stagnant. This ongoing adjustment enhances my sensitivity and helps me connect with new creative channels. By doing so, I maintain my life's rhythm while actively engaging in new forms of design expression.

● **Yukari Okada:** When I first began designing, I sought new forms of expression by attending exhibitions and learning new techniques. Recently, however, I've found greater inspiration in nature—the intricate veins of a leaf I picked up while playing in the park with my daughter, the resilience of a cherry tree branch, or the silhouette of a person momentarily illuminated by the setting sun. These natural elements—dots, lines, and planes—are never static; they shift and evolve with nature itself. Observing this constant transformation has become one of my most valuable lessons.

● **Yu Miyama:** Observe the world around you, experiment with different tools—sometimes, unexpected discoveries arise. For example, in my work *Imagination & Technology* (see page 303), published in *Brain* magazine, I chose to use the English transliteration of each Chinese character instead of dots. This idea came to me after realizing one day that letters could be used for holographic anti-counterfeiting. ○ I always begin with hand-drawn designs before converting them into final digital data, and throughout each step of the process, I continue to uncover new insights. My interest in woodblock printing began when I started feeling constrained by working solely with digital outputs. I was also drawn to the unique lines and surface textures that woodblock printing offers. ○ Today, it's possible to complete an entire design—from concept to execution—on a single computer. However, I believe that stepping outside, experiencing different things, and creating with my own hands leads to better design.

● **Yusei Oi:** This is a continuous cycle of input and output. I immerse myself in various experiences—appreciating design, observing paintings, and taking walks in the park. I document these thoughts, sketch ideas, and experiment with new shape combinations. Through this process, I create timeless visuals.

● **Yuto Tamura:** I don't actively chase the latest design trends. Instead, I immerse myself in daily life, observing what naturally enters my field of vision. Rather than deliberately adopting external perspectives, I let my instincts guide me, allowing whatever unconsciously surfaces to take shape and find expression.

● **Yuuri Mikami:** It is essential to keep learning continuously, to strive to understand others, and to never spare effort in the pursuit of knowledge.

● **Zin Nagao:** I believe that simply chasing current trends and creating based on them does not lead to truly new design. What's important is having the potential to shape trends yourself by exploring design's evolution across different countries and eras. ○ Additionally, by accumulating cultural knowledge and insights beyond design, you can refine ideas and techniques that others may not have considered. However, refining ideas alone is not enough—presenting your work is just as crucial. Through this process, you gain an objective perspective on how things appear, which colors and shapes are compelling, and where improvements can be made.

CONCLUSION

● The uniqueness of Japanese graphic design stems from its deep cultural roots and distinctive aesthetic values. It cleverly blends the minimalist beauty of Zen philosophy, the charm of Chinese characters, inspiration from nature, the fusion of technology and tradition, the art of visual storytelling, and the Japanese spirit in art. This fusion is not merely an accumulation of elements, but a design language that has emerged from the unique melting pot of Japanese culture.

● The core philosophy of Japanese graphic design is to reveal the essence of life through the construction of "permanence in impermanence." It is a response to the fleeting nature of life and a deep exploration of existence, a profound expression of the design philosophy. Designers, through the combination of dots, lines, and planes, aim to transcend mere formal beauty and pursue a deeper philosophical contemplation that arises from within.

● **Design is an iterative process, and design thinking should evolve with it.** Designers should be sensitive to the pulse of new ideas and technologies, integrating different philosophical thoughts into their design practices to drive the updates of design thinking. This is not only a continuation of the philosophy of "permanence in impermanence" but also a continuous exploration of the unknown. With an open mindset, designers embrace new ideas, skillfully integrate them into the design process, and revitalize the ongoing development of design thinking.

INDEX

A

Agata Yamaguchi
https://www.collé.co.jp
info@colle.co.jp
290-295

Aki Kainai
https://kanaisasaki.com/
contact@kanaisasaki.com
188-201 | 284-287 | 336-337

Arata Kubota
https://www.aratakubota.net
info@aratakubota.net
126 | 248-249

D

Daigo Daikoku
https://www.ndcla.us/
ndcla@ndc.co.jp
36-53 | 130 | 168-169 | 182-183 | 202-203 |
214-215 | 246-247 | 282-283 | 288-289

Daisuke Kobayashi
https://www.sukedachidesign.jp/
info@sukedachidesign.jp、
181

E

Eriko Kawakami
https://erikokawakami.com/
eriko@erikokawakami.com
306-307 | 322 | 325

H

Hirokazu Matsuda
https://matsudahirokazu.com/
matsuda@hekichi.info
137 | 226 | 324

Hiroko Sakai
https://coton-design.com
info@coton-design.com
216 | 224-225 | 251 | 302

Hiroyuki Masuda
https://taro-inc.jp
info@taro-inc.jp
67 | 223

J

Josephine Grenier
https://www.josephinegrenier.com
j.grenier.furukawa@gmail.com
94-95 | 140-141

K

Koji Iyama
http://iyamadesign.jp/
iyama@iyamadesign.jp
58-59 | 68 | 132

M

Maehara Shoichi
https://www.maeharashoichi.com/
m@maeharashoichi.com
128-129 | 136

Masashi Murakami
https://emuni.co.jp/
manager@emuni.co.jp
120-121 | 139 | 236-237 | 316-317

Masunaga Akiko
https://masdb.jp/
masunaga@masdb.jp
165 | 217

Miharu Matsunaga (Hami)
https://www.miharumatsunaga.com/
miharumatsunaga.hami@gmail.com
hami@7m.agency
70-71 | 124-125 | 152-153 | 204-207 | 244-245 | 254-257

Minako Izumi
http://pinhole-db.com
info@pinhole-db.com
92-93 | 163

Mitsuki Kashiwagi
https://www.i-k-do.com/
ikdo@i-k-do.com
56-57 | 61 | 222 | 230-231

Mitsutaka Nakao
https://www.econosys.jp/
office@econosys.jp
69 | 133-134 | 166-167

Muramatsu Takehiko
https://mu-design-room.com
mu.design.room@gmail.com
240-241 | 300-301 | 304-305 | 320-321

N

Naoko Fukuoka
https://woolen2010.tumblr.com
fukuoka@woolen2010.com
78-79 | 151

Naonori Yago
https://naonoriyago.com/
yagonaonori@gmail.com
96-101 | 104-115 | 178-180

R

Ryohei Miyata
https://miyataryohei.com/
ryoheimiyata11@gmail.com
308-309

Ryuichi Kawajiri
https://ka-wa.jp/
kawajiri@ka-wa.jp
64-65 | 176

S

SAKIE
https://www.instagram.com/ske_artwork/
SAKIEsuzuki16@gmail.com
160-162

Sakura Kashiwazaki
https://s-kashiwazaki.com
kashiwazaki39@gmail.com
62-63 | 142-143 | 314-315

sanzui
https://www.instagram.com/sanzui0000/
sanzui0000@gmail.com
66 | 145

Shimizu Kango
https://shimizukango.com/
shimizukango@gmail.com
144 | 154-155 | 184-185 | 310-311

Shogo Kishino
https://www.6d-k.com/
info@6d-k.com
74-75 | 123 | 131 | 156-157

Shunta Sakamoto
https://new-creators.club
https://sakamoto.app
shunta.sakamoto@new-creators.club
info@sakamoto.app
228-229 | 250 | 296-297 | 326-327

STUDIO WONDER
https://studiowonder.jp/
hello@studiowonder.jp
89 | 138

T

Tadashi Ueda
https://tadashi-ueda.com/
studio@tadashi-ueda.com
146-147 | 258 | 323

Taichi Tamaki
https://taichitamaki.com/
taichitamakidesign@gmail.com
72-73 | 90-91 | 148-149 | 172-173 | 253

Taku Sasaki
https://kanaisasaki.com/
contact@kanaisasaki.com
188-201 | 284-285 | 336-337

Tasuku Matsuo
https://www.instagram.com/tasuku_matsuo/?locale=zh_CN&hl=da
tasukumatsuo.info@gmail.com
135 | 150 | 318-319 | 328-331

Tomomi Mizukoshi
tomomimizukoshi.com
mimizukoshin@gmail.com
332-333

U

UESATSU
https://www.uesatsu.com/
memesatsu@gmail.com
334-335

Y

You Kojima
https://you-you.jp/
KIBI: https://www.instagram.com/kibi.obuse/
yu.kojima1013@gmail.com
220-221

Yukari Okada
http://www.cyandesign.jp/
yo@cyandesign.jp
208-209 | 227 | 232-233

Yu Miyama
https://www.instagram.com/u380/
uyumayamiii@gmail.com
210-211 | 238-239 | 298-299 | 303

Yusei Oi
https://www.instagram.com/soboku_design
design.oioi.0127@gmail.com
60 | 218-219

Yuto Tamura
https://tm-inc.jp/
info@tm-inc.jp
84-85 | 116-119 | 122 | 127 | 170-171 | 174-175 | 234-235 | 312-313

Yuuri Mikami
https://yuurimikami.com/
mail@yuurimikami.com
164 | 177 | 259

Z

Zin Nagao
https://www.foznt.com
abc@foznt.com
54-55 | 80-83 | 86-88 | 212-213 | 252 | 260-263 | 266-281

JAPANESE WOW FACTOR:
REDEFINING DOTS, LINES, AND PLANES IN DESIGN

English edition © 2025 SendPoints Publishing Co., Ltd.
First printing of the first edition, October 2025

sendpoints

PUBLISHED BY SendPoints Publishing Co., Ltd.
ADDRESS: Unit 23, L1/F Mirror Tower, 61 Mody Road, Tsim Sha Tsui, Kowloon, Hong Kong, China
PUBLISHER: Lin Gengli
CHIEF EDITOR: Wu Dongyan
DEVELOPMENT EDITOR: Wu Dongyan
EXECUTIVE EDITORS: Zhang Yiyu, Liang Xinyi
COVER DESIGNERS: Aki Kainai, Taku Sasaki
EXECUTIVE ART EDITOR: Zhang Zichen
TRANSLATORS: Zhang Yongzheng, Qi Yang, Zhang Yiyu
PROOFREADERS: Zhang Yiyu, Huang Chujun, Zeng Wanting

SALES DIRECTOR: Philip Tsang
TEL: +852 6296 2246
EMAIL: sales@sppub.com
WEBSITE: www.sppub.com

ISBN 978-988-77573-7-5

All rights reserved. No part of this publication may be reproduced, stored in a retrieval system or transmitted in any form or by any means, electronic, mechanical, photocopying, recording or otherwise, without prior permission in writing from the publisher. For more information, please contact SendPoints Publishing Co., Ltd.
Printed and bound in China.

Facebook Instagram X

ACKNOWLEDGEMENTS

We would like to thank all the designers and contributors who have been involved in the production of this book; their contributions have been indispensable to its creation. We would also like to express our gratitude to all the producers for their invaluable opinions and assistance throughout this project. And to the many others whose names are not credited but have made specific input in this book, we thank you for your continuous support.

FUTURE COOPERATIONS

If you wish to participate in SendPoints' future projects and publications, please send your website or portfolio to editor02@sendpoints.cn.